Working With Parents
and Families of Exceptional
Children and Youth

Working With Parents and Families of Exceptional Children and Youth:

Techniques for Successful Conferencing and Collaboration

Fourth Edition

Richard L. Simpson
and Nancy A. Mundschenk

8700 Shoal Creek Boulevard
Austin, Texas 78757
800/897-3202   Fax: 800/397-7633
www.proedinc.com

#298112237

An International Publisher

© 2010, 1996, 1990 by PRO-ED, Inc.
8700 Shoal Creek Boulevard
Austin, Texas 78757-6897
800/897-3202   Fax 800/397-7633
www.proedinc.com

Library of Congress Cataloging-in-Publication Data

Simpson, Richard L., 1945–
Working with parents and families of exceptional children and youth : techniques for successful conferencing and collaboration / Richard L. Simpson, Nancy Mundschenk.
     p. ; cm.
  ISBN-13: 978-1-4164-0433-0
  1. Parent-teacher conferences—United States.   2. Parents of exceptional children—Counseling of—United States.   3. Special education—United States.   4. Exceptional children—Family relationships—United States.   I. Munschenk, Nancy A.   II. Title.
  LC225.5.S55 2010
   371.9—dc22
                                        2008055813

Notice: PRO-ED grants permission to the user of this material to make unlimited copies of the reproducible forms for teaching or clinical purposes. Duplication of this material for commercial use is prohibited.

Art director: Jason Crosier
Designer: Lissa Hattersley
This book was designed in Avenir and Fairfield LH

Printed in the United States of America
1   2   3   4   5   6   7   8   9   10   18   17   16   15   14   13   12   11   10   09

*To our families and families everywhere—
by birth, by marriage, or by choice—
and to the professionals who work with them.*

Contents

PART 3

Addressing the Issues and Needs of Families
Across the Years

PART 1

The Family of the Child With an Exceptionality

Chapter 1

Understanding and Responding to the Needs of Parents and Families

The importance of developing and maintaining meaningful and effective relationships between parents, family members, and professionals is a topic that has received widespread attention during the past decades. Numerous books, articles, and conferences have reflected the importance of an effective relationship between the parent or family and the professional and suggested methods for facilitating such cooperative involvement (Fine & Simpson, 2000; Lambie & Daniels-Mohring, 1993; Seligman & Darling, 2007; A. Turnbull, Turnbull, Erwin, & Soodak, 2006). In spite of such attention, however, educators and other professionals involved with children and youth with exceptionalities are often ill at ease and ineffective when attempting to advocate for parents and family members, to communicate and collaborate with them, or to meet their needs in general. Even professionals with expertise in directly servicing children and youth and in relating to other professional disciplines often find it difficult to extend their services to parents and families (Elwy, 2005; Friend & Cook, 2007; Seligman, 2000; A. Turnbull & Turnbull, 2001; Ulrich & Bauer, 2003; Wilford, 2004).

The factors associated with this situation are multiple and complicated, yet four primary considerations emerge. First, many professionals' lack of understanding of the American family and its changing role is at least partially responsible for professionals' deficiencies in the area of parent and family conferencing. In the past, teachers were often familiar with the parents and families of all the students in their classes. Teachers tended to be a part of a community, and families generally remained for generations in one locale. Families are now much more mobile, however, in pursuit of jobs or the "good life" or simply for the sake of change. In addition, today's professionals are much less apt to be a part of the community in which they work. To be able to offer appropriate, effective services to parents and families, professionals must possess an understanding of the nature of today's family, its attitudes and values, and the background against which the latter were developed.

A second factor relates to a general confusion about the relationship between educators and other professionals and parents and families. That is, there is a lack of scientifically based understanding regarding which professionals are responsible for meeting various parent and family needs and how they should go about meeting these needs in an organized and orchestrated fashion. Hence, it is not surprising that a lack of clarity and agreement in this respect should create service-delivery problems.

The third issue concerns how to properly identify and serve the needs of parents and families of children and youth with exceptionalities. In spite of numerous efforts, the needs of parents and families with exceptional members and the skills and procedures required of professionals to serve these needs have not been clearly identified.

Finally, the widespread lack of parent and family conferencing skills can be attributed to training deficiencies. In spite of recent improvements, efficacious and appropriate curricula and training experiences in this area are still lacking, particularly in teacher education programs.

This chapter will discuss factors that are essential for improving services to parents and families of exceptional children and youth, including (a) trends in parent and family patterns, (b) educators' roles in interacting with and serving the needs of parents and families, (c) a model for parent and family involvement, and (d) the impact of children and youth with disabilities on families.

Historical Perspective

The nature and function of the American family has changed dramatically over the past decades, as has the relationship parents have with the educational institutions attended by their children. Prior to the 19th century, most day-to-day activities centered almost exclusively on the family. Parents and other members of extended families worked at or near their homes, and the family functioned as the primary educational and social institution for children and youth. In fact, parents were frequently responsible for educating their own children. In the mid-17th century, for example, a provision in the Massachusetts Bay Colony stipulated that parents could be fined for failing to educate their children. Early American society was based on an agrarian economy, a way of life that required the participation of entire families, including relatively young children, to produce the basics necessary to sustain life. This lifestyle was characterized by strict role assignments and well-established family and community values. Thus, rules, policies, and values reflected the position of the family and the roles of individual family members and were compatible with the philosophy of rural America. In keeping with this tradition, schools, whenever available, were designed to both reflect and perpetuate family and community values. Consequently, close cooperation between educators and parents was a necessity (Bayles & Hood, 1966). Few of the problems experienced by present-day educators were common to that era. It is difficult, for example, to imagine debates over which reading series to use with students, whether a particular teacher-applied intervention might result in a lawsuit, or whether a student's Individualized Education Program (IEP) had sufficient parental input.

With the Industrial Revolution came the transformation of agrarian life to what eventually became modern urban society. This large-scale social and economic development brought about two profound changes: the movement of families from farms to cities, and the inclusion of women (in some instances children) in the workforce (Goode, 1971). As families moved from farms to cities, contact with extended family members often decreased and, thus, so did the opportunity for children to be exposed to a variety of adult family role models. In addition, city life resulted in exposure to families that represented different attitudes and value systems. Gradually such contacts came to exert more influence on children's attitudes and values than exposure to extended family members and the more restricted beliefs of small agricultural communities. Furthermore, the induction of women into the workforce during the Industrial Revolution resulted in less contact between children, parents, and other adult family members. Hence, children and youth began to spend relatively long periods of time without parental supervision, and their peer groups came to assume a much stronger role in attitude and value formation.

During the period between the Industrial Revolution and the Civil War, American education began to exhibit many of the characteristics that are prevalent today. Children and youth were given an opportunity to attend publicly supported schools; graded schools and self-contained classrooms proliferated; formal teacher training programs in colleges and universities developed; curricular options increased; and consolidated schools staffed and operated by professional educators became the rule.

Since World War II, major technological, political, and economic events have caused monumental changes in the American family. Children and youth are presently a part of family units that rarely include grandparents and other extended family members; frequent moves have become commonplace; single-parent and reconstituted families are common; and families where both parents are employed full-time outside the home are becoming the norm. As a result of these changes, parents commonly expect the schools to fulfill roles traditionally assumed by the family.

School Reform

A new national agenda emerged in the 1990s and continued into the 2000s that includes initiatives largely focused on such issues as identifying educational goals and outcomes, raising academic and behavioral standards, using standardized assessments to measure and evaluate performance, making resources dependent on performance, empowering teachers and students, increasing cultural sensitivity, fostering local educational autonomy, and increasing not only the quantity and quality of what is taught but also the quality of the teachers providing the instruction (Individuals with Disabilities Education Improvement Act, 2004; No Child Left Behind Act, 2002).

Parents and families have felt the effects of school reform. As a result, many parents and families of individuals with disabilities have found themselves advocating for a restructured educational program that will address the needs of both exceptional and nonexceptional students (Barclay, 2005; Christenson, 2004; Simpson & Zurkowski, 2000). Similarly, educators involved in educating students with special needs have increasingly been confronted with difficult issues associated with school reform, including extended school days and extended school years, changing staff roles (e.g., more collaboration, more consultation models), adoption of more stringent accountability systems, adoption of high school core curricula, agreement on what constitutes an effective school and the accompanying programs to make sure such schools are available, open enrollment choice in education, stricter conduct policies, adoption of systems based on rewards and penalties for schools based on performance, and increased parental responsibility for student learning. Obviously these are difficult issues, and acceptable solutions will require the collective efforts of both professionals and families.

Historically, parents were generally denied opportunities to participate as partners in the educational system outside of the traditional PTA activities. Rather, they were more commonly considered unqualified to be part of the educational decision-making process or to employ procedures in the natural environment that would facilitate their children's educational or social development. Even more inequitably, they often were looked upon as being the cause of a child's problems and, thus, in need of treatment themselves. In response, parents have been able to establish their position and role primarily because of legal, legislative, advocacy, and political maneuvers.

Fortunately, the recognition of parents and families as significant contributors to children's education and development is occurring. Schools are increasingly working to establish and enhance partnerships that will combine family and professional resources to promote the social, emotional, and academic growth of children. Parents and families, especially those with exceptional children and youth, are being urged more and more to become collaborators in their offspring's educational programs and consequently are assuming major roles in decision making that will affect their children's future. This heightened parent–school involvement has stemmed partly from the acknowledgment by educators and other professionals of the importance of parental participation and cooperation and the recognition that parents and families can be a valuable resource and are experts with regard to their own children.

Parental involvement has undergone significant change, and parent participation, collaboration, and influence will continue to characterize program offerings. Professionals recognize that parents and families must have an opportunity for partnership in their children's education. History attests to the fact that when parents are denied opportunities for participation, collaboration, and involvement, they will seek other avenues of recourse. The most effective courses of action are not necessarily those where parents are forced to exercise their right to input via political, legal, and legislative strategies. When this happens, everyone suffers (Cronin, Slade, Bechtel, & Anderson, 1992; Dominguez, 2003; Fiedler, Simpson, & Clark, 2007; Sailor, 2002).

The Changing Nature of "Family"

Without argument, the family has changed along with the other social institutions in this country. No longer is the family a self-sufficient entity where parents, children, and other extended family members jointly work together to provide for the economic security of the members and where most educational, social, and ethical development takes place. Presently both children and parents spend increased amounts of time outside the home.

Although disagreement abounds on the nature and ultimate result of these trends, schools are the major social institution to feel the impact of the following statistics:

- In 2001, almost 6% of youth with disabilities lived with a
  family member other than a parent—a rate twice that of

1987—and were significantly more likely to be living in a household with an adult with a disability than they were previously (Wagner, Cameto, & Newman, 2003).

- Data released by the U.S. Census Bureau (2003) showed that by 2003 Latinos had become the largest and fastest-growing minority group in the United States.
- In 2001 more than half of Hispanic youth with disabilities spoke primarily a language other than English at home (Wagner et al., 2003).
- Approximately 5.6 million children, or 8 percent of the total population of U.S. children, lived in a household that included a grandparent. The majority of these children (3.7 million) lived in the grandparent's home; of these, two thirds had a parent present (Fields, 2003).
- Although the percentage of girls aged 15 to 19 years who gave birth declined from a high of 9.6% in 1957, still 4.2% of girls in that age range gave birth in 2003 (Fields, 2003).
- According to U.S. census data, 12.5 million children younger than the age of 18 years living in families were living below the poverty line in 2000.
- In 2002 an estimated 896,000 children were determined to be victims of child abuse or neglect caused by a parent or primary caregiver (National Clearinghouse on Child Abuse and Neglect Information, 2004).
- In 2003, 20% of females aged 12 to 17 years (2.4 million) reported taking part in one or more serious fights at school or work during the previous year, an increase over the percentage reporting this behavior in 2002 (16.2%) (Substance Abuse and Mental Health Services Administration, 2003).
- The percentage and number of children younger than the age of 18 years without health insurance increased between 2004 and 2005, from 10.8% (7.9 million) to 11.2% (8.3 million) (DeNavas-Walt, Proctor, & Lee, 2006).

In spite of irrefutable data and other signs of familial change, however, little evidence exists to indicate that the world's oldest social institution will fail to endure. The family, though the definition of it may have changed, continues to serve a major social function and will most likely persist as the major lifestyle model in the future.

For these reasons educators and other professionals involved with children and their families must recognize changing family patterns and develop responsive programs for children, youth, and families. Specifically, professionals must recognize and accept that many children and families will be impermanent community members; that current divorce and blended-family rates will likely continue; that cultural, racial, economic, and value diversity characterizes every community and school; that schools may function less as recreational and social centers of the community; and that disagreements will occur among professionals and families regarding the extent to which the education and socialization of children is the exclusive function of professional educators.

At the same time, educators must recognize that parents must be part of any instructional program—especially those designed for children and youth with exceptionalities—and that functional and efficacious models and solutions can be developed to help solve family problems and facilitate the growth and development of children and youth.

The unique and changing nature of most families and the complex social and economic issues affecting parents, professionals, and children make cookbook approaches to parent conferencing insufficient. Instead, today's educator needs pragmatic strategies to form useful alliances with families to increase parent participation in all aspects of educational programming for children and youth with disabilities. The challenge is significant; however, the procedures and technology needed for successful parent and school involvement can be acquired by those willing to develop appropriate conferencing skills.

Diverse Value Systems

Accompanying the technological changes of the past decades have been major value changes. Moreover, the increased presence of American families representing a variety of racial and cultural groups has intensified the educational significance of value differences (Blue-Banning, Summers, Frankland, Nelson, & Beegle, 2004; Hodgkinson, 1992; Keyes, 2002).

Professionals will come into contact with children, parents, and families who represent a variety of value systems, some of which may be dramatically different from their own. Recognition of this possibility is crucial if the educational conferencer is to work effectively with children, parents, and families who present variant socioeconomic, religious, ethnic, cultural, and political persuasions (Bentley, Tinney, & Chia, 2005; Mundschenk & Foley, 1997; Obiakor, Algozzine, & Ford, 1993). As previously mentioned, educators must be able to understand their own value systems because people tend to base their decisions and overall behavior on their own values (Dettmer, Thurston, Knackendoffel, & Dyck, 2009; Keyes, 2002;

L. G. Nelson, Summers, & Turnbull, 2004; A. Turnbull & Turnbull, 2001). Thus, individuals unfamiliar with their personal values may find it difficult to understand their interactions or the basis of their behavior. Although clarifying one's own values is not a simple process, several sources are available to help conferencers in this task (see, for example, Bentley et al., 2005; Kroth & Simpson, 1977; L. G. Nelson et al., 2004; C. Smith, 1993).

In addition, conferencers must be able to understand (and accept!) the values of the different individuals and families with whom they become associated in their professional dealings. Without such a basis the effectiveness of any interaction will be undermined. Perhaps because almost everybody has experienced school in some form, there are many self-proclaimed experts on the subject of education. The varying values of parents and families accompanied by such self-proclaimed expertise about education can potentially result in clashes. A simple acknowledgment, on the part of the conferencer, of the presence of different values and an attempt to understand these systems will frequently serve to turn conflicted encounters into meaningful and fruitful exchanges (Blue-Banning et al., 2004; Pogoloff, 2004; Salend & Taylor, 1993; A. Turnbull et al., 2006; Wilford, 2004).

The educational conferencer must recognize not only that values have changed and will continue to do so but also that personal values form the basis on which meaningful interactions and collaboration will take place (Friend & Cook, 2007; Keyes, 2002).

Consideration of Family Needs

Professionals are increasingly recognizing the benefits of interacting with families of exceptional children and youth, not just their parents. This change of perception and professional practice stems from the belief that all elements of a family are interconnected and that events and circumstances that affect one family member will impact others (Fleming, 2004; L. G. Nelson et al., 2004; Pogoloff, 2004). Thus, because a child or youth with an exceptionality will influence and be influenced by his or her entire family, professionals are being advised more and more to focus on others besides the parents.

Consistent with this viewpoint, professionals cannot adequately understand individuals, including those with disabilities, without analyzing how they fit into the family structure (Dattilio, 2005; Keogh, Garnier, Bernheimer, & Gallimore, 2000; Lambie & Daniels-Mohring, 1993; Mullis & Edwards, 2001; A. Turnbull & Turnbull, 2001), thus professionals must consider the interaction influences of each family's structure, functions, and life cycles. In this context, programs, procedures, and methodology should be based on a variety of family-related factors, as opposed to focusing exclusively on family members with exceptionalities or their parents. These factors include unique family characteristics (e.g., size, extrafamilial support, socioeconomic status), cultural styles (e.g., family values, ethnicity), ideological characteristics (e.g., parent and family attitudes), roles (e.g., unique economic, education, guidance, socialization functions), and life-cycle changes (e.g., retirement-age parents, birth of a sibling, death of a parent). Failure to consider family needs in program development may result in (a) overinvolvement by parents with their exceptional children (i.e., to the exclusion of other family members' needs), (b) unrealistic expectations on the part of professionals, and (c) poor family–professional communication.

Fortunately, increased professional attention has turned to the needs of families of children and youth with exceptionalities. Increased sensitivity to these needs should enhance family–professional partnerships as well as the maximum development of children and youth with disabilities in a variety of settings (Christenson & Sheridan, 2001; Fox, Vaughn, Wyatte, & Dunlap, 2002; Ogletree, Bull, Drew, & Lunnen, 2001; T. E. C. Smith, Gartin, Murdick, & Hilton, 2006).

The Educator's Role

Along with the increase in services provided to children and youth with exceptionalities has come the development of programs for parent and family involvement. Accordingly, most individuals assigned the task of interacting with parents, particularly those with special needs, have acquired some basic conferencing skills. Nevertheless, parent conferencing techniques and procedures for educational personnel have been developed and refined at a much slower pace than other educational components. Consequently, even though advancements have been made in parent and family conferencing and counseling, this area remains one of the most neglected and underdeveloped skills in the repertoire of most educators (Seligman, 2000).

Educators Are in the Best Position to Conference With Parents and Families

Extensive evidence suggests that instructional programs are most effective when parents and families participate in supportive roles (Cronin et al., 1992; Darch, Miao, & Shippen, 2004; Hallahan, Kauffman, & Pullen,

2009; O'Shea, O'Shea, Algozzine, & Hammitte, 2001; Rupiper & Marvin, 2004) and when families and professionals are able to build and maintain satisfactory lines of communication (Blue-Banning et al., 2004; Lawson & Sailor, 2000; L. G. Nelson et al., 2004; Salend, 2008a; Ulrich & Bauer, 2003; Webster-Stratton, Reid, & Hammond, 2004). One salient feature of good communication in this respect is the dissemination of accurate and current information. Although parents and families may have additional needs, the vast majority will be interested in learning about their child's classroom and school-related functioning. The individual with the closest and most consistent student contact will be most capable of providing information and making necessary procedural changes. Consequently, educators must again play an instrumental role in disseminating parent and family information. In addition, parents frequently report that they feel most comfortable in discussing their child with his or her classroom teacher. Thus, educators almost universally have access to the most relevant and current information about a given child. At the same time, parents may demonstrate a level of trust and openness toward them not found with many other individuals in the helping professions. It seems logical, therefore, to take advantage of educators' favorable position by training them to serve as many parent and family needs as appropriate.

A Model for Parent and Family Involvement

Although important, basic human relations skills and an aptitude for parent and family involvement are insufficient as components of parent and family conferencing. Instead, successful parent and family involvement necessitates a comprehensive service-delivery program with sufficient breadth to encompass the many individual needs experienced by families of children and youth with exceptionalities. Needs within and across families vary; needs also vary over time (Adelizzi & Goss, 2001; Heward, 2009; Keogh et al., 2000; A. Turnbull et al., 2006). Thus, within a comprehensive model, individualized planning is fundamental. Such a strategy allows for general planning within commonly acknowledged need areas while at the same time allowing individualization.

The model of parent and family involvement shown in Figure 1.1 identifies and briefly describes five major parent and family needs: information exchange; partnership and advocacy training; home and community

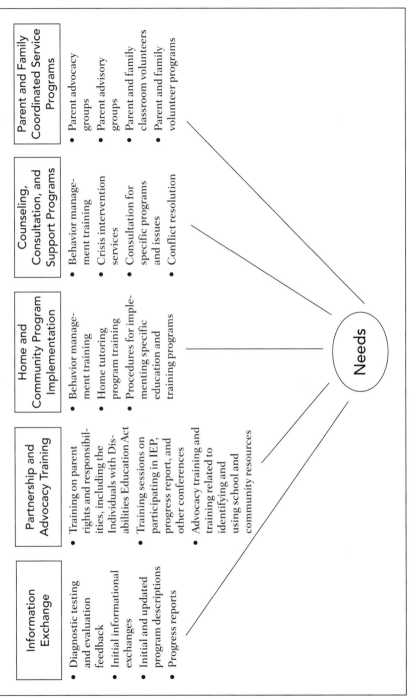

Figure 1.1. Model of parent and family involvement.

program implementation; counseling, consultation, and support programs; and parent and family coordinated service programs. The basic premise of the model holds that these are major needs experienced by parents and families of children and youth with exceptionalities and that each element requires an appropriate and individualized professional program. Thus, educators and other professionals must be able to assess and appropriately respond to the parent and family needs listed within each of the basic components of the model.

It is unlikely that every family will have needs in all five areas at any given time. It is likely, however, that a group of parents and family members of children and youth with exceptionalities—as might be encountered by a special education teacher—will reflect all needs at some point. Accordingly, educators who are involved with children and youth with special needs are urged to develop basic knowledge and skills in each of the five major areas, descriptions of which follow.

Information Exchange

This element of the model refers to parents' and family members' need for information as well as a basic professional need for accurate and ongoing information coming from parents and families. Thus, the educational conferencer must obtain relevant facts about children and families (e.g., developmental history, school history, family expectations) while also providing appropriate information to the parties, including progress reports.

Sharing information with parents and family members should include not only the assessment data but also a chance to discuss the findings. Even though parents and families may have received an interpretation following an assessment of their child, most likely they will benefit from a review of the information and from discussing issues associated with the assessment and subsequent recommendations.

Parents and families should also be given a description of the educational program to be provided to their child, including the teacher's educational philosophy and strategy, the academic and behavioral remediation programs scheduled for use, the auxiliary services to be provided, and the available parent and family support programs.

The mother of one child with a severe disability reported that upon moving to a new community, "our entire family was consumed with getting things set up for Cindy." The mother indicated that only after enrolling her daughter in an appropriate school program, identifying a pediatrician knowledgeable in children with special needs, and finding acceptable after-school care was her family able to direct full attention to other matters.

She also observed, "When I see Cindy's bus pick her up for school in the morning, I know my child is being provided for—then I can go about other things."

Responding to parents' and families' needs for appropriate programs and services for exceptional members is often taken for granted. Yet professionals must recognize this basic need as a linchpin of family adjustment and parental and family involvement and, accordingly, not underestimate it.

Other information to be disseminated includes the procedures planned for evaluating student progress and the manner in which these data will be communicated. In this regard, many parents and family members prefer regularly occurring and informal contacts (e.g., phone conferences, notes sent home, e-mail).

Effective information exchange is basic to a family–professional partnership. Educators should assume that all parents and families need ongoing information exchanges just as all professionals require accurate home and family information.

Partnership and Advocacy Training

Even though parents have been granted significant input in determining what educational procedures will be used with their children (particularly those with special needs), more has to be done to provide the knowledge, training, and confidence needed to serve in this participation role (Blue-Banning et al., 2004; Dettmer et al., 2009; Olsen & Fuller, 2003; Trussell, Hammond, & Ingalls, 2008). In spite of being eligible to participate in IEP conferences and other parent–teacher meetings, parents have not been trained in how to do so effectively. Indeed, historically, empowered parents and families have achieved their skills and knowledge with little or no assistance from professionals. Parents and family members, however, must be provided opportunities for appropriate training if they are to be expected to collaborate with professionals and to function at a level consistent with their assigned rights, needs, and personal motivation. As Simpson and Poplin (1981) pointed out,

> In order for professionals to be willing to train parents in procedures for participation in educational conferences and other related activities, they must believe that a majority of parents, with training and encouragement, are willing to become involved with schools in generating and sharing concerns and goals for their child's education and that this participation adds to the school's ability to help the child. (p. 21)

Unless educators meet parents' needs for sufficient information in this area, they cannot be expected to participate in parent–teacher conferences in a manner that will maximize the school's efforts.

This component of the parent and family involvement model taps several training elements, including (a) the procedures for how to participate in conferences and meetings and (b) the rights and responsibilities of parents and families of children with exceptionalities. This aspect of the model also relates to how to prepare parents and families to serve as advocates for children and youth with exceptionalities and to act as effective consumers of community, school, and agency services and resources. That is, the partnership and advocacy training component of the model focuses on *empowering* parents and families to the extent that they are seeking such a role. One cannot assume, however, that all parents and families need or desire partnership, advocacy training, collaboration, or empowerment; however, many parents and families will make use of programs designed to develop such skills and knowledge, if available (Kahne & Westheimer, 1993; Matuszny, Banda, & Coleman, 2007; Rock, 2000; Simmons, 2003).

Home and Community Program Implementation

Research has confirmed that parents and families can be effectively trained to implement education-related services with their own children (Baker, 2003; Buschbacher, Fox, & Clarke, 2004; Gortmaker, Daly, McCurdy, Persampieri, & Hergenrader, 2007; Obiakor et al., 1993; Reid, Webster-Stratton, & Baydar, 2004; Simpson, 2004). Both as academic tutors and agents of behavior management, parents and other family members have proved to be valuable resources for extending professional intervention and academic programs beyond the classroom setting. For example, under professional direction, parents and family members can be trained to implement individualized tutoring programs with their own child. Such tutoring serves both to involve these individuals in a child's academic program and to appropriately communicate their concern to the child. In addition, this type of activity provides a means for structuring interactions between the family and child and for bridging the gap between home and school.

Parents and families have also been trained to employ behavior management procedures with children. This approach has allowed them to effect planned behavior changes in the natural environment and thus to extend the therapeutic influence of professionals beyond the classroom.

Although some parents and families may be unmotivated or unsuited for this role, others will be highly appropriate. Training parents and families to serve in this capacity provides a vehicle for extending problem-solving efforts into noneducational environments and for coordinating parents' motivations for collaboration and participation.

Counseling, Consultation, and Support Programs

Although only a small percentage of parents and families will need in-depth therapy and counseling, the necessary resources must be available to those who require them. In most instances, the educator's role in this area will consist of putting parents in touch with those professionals who are best equipped to serve them. The most common referrals include family counseling, psychotherapy, crisis intervention, and other clinical and social agency assistance.

Other parent and family needs within this domain are more widespread. For instance, many families will benefit from participating in support groups (Evans, 2003) at some point, a family crisis may require professional intervention, conflicts between professionals and parents and families may necessitate professional resolution programs, and many parents periodically require consultation regarding particular issues (e.g., feeding issues, peer relationships, sleeping problems) (Adelizza & Goss, 2001; Heller, Forney, Alberto, Schwartzman, & Goeckel, 2000; C. D. Hoffman et al., 2008; Taylor, 2000).

Parent and Family Coordinated Service Programs

Some parents and families wish to go beyond their own needs and those of their offspring to serve the larger community of children with exceptionalities and their families. This may include serving on advisory boards, participating in community service programs, engaging in "parent-to-parent" groups, or working as volunteers in programs for children and youth with special needs.

Noting that basically all major amendments in policies and services for children with exceptionalities have been effected by the work of parent groups can highlight the importance of these activities. Such results, along with the need for continued progress, may motivate certain parents and families to work at local, state, and national levels to secure more and better services for all individuals with disabilities. For those parents and families who have the time, ability, and energy, opportunities for such service to the larger community of exceptional citizens should be made available.

Analysis of Parent and Family Needs

Successful parent and family involvement is associated with awareness and sensitivity to the unique needs and circumstances of families with exceptional members. As noted previously, these families must contend with myriad issues, only some of them related to education (A. Palmer, 2004; Simpson & Carter, 1993; A. Turnbull et al., 2006). These issues may include social isolation and feelings of guilt and embarrassment, financial strain (e.g., medical expenses, "special baby-sitter" expenses), limitations on recreational options, pessimistic perceptions of the future, household routine delays and disruptions (e.g., additional time to feed, bathe, and dress a disabled family member), and interference with other family members' needs and gratification.

Sensitivity to the demands and stresses commonly experienced by families of exceptional children and youth will aid educators in keeping educational matters in proper perspective and in assisting families with the numerous noneducational issues with which they must contend. Without such a perspective, educators lack a basic ingredient of successful parent and family involvement.

Because there are no reliable and valid standardized measures for identifying parent and family needs, assessing such needs is an informal process. In this regard, the model of parent and family involvement can become a frame to identify possible parent and family requirements.

One should consider two general factors in identifying parental needs: professionals' perceptions of parent and family needs, and parents' and families' self-perceived needs. The first consideration involves professionals sharing with parents or family members their perceptions of a family's needs along with possible program and service options for addressing those needs. Although no standard formula exists for gauging parent and family needs and preferences, consideration of the following factors is recommended: (a) analysis of the family's perceived and stated needs, as per the model of parent and family involvement, including programs and services used and requested by parents and families; (b) family makeup and characteristics, including number and ages of members and cultural, socioeconomic, and ethnic factors; (c) disabled member's exceptionality, including severity level and impact on family members; (d) human, financial, and community resources available to the family; (e) family restrictions and problems associated with the disability; (f) degree of family communication and support; and (g) age of the child with a disability. Although consideration and interpretation of these data may vary from professional to professional, these factors should serve as guidelines for how to identify parent and family needs.

Because professionals are not always able to accurately identify parental and family needs (especially if family members are not forthcoming about their concerns, circumstances, and requirements), and because parents and families may be unaware of their own needs (e.g., a parent may be unaware of advocacy training options), conferencers should apprise parents and families of potential needs they may experience. This process involves assuring parents that it is predictable that they will have various needs over the course of caring for and educating a child with an exceptionality and that their needs can be addressed. Hence, a combination of professional analysis and solicitation of parents' self-perceived needs is recommended.

Although professionals' analyses of child and family requirements and related programs are important, parents' and families' self-perceived needs and their willingness to invest in addressing them are also obvious salient determinants of family involvement. Too frequently parents have reported encountering little or no flexibility in the manner in which their needs are perceived and the degree to which they are expected to be involved in their child's intervention and education program. Thus, professionals must be sensitive to families' self-perceived needs and their preferences for involvement and collaboration with school personnel and agencies. Although professionals must identify what they consider to be a parent's or family's needs, in the final analysis these perceived requirements are acted on only with parent and family support and endorsement. For example, a professional may observe that a parent appears to need home management training. Home management skill training, however, can (and should) be provided only if the parent agrees with the professional's assessment and seeks collaborative training support.

Individualization Within the Model of Parent and Family Involvement

The Individuals with Disabilities Education Improvement Act has effectively established that students with disabilities are to be provided an education that is based on their individual needs. It is ironic that this enactment has not applied the principle of individualization to parents and families. That is, parents and families are frequently perceived as though they are all experiencing the same needs and program requirements. Accordingly, the model of parent and family involvement is designed to accommodate individualization, based on three assumptions: (a) parents and families are unique in terms of needs, time, resources, motivation, skills, commitment, and interests; (b) professionals should encourage a range of parent involvement matched to individual interests and needs; and (c) increased involvement by parents and families in their children's education and development does not necessarily mean more effective involvement. In accordance with these underlying assumptions, decisions regarding the degree and type of parent and family involvement and the most appropriate methods for satisfying parent and family needs should come from individual and family preferences and needs (Fox et al., 2002; O'Shea et al., 2001; Simpson & Carter, 1993; A. Turnbull & Turnbull, 2001).

The model of parent and family involvement accommodates individualization by offering parents and families various levels of participation and collaboration options for satisfying their needs: (a) recognition and awareness, (b) ongoing communication, (c) advocacy and skill development, and (d) partnership. The levels of involvement are not hierarchical; that is, advocacy and skill development for a particular family are not necessarily better, for example, than ongoing communication. Rather, needs, motivation, abilities, and other factors serve as the basis for identifying the appropriate degree of parent and family involvement. In addition, a family's level of involvement may vary over time. For instance, a family experiencing divorce or other significant changes might temporarily have fewer resources to invest in training a disabled member. Finally, the levels of participation apply across need components. For example, within the counseling and consultation component, family participation may vary from recognition and awareness of educators' ability and willingness to make referrals to community agencies to partnership in conducting parent and family support groups.

The first level of participation, recognition and awareness, represents the baseline expectation for all parents and families across all needs. Specifically, this basic level of involvement requires (a) parent and family awareness of school and agency personnel, including their roles; (b) recognition of parent and family services available through the child's program and community, especially those associated with parent and family needs; and (c) basic information about the child's instructional program and the manner in which families may obtain information and access services.

Ideally, ongoing communication is a level of involvement that one may achieve with all parents and families, in all areas of need expressed in the model of parent and family involvement. This degree of collaborative involvement entails regularly occurring information exchange between parents and families and professionals. Included are progress reports by families and professionals, within their respective settings; formal and informal exchanges of progress and developments potentially affecting children's performance (e.g., family crisis); progress related to parent-applied home intervention programs; and other open exchanges of information, such as expectations, attitudes, and feelings.

Advocacy and skill development refers to parents and families responding to the expressed or perceived needs of the model of parent and family involvement through various empowerment and skill application activities. For instance, involvement at an advocacy and skill development level may be appropriate for parents and families who have the need and ability to represent their child with a disability, to participate collaboratively in making relevant educational and intervention decisions, and to implement collaborative home and community programs and procedures, typically under the direction of a professional. Hence, this includes identification of IEP goals and objectives; participation in educational conference training programs; participation in advocacy and volunteer training programs, including those designed to empower parents and families; and involvement in home-based tutoring and behavior management programs.

Involvement at the partnership level of participation is reserved for parents and family members who demonstrate the needs, skills, motivation, time, and energy to assist children and youth with exceptionalities on an equal level (or near-equal level) with professionals. Examples of collaborative activities at this level of participation include independently applying home-based programs; training other parents and family members to represent, advocate, or train children; and serving as leaders or coleaders of a family support group.

Developing a Personalized Conferencing Philosophy and Style

The unique nature and needs of parents and families as well as the variant characteristics of educators necessitate the development of an individually formulated conferencing philosophy and style. Hence, although certain general aptitudes and specific skills are necessary for successful parent and family interaction, these must be applied in accord with the conferencer's strengths and weaknesses. For reasons discussed previously, ready-made approaches and universally applicable strategies are neither appropriate nor effective with all parents and families.

Consequently, conferencers must work to develop styles that are pragmatic and compatible with their individual qualities, temperaments, and preferences. Furthermore, although recognizing that all theoretical positions may be potentially valuable and contributory to the goal of serving parents and families, conferencers must also be aware of the dangers inherent in accepting any single position as sufficient for meeting the needs of all parents and families. Although adherence to a single philosophy or approach may satisfy a conferencer's need for security, it is rarely adequate for serving a wide variety of parents and families. As previously noted, the American family has undergone significant change in past decades. American families' changed and variant needs can be served most adequately by conferencers who have developed a personal style and who are flexible enough to employ different approaches to meet the unique needs of those with whom they work. If educational conferencers are truly to meet the challenges presented by today's parents and families, they must possess a repertoire of skills that align with their own character and can be individualized for a variety of parents and families.

Impact of Children and Youth With Exceptionalities on Parents and Families

Families of children with exceptionalities have experienced the same changes and exist as heterogeneously as other parents and families. Yet, traditionally, parents of children and youth with exceptionalities have been regarded as sharing so many commonalities that they present a homogeneous population—as having unique features not shared by others. Parents and families of exceptional children, however, are as individualized and diversified as those without "special" children; their only common denominator is at least one child who deviates from the norm to such an extent that he or she requires some type of curriculum modification, specialized educational program, or other considerations to function at a level commensurate with his or her ability.

In spite of their heterogeneity, parents and families of children with exceptionalities experience increased levels of frustration and certain problems not encountered by other parents and families (Fleming, 2004;

Marshak & Prezant, 2007; A. Palmer, 2004). For example, C. D. Hoffman and colleagues (2008) examined the relationship between children's sleep problems (e.g., bedtime resistance, night wakings) and maternal stress. They concluded that children's sleep problems were related to the severity of their autism and in turn to their mothers' reports of sleep difficulties and stress. Clearly, sleep difficulties in parents will affect other family functions and may well exacerbate the sleep and other problems of their child, because maternal sleep deprivation will almost certainly diminish the mother's effective parenting behavior.

Equally important, parents of children with exceptionalities may lack those feelings of accomplishment and satisfaction that are so necessary to effective parenthood. Instead, such parents experience hurt because their child may not become an independent adult, frustration because he or she may lack the physical capacity to respond to a parent's efforts to interact, or anger because their son or daughter is rejected by other children. As a result of such feelings, some parents perceive themselves as failures or consider their life one of shattered dreams. Whatever the particular response, it is safe to conclude that it will have significant impact and, in most instances, will intensify stress on the family (Baxter, Cummins, & Yiolitis, 2000; Lessenberry & Rehfeldt, 2004; Lustig, 2002; Orsmond, Seltzer, Greenberg, & Krauss, 2006). In no way does this suggest that the presence of a child with an exceptionality precludes family harmony and parental happiness. It does suggest, however, that typical parental and family pleasures may take nontraditional forms when a child or youth with a disability is involved. That is, parents and families may find themselves learning to use sign language so they can communicate more effectively with a child with a hearing impairment or becoming involved in a community action program designed to benefit all individuals with developmental disabilities. At the very least, the presence of an exceptional child creates unique challenges for both parents and the family (Fine & Nissenbaum, 2000; Marshak & Prezant, 2007; A. Turnbull & Turnbull, 2001).

Children's social, intellectual, and other forms of development are greatly influenced by their parents and families. Within these relationships, it is equally obvious that children influence the families of which they are a part. This reciprocity of influence is apparent even in young child–family interactions, and it becomes particularly significant when a child is exceptional (Kauffman, 2005; Paul & Simeonsson, 1993; A. Turnbull & Turnbull, 2001). Although the degree of such an influence relates to a variety of factors, including the severity and nature of a child's exceptionality, any disability of a family member exerts a significant effect on the entire family.

The unique challenges experienced by many families of children and youth with exceptionalities require that educators and other professionals be able to understand an atypical child's impact on the family system and be knowledgeable about procedures and strategies for aiding families with disabled members meet their needs. Without this added dimension of the role performed routinely by educators, programs for children and youth with exceptionalities will probably not adequately serve the needs of both students and their families.

In her book *The Child Who Never Grew* (1950), Pearl S. Buck wrote the following:

> The first cry from my heart, when I knew she would never be any-thing but a child, was the age old cry that we all make before in-evitable sorrow: "Why must this happen to me?" To this there could be no answer and there was none. (p. 34)

Buck's analysis remains relatively current. That is, in spite of the growing volume of information available on the impact of a child with an exceptionality on the family, empirically valid data on the exact nature of this impact remain scarce (Singer, 2002). Indeed, most information on the topic is based on case studies and subjective reports (Ferguson, 2002; Seligman & Darling, 2007; A. Turnbull & Turnbull, 2001).

Parental Reactions

As a function of its subjective and anecdotal nature, the literature dealing with parental reactions to having a child with an exceptionality is diverse and rather inconsistent. In spite of such variance, however, parents of children with exceptionalities appear to experience some commonality of feeling. Some researchers have contended that parents go through emotional reactions in relation to their child's disability that are much like those, as articulated by Kübler-Ross (1969), expressed by people when they are talking about death and dying (Ferguson, 2002; Volkmar & Wiesner, 2004; Zolko, 1991). These reactions are not experienced by all parents and may vary in duration and strength of response when they do occur. In fact, because of changes in public attitudes and supports for children with disabilities and their families, the participants in current research on family reactions may reflect a group that is very different from those participating in earlier studies. In addition, current research has begun to look beyond the nature of the impact on parents and their adjustment to having an exceptional child to the identification of factors that contribute to the resiliency and successful adaptation of families (Ferguson, 2002; Kochhar-Bryant, 2008; Lin, 2000; Scorgie & Sobsey, 2000).

Nonetheless, it is imperative that conferencers be aware of the factors that correlate with parents' reactions. These include the child's age at the time of diagnosis, the nature and severity of the disability, and other factors such as family adaptability, social supports, and emotional bonding within the family (Fine & Nissenbaum, 2000; Hardman, Drew, & Egan, 2002; Lin, 2000; Lustig, 2002; Symon, 2001). Some parents learn of the disability at the birth of their child, and the etiology may be clear. Others have concerns and suspicions that something is not quite right that are later confirmed by professionals. One parent expressed her frustration at the series of physicians she consulted before her son was diagnosed with a hearing impairment that she had suspected for the previous year. Still other parents are surprised to hear for the first time that their school-age child has a disability.

A major topic related to parental reaction has been the manner in which the parents were initially apprised of their child's exceptionality. A number of authorities have reported that contact with professionals is a topic parents of children with exceptionalities frequently wish to address (Fleischmann, 2004; Lambie & Daniels-Mohring, 1993; Nissenbaum, Tollefson, & Reese, 2002; Simpson & Carter, 1993).

Thus, although it is unlikely that the parents of a child with a mild learning problem would respond in the same manner as the parents of a child with a severe disability, in each situation the parents will wrestle with the impact of that diagnosis on the family and deal with the myriad reactions to the ongoing accommodations they will make to adapt to the changing needs of their child.

Almost without exception, parents of children with disabilities report difficulties directly associated with their child's condition. In addition to the required daily responsibilities and accommodations, parents of children with disabilities frequently face the need to secure services and consideration for their children in a society that is often not comfortable with the differences those children display and that places little value on persons with exceptionalities (Murdick, Shore, Chittooran, & Gartin, 2004). Worcester, Nesman, Raffaele Mendez, and Keller (2008) reported one mother's reflections on her struggle to coordinate services for her daughter:

> I managed to get everything we needed, but I had to fight for every freaking bit of it. So early intervention made my life more difficult because instead of giving me the services that my daughter needed,

> every conversation with them was stressful. I had to do major re-
> search and documentation to justify any decision. (p. 518)

Without attempting to recount the numerous—both positive and negative—experiences encountered by parents of children with exceptionalities in interacting with professionals, suffice it to say that the initial encounter is frequently identified as significant.

The well-established importance of the professional's relationship
with families underlies a frequent criticism by parents of many educators' lack of skill in this area (Elwy, 2005; Simpson, 2004; A. Turnbull
et al., 2006; Ulrich & Bauer, 2003; Wilford, 2004). Parents and families
have recounted instances of gross insensitivity and brusqueness at a time
when they are most vulnerable. Although parents on occasion may exag-
gerate their negative experiences with professionals, the latter must become more skillful in their initial contacts with parents, including those
instances when such contacts involve dissemination of diagnostic and
classification information. Thus, professionals must accurately and com-
passionately communicate diagnostic findings and recommendations, help
families secure appropriate services, and support families through what
is an extremely difficult time. As suggested, initial positive and supportive interactions between parents and families establish a basis for future
effective communication and an overall effective parent–professional
partnership (A. Turnbull et al., 2006; Webber, Simpson, & Bentley, 2000;
P. Zionts, Zionts, & Simpson, 2002).

Because parents and families of children and youth with exceptionalities are clearly unique, it is difficult to draw meaningful generalizations
about what they think, feel, and experience relative to living with an exceptional child. Yet a basic element of success in interacting and working with
these families is an awareness and sensitivity to their experiences and feelings. In an attempt to facilitate professionals' understanding and empathy
for these families, parents offer personal perspectives on their experiences
in living with and raising a child with an exceptionality in *Exceptional Parent* and similar periodicals.

One mother of a child with autism described her perspective this way:

> Life with a special needs child is a long journey, filled with hills
> and valleys, triumphs and defeats. It is a journey without end. A
> journey with unexpected twists and turns, exuberance, joy . . . and
> oftentimes sorrow. It is a journey that we never expected to take,
> but that we will join nonetheless . . . for the love of a child.
> (Fleischmann, 2004, p. 37)

Sibling Reactions

Research on the impact of a child with disabilities on siblings has generated equivocal results. The notion that a child with a disability can have a deleterious influence such as depression, social difficulties, or anxiety on other children in the family has persisted for a long time (Damiani, 1999; Fleming, 2004; Hutton & Caron, 2005; Rossiter & Sharpe, 2001; A. Turnbull & Turnbull, 2001). Such negative influence, however, has been refuted by other authorities (Damiani, 1999; Orsmond & Seltzer, 2007; Rossiter & Sharpe, 2001). For example, Cuskelly and Gunn (2006) concluded that having a sibling with Down syndrome may also produce increased levels of empathy and appreciation for individual differences.

The relationship between siblings with and without disabilities has been reported to be generally positive. Encouraging effects on siblings were identified by mothers in one study who reported that siblings without disabilities developed greater maturity and a greater sense of responsibility (Taunt & Hastings, 2002). In other studies, on a measure of global self-concept, no statistical differences were found between siblings of students with learning disabilities and a comparison group of siblings of students without learning disabilities (Dyson, 1996) or between students with learning disabilities and their siblings without disabilities, both aged 7 to 15 years (Dyson, 2003).

Some researchers have looked at gender as a prominent and contextual factor in the relationships of brothers and sisters of adults with mental retardation. For mixed-gender sibling pairs, mothers reported sisters were more likely to be the most involved sibling for a brother with mental retardation than were brothers for a sister with mental retardation. Orsmond and Seltzer (2000) reported that brothers were more pessimistic about the future of their sisters with disabilities than they were about the future of their brothers with disabilities. Moreover, and as in previous research (Damiani, 1999; Stoneman & Berman, 1993), sisters provided more care and companionship than their brothers. During their 5-year study, however, Orsmond and Seltzer found that positive affect toward the sibling with mental retardation increased for both brothers and sisters.

In spite of equivocal findings regarding the influence of children with disabilities on their siblings without disabilities, evidence indicates that the latter will be affected by an exceptionality (Fleming, 2004; A. Turnbull & Turnbull, 2001). Commenting on this assumption, Crnic and Leconte (1986) concluded the following:

> Although it seems clear from both research and clinical reports that the effects of having a handicapped sibling vary greatly from

individual to individual, and we cannot automatically assume that the effects will be deleterious, normal siblings are at risk for any number of social, behavioral, or emotional difficulties. This at-risk status is a function of the ongoing stress associated with the presence of a handicapped sibling, and it is likely that the nature of these risks and stress vary across the sibling's life-span. (p. 93)

Current research efforts have increased attention on the comparative impact on siblings of children with disabilities across diagnostic categories such as Down syndrome, developmental disabilities, autism (Hodapp, 2007; Hodapp & Urbano, 2007; Orsmond & Seltzer, 2007; Rossiter & Sharpe, 2001), and acquired brain injury (Boschen, Gargaro, Gan, Gerber, & Brandys, 2007) and highlighted the need to identify specific child characteristics or other factors that impact the sibling relationship. Additional research should take a life-span developmental approach that helps identify how the sibling relationship and sibling well-being changes over time (Dew, Balandin, & Llewellyn, 2008; Hodapp, 2007; Lin, 2000; Orsmond & Seltzer, 2007; L. White, 2001). For example, as parents age or experience illness or health limitations, siblings will likely anticipate assuming a more primary role in the care of the person with disabilities. They may become concerned about long-term outcomes for their brother or sister with disabilities, such as employment opportunities and the availability of adequate supports for successful employment and independent living (Hodapp & Urbano, 2007; Orsmond & Seltzer, 2007).

Support and Consideration of All Family Members

From a family systems perspective, all elements of a family unit are interconnected, and events affecting one member impact others. For example, cancellation of a family trip because vacation monies went toward therapy or medical services, or excessive child care responsibilities that restrict siblings' participation in school activities, or increased mealtime anxiety because of implementing a language training program cannot help but affect everyone in the family. Because each family member feels the impact uniquely, individual needs must be recognized and accommodated for families to function effectively.

A. P. Turnbull, Summers, and Brotherson (1983) developed a family systems model for understanding and accommodating the needs of families with disabled members that consists of three major components: (a) family structure (membership characteristics, cultural style, ideological style), (b) family functions (economic, physical, rest and recuperation, socialization, self-definition, affection, guidance, education, and vocational), and (c) family life cycles (family members aging and passing through various family roles). Thus, events that affect husband and wife, parental, sibling, and extrafamilial interactions will impact all family members. As a specific example of this process, A. P. Turnbull et al. (1983) offered the following:

> Consider the example of a mother who has agreed to work on a home training program in the area of feeding with her severely retarded child. Allowing her child to feed himself triples the time involved in each meal. While the mother is working with the child on feeding, her dinner conversation with her husband and other children is substantially limited. After the other family members finish dinner, the father cleans the kitchen and the siblings proceed to their homework all feeling that some of their needs have been overlooked. Meanwhile, the mother is feeling isolated from the rest of her family and frustrated over all the tasks to which she must attend before midnight. (p. 5)

A. Turnbull and Turnbull (2001) contended that effective family interactions are characterized by cohesion, adaptability, and communication. Cohesion refers to the force that unites family members. If a family is to effectively meet the needs of all members, it must avoid becoming enmeshed (i.e., overly concerned or overly involved) or disengaged (i.e., rigid in meeting needs) in interacting with family members who have disabilities. Another determinant of effective family interactions is adaptability; that is, family members must be able to conform to new or changed circumstances. Functioning families also display effective communication skills, including receiving and sending clear messages and displaying effectual listening behaviors.

As some of the interaction elements emphasized in the preceding models may not occur naturally, professionals assisting the families of children and youth with exceptionalities must help identify strategies and procedures for facilitating such interactions. Families may need assurance and confirmation that it is acceptable to feel ambivalent or even negative about having a child with an exceptionality. Some parents and family members may need encouragement to pursue interests and activities other than serving and advocating for the child with a disability. That is, parents and families should be encouraged to attend to their own needs as well as to those of other family members and to recognize that being the parent or sibling of a child with a disability need not and should not be their main responsibility and pursuit. Overcommitment on the part of parents and families can sometimes be as detrimental as inattention.

The presence of a child with an exceptionality will inevitably exert a significant impact on a family, and that impact will be mediated by socioeconomic status, availability and use of support systems, marital stability, family constellations, psychological health of parents, cultural beliefs, religious beliefs, coping strategies, and the nature and visibility of the disability (Stainton & Besser, 1998; Turner, 2000). Little research on family functioning has focused on the positive impact of exceptional children (Taunt & Hastings, 2002). Most investigations ask families how they have adjusted to and coped with the presence of the child with disabilities. Poyadue (1993) proposed a stage beyond acceptance and adaptation that reflects the families' genuine appreciation of the positive aspects of family life with an exceptional child.

Stainton and Besser (1998) interviewed parents regarding the positive impact of their children with disabilities on their family. Responses of the parents interviewed suggest that although there are expected difficulties and stresses, reports of positive impacts are real, not a defense mechanism or the result of parental denial. As one parent offered in relation to the development of advocacy skills, "It gave us more strength and we'd go and say, 'way to go Caroline, you know. Look at what you have made of us. You made us "door openers" and we're getting really good at it' " (Stainton & Besser, 1998, p. 65).

A primary goal for the educational conferencer and other professionals must be to help parents and family members understand and plan for a child or youth with an exceptionality. Regardless of his or her stated role, the parent conferencer must work for the preservation of family unity and employ the necessary procedures to support accommodation of the child within the family.

Planning for Accommodation of a Child With an Exceptionality

Accommodating a child or youth with an exceptionality within his or her family usually entails a gradual process associated with a variety of factors, some of which extend beyond the control of professionals. Nevertheless, the latter must realize their potential positive influence on this process. This facilitative effect can be accomplished best through well-planned procedures and strategies, including the following:

- Listen to parents and family members. As this is very frequently what they are looking for, it can be the most therapeutic offering a professional can make.
- Avoid hasty attempts at problem solving, advice giving, and information dissemination. Frequently parents and family members are simply seeking an opportunity to share their concerns with someone who can understand and empathize with their situation.
- Do not attempt to convince parents and family members that a child or youth with an exceptionality is good or beneficial for them and their family. In fact, conferencers should refrain from making judgmental statements of any kind and focus instead on aiding families in accommodating the member with special needs.
- Apprise parents and family members of the potential impact of a child or youth with an exceptionality on the family. Although conferencers obviously cannot forewarn parents and families of every eventuality, they can advise about the common problems and conditions that crop up.
- Encourage parents and siblings to pursue interests and responsibilities other than those exclusively concerning the family member with an exceptionality. Although positive action programs can benefit the larger community of exceptional children, parents generally should be dissuaded from committing their lives solely to their own exceptional child or to programs for persons with exceptionalities.
- Provide parents with alternatives and opportunities for working appropriately with their own child and for participating in programs designed to serve other persons with exceptionalities. Such involvement is most effective when it is individualized and compatible with individual and family needs.
- Encourage parents and family members to share their thoughts and feelings about having a member with an exceptionality. Make them aware of the advantages of having someone to talk with about their concerns.
- Encourage parents to think about their child's future, including identifying alternatives available to both the child and the family.
- Identify procedures that the parents and family can employ with their child to train and develop functional skills and accomplish agreed-upon goals. Such procedures often facilitate

family communication and satisfaction of all members' needs.

- Aid parents and siblings in identifying areas of growth and accomplishment shown by a family member with a disability.
- Avoid responding negatively or discouragingly to lofty goals set by families for their member with an exceptionality. A certain measure of overestimation can be advantageous.
- Help parents and families understand that a child with an exceptionality is only one among several members of the family and therefore should be responded to accordingly.
- Be aware of value system differences between the home and school support and helping organizations.
- Do not produce or use guilt to motivate parents and family members.
- Do not create a false sense of security or progress for parents and family members. Be realistic and truthful.
- As necessary, review materials and issues that have previously been discussed. It is not unusual for parents and family members to periodically wish to review old information and share their perceptions and feelings about it.
- Encourage parents to present their own agendas at conferences.
- Inform parents and family members of community resources that may help them accommodate their child or youth with an exceptionality.
- Remind parents that all children in the family, regardless of whether they have an exceptionality, have needs and require appropriate attention.
- Apprise parents and family members that their needs, as well as the needs of their child with an exceptionality, may likely change over time.

Summary

The needs and characteristics of families are not only varied but also dynamic and thus in a state of constant change. Accordingly, parent and family involvement requires that professionals be familiar with the range of needs encountered by parents and families with exceptional members, the methods for individualizing parent and family involvement, and the strategies appropriate for serving their needs. A child or youth with an exceptionality almost always will have a significant impact on his or her parents and family. The conferencer can help families more adequately understand their situation and identify strategies for most successfully providing for the overall well-being of a child with an exceptionality. As any experienced professional can attest, it is only with such efforts that a child or youth with an exceptionality can benefit maximally from available services and hence progress at a rate commensurate with his or her abilities while the family maintains the integrity of its structure.

Exercises

1. Apply the model of parent and family involvement to at least one family of a child or youth with an exceptionality. As a part of your application, identify the needs you perceive the family to have, a brief plan for best serving those needs, and your perception of an appropriate level of participation for the family.

2. Develop a list of community and school resources that offer parent and family counseling and support services.

3. Discuss with some parents the impact their child with an exceptionality has had on the family. Discuss with a brother and/or sister the sibling relationship.

4. Scan newspapers, magazine articles, movies, and other media outlets for story lines that reference persons with disabilities. Analyze how the persons with disabilities are portrayed, and the impact those portrayals might have on their families and on other individuals who interact with children and adults with exceptionalities.

5. Ask parents to suggest procedures, techniques, and services that professionals could offer to help families more effectively integrate and accommodate a child or youth with an exceptionality.

6. Invite a panel of parents of children and youth with exceptionalities to visit with a group of professionals (such as those taking a parent conferencing class, an in-service session, etc.) to discuss experiences in raising and living with an individual who has an exceptionality. As a part of the discussion, encourage the parents to identify steps that professionals could have taken to assist them in better understanding and accommodating the family member with special needs.

Chapter 2

Accommodating Cultural, Linguistic, and Family-Structure Diversity

Levinda is a single parent. Money has always been tight but particularly now that she is going back to school. Her only child, Devonne, had difficulty as soon as he entered first grade. He didn't sit quietly as his teachers read stories and presented the lessons. He interrupted class activities to make his suggestions, was often out of his seat, and began to passively refuse to do what he was asked to do. Levinda's meetings with school personnel were often thorny.

"We had meeting after meeting to talk about all the inappropriate things my son was doing. I'm fortunate because I have a reliable car so I could attend the meetings at school . . . other parents aren't so lucky. I tried to give them examples of what I do at home, but they just said, 'We can't do that' or 'We don't do that,' or they just went through the motions. There'd be 13 to 15 people to those meetings, and they cut me out of the loop. After a while I thought they just wanted to ship him off to a BD class. Devonne figured out the system. If you're a White kid, you get away with things, you can talk your way out of just about anything, but if your skin is dark—you're SOL. In fifth grade he became argumentative and disrespectful even to me, skipped school, and at some point just stopped communicating, so I signed the papers for placement in a BD room. . . . I thought it was either do that or risk that he'd end up in jail.

His teacher is wonderful! She admits that she doesn't know everything, and we brainstorm ideas. She invited me to come to class and see what she is doing. She doesn't believe in baby work just 'cause you're in special education. She actually works on academic subjects and recognized that Devonne was doing his homework and sharing it with the other kids but wouldn't turn it in. He didn't want anyone to know that he was smart. Now that I'm going back to school, I try to be a good role model for him.

Devonne's dad has another family now and lives in town, but he hasn't seen Devonne since he was a baby. It has been rough on Devonne to see his half brothers, sisters, and cousins around town but not see his dad. He recognizes them when he sees them on the streets and sometimes will say hi, but they don't talk. I know it hurts him and makes him feel less, but he won't talk about it. I think it's why he gets belligerent and combative with his teachers and me. We're all trying to work on that now."

This scenario helps to illustrate the complexity of issues often surrounding the families of children with special needs. These families represent the changing nature of "family" that reflects increasing cultural, ethnic, and linguistic diversity, as well as the way we define the family unit itself.

Culture refers to group relatedness or the way that people identify or associate with each other through shared implicit and explicit rules and traditions that express the beliefs, values, and goals of the group (Kalyanpur & Harry, 1999). Most discussions of cultural diversity begin with race and ethnicity. Superficial considerations interpret these terms to be synonymous; however, *race* refers to presumed biological differences, whereas *ethnicity* indicates regional and cultural differences (Atkinson, 2004; Tate & Audette, 2001). This distinction is important given the tendency by some to consolidate several culturally diverse groups into racial categories, suggesting that people of the same race share the same culture. The largest and most clearly identified ethnic minority groups include African American, Native American Indian, Asian American, and Hispanic or Latino (Atkinson, 2004; U.S. Census Bureau, 2002), although these groups represent an oversimplification of the diversity in the United States.

Teachers should recognize the differences among specific groups of individuals from the same general minority classification and not assume that they share common characteristics. For instance, the umbrella category "Hispanic" includes groups such as Mexican Americans, Puerto Ricans, South Americans, and Cuban Americans, all of which have many unique characteristics. The group "Asian Americans" includes families from diverse countries of origin such as Korea, China, Laos, Cambodia, India, and Japan. Teachers can expect to find significant between-group differences (e.g., Chinese families versus Japanese families) as a result of differences in language, values, and religion. In addition, there are within-group differences among ethnic minorities as a result of the specific region of origin, recent immigration versus third generation, socioeconomic status, life experiences, and the degree to which the family has assimilated into the mainstream American culture (Atkinson, 2004; Harry, 2002; Kalyanpur & Harry, 1999). Certainly the experiences of an affluent Asian American entrepreneur in Silicon Valley and those of a recent immigrant who drives a cab in New York would be vastly different, even though they may share the same ethnic group and may even speak the same language (Kim, 2004). This within-group diversity, along with the recognition that culture evolves and has a dynamic nature, suggests that lists of cultural characteristics for specific groups will be helpful to the practitioner only to the degree that the characteristics are accurate for that individual family. Teachers should recognize the commonalities of parents and families and yet demonstrate an understanding of cultural differences and contemporary family experiences without reinforcing stereotypes.

The exact number of culturally and linguistically diverse students who receive special education services in schools in the United States is unknown. Although the amendments of the 2004 Individuals with Disabilities Education Improvement Act (IDEA) require that states collect and report data on the race and ethnicity of students for all disability categories, reporting of these data continues to be a problem for states, and some data are missing (U.S. Department of Education, 2002). In addition, the interpretation of these data is complex. Table 2.1 provides the percentage of students ages 6 through 21 served by race and ethnicity and disability category during the fall of the 2002 school year. As the table illustrates, compared with the percentage of all students with disabilities, a striking percentage of African American students received services for mental retardation and serious emotional disturbance. It is also notable that among Hispanic and American Indian/Alaska Native students, the percentage was higher for learning disabilities, and American Indian/Alaska Native students received services under the developmental delay category at a higher rate than other groups. It is unclear why the disability distribution rates vary by ethnic group.

Although abundant evidence shows that no cultural, ethnic, or racial group is immune to social problems, teachers nonetheless must be sensitive to several facts: (a) culturally and linguistically diverse groups experience a great number of social and economic problems (Atkinson, 2004; Blair & Scott, 2002; Fujiura & Yamaki, 2000; A. G. Gill, Wagner, & Vega, 2000; Minino & Smith, 2001), (b) culturally and linguistically diverse children have been overly represented in special education programs

TABLE 2.1.
Disability Distribution, by Race and Ethnicity,
of Students Ages 6 Through 21 Receiving Special
Education and Related Services: Fall 2002

Disability	American Indian/Alaska Native (%)	Asian/ Pacific Islander (%)	Black (not Hispanic) (%)	Hispanic (%)	White (not Hispanic) (%)
Specific learning disabilities	55.3	40.8	45.1	58.3	46.8
Speech/language impairments	16.2	25.6	14.4	18.1	20.1
Mental retardation	7.8	9.1	16.8	7.8	8.3
Serious emotional disturbance	7.9	4.7	11.3	4.9	7.9
Multiple disabilities	2.3	2.7	2.2	1.9	2.3
Hearing impairments	1.0	2.9	1.0	1.6	1.1
Orthopedic impairments	0.7	1.8	0.9	1.3	1.4
Other health impairments	5.0	4.8	5.1	3.6	8.0
Visual impairments	0.4	0.9	0.4	0.5	0.4
Autism	0.9	4.9	1.6	1.3	2.2
Deaf-blindness	<0.05	0.1	<0.05	<0.05	<0.05
Traumatic brain injury	0.3	0.4	0.3	0.3	0.4
Developmental delay	2.2	1.4	1.1	0.5	1.0
All disabilities	100.0	100.0	100.0	100.0	100.0

Source. From *Twenty-Fourth Annual Report to Congress on Implementation of the Individuals with Disabilities Education Act,* Tables 1-16a through 1-16m, Vol. 2, by U.S. Department of Education, 2002, Washington, DC: Author. These data are for the 50 states; Washington, DC; Puerto Rico; Bureau of Indian Affairs schools, and the four outlying areas.

(Artiles, Harry, Reschly, & Chinn, 2002; Coutinho & Oswald, 2000; Ferri & Connor, 2005) and underrepresented in programs for gifted and talented students (Donovan & Cross, 2002; Elhoweris, Mutua, Alsheikh, & Holloway, 2005), and (c) discriminatory and otherwise biased assessment procedures represent significant concerns for culturally and linguistically diverse children experiencing school-related problems (Artiles et al., 2002; Demmert, 2005; Oswald & Coutinho, 2001; Shealey, Lue, Brooks, & McCray, 2005). Just as significantly, educators must recognize the need to address specific communication-related issues when interacting with parents and families of children with exceptionalities whose cultural, linguistic, educational, or religious background is markedly different from their own.

Poverty

Poverty is one of the most intractable problems affecting our society and the welfare of our children. The link between low socioeconomic status and family structure, particularly single-parent households, and the prevalence of disabilities is well established; as poverty has increased, so has the number of children with disabilities (Birenbaum, 2002; Fujiura & Yamaki, 2000; Park, Turnbull, & Turnbull, 2002). Although the exact relationship between poverty and disability is not fully understood (whether it causes or contributes to disability), the risk factors associated with socioeconomic disadvantage, such as low maternal education, lack of prenatal care, low birth weight, and poor nutrition, significantly increase the chances of special education placement (Blair & Scott, 2002; Donovan & Cross, 2002; E. Emerson, 2007; C. A. Mason, Chapman, & Scott, 1999).

In 2003, both the poverty rate and the number of children younger than the age of 18 living in poverty rose to 17.6%, or 12.9 million children, up from 16.7% in 2002 (DeNavas-Walt, Proctor, & Mills, 2004). Poverty rates among African American and Hispanic children are more than twice those of their White counterparts (Donovan & Cross, 2002). Twenty-eight percent of children with disabilities aged 3 to 21 are living in families earning a total income below the poverty threshold set by the U.S. Census Bureau (Park et al., 2002). In addition, when investigations of poverty focus on predictors beyond family income, the picture for families with children with disabilities becomes clearer. In a study of 42,000 households responding to the *National Survey of America's Families*, researchers compared families raising children with disabilities and families raising children without disabilities on measures of material hardship (e.g., skipping meals because of lack of money, being unable to pay rent, having phone disconnected). Results indicated that children with disabilities and their families fared worse than families of children without disabilities for 8 of the 11 indicators measured (Parish, Rose, Grinstein-Weiss, Richman, & Andrews, 2008). For example, these families had a 78% greater likelihood of reporting that the food they bought did not last, had a 89% greater likelihood of skipping meals because of lack of money, and were 81% more likely to report that their phone service was disconnected because of nonpayment (p. 84). In addition, as family income rose above the poverty line, family hardship declined sharply for families of children without disabilities but not for families with children with disabilities. Raising a child with disabilities may have financial implications for families that are not completely addressed by social programs aimed at families who fall at or below the poverty threshold. In fact, many middle-class families may also be struggling with material hardships (Parish et al., 2008), and conferencers must be aware of possible financial stresses. Finally, too many children live in neighborhoods plighted by violence, drugs, and urban decay so symptomatic of the living environment of urban minority children and their families.

Although these descriptions are representative of some culturally and linguistically diverse children and their families, they are not presented here as the norm. It is important to realize that not all minority families are poor. Although approximately 10% of Asian American families in 2002 were living in poverty, one in three had annual incomes over $75,000. Disparate socioeconomic backgrounds also exist for African American families. Although family income for African Americans lags behind that of White families, with a median income of $33,589 compared to $57,320 for White, non-Hispanics, 20% of African American families earn an annual salary above $110,000 (National Population Projections, 2002; U.S. Census Bureau, 2002). In addition, Native American Indians living off reservations earn, on average, $11,000 more than those living on reservations (DeNavas-Walt et al., 2004).

Nevertheless, teachers must recognize that many families with whom they work will vary significantly from the often romanticized, majority-culture, middle-class family. Consider, for example, that although African American citizens compose only a fraction of the total population, they represent a significantly greater proportion of the nation's poor. Hispanic and Native American groups also contain a disproportionate number of individuals existing at a poverty level (Atkinson, 2004).

African American youth and young adults experience significant unemployment and underemployment problems, a higher death rate (28.7 deaths per 100,000 compared to 17.5 for White youth aged 5 to 14), and a teen pregnancy rate that places both the children and their mothers at greater risk of negative consequences such as low birth weight, infant mortality, and poverty (Minino & Smith, 2001; Wicker & Brodie, 2004).

Alcoholism, poverty, prolonged unemployment, and substandard housing are common among Native Americans, particularly those living on reservations. Native Americans also have the highest rate of completed suicides of any ethnic group (Herring, 2004; Indian Health Service, 2002).

Nearly 4 in 10 African American and Hispanic children are living below the federal poverty threshold, and the majority of these families are headed by a single parent—two variables highly correlated with increased risk for disability (Fujiura & Yamaki, 2000). Approximately 1.35 million children younger than the age of 18 (10% of all poor children) will likely experience homelessness over the course of a year (Burt & Aron, 2000), and a significant proportion of them have disabilities and are from minority groups (Waldman & Perlman, 2008). In fact, the U.S. Department of Education (2008) reported that during the 2006–2007 school year, 51,924 homeless students with disabilities were served by local school districts with funds for homeless education (McKinney-Vento subgrants). This figure does not include children younger than 6 years of age who have not been enrolled in school or those children served with only local funds, thus this figure underestimates the incidence of homeless children with disabilities. These and similar statistics point to the need for teachers to be cognizant of and sensitive to the factors associated with minority status and poverty and be willing to accommodate these circumstances.

Although conferencers may be able to do little to correct the underlying conditions and circumstances facing culturally and linguistically diverse families, they must demonstrate sensitivity to the circumstances that impact these groups. Specifically, professionals must recognize that for some parents and families, the least of their worries will be their child's school performance; that attending school conferences may create significant logistic, economic, and child care burdens; that trust and rapport with school personnel may be slow in developing; and that the perceived value of education as a facilitator of survival in certain environments may be minimal. Teachers' failures to demonstrate this sensitivity will likely lead to significant communication problems.

Professionals also should note that the detrimental effects of poverty on many aspects of family functioning, including health, productivity, and family interactions, may impair minority group members' ability to effectively consume available services. Accordingly, teachers should be sensitive to strategies for strengthening entire families (rather than focusing exclusively on children with disabilities, independent of their families) and should help parents and families more effectively use available resources to improve the quality of life for all family members. Without these efforts, educators may find that some culturally and linguistically diverse families struggle to meet the needs of a child with disabilities as they face multiple challenges associated with poverty (Boushey, Brocht, Gundersen, & Bernstein, 2001; E. Emerson, 2007; Fuller, 2008; Parish et al., 2008; Park et al., 2002).

Educational Challenges Facing Culturally Diverse Students With Exceptionalities

When it comes to accessing the American dream of educational opportunity, many students from diverse backgrounds fall far short of achieving their goals. For example, approximately 17% of African Americans and 11% of Hispanics graduate from college compared with 28% of White students (National Population Projections, 2002; U.S. Census Bureau, 2002).

Minority children more commonly attend schools that have larger average class sizes than do nonminority children, and they are likely to be taught by inexperienced instructors who have not mastered the critical skills and competencies required for effective academic instruction and behavior management (Boyer & Mainzer, 2003; Cartledge, Tillman, & Johnson, 2001; Darling-Hammond, 2004). For example, students enrolled in schools where 75% or more of enrollments were minority students or in poor schools where 75% or more of the students were eligible to participate in federal free or reduced cost lunch programs were almost twice as likely as students in nonminority and nonpoverty schools to have math, English, science, and social studies teachers who were not certified or did not have a major in those academic areas (Darling-Hammond, 2004).

According to the Civil Rights Project of Harvard University, nationwide more than 60% of Black and Hispanic students attend high-poverty schools (more than 50% on free and reduced cost lunch) compared with 30% of Asian Americans and 18% of White students. Black and Latino students are more than 3 times as likely as Whites to be in high-poverty schools and 12 times as likely to be in schools where almost everyone is poor. Students in high-poverty schools experience higher teacher turnover, lower educational standards and aspirations, more limited curriculum and educational opportunities, and higher dropout rates (Orfield & Lee, 2005; Orfield, Losen, Wald, & Swanson, 2004). In addition, linguistically diverse students may be disadvantaged when the primary language for instruction is English and when students are actively engaged in academic behaviors for less than half of a typical school day (Arreaga-Mayer, Utley, Perdomo-Rivera, & Greenwood, 2003).

It is not surprising that these students tend to perform more poorly on standardized achievement tests, particularly in the upper grades, than nonminority students and have less access to educational facilities and experiences related to academic achievement. In support of the notion that minority students frequently are exposed to fewer opportunities than their majority culture peers, the National Center for Educational Statistics (2003) reported that although more Black and Hispanic 12th-grade students are taking advanced placement examinations, in 2000 those numbers represented a considerably smaller proportion of Black and Hispanic students taking those examinations than White students. In addition, although graduation rates for minority students are increasing and dropout rates are improving, clear evidence points out the particular vulnerability of culturally and linguistically diverse students to leaving school prior to graduation, and so ensuring that students have access to the full range of education curricula and programs remains a challenge for schools (Gravois & Rosenfield, 2006; Holzman, 2004; National Center for Educational Statistics, 2003; Orfield & Lee, 2005; Pluviose, 2006; U.S. Department of Education, 2002; Wagner & Cameto, 2004).

Assessment

Assessment issues have long been significant relative to evaluation and placement of minority children into programs for students with exceptionalities (Artiles et al., 2002; Demmert, 2005; Grossman, 1995; MacMillan & Reschly, 1998). As a result, questions regarding nondiscriminatory assessment procedures are likely to occur in conferences with parents of minority pupils. There has been criticism of the perceived cultural and linguistic biases in standardized tests and the norms used to interpret results (Demmert, 2005; Ferri & Connor, 2005; Oswald & Coutinho, 2001; Shealey et al., 2005). The assumption implicit in these concerns harkens back to Dunn's (1968) criticism of placement of minority students in segregated special education classrooms because of purported harmful consequences including detrimental effects of labeling and ineffective educational dispositions. Although we might assume that the hallmarks of special education (e.g., individualized instruction based on current performance levels, empirically based instructional methods, data-driven decision making) could be only of benefit to any student, it is critical that our assessment procedures identify all eligible students with disabilities and not simply reinforce stereotypes of minority groups.

Most teachers recognize the difficulties in assessing and interpreting scores for students with limited English proficiency using assessments administered in English. The results most likely reflect the student's ability to read and comprehend the English language. Might culturally diverse students also be disadvantaged in assessment procedures that fail to consider the influence of culture on students' interpretation of test questions, their comfort level with the testing context, or their level of engagement? As a result, increased attention has been turned to the IDEA mandate that schools consider a child's native language and culture when conducting assessments and evaluations (Demmert, 2005; Shealey et al., 2005).

Parents want to know that during the assessment process, educators have obtained an unbiased, thorough, and accurate picture of their child's needs and abilities and hence that their own child's diagnosis and placement are valid. Professionals' ability to respond to questions and demonstrate to parents and family members that the assessment procedures were nondiscriminatory, multidisciplinary, and comprehensive is closely aligned with developing and maintaining rapport, trust, and effective parental involvement.

Placement

National statistics indicate that students from culturally and linguistically diverse backgrounds are disproportionately placed in special classes, particularly for children with mental retardation and behavioral disorders, and are underrepresented in gifted and talented programs (Artiles et al., 2002; Elhoweris et al., 2005; Friend, 2005; Losen & Orfield, 2002; U.S. Department of Education, 2002). This issue has been debated for decades (Artiles & Bal, 2008; Dunn, 1968; Hallahan, Kauffman, & Pullen, 2009; Harry & Klinger, 2006; Hosp & Reschly, 2003; MacMillan & Reschly, 1998; Ndura, Robinson, & Ochs, 2003; J. M. Patton, 1998).

For some parents and professionals, the overrepresentation of culturally and linguistically diverse students in special education classes and the underrepresentation of them in gifted and talented programs are indicators of systemic bias and foster feelings of mistrust for educational institutions. The measurement of disproportionality and the interpretation of those data is complex. One way to interpret overrepresentation is to calculate a risk index for each disability category for each ethnic group. The risk index is calculated by dividing the number of students with the disability in the racial and ethnic group by the total number of students in that racial and ethnic group in the population, multiplied by 100 to produce a percentage. A ratio of 1.0 indicates exact proportionality, whereas a ratio above 1.0 or below 1.0 indicates over- and underrepresentation, respectively (Skiba et al., 2008). Data provided by the annual reports to Congress on the implementation of IDEA indicate that the percentage of the population receiving special education services varies by race and ethnicity. In 2003 the percentage receiving special education (risk index) was largest for American Indian/Alaska Native (13.8%), followed by Black (12.4%), White (8.7%), Hispanic (8.2%), and Asian/Pacific Islander (4.5%) students (U.S. Department of Education, 2007). Likewise, the risk index for ethnic groups for specific disability categories can be compared by constructing a risk ratio (Hosp & Reschly, 2003; Parrish, 2002). Using the 2003 data, risk ratios indicate the following:

- American Indian/Alaska Native students were 1.8 times more likely to receive special education and related services for specific learning disabilities and 3.6 times more likely to receive services for developmental delay than all other racial and ethnic groups combined.
- Asian/Pacific Islander students were 1.2 times more likely to receive special education and related services for hearing impairments, autism, and deaf-blindness than all other racial and ethnic groups combined.
- Black students were 3.0 times more likely to receive special education and related services for mental retardation and 2.3 times more likely to receive services for emotional disturbance than all other racial and ethnic groups combined.
- Hispanic students were 1.2 times more likely to receive special education and related services for hearing impairments and 1.1 times more likely to receive services for specific learning disabilities than all other racial and ethnic groups combined.
- White (not Hispanic) students were 1.6 times more likely to receive special education and related services for other health impairments than all other racial and ethnic groups combined (U.S. Department of Education, 2007).

Conversely, a low percentage of children from culturally and linguistically diverse backgrounds are found in programs for gifted and talented students (D. Y. Ford, Grantham, & Whiting, 2008; U.S. Department of

Education, 2002). Elhoweris et al. (2005) reported that elementary school teachers treated identical information regarding a gifted and talented student presented in a descriptive vignette differently according to student ethnicity. Teachers were slightly more likely to refer students of unspecified ethnicity than the African American students to gifted and talented programs.

The issues of disproportionate representation have not only been debated; some of those discussions are often emotionally charged. Of particular concern is the number of culturally and linguistically diverse students who are determined to be eligible for special education under the more subjective categories (those reliant on clinical judgment) such as learning disabilities (LD), mental retardation (MR), and behavior disorders (BD) compared with less subjective categories such as blindness or deafness (Ferri & Connor, 2005; Losen & Orfield, 2002). One hypothesis posits the cause is the result of cultural biases inherent in the referral, assessment, eligibility, and placement process in special education. Consequently, initial referrals for special education evaluation result from teacher–student and home–school discontinuities and conflicts that are based on cultural differences, not on the presence of actually disabilities (Coutinho & Oswald, 2000). The assessment process exacerbates the differences by overreliance on standardized tests and procedures inappropriate for use with culturally and linguistically diverse students. Subsequent educational placements are made based on factors such as socioeconomic status and ethnicity rather than on student needs (Blair & Scott, 2002; Blanchett, Mumford, & Beachum, 2005; Ferri & Connor, 2005; A. Frey, 2002).

Only a small percentage (14% or less) of the professionals who work in public schools represent culturally or linguistically diverse backgrounds (Billingsley, 2002; National Collaboration on Diversity in the Teaching Force, 2004); in contrast, the student population is becoming increasingly diverse, and by some estimates students who are culturally or linguistically different will become the majority within a few decades (Boyer & Mainzer, 2003; Cushner, McClelland, & Safford, 2003; Tyler, Yzquierdo, Lopez-Reyna, & Flippin, 2004). The number of culturally and linguistically diverse special education teachers is not projected to keep pace with the growth in diversity within this student population (Olson, 2000; Tyler et al., 2004). This situation results in a lack of role models for students, creates the potential for negative stereotypes and inaccurate perceptions among teachers, and engenders parents' perceptions that teachers do not understand them. Because teachers initiate most referrals, and those teachers likely come from a cultural background different from their students', some researchers have suggested that the mismatch between teaching style and learning style is a factor in disproportional placements (Atiles et al., 2002).

Low socioeconomic status (A. Frey, 2002) and minority status are significant predictors of referral for special education and teachers' recommendations for special education placement (Blair & Scott, 2002; Mutua, 2001; D. Zhang & Katsiyannis, 2002), resulting in disproportionate placement of culturally and linguistically different students in special education programs. Few studies, however, have been conducted to examine referral rates by comparing them to population rates, and those few were in individual school districts (Hosp & Reschly, 2003). In addition, disproportionality of African Americans and Native Americans has been observed at the national and local level; nevertheless, referral and placement patterns vary at the district and school levels based on such factors as program size and representation of the group in the district (Artiles, Rueda, Salazar, & Higareda, 2005). Clearly, there are a number of student and sociodemographic variables mediating special education placements for culturally and linguistically diverse students.

A study by Hosp and Reschly (2002) illustrated the complexity of the issues underlying overrepresentation. In their analysis of specific variables and patterns of variables related to the restrictiveness of students, they concluded,

> Overall, decisions regarding restrictiveness of a student's placement appear to be influenced by three general factors: the severity of the student's academic difficulties, the presence of behavior problems, and the involvement of the student's family. These factors appear to be consistent for African American and Caucasian students. This would suggest that disproportionate placement in more restrictive programs, when it exists, is not a matter of bias in the process of special education placement. (p. 235)

They also noted, however, that African American students who did not receive individual help from teachers as a prereferral intervention were more likely than their White peers to spend more time in placements outside the general education classroom (Hosp & Reschly, 2002). It is unclear why students did not receive prereferral interventions or why this would result in differential placement for African American students.

A second hypothesis suggests that because minority groups experience more poverty, limited school and community financial resources, and limited access to educational options (Blair & Scott, 2002; Cartledge et al., 2001; Fujiura & Yamaki, 2000), they may be differentially vulnerable to educational disabilities (Coutinho & Oswald, 2000).

Coutinho, Oswald, and Best (2002) investigated individual student and school district-level variables that influence LD identification rates for minority students. Using data collected by the U.S. Office of Civil Rights and the National Center for Educational Statistics, the authors examined the effects of gender, ethnicity, and sociodemographic factors such as student–teacher ratio, per-pupil expenditures, and percentage of non-White and limited English proficient students enrolled on the proportion of students identified as having LD. Their analysis suggests that both individual student characteristics and sociodemographic conditions of a school district are strongly associated with the proportion of students identified as having LD, and the impact of the sociodemographic characteristics is different for various gender and ethnicity combinations. For example, LD identification rates for gender and ethnic groups, except Native American Indian, decline as the proportion of non-White students in the school district increases. Black and Hispanic students and male Asian American students, however, are more likely to be identified as having LD as the percentage of households below the poverty threshold increases (Coutinho et al., 2002). Clearly, additional research is needed to determine the relationship between poverty and district-level variables on the identification of culturally and linguistically diverse students.

The multifactored nature of overrepresentation clearly warrants further examination of the relationship between cultural and linguistic differences and the referral, assessment, and placement processes in special education. Additional research will address whether overrepresentation is the result of inadequate referral and screening procedures, invalid assessment practices, teachers' misinterpretation of cultural or linguistic differences, placement procedures in response to increasing social and political pressures for educational accountability, poverty, or some combination of these and other factors.

In the meantime, educators can respond to the issue of disproportionate placement by ensuring that they implement scientifically validated interventions effective across cultures, such as early detection and primary prevention, prereferral procedures, social competence, resiliency, and self-determination strategies (Cartledge & Kourea, 2008; Donovan & Cross, 2002; D. Y. Ford et al., 2008; Gravois & Rosenfield, 2006; Serna, Forness, & Nielson, 1998).

Disciplinary Actions

Minority students, particularly Black males, are vulnerable for more severe punishments than White students for the same behavioral infractions and are expelled at rates two to three times higher than White students (Cartledge et al., 2001; Day-Vines & Day-Hairston, 2005; Pauken & Daniel, 1999). Several ecological factors have been suggested to account for this difference. The dynamic interaction between poverty and minority status, discussed previously in this chapter, also impacts student behavior. The high density of students in overcrowded classrooms, inadequate facilities, inexperienced teachers who do less to challenge their students academically, high levels of crime and violence, family challenges, and myriad other factors strain a student's ability to conform to school demands and expectations (Bireda, 2002; Day-Vines & Day-Hairston, 2005; Mendez, Knoff, & Ferron, 2002), particularly if those demands and expectations are translated into zero-tolerance policies that are vague and inconsistently applied.

Students who feel disconnected from their school may adopt a posture of false bravado when academic achievement, prosocial behaviors, and personal vulnerability are ridiculed by their peers. They engage in acting-out behaviors, hostility, and aggression in the absence of appropriate outlets for their personal distress (Day-Vines & Day-Hairston, 2005; Wicker & Brodie, 2004), prompting schools to respond with reactive punitive measures such as suspension and expulsion.

Some students from minority groups demonstrate communication patterns that are described as loud, intense, and confrontational because they stand in sharp contrast to the more reserved, dispassionate, and impersonal style demonstrated by majority culture students. As a result, minority students may be disciplined for verbal behavior that is interpreted as rude, disrespectful, or even volatile by their teachers (Day-Vines & Day-Hairston, 2005). In addition, those minority students who retain a spontaneous and interactive communication style rather than the sequential turn-taking common in public school classrooms may be identified as disruptive or impulsive (Day-Vines & Day-Hairston, 2005; Gay, 2000).

The concept of cultural capital, or the funds of knowledge and experiences that enable parents to understand and negotiate the majority culture (Barrera, Corso, & Macpherson, 2003; Kalyanpur & Harry, 1999; Valadez, 2002), may play a part in this misinterpretation. The knowledge of how educational systems operate, and positive experiences negotiating those systems, helps parents prepare their children for the academic and behavioral requirements of school. Lacking that knowledge and experience, parents may be at cross-purposes with school. Their expectations may not match those of the school (Aaroe & Nelson, 2000), and parents send conflicting messages to their child about appropriate behavior. In summarizing research on parental views of disabilities, Harry (2002) noted that minority parents of children with mild disabilities held broader parameters of normalcy than those allowed by the school-based evaluations by which children were classified, only considering "disability" an appropriate label when the child's cognitive and social functioning was obviously impaired. Others have suggested that some parenting styles do not instill in children a sense of personal accountability (Bireda, 2002).

Likewise, children whose perceptions of rules, routines, and expectations closely mirror those of their teachers are less likely to demonstrate challenging behaviors that often result in punitive disciplinary actions. Cultural norms impact both teacher and student behavior and may contribute to dissonance in teacher–student interactions (Cartledge et al., 2001). For example, a high school teacher may misinterpret a Black male student's attempts at verbal sparring during class discussions as a challenge to her authority or competence or even as an indication of disrespect. In response, she is likely to issue a disciplinary warning or some other punitive consequence. The student then responds with an intentional disrespectful or flippant remark because he feels that he was appropriately participating in the discussion and has been unfairly treated by the teacher.

Establishing fair and appropriate policies for determining when and for how long students should be excluded from attending school is quite important, given that students from diverse cultural groups are especially vulnerable to dropping out of school and experiencing out-of-school problems. Teachers should use their understanding of the impact of culture on behavior to ensure that minority students are taught the necessary strategies, self-management skills, and appropriate replacement behaviors to succeed in school. At the same time, they should be aware of other variables such as poverty, poor academic achievement, and negative school experiences that may more fully explain the inappropriate behavior exhibited by culturally diverse students (Aaroe & Nelson, 2000; Marsh & Cornell, 2001).

Community Services

Community services issues relative to students and families from minority culture and language groups also warrant the consideration of teachers. These families are more likely to have problems associated with substance abuse, mental illness, family conflict, and domestic violence (Abreu, Consoli, & Cypers, 2004; Anderson-Butcher & Ashton, 2004; Atkinson, 2004; Bowen & Richman, 2002; Dodge, Keenan, & Lattanzi, 2002; Talbott & Fleming, 2003; Weist et al., 2000; Wicker & Brodie, 2004). These problems are compounded by family poverty and a lack of resources in the community. In 2003, 11.4% of all children, or 8.4 million, were uninsured (DeNavas-Walt et al., 2004), increasing the inaccessibility of needed care for these students who must rely on publicly funded mental health services. In many poor communities, the services are few, agencies are understaffed, and parents may have to travel to other communities for assistance. Lack of reliable transportation, lack of access to child care, or scheduling difficulties associated with working multiple low-paying jobs may also hamper access to services.

Burns and colleagues (2004) reported that nearly half (47.9%) of youths aged 2 to 14 who had been investigated by child welfare agencies after reported maltreatment displayed significant emotional or behavioral problems, yet only one fourth of those youths received appropriate mental health services. Moreover, minority youth are less likely to receive care (Garland, Landsverk, & Lau, 2003; Yeh, McCabe, Hough, Dupuis, & Hazen, 2003). Many students, particularly those with multiple problems, fall through the cracks and are overlooked by local social services (Dodge et al., 2002) or don't actually receive the care they have been scheduled to receive (Harrison, McKay, & Bannon, 2004; McKay, Lynn, & Bannon, 2005). This may be the result, in part, of miscommunication between parents and agency providers or a failure on the part of agencies to identify parents' attitudes and beliefs about mental health services or to problem-solve obstacles identified by parents to accessing and continuing with those services (Hoagwood, 2005). This is illustrated by the families who reported that they wanted services even after they missed the initial session (Harrison et al., 2004). Interestingly, families who receive the specific services they request for their child attend more treatment sessions (Bannon & McKay, 2005). Clearly, responsiveness to family needs is related to ongoing utilization of services and must be carefully considered to improve outcomes for youth and their families.

The families most in need of community services may be the most difficult to engage. Minority families may be reluctant to seek assistance from community services because they are suspicious of majority institutional structures (e.g., law enforcement, education, social services) as being potentially threatening environments or systems (Neville & Walters, 2004). This cultural mistrust can also extend to interpersonal situations with personnel from these systems and may result in avoidance of initial contact or follow-up visits. Some parents feel that seeking help outside of the family is inappropriate or to be used only as a last resort, or they are skeptical of any positive outcomes (Day-Vines & Day-Hairston, 2005; McKay, Pennington, Lynn, & McCadam, 2001). In addition, some family members may feel that to seek services brings shame on the family by suggesting they are unable to care for their own children. The fear of stigma, shame, or disgrace prevents some families from accessing community services that would be of great benefit.

In a study by Cho, Singer, and Brenner (2003), Korean immigrant mothers reported episodes of suicidal ideas and feelings especially when they first heard that their child had severe disabilities, and they reported that these intense emotions could last from several months to 2 years. These feelings often returned when their child exhibited inappropriate behavior that caused them to feel shame or even humiliation. Asian cultural values include a collectivist family orientation that places the needs of the family over the individual's needs, and family honor and reputation in the community are essential (Atkinson, 2004). For some Asian American parents, suicide may be considered an acceptable mechanism to remove shame. Therefore, the need for counseling services that are culturally sensitive are of critical importance, particularly in cases where family members may be experiencing extreme psychological distress or when suicidal ideation is reported (Cho et al., 2003).

Given the significant unmet needs, professionals have advocated for improved linkages between social service agencies and public schools to make services more effective and accessible to students and their families (Altshuler, 2003; Anderson-Butcher & Ashton, 2004; Dodge et al., 2002; Zanglis, Furlong, & Casas, 2000). In response, collaborative planning teams have adopted an approach often called "wraparound" to design and implement individualized service plans for children and families. The purpose is to wrap an array of services (e.g., mental health, substance abuse, health, education) around students with multiple or complex needs in a coordinated and comprehensive plan. Wraparound teams share a common value base reflected in a collaborative planning process that is family driven, culturally competent, individualized, and based on the strengths of the child, family, and community (Anderson-Butcher & Ashton, 2004; Burns, Schoenwald, Burchard, Faw, & Santos, 2000; J. S. Walker & Schutte, 2004). Proponents of a wraparound approach assert that services and service planning are likely to be more effective if families are included as collaborative partners because this builds family optimism and empowerment, which results in increased capacity for adaptive problem solving (J. S. Walker & Schutte, 2004).

Some schools have also extended traditional links with community agencies and organizations to form "extended-service schools," "full-service schools," "community schools," or, more generally, "school–community initiatives" (U.S. General Accounting Office, 2000). These collaborative structures are designed to provide the support necessary for students to be successful in school and beyond and to strengthen their families and communities. They use some federal funds but are mostly funded at the local or state level or by private organizations.

One example is the Juvenile Services Task Force in Alliance, Ohio (later renamed the Alliance Family Council), which brought together representatives from area service agencies to develop a tighter net of services for students and their families through collaboration and service coordination (Dodge et al., 2002). The goal was to empower parents, other adults, and community institutions to address juvenile issues such as classroom and community behavior, academic performance, mental health needs, graduation rates, and criminal activity. To avoid duplicating or complicating the efforts of community agencies working with students and families, the school provided appropriate agency referrals to students in need of services. They maintained a coordinated service plan so families registered for services with a single agency, and all involved agencies had important information about the clients; there was a seamless system of services. To reduce the stigma often associated with seeking out mental health services, a mental health clinic was provided within the school, and therapy sessions were scheduled during the school day (Dodge et al., 2002). They also recommended other services such as parent training, mentorship services, and a summer meals program. What began as a meeting of a small group of service providers at the school district office developed into a system of care for students and their families to address identified needs within their local communities.

Although these coordinated services programs have not been rigorously evaluated through comparison of their participants and similar students and families, they have demonstrated preliminary positive outcomes and garnered support from their respective communities such that they hold great promise for students with disabilities and their families and communities.

Forming Partnerships With Culturally and Language Diverse Families

Developing effective partnerships with parents and families who have diverse cultural and/or language characteristics is basic to effective education and requires that teachers remain aware and accepting of various cultures and other differences. Understanding and accepting that members of different cultures will vary in the value they attribute to certain issues (e.g., educational progress) will facilitate the professional's ability to interact more effectively with a wide range of families. Thus, for example, such awareness should aid in understanding some Hispanic families' concern over academic competitiveness and some Native American families' resistance to the use of public praise in social reinforcement programs.

An important cautionary note must accompany teachers' attempts to understand individuals of cultures different from their own. First, it is critical to invest sufficient effort in the task of learning and understanding that one can transcend stereotypical descriptions—negative or positive—of other cultures. Thus, educators must become familiar with the day-to-day background, culture, and traditions of students and their families rather than with just the popular folklore regarding a particular group.

Developing an Awareness of Value Differences

The cultural beliefs and values held by minority families may differ significantly from those held by the majority culture, particularly regarding educational issues (Correa & Jones, 2000; Day-Vines & Day-Hairston, 2005; Garrett, 2004; Herring, 2004; Lai & Ishiyama, 2004). Those beliefs and values will impact the interactions between school and home and will be reflected in parents' goals for their children and in their willingness to implement certain intervention strategies. Understanding and building on a family's cultural interpretations of disability and beliefs about and participation in the intervention process are essential for creating partnerships with parents (Lamorey, 2002). The degree to which schools form respectful and comfortable partnerships with diverse families will also be reflected in parents' satisfaction with special education services (Bailey, Skinner, Rodriguez, Gut, & Correa, 1999; L. T. Zionts, Zionts, Harrison, & Bellinger, 2003).

It is important that professionals scrutinize their own attitudes toward specific minorities. In particular, teachers should attempt to pinpoint personal beliefs, prejudices, fears, and concerns regarding culturally and linguistically diverse groups as well as to try to better understand the nature and origin of these perceptions. The middle-class majority culture educator should be aware, for instance, that public school curricula and procedures have historically accentuated the "rightness" of the White and European tradition. Although some schools have attempted to focus on the "melting pot" composition of this country and its ability to accommodate "other peoples," this traditionally has been pursued under the guise that minority groups would eventually adopt the values, ideals, and practices of the majority culture. As a result, we can expect that an educator reared in the tradition of the dominant culture (particularly if from a middle-class background) has developed certain beliefs and perceptions regarding minority groups as either wishing to retain their own traditions and values or having been prevented from becoming a legitimate part of the majority culture. This should in no way be interpreted as an endorsement of biased or inappropriate attitudes and prejudices; rather it is a position based on the premise that individuals must first understand their own values and sentiments before they can effectively communicate with persons of different beliefs (Harry, 2008; Kalyanpur & Harry, 1999; Lamorey, 2002). Though individuals with particularly strong biases may need to explore strategies for modifying their attitudes, the primary benefit of self-scrutiny is better self-understanding.

As a means of gaining a clearer understanding of minority-related beliefs, readers are encouraged to complete the self-assessment survey that appears in Figure 2.1. Those who belong to culturally diverse groups themselves should complete the form on the basis of their perceptions of other minority groups. For each item, the respondent should check the column (strongly agree, mildly disagree, etc.) that most closely corresponds to his or her attitude. Respondents should base their answers on initial impressions rather than attempt to "talk themselves" into or out of certain choices. After completing and reflecting on their responses, readers are encouraged to ask a colleague to evaluate them using the same scale. Areas of discrepancy should be discussed along with attitudes that may require modification. The instrument also can serve to assess patterns of growth and change over time and to solicit feedback from minority parents and families. Although no norms are associated with this scale, it can make professionals more familiar with their diversity and minority-related values and attitudes. Such self-understanding provides the basis for more effective communication and programming efforts.

Garrett (2004) and Herring (2004) identified several value-related differences between Native Americans and the majority culture. They observed, for instance, that Native Americans tend to respect and honor their elders more, their family life more often includes extended family members, they more commonly accept and conform to Nature instead of attempting to dominate it, they put less emphasis on personal competition and prestige, and they more frequently express themselves through actions rather than through words than do members of the majority culture. They emphasize the connectedness of family and community members, and the group takes precedence over the individual. Similarly, African American cultural values promote a collective orientation that includes an extended

	Strongly Agree	Agree	Mildly Agree	Neutral	Mildly Disagree	Disagree	Strongly Disagree
1. I am uncomfortable in conferences with individuals with skin colors different from my own.	☐	☐	☐	☐	☐	☐	☐
2. I consider culturally and linguistically diverse educational problems basically to be a function of a lack of parental emphasis on doing well in school.	☐	☐	☐	☐	☐	☐	☐
3. I am intimidated by individuals from cultures that I do not fully understand.	☐	☐	☐	☐	☐	☐	☐
4. I believe that the dominant language of the home, even if not English, should be accommodated in public school.	☐	☐	☐	☐	☐	☐	☐
5. I believe that the dominant language of the home, even if not English, should be taught in public schools.	☐	☐	☐	☐	☐	☐	☐
6. I believe that certain cultural and ethnic groups are innately inferior in educational potential to the majority culture.	☐	☐	☐	☐	☐	☐	☐
7. I am uncomfortable in conferences with parents who are unable to speak standard English.	☐	☐	☐	☐	☐	☐	☐
8. I frequently become angry in conferences with parents who are unable to speak standard English.	☐	☐	☐	☐	☐	☐	☐
9. I share many similarities with the minority pupils and families with whom I am associated.	☐	☐	☐	☐	☐	☐	☐
10. I am usually as satisfied with my conferences with minority parents as with those that include nonminorities.	☐	☐	☐	☐	☐	☐	☐

Figure 2.1. Minority Attitude Self-Assessment Survey.   (continues)

	Strongly Agree	Agree	Mildly Agree	Neutral	Mildly Disagree	Disagree	Strongly Disagree
11. I would prefer to work in a school serving children and families from cultures and backgrounds similar to my own.	☐	☐	☐	☐	☐	☐	☐
12. I believe that most cultural and language-related social problems could be solved if groups made up their minds to improve their conditions.	☐	☐	☐	☐	☐	☐	☐
13. I do not believe that schools can solve many of the problems experienced by minorities.	☐	☐	☐	☐	☐	☐	☐
14. I am surprised when parents from culturally diverse groups show an interest in their child's school-related performance.	☐	☐	☐	☐	☐	☐	☐
15. I resent certain groups of parents calling me at home more than others.	☐	☐	☐	☐	☐	☐	☐
16. I am equally at ease in accepting a dinner invitation to the homes of my minority and nonminority students.	☐	☐	☐	☐	☐	☐	☐
17. I find it easier to empathize with parents whose background is similar to my own.	☐	☐	☐	☐	☐	☐	☐
18. I am more inclined to give advice to parents from culturally diverse groups than to parents from other groups.	☐	☐	☐	☐	☐	☐	☐
19. I find it easier to admit to a minority parent than to a nonminority that I was wrong.	☐	☐	☐	☐	☐	☐	☐
20. I am more inclined to ask minority parents to participate in home-based programs.	☐	☐	☐	☐	☐	☐	☐

Figure 2.1. *(continued)*

family network and incorporates religion as an integral aspect of life (Day-Vines & Day-Hairston, 2005).

Correa and Jones (2000) provided examples of cultural beliefs of some minority groups that may assist educators in successfully working with these families. Shown in Table 2.2, these examples extend the notion that diverse groups often hold unique beliefs that may affect educational services. Teachers must remember, however, that each family is unique and that family culture exists within their individual context.

Educators must become knowledgeable regarding the particular traditions and values of the minority families with whom they work. Teachers should be aware of how culture has shaped their own perceptions of what is right and wrong in parenting and in parent–child relationships, just as minority groups will have developed their own practices. For example, Native American parents may be more indulgent and less punitive to their children (Herring, 2004), and African American parents may be more accepting of physical punishment (McLoyd, Cauce, Takeuchi, & Wilson, 2000). Familiarity with and acceptance of these perceptions form the basic components of successful conferencing and culturally sensitive and appropriate interventions for families and their children.

Strategies Appropriate to Particular Minorities

Ideal parent–professional interactions are based on a free and accurate exchange of information and an atmosphere of trust, mutual respect, and cooperation. Actual interactions between parents and professionals, however, do not always meet these goals, and in particular, conferences between professionals and minority parents have tended to stumble because of misinterpretations and suspicions. Some communication problems are associated with misunderstood body language, verbalizations, or other unique expressions associated with an individual's culture. Because these and similar responses can significantly influence communication in a conference situation, professionals must become aware of their personal interaction style and its effect on specific groups of people. In addition, professionals must become familiar with the interaction styles of particular minorities and with the impact of this factor on the conferencing process. One school psychologist, for example, misinterpreted the absence of eye contact in a Native American mother to be a sign of "emotional shock" rather than the cultural manifestation that indeed it was.

Identifying all the characteristics of minority groups that warrant attention as well as the idiosyncratic habits of professionals that may affect

TABLE 2.2.
Examples of Cultural Values or Beliefs Affecting Intervention With
Culturally Diverse Families of Children With Disabilities

Ethnic Group	Cultural Values or Beliefs	Implication for Services
Mexican	machismo	• respect the role of the father in American family governance • understand that the father is the "provider" and may be uncomfortable with the child care role • provide "male-oriented" activities for the family involvement • use male professionals when possible • respect the mother's need to postpone decision making until she speaks with her husband
Puerto Rican	confianza (trust)	• understand that the families may not openly accept service providers into their lives • anticipate that it might take some time for families to develop trust in a new service provider • acknowledge that bilingual and bicultural service providers may develop confianza earlier than non-Spanish-speaking professionals • demonstrate genuine concern, care, and advocacy for the child with disabilities to advance the development of trust • develop respect from the family by learning simple Spanish phrases and appreciating their cultural traditions
	compadres	• include extended family members such as god-parents, close friends, and neighbors in school activities • respect the involvement of nonfamily members in the decision-making process • use extrafamilial subsystems to provide support for parents
Japanese	avoid confrontation	• understand that parents are not likely to challenge professionals in a meeting, even if they are unhappy with the recommendations
Native Americans	acceptance of fate	• recognize the families' acceptance of the child's disabilities, and focus on the child's strengths

Note. From "Multicultural Issues Related to Families of Children With Disabilities," by V. I. Correa and H. Jones, in *Collaboration With Parents and Families of Children and Youth With Exceptionalities,* by M. J. Fine and R. L. Simpson (Eds.), 2000, Austin, TX: PRO-ED.

certain groups obviously extends beyond the scope of this book. Moreover, diversity among individuals from the same diverse groups would make such an effort inappropriate. Accordingly, teachers must analyze their own styles and the general cultural norms of the groups with whom they relate. Awareness and sensitivity to these factors enable professionals to increase their communication effectiveness and to involve parents of minority students who might otherwise choose to withhold cooperation and involvement (Blue-Banning, Summers, Frankland, Nelson, & Beegle, 2004).

Above all else teachers must attempt to understand culturally and linguistically diverse parents in accordance with the culture of which they are a part. They must also recognize that their own demeanor and heritage will affect any interaction with minority families. Recognition of these significant factors should result in more productive conferences and increased parent and family involvement.

Involvement With Nontraditional Parents and Families of Children With Exceptionalities

Educators regularly interact with families of divorced parents, blended or reconstituted families, unmarried single parents, grandparents who raise their own children's offspring, and other atypical parent configurations (e.g., gay or lesbian parents, foster parents). Regardless of one's personal perspective regarding these changes, professionals obviously must be able to communicate and interact effectively with a variety of family groups. Moreover, it is beneficial to be able to comprehend the circumstances involved in family transitions or unique situations (e.g., divorce, family reconstitution), to possess knowledge of procedures and strategies for facilitating the growth of involved family members during stressful times, and to recognize that these often difficult or stressful circumstances will likely be further complicated when a child in an involved family has an exceptionality.

Single-Parent Families

The vast majority of one-parent homes are headed by women, even though numbers of custodial male parents have increased (Fields & Casper, 2001; Hobbs, 2005; U.S. Census Bureau, 2008). Some single mothers, unlike teenage mothers, are mature women who have opted to have children. These women are typically well educated and financially independent, and parenthood is a well-thought-out decision (Olsen & Fuller, 2003). Many single mothers, however, are resolving the issues related to single parenthood as a result of divorce, and a major issue facing many single parents is economic survival (Boushey et al., 2001). Though both men and women may have a lower standard of living after their divorce, it is the mother-headed family that seems most vulnerable to financial problems. Over half (57%) of female-headed households have family incomes below the national poverty line, and more than 90% of custodial parents are women (Fields & Casper, 2001; H. P. Johnson & O'Brien-Strain, 2000). Half of all poor households in the United States are families headed by single mothers even though they make up only one fifth of total U.S. families (Gunn, 2003). Accordingly, women who head homes must concern themselves not only with the impact of personal economic change at a time when they are most vulnerable but also with the influence of this change on their children.

In addition to financial concerns, single parents may also wrestle with stressors such as having sole or primary responsibility for the care of children; dealing with continuing conflicts with the ex-spouse over child support, visitation, or parenting practices; facing the loss of emotional support from family or friends; and dealing with other disruptive events (Amato, 2000; Cohen & Petrescu-Prahova, 2006; Olsen & Fuller, 2003; Tein, Sandler, & Zautra, 2000).

Conventional wisdom indicates that divorce has a negative, and some would argue long-lasting (see the work of Judith Wallerstein), impact on children and families. Much of the research over the past 20 years on the impact of divorce has focused on adult adjustment and academic or psychological and behavioral outcomes for children (Amato, 2000; Clarke-Stewart, Vandell, McCartney, Owen, & Booth, 2000; Jeynes, 2001; Kelly & Emery, 2003; Leon, 2003). The research, although plentiful, has generated equivocal results and positions. Although research has demonstrated that children from single-parent or divorced homes differentially suffer ill effects compared with their nuclear family counterparts, the contributing factors responsible for these findings are not clearly understood. In most cases correlations were calculated on specific variables of interest, such as behavior problems or academic achievement, between children in a variety of family structures (e.g., single parent, nuclear family, blended family). The data reliably revealed significant differences between groups. The studies, however, often confound correlation with cause such that they interpret any problems found among children in divorced families as being caused by the divorce, and they fail to include in their analysis other variables in the family context. For example, Clarke-Stewart and colleagues (2000) conducted a longitudinal study of 370 mothers in one of three categories: never married, separated or divorced, or continuously married. They found that marital status did not predict child outcomes, but other variables such as maternal education, family income, and parenting ability were significantly associated with child outcomes.

All in all, indications are strong that separation and divorce can have a negative influence on children, yet it is possible that children whose parents divorce would have demonstrated those difficulties or different problems if their parents had remained married (Leon, 2003). Before definitive conclusions can be drawn, the complexity of the variables involved requires a thorough analysis of factors such as the age of the child at the time of separation; the relationship of the child and parents prior to, during, and after the separation and divorce; coping and parenting skills; and family income, parent education, and supports available for the family.

The results of a recent study may be of particular interest to teachers. Brody, Dorsey, Forehand, and Armistead (2002) investigated parent and school contexts with 277 African American single-mother-headed households with children ages 7 to 15. It is not surprising that they observed that children benefited from parenting and school practices that were organized, predictable, and affirming. They also concluded, however, that classroom experiences can serve as a protective or stabilizing influence even when parenting was compromised. Other studies have focused on protective factors such as maternal education (Clarke-Stewart et al., 2000), positive supportive parent–child interactions (Leon, 2003), parental involvement in the child's education (Halpern-Meekin & Tach, 2008), and ways that parents and children communicate about the stressful changes before, during, and after the divorce (Afifi, Huber, & Ohs, 2006) that may buffer the negative outcomes associated with divorce and improve adaptation of children.

Finally, teachers should note that most children of divorce (75% to 80%) not only do not suffer psychological problems but achieve their career goals, retain close ties with their families, and enjoy intimate relationships, and although they may have painful memories, they are not permanently scarred (Amato, 2000; Hetherington, 2002; Laumann-Billings & Emery, 2000). Although a cliché, it seems apparent that the quality of parent contact in a home is far more significant to children than the number of parents a child lives with.

Blended Families

Although a significant number of divorced parents will reconstitute their families though remarriage (Amato, 2000), there is surprisingly little research on these blended families. Perhaps this is because there has tended to be a collective sigh of relief from some policy makers, educators, and researchers when blended families are constituted because of an assumption that two-parent households are more beneficial for students than single-parent family structures (Olsen & Fuller, 2003). Interestingly, current research suggests that, in relation to academic outcomes, stepchildren and half siblings in blended families achieved similar academic outcomes, but those outcomes were substantially worse than those for children in traditional nuclear families (Ginther & Pollak, 2004). In addition, children in blended families scored no higher and sometimes lower (especially in math) than children from divorced single-parent homes (Jeynes, 1999). When family background characteristics such as parent education and income were controlled, however, the differences diminished substantially. For example, when family income is included in the analysis, the effects of living in a single-parent home are insignificant (Ginther & Pollak, 2004; Jeynes, 1999). Ginther and Pollak (2004) discussed the possible experiences of multiple children in different blended family structures. For example, in a blended family the youngest son may spend his childhood with both biological parents, whereas the eldest child may be raised first by his biological parents, then by a single mother following divorce, then by his biological mother and stepfather, and later with his half brother. In another blended family both biological parents may remarry spouses who also bring children into the new family, and children shuffle between two separate households. Thus, the actual family structure is complex, changes over time, and can take a variety of forms, making determinations about causal relationships more difficult.

There are strengths observed in blended families, including an increase in family income, increased access to multiple positive adult role models and caregivers, a larger extended family, exposure to a positive model of marital interaction, and opportunities to improve negotiation skills (Olsen & Fuller, 2003). At the same time there are also a number of challenges.

Children in blended families may resist complying with the wishes of stepparents, natural parents may not want their spouse disciplining their children, and stepparents may feel uncomfortable assuming a parental role. Many children will experience conflict in remaining loyal to a natural parent while living with and relating to a stepparent or while interacting with a stepbrother or stepsister in the same manner as a natural sibling. There may be rivalries with stepsiblings, jealousy toward the stepparent, and conflicts regarding distribution of family resources for individual members (Ganong & Coleman, 2004; Halpern-Meekin & Tach, 2008).

All of these issues will affect a child's performance in school. Accordingly, teachers should be cognizant of and sensitive to such matters as previous emotional ties and children's loyalties to their noncustodial parents and other relatives, the distribution of authority within the family structure, and role development and enforcement. Teachers must be able to aid stepparents in recognizing that they can neither expect nor demand that their stepchildren respond to them as a natural parent or relinquish feelings of allegiance for their natural parents. Teachers may be asked to become involved in formulating disciplinary techniques and developing strategies for clarifying authority and communication lines. Finally, they must be sensitive to the changing needs of the family over time and respond accordingly.

Other Nontraditional Families

Identification of the myriad types of families that currently compose the American landscape clearly extends beyond the scope of this work. It can be said without argument, however, that educators increasingly find themselves involved with ever-increasing numbers of nontraditional families.

FAMILIES HEADED BY GRANDPARENTS

Grandparents are assuming important roles in the upbringing of their grandchildren. For some grandparents this involves providing support in the form of child care, financial assistance, or temporary housing when their adult children move back home and bring grandchildren with them. For an increasing number of grandparents, it means assuming primary responsibility for raising their grandchildren. In most cases grandparents assume primary care (are custodial grandparents) of these children when the parents are absent because of mental illness, substance abuse, a prison sentence, illness, or death or when the teenage parent is unable to care for the child (Glass & Huneycutt, 2002; Reynolds, Wright, & Beale, 2003; R. G. Sands & Goldberg-Glen, 2000).

Custodial grandparents are a diverse group—some are 35 years old, and others are in their 70s (Glass & Huneycutt, 2002)—but the median age is 53 to 57 (Reynolds et al., 2003). This means that baby boomers may find themselves caring for their grandchildren at the same time they care for aging parents. Although there are more White children being raised by grandparents, a larger percentage of African American children are in the care of their grandparents. In the late 1990s, figures indicated that 13.5% of African American children compared with 6.5% of Hispanic and 4.1% of White children were being raised by grandparents (Waldrop & Weber, 2001). In addition, a disproportionate number who care for their grandchildren for 10 years or longer are single African American women with low incomes (Reynolds et al., 2003).

There are a number of contextual conditions that impact the grandparents' ability to care for their grandchildren and their interactions with school. For most grandparents, their routines, finances, social life, and emotional state have been impacted by the realities of raising a grandchild (Fitzpatrick & Reeve, 2003; Glass & Huneycutt, 2002). If they are also caring for aging parents, they experience additional stress, fatigue, and scheduling difficulties and have less energy to help their grandchild with activities and homework (Reynolds et al., 2003). They may feel socially isolated because they are living a different lifestyle from their peers who have transitioned beyond child care concerns, and they have little in common with the young parents of their grandchildren's peers (Waldrop & Weber, 2001). Because many of these grandparents are poor and have no health insurance, they may also have stress related to inaccessibility of appropriate health care for themselves or their grandchildren. In addition, because they don't fully understand the current educational system and because approximately one third of the grandparents have not earned a high school diploma, they may feel overwhelmed with school and educational responsibilities (Glass & Huneycutt, 2002; R. G. Sands & Goldberg-Glen, 2000). In addition, because family crisis and disruption usually trigger grandparents' assuming care for their grandchildren, they may experience feelings of sadness for the dashed hopes they held for their child, anger at them for their inability to function as a parent, feelings of guilt or blame for their own errors in parenting, and disappointment at the negative impact on the family (Glass & Huneycutt, 2002; Waldrop & Weber, 2001).

Grandparents of children and youth with disabilities face additional challenges. Compared with grandparents raising grandchildren without disabilities, they report a greater need for assistance from the school in dealing with disability-related issues and access to related services for their grandchild such as transportation and speech and language therapy (Force, Botsford, Pisano, & Holbert, 2000). Abused and neglected children and those placed under the care of someone other than their parent are more likely to have emotional or behavior problems, making them more difficult for grandparents to manage, particularly as they enter adolescence (Glass

& Huneycutt, 2002; Reynolds et al., 2003). In addition, psychological and physical problems in their grandchildren are significantly related to grandparents' stress (R. G. Sands & Goldberg-Glen, 2000).

IDEA mandates that a surrogate parent be appointed for children with disabilities whose parents are unavailable or unable to act on behalf of their child. In many cases custodial grandparents assume the role of surrogate for their grandchildren (Reynolds et al., 2003). Negotiating the special education system, participating in a meaningful way in program development and implementation, and navigating the variety of social service and legal agencies involved can be daunting.

Grandparents can serve as an important stabilizing force in families. They act as surrogate parents, help to maintain the family network, transmit family culture and values, provide a stable environment for vulnerable children, and share in those children's accomplishments. Schools can assist grandparents in their efforts by identifying the grandparents' knowledge and capacity to deal with the challenges of their grandchild with disabilities, providing the necessary professional and emotional support, providing referrals to appropriate social services agencies, and creating family-centered activities inclusive of grandparents.

FOSTER FAMILIES

Foster parents care for children who have been removed from their birth home by child protective services because remaining in the home is not in the best interest of the child. They may be relatives of the child or unrelated foster parents. Currently, there are approximately 420,000 school-age children in foster care in the United States (J. Emerson & Lovitt, 2003). Data from the U.S. Department of Health and Human Services (2001) suggest that African Americans are overrepresented, with 39% of the children in foster care identified as Black, 34% as White, 17% as Hispanic, 2% as Native American, and 1% as Asian. Many of these children are also placed in special education programs (J. Emerson & Lovitt, 2003; Zetlin & Weinberg, 2004).

Although the intention of foster care is to provide alternative temporary placement, many children remain in foster care for 3 or more years, and the longer they remain in the system, the more likely they are to be suspended or expelled from school (Zima et al., 2000). These students have experienced abuse, neglect, parental substance abuse, or incarceration. They are more likely to be absent from school and to display behavioral and psychiatric problems, significant academic skill delays, and school failure (J. Emerson & Lovitt, 2003; Hussey & Guo, 2005; McMillen et al., 2005; Zetlin & Weinberg, 2004; Zima et al., 2000).

Approximately 20,000 children a year "age out" of the foster care system when they reach the age of majority, and only about a third of those graduate from high school (Zetlin & Weinberg, 2004). The long-term outcome for those who do not complete high school is sobering; many will become part of the criminal justice or public assistance systems (Zetlin & Weinberg, 2004) or end up homeless and unemployed (J. Emerson & Lovitt, 2003). Clearly, there is a moral imperative to see that these students receive appropriate services, including transition planning for postschool adjustment and increased attention to keeping them in school.

These students also experience placement instability (Hussey & Guo, 2005) as a consequence of frequent movement in child welfare placements, resulting in absenteeism and frequent school transfers. Teachers may be less likely to invest time and effort in children who they perceive to be transients in their classroom, and they may have little time to get to know the student well. Compounding this challenge is the increased likelihood that school records will be lost or incomplete (e.g., credits transferred) and difficult to access, sometimes taking weeks or months to obtain (Zetlin, Weinberg, & Luderer, 2004). As a result, students with Individualized Education Programs (IEPs) may not be placed in appropriate school programs or given necessary related services while the district completes its own assessment and IEP (Zetlin & Weinberg, 2004; Zetlin et al., 2004). Given the high residential mobility, these students may never receive the free appropriate public education to which they are entitled. Teachers may not be able to impact mobility rates, but they can ensure that accurate and up-to-date records are kept on all of their students. Educators should also be aware that foster parents may not have current educational records; nonetheless, these parents can be contacted immediately to identify any information they might have and asked to provide ongoing information for teachers to address the academic, social, and emotional needs of the children in their care. In addition, foster parents may have had little or no contact with special education systems, and teachers may need to educate them about the policies and procedures that govern delivery of special education services and the foster parents' role as advocate for the child.

Beyond relationships with foster parents, teachers will have ongoing contacts with social services caseworkers, some of whom may have concerns about confidentiality constraints when communicating with teachers. Caseworkers are initially concerned with the safety and well-being of the child and may feel that some requests for information by the school are inappropriate and unrelated to educational concerns (Altshuler, 2003). In addition it may be unclear who bears responsibility for initial and ongoing contacts. These caseworkers often act as a conduit between foster parents and the school. It is important for teachers to make an active commitment to establish trusting and collaborative relationships with caseworkers to facilitate meaningful involvement of foster parents in the schools.

Finally, students from cultural groups where multigenerational support is natural may be adjusting to the absence of not only their biological parents but their extended family members as well. Teachers can refer foster families to community agencies or organizations that provide culturally appropriate activities and opportunities for students to interact with the minority community in their area.

FAMILIES HEADED BY GAY AND LESBIAN PARENTS

Gay and lesbian parents are becoming more common and more visible in schools. Although there is a dearth of statistical information on the number of children raised in gay or lesbian families, the estimates range from 6 to 14 million (Kershaw, 2000; Lamme & Lamme, 2003). Exact numbers are difficult to obtain because of parents' hesitancy to reveal their sexual orientation in a social context that is less accepting of their lifestyle. Some research indicates that 10% of gay men and 15% to 20% of lesbian women are parents (American Civil Liberties Union, 1999; Millbank, 2002), suggesting that teachers will likely have greater contact with lesbian mothers.

Much of the research on gay and lesbian families has been in response to legal challenges to child custody and concerns regarding the adjustment of children in those family configurations. Kershaw (2000) and C. Patterson (2000) identified several key issues cited as concerns. For example, in the development of appropriate gender role behavior, boys would be less masculine and girls less feminine than those brought up in heterosexual families. Children living in those environments would be at greater risk of being sexually abused or have parents with less desirable assessments of psychological health. Finally, these children would have difficulties in relationships with peers and feel stigmatized by having a parent who is different.

The research to date is limited in that most of the samples have included White, middle-class, largely professional families; however, they provide no evidence that the psychological adjustment of these children is impaired. In addition, these families provide environments just as likely as those provided by heterosexual parents to enable normal psychosocial growth in their children (C. Patterson, 2000; Tasker, 1999). Specifically, no differences have been found between heterosexual and lesbian mothers on measures of self-concept, happiness, overall adjustment, parenting style, and general ability to parent effectively (Millbank, 2002; C. Patterson, 2000). Some have identified positive outcomes associated with growing up with gay or lesbian parents, including flexible gender roles, increased tolerance of diversity, an open climate regarding sexuality issues, and a wide range of positive role models for the children (Kershaw, 2000; McNair, Dempsey, Wise, & Perlesz, 2002). Research is now moving away from investigating the impact on the child to understanding how the family functions (Kershaw, 2000).

The way that gay and lesbian adults become parents (i.e., through heterosexual relationships, adoption, foster parenting, surrogate parenting, or artificial insemination) impacts the family adjustments that they will make. For example, children born or adopted within the context of a heterosexual relationship that ended in divorce because one parent identified as gay or lesbian will wrestle with the same challenges and reorganization that are characteristic of parental divorce and separation, previously discussed in this chapter. Those born or adopted after the parent affirmed his or her gay or lesbian identity will not necessarily experience these transitions (C. Patterson, 2000).

One lesbian parent, newly divorced and living with her partner, expressed frustration at the school staff's unwillingness to address her perception that her son's behavior problems were the result of his having difficulty adjusting to being shuffled between the homes of his mother and father, the inconsistent parenting in the two environments, and to the demands and expectations in kindergarten. The school dismissed her observations, implying instead that his behavior was in response to learning that his mother is a lesbian.

An important issue for teachers is to learn how to create supportive and respectful school environments for all families. Support from family, teachers, community, and social service agencies can play a critical role in mitigating the adverse effects of discrimination experienced by these families and are predictive of family functioning and child well-being (Lamme & Lamme, 2001/2002; McNair et al., 2002).

Professionals should remind themselves that their personal attitudes toward atypical families must not interfere with their commitment to support, communicate, and collaborate with them in an environment free from harassment and discrimination. This is particularly important because many nontraditional parents and families involved with children and youth who have disabilities will experience the need for close contact and support from school personnel.

Working With Nontraditional Families

Regardless of the attitude and personal position a teacher assumes relative to the increased prevalence of nontraditional families, these trends do represent reality. Hence, professionals have no choice but to contend, either effectively or ineffectively, with these situations. Though educators may not be trained to provide family or marital counseling, they must nonetheless be sensitive to the issues facing families within diverse configurations and be cognizant of these families' special needs. Furthermore, professionals must recognize that the changes associated with divorce, family reconstruction, adoption, and so forth will have a significant impact on both children and adults; accordingly, teachers must also recognize that only with sensitivity and appropriate strategies can the special needs of these families be met. The following are considerations for educators relative to serving the special needs of nontraditional families.

Be able to suggest resources and services for single-parent, reconstituted, and other nontraditional families. Although educational personnel must not automatically assume that single-parent, reconstituted, and other nontraditional families universally require community and professional services, they must recognize that these families will in many cases present in their most vulnerable state. Accordingly, teachers should keep available a list of appropriate resources to serve the various needs of such families. Included should be family counseling, mental health, and social agency contact persons; support groups for adults and children encountering particular types of change; agencies that can aid parents in such areas as establishing credit, securing child support and alimony, and understanding their various rights under the law; community recreation facilities and programs; day care programs; and various other problem-solving agencies. Even though educators may not directly provide the services needed to satisfy the multiple needs of these families, they can effectively assume the essential role of referral agent.

Be aware that the priority concerns of single-parent, recombined, and other nontraditional families may differ from those of the educator. Even though parents will be concerned about their children's progress in school, one must recognize that single, unmarried, recently divorced, and separated parents—as well as those involved in reconstituting or restructuring a family—will have other concerns that they may allow to take priority. This implies not that these parents should not be apprised of or allowed to be involved in their child's educational program but rather that the educator should be aware of the other issues that may be impinging upon these families. A recently divorced mother experiencing difficulty earning enough to feed and shelter her children may be understandably callous to learn that her daughter is having difficulty in math. Hence, the educator must be able to involve parents in their child's educational program while allowing them to put school-related concerns in proper perspective.

Be aware that some nontraditional parents may have severe time, energy, and financial restrictions. As noted previously, single-parent families are routinely beset by monetary problems and time restrictions. One recently divorced mother reported that her day started at 5:15 A.M. and ended at about 9:30 P.M. She confessed that even though she was deeply concerned about her child's school progress, she had neither the time nor the energy for close involvement. Awareness of this common issue for single-parent homes should sensitize educators to the need for flexible conference schedules, alternatives to face-to-face contacts (e.g., notes, phone calls, etc.), properly spaced contacts, and a variety of ways that parents can be involved in school.

Attempt to include noncustodial parents and other involved adults in conferences and programs. Even though a child may be legally assigned to live with one parent or may be part of a reconstituted family, both parents and teachers must recognize the ramifications that occur when the child has another parent with whom he or she maintains regular contact. Accordingly, efforts must be extended to apprise both parents of their child's school-related progress and to include them, as much as appropriate, in the intervention programs. Such measures allow disrupted families not only to receive significant information but also to extend therapeutic programs to a greater number of settings within the natural environment.

Become familiar with your family-related values. People tend to act on their values. Hence, the attitudes and perceptions that educators have toward marriage, divorce, family blending, and family composition will undoubtedly affect the manner in which they relate to individuals in nontraditional families. Simply becoming aware of one's values in this area can significantly improve the conferencing process.

Be able to apprise parents and family members of the potential impact of divorce, reconstitution, and other nontraditional factors on the family structure. It is not at all unusual for the teacher to be a major referral and support resource for single-parent, reconstituted, and other nontraditional families. In fulfilling this role he or she must be able to inform parents of the potential impact of the change process. In some instances this will take the form of providing reassurance that turmoil and confusion are expected by-products of divorce and family reconstitution and that eventually more satisfying experiences will replace these problems. In other situations teachers may be able to direct families in procedures for facilitating the growth and stabilization of the family unit. Finally, educators may find it appropriate to relate to parents that cooperation between home and school can serve to stabilize at least one significant environment for children in the face of an otherwise changing world. Regardless of the role played, teachers must acquire at least a basic understanding of the potential impact of divorce, family reconstitution, and other nontraditional factors on families and be able to relate this information appropriately to parents.

Aid divorced parents, stepparents, grandparents, and others to be effective in their respective roles. Helping parents and other family members to adequately fulfill their respective roles involves using effective listening techniques (including attention to feelings), exercising care in voicing opinions about an individual's lifestyle and behavior (e.g., "I just don't think divorced women with children should date"), avoiding taking sides in marital and family conflicts, making available appropriate intervention strategies and resources for solving particular problems, and allowing for parent and family individualization.

With support and appropriate resources, most parents and other members involved in nontraditional families can learn to effectively serve the needs of their children. It is mandatory that the educator be available to serve as a facilitator in this process.

Anticipate atypical behavior in parents and children experiencing turmoil and change. As suggested previously, families in transition may experience a significant amount of pressure and family turmoil. Because frequently these influences can produce changes in behavior, teachers should be sensitive to deviations in the academic and social behaviors of children involved in a change process and be willing to take necessary actions to reduce their long-term injurious effects. In the same manner the teachers must recognize that many changes in parental behavior, including even irrational actions, may be a function of the difficult situation the person is in. Hence, professionals must be cautious in drawing hasty conclusions under these circumstances.

Summary

The plurality and diversity of Americans has always been a feature of this society. At the same time, however, many have assumed that the "melting pot" characteristics of the United States would eliminate the qualities that differentiate minorities from the majority culture. Most farsighted individuals, including educators, have now abandoned this naive position and recognize that the distinct qualities of all groups must be acknowledged and accommodated.

Teachers must hone the skills required to deal effectively with a variety of parents and families of various configurations, including those with different languages, cultural practices, lifestyles, and values. Professionals who understand their own beliefs, values, and assumptions will find it easier to respect and work more effectively with the diversity of families whose children are entitled to benefit from special education. Finally, teachers must recognize that adults find fulfillment and children flourish in a variety and ever-changing array of family structures.

Exercises

1. Complete the Minority Attitude Self-Assessment Survey (Figure 2.1) in accordance with the directions and suggestions provided in the text.

2. Identify leaders and contacts in the multicultural and diverse communities with whom you might consult to increase your understanding of the diverse families in your school. For example, develop connections with church leaders of minority congregations, coordinators of gay and lesbian family resource centers, or bilingual education coordinators.

3. Identify services available through your school, agency, or community that can be used to aid parents and families contending with divorce or family reconstitution and to support other types of nontraditional families.

4. Interview parents and other members of a nontraditional family regarding their needs. Furthermore, request that they indicate those measures that educators could employ to support the family and improve collaborative interactions.

Chapter 3

Basic Skills and Strategies Needed for Successful Conferencing and Collaboration

Vignette

[My son's teacher] came to my house to meet with me. That just meant so much to me that she would take the time out of her day to come to my house—before she left the house she gave me her pager number, her home number . . . in all the previous schools not one teacher gave me their home phone number—so I think one of the characteristics of these [collaborative professionals] is that they truly, truly have a genuine interest into the well-being of that child and they believe that in order to serve the child properly they have to have a close personal relationship with the parent. They can't educate just the child academically; they really have to get into the workings of the family (Blue-Banning, Summers, Frankland, Nelson, & Beegle, 2004, p. 176).

Establishing Home–School Partnerships

In recent years there has been a shift in home–school relationships from relatively separate roles and responsibilities to a partnership approach to meet the complex needs of students with disabilities (Dettmer, Thurston, Knackendoffel, & Dyck, 2009; Fine & Simpson, 2000; B. A. Ford, 2004; Olsen & Fuller, 2003; O'Shea, O'Shea, Algozzine, & Hammitte, 2001; A. Turnbull, Turnbull, Erwin, & Soodak, 2006). This shift is due in part to recognition that the relationship between parents and teachers is likely to have a significant effect on the child's attitude, commitment, and achievement at school (Kyriakides, 2005; T. E. C. Smith, Gartin, Murdick, &

Hilton, 2006). Interestingly, although most parents recognize that success at school is a key to their child's future, they often underestimate their own potential for influencing learning (Masten, 2001). And most experienced teachers will affirm that not all parents are as involved as the teachers would like them to be. The interface of home and school is strong for some families and weak or nonexistent for others (Christenson, 2004).

We know that both home and school act as reciprocal influences on student outcomes. For example, difficulties that students experience at school impact family life, and, conversely, family problems influence students' achievement and behavior (Christenson, 2004). Likewise, skills or concepts that a student is taught at school can be reinforced with the assistance of parents at home, and goals identified by parents can be addressed through school interventions. Coordinating efforts between home and school are likely to achieve more than either one alone. Consistent congruent messages across home and school will enhance positive outcomes for students and families (K. S. Adams & Christenson, 2000; Olsen & Fuller, 2003), and this congruence is possible when meaningful partnerships are forged.

Christenson and Sheridan (2001) identified the following defining features of family–school partnerships:

- a student-focused philosophy wherein teachers and families collaborate and cooperate to enhance learning opportunities, educational progress, and school success in academic, social, emotional, and behavioral domains;
- a belief in shared responsibility, parents as essential partners, and a place where options for active, realistic participation are created;
- an emphasis on the quality of the interface and ongoing connection between families and schools to create a constructive relationship; and
- a preventive, solution-oriented focus in which families and educators strive to create conditions that facilitate student learning, engagement, and development (pp. 37–38).

Communication is the basis for establishing strong home–school partnerships and is key to successful collaborative activities (K. S. Adams & Christenson, 2000; Swick, 2003; Welch & Tulbert, 2000). When K. S. Adams and Christenson (2000) asked teachers and families of students in kindergarten through 12th grade for recommendations to improve their relationships, particularly in regard to the trust between home and school,

53% of parents and 33% of teachers identified communication as the primary means. In addition, in those relationships, the perceived quality of the home–school interaction was a better predictor of trust than the frequency of contact or demographic variables (e.g., gender, ethnicity, parent education) often associated with efficacy of the partnership. Clearly, ongoing effective communication between home and school is the essential foundation for satisfying and productive relationships (Lake & Billingsley, 2000).

Effective communication structures enhance dialogue and mutual understanding (Christenson, 2004). As a result the communication is two-way, with both parties actively participating. These exchanges will occur only when teachers are talking with parents, not at them. One of the first steps is to establish positive rapport.

Developing Rapport With Families

Establishing rapport with parents requires teachers to connect with them as individuals. Development of initial rapport may be particularly vulnerable to factors associated with cultural and linguistic differences. That is, during early meetings parents and professionals may be adversely influenced by the subtle (and not so subtle) characteristics associated with minority and majority interactions. In particular, professionals may find it difficult to empathize with persons who are different from themselves, and parents from minority cultures in turn may doubt the professional's ability to understand their current situation or overall heritage. Minority parents have often been included in traditional roles such as fund-raiser or chaperone but not in more collaborative partnerships because of erroneous beliefs that these parents would choose not to collaborate or are unable to because of language barriers or limited education (Obiakor & Ford, 2002; Peña, 2000). In addition, teachers have difficulty influencing some factors that act as barriers to parental involvement such as socioeconomic status, family size, and urban school versus suburban school (Feuerstein, 2000; B. A. Ford, 2004; Peña, 2000), and as a result they may be inclined to minimize the potential of parents as partners, neglecting efforts to establish rapport.

Nonetheless, as rapport is an essential ingredient of communication success, educators must identify mechanisms for developing this fundamental trust. Accordingly, teachers should become familiar with the effect of different rapport-building procedures on different groups. In spite of significant variance within groups, certain commonalities exist. For example, some minority groups are suspicious of "small talk" at the beginning of a conference, believing that such behavior poses a delay tactic or a strategy for avoiding an unpleasant topic rather than offering a means of establishing rapport. Conversely, other groups (e.g., Asian American and Pacific Islander) may prefer an opportunity to discuss matters unrelated to the business at hand for a few minutes before focusing on the primary agenda.

Majority culture teachers should also recognize that some minority parents are anxious and suspicious during initial encounters. Because some minority parents may have had limited prior face-to-face contact with professional personnel, they may require special support and clarification regarding the nature of the session and their own role in the conference. For example, one Hispanic father who had been asked to attend a progress report conference about his son confided that he had punished his child prior to coming to the meeting because he assumed that it was called in response to the boy's "bad classroom behavior." Asian American parents may view the teacher as the expert or authority and therefore expect a more directive and prescriptive approach, not the collaborative interaction the teacher expects (Atkinson, 2004). Teachers may need to speak candidly about the variety of roles families may assume in partnership with the school so that parents' cultural expressions are respected, yet they are fully aware of the importance of their involvement. More time may be needed to develop rapport and establish relationships when working with diverse families; teachers should also be aware that schools often represent a different culture for parents (Behring, Cabello, Kushida, & Murguia, 2000).

Educators must also be sensitive to language-related issues when conferencing with parents with limited English proficiency. In some instances, interpreters are required to participate in meetings with parents to address language differences and avoid communication barriers. In such cases teachers should be aware that interpreters may create a barrier to effective communication. Lopez (2000) and Sheridan (2000) identified several possible barriers to working with interpreters. First, introducing another person into the interaction will likely influence the pace because of the needed lag time in translating messages between teachers and parents. This delay can hamper the natural flow of communication and make the interaction seem stilted or awkward. In addition, during the translation process the listener will be turned toward the interpreter, establishing eye contact with him or her rather than with the person who originated the message. This may be a hindrance in establishing rapport with parents and families. Finally, the interpreter may also translate the essence of the message as he or she comprehended it rather than everything that was said. Errors in the translation, particularly related to complex terms, can compromise authentic communication between participants.

To avoid any potential negative effects, teachers should meet with the interpreter prior to scheduled meetings if possible or before the meeting begins to discuss the purpose and structure of the meeting or contact. Teachers should be clear in their instructions to the interpreter that they want the two-way communication translated in its entirety, not just the gist of what the teacher or parents are saying. Any potentially novel or complex terms should be fully explained to the interpreter. Finally, teachers should often clarify and validate both the parents' and the interpreters' understanding of the communicative interactions.

Most frequently language differences will take a more subtle form. For example, teachers should be aware that (a) some groups, such as Native Americans, may be parsimonious and concrete in their use of language; (b) some minority parents may fail to use standard English; (c) even bilingual educators may be unable to converse with some parents because of dialectal differences; and (d) idioms and phraseology specific to a group or region may be encountered. When language differences, albeit subtle, come up, both educators and parents must feel comfortable in asking for clarification. Failure to do so will almost certainly impede the communication process.

As a general rule, teachers must take care not to act overly sympathetic, indulgent, or patronizing of minority parents. In a like manner, professionals should avoid attempting to convince minority parents that they truly know the plight of a particular group (unless, of course, this is true because they are a member of that minority, were raised in that cultural context, etc.) or that they are different from other professionals with whom the parents may have had contact. Although one hopes that such understanding and trust will develop during the course of the conferencing process, such sentiments should not be expressed in an initial overt message to parents.

Teachers should also recognize the potential impact of their gender on interactions with some minority parents. Female educators, for example, should be aware that some Hispanics may be reluctant to take advice from women. Similarly, members of certain minority groups may avoid eye contact solely on the basis of gender.

Some families are particularly vulnerable and more difficult to engage in meaningful dialogue, such as those who are homeless. Despite the incredible challenges, many parents want to participate in their child's education but may feel powerless and helpless because of their living situation and the negative stereotypes and assumptions teachers may hold regarding the causes and realities of homelessness (Swick & Bailey, 2004). The McKinney-Vento Homeless Act of 2001 requires schools to communicate with parents and families to enhance parental involvement and to ensure that all homeless children have access to a free appropriate education (Berliner, 2002). Clearly, schools have the responsibility to reach out to these families. If teachers are to establish strong partnerships, they must strive to establish rapport and maintain ongoing communication while demonstrating sensitivity to the situation of parents who are homeless. Swick and Bailey suggested the following questions to guide efforts in developing communication with families who are homeless:

1. Are we responsive to the stressors families are experiencing?
2. What steps have we taken to encourage ongoing communication with families?
3. Are we engaging families in setting up the agenda for our various communicative activities?
4. What specific steps have we taken to help homeless families feel invited and important in our program?
5. What are we doing to continually evaluate and improve our communication strategies (p. 214)?

Communicating With Parents and Family Members

John Dewey (1938) observed that one of man's strongest urges is to be important. Listening, and the attention that accompanies the process, offers a primary means of facilitating a feeling of acceptance and value in another person. Others have also described the impact of the attention that comes from good listening. Publilius Syrus, the poet of ancient Rome, remarked, for example, that "we are interested in others when they are interested in us," and Dale Carnegie (1936) observed that a demonstration of interest in another person is the most effective means of establishing rapport.

Though documented long ago, these observations are by no means out of step with current parent and family conferencing goals and practices (Hanhan, 2003; Hepworth-Berber, 2000; Lawrence-Lightfoot, 2004b; Seligman, 2000). Without question the ability to communicate interest and attention will largely depend on the professional's ability to follow the parent's topics and to communicate an accurate understanding of what he or she is saying and feeling. In the words of Carl Rogers, "I believe the quality of my encounter is more important in the long run than is my scholarly knowledge, my professional training, my counseling orientation, the techniques I use in the interview" (1962, p. 416).

Teachers and other professionals agree that educational and related service programs that are responsive to the needs of families and the formation of effective collaborative relationships develop most effectively in an atmosphere of mutual respect, acceptance, and a willingness to listen (Idol, Nevin, & Paolucce-Whitcomb, 2000; Lake & Billingsley, 2000; Miretzky, 2004; Salas, 2004). Benjamin (as cited in Seligman, 2000) described this atmosphere:

> Basically, to me acceptance means treating the interviewee [parent] as an equal and regarding his thoughts and feelings with sincere respect. It does not mean agreeing; it does not mean thinking or feeling the way he does; it does not mean valuing what he values. It is, rather the attitude that the interviewee [parent] has as much right to his ideas, feelings, and values as I have to mine and I want to do my utmost to understand his life space in terms of his ideas, feelings, and values rather than in terms of my own. (p. 121)

Though listening may be a skill frequently taken for granted, its importance to the successful conference is such that one cannot overestimate it. In addition, contrary to popular belief, listening is not a natural aptitude for most people. True listening requires diligence and practice, and it rarely occurs spontaneously. It is a difficult skill that requires discipline and concentration to master (DeVito, 2001; Friend & Cook, 2007; Hamilton, 2001). Accordingly, educators should remember that one of their most important assets is their ability to effectively attend and listen to parents.

Empathy: A Basis for Listening

Effective communication appears to be most feasible in situations where professionals can listen empathically. *Empathy,* from a Greek term that literally means "suffering in," describes an attitude of understanding that goes beyond the surface. To empathize is to attempt to experience and understand another person's world and situation in a fashion similar to what he or she is experiencing; in essence, "to walk in their shoes." Although obviously one can never totally achieve true empathy, the climate created by attempting to understand another person's view can establish an attitude of acceptance that will facilitate the conferencing process.

Empathy facilitates the listening process by increasing one's acceptance of the parents' or families' situation and position. The empathic listener is able, within obvious limits, to relate to another individual's frame of reference as if it were his or her own. By relating to and understanding the internal world of the parent or family member, the professional can better create an accepting and supportive listening environment. Although empathic relationships are achievable, teachers must appreciate that they occur only with significant effort; ordinarily, attempts to truly understand the position and perception of parents are less common than attempts to analyze situations or arrive at solutions to problems. Hence, we tend to use language that focuses on deficit areas and difficulties to ameliorate or minimize problems. Although these strategies are not necessarily incorrect, they are frequently incompatible with true understanding and empathic listening. Teachers should afford parents opportunities to describe their children and articulate dreams for their children to see the parents' perspective of the whole child (Lake & Billingsley, 2000).

Empathy involves a cognitive component where there is understanding of another's feelings as well as an affective component where emotions expressed by another are felt vicariously (M. L. Hoffman, 2001; Snow, 2000). Empathy is distinguished from sympathy, as sympathy generally refers to feelings of sorrow or concern *for* another person, and empathy reflects feeling *with* the other person (Snow, 2000). Accordingly, empathy goes beyond the mere cognitive level to connect to the emotions and feelings of the parent or other family member. It has been said that to the parents, the child is the most important person, the one who arouses their deepest passions, greatest vulnerabilities, and fiercest protection (Lawrence-Lightfoot, 2004a). Clearly, if teachers genuinely empathize with parents and families, they will put the child's strengths, challenges, achievements, and needs at the center of conversations.

Once this atmosphere has been achieved, teachers should have in place the basic ingredient for an effective relationship and thus be able to more fully meet parents' and families' needs.

Developing Listening Skills

Although not an easy task, the capacity to listen can be learned (DeVito, 2001; Guilar, 2001; Hamilton, 2001). Though perhaps an oversimplification, at its core this skill just allows another person the opportunity to talk, with assurance that what he or she is communicating is important enough to capture the full attention.

There are two varieties of listeners: passive and active (Seligman, 2000). The passive listener allows another individual the opportunity to talk without playing an overly intense role and without making numerous responses. Passive listeners are frequently sought out by others because they offer speakers the opportunity to hear themselves. This type of listener, although perhaps not appropriate in all situations, offers parents and family members of children with exceptionalities what they may need most—the chance to talk about their attitudes and feelings relative to the child with an interested yet quietly accepting professional person. Carnegie (1936) provided the following historic example of passive listening: Abraham Lincoln sought out a friend during the Civil War to discuss the issue of slavery. As the story was related, President Lincoln spent a great deal of time verbalizing the pros and cons of abolishing slavery. After going on for hours about the situation without asking the friend's opinion, Lincoln thanked his listener for talking with him. Carnegie noted, "Lincoln hadn't wanted advice. He had wanted merely a friendly, sympathetic listener to whom he could unburden himself. That's what we all want when we are in trouble" (p. 113).

Parents and family members of children with exceptionalities frequently desire and require nothing more than the opportunity to be listened to. Though teachers must be able to disseminate information and respond to questions when answers or guidance is truly being requested, they must also allow parents and families the opportunity to derive the benefits of a good listening atmosphere.

Active listeners, as opposed to the passive variety, will assume a far more vigorous and enthusiastic role in the parent conference. This intensity will take the form of increased levels of responding, body animation, and question asking. Active listening also implies a well-established degree of rapport between respondent and listener. Lake and Billingsley (2000) noted the need to convey sincere validation of the other person's ideas. P. Zionts, Zionts, and Simpson (2002) highlighted the connection between effective communication and acceptance and interpersonal security. Swick (2003) revealed similar beliefs, noting that the process of active listening conveys that the listener values and appreciates the message and is open to what is being said.

As noted previously, effective communication between parents and family members and professionals will not occur without an adequate listening environment. It is obvious, however, that many professional people, including teachers, are far more adept at talking than listening. Swick suggested that the active listener (a) displays an attentive body and head position, (b) maintains appropriate eye contact, (c) shows authentic facial expression, (d) uses appropriate touch, and (e) provides meaningful verbal responses.

Listening is a learned behavior, one that must be consciously developed and practiced. Consequently, the listening process must include the willingness of both parents and teachers to listen to the others' points of view. As Blue-Banning and colleagues (2004) pointed out,

> Professionals need to hear directly from families their stories about how various actions or inactions have impacted their family, and about how well intentioned actions or comments did or did not have the intended effect. On the other side, parents need to hear and experience professionals' perspectives about how and why certain actions were taken, and what the limitations of their own lives might be. (p. 181)

The professional who attempts to respond to parents prior to listening to them or the educator who too hastily assumes the position of telling parents what to do or answering their questions when they simply desire the opportunity to talk will rarely establish the most satisfactory conferencing relationship. Thus, an important step is to recognize factors that may interfere with active listening, such as those described by DeVito (2001):

1. Some professionals may be hearing what is being said but are not truly listening. Instead they are mentally rehearsing the response they will give when the speaker has finished.
2. Some professionals merely tolerate the parents' talking, without really listening.
3. Some professionals reduce and analyze the content of the parents' messages without really listening to what they are saying, or they filter out the parts they are not interested in or do not want to hear.
4. Some professionals seem preoccupied, perhaps even daydreaming, while parents and family members are talking; they obviously have something else on their mind.
5. Some professionals stumble on hot-button words that elicit a strong emotional response such as *inclusion* or *fairness* and shift their focus from active listening to thinking about what the hot-button issue means to them.
6. Some professionals are distracted by extraneous details irrelevant to the speakers' message such as the clothes they are wearing, their accent, or even other sounds or conversations occurring nearby.

Specific Techniques

The effective conferencer, in addition to demonstrating the skills of attention, acceptance, and empathy, must also possess specific strategies for facilitating the communication process. These elements include door-opening statements, clarifying responses and questions, paraphrasing, reflecting, nonverbal behaviors, silence, and summarization.

Door-Opening Statements

Door-opening statements (and questions) are designed to demonstrate an interest in the parent or family member and thus indicate a willingness to listen. These efforts at stimulating the interaction process are not aggressive attempts to interrogate the parent or family member or analyze a situation, and they are not necessarily intended to obtain information or to establish a routine of questions and answers. Rather, these remarks should set an appropriate interaction tone. Implicit in the use of door-opening statements is the message that the professional does not intend to do all of the questioning and have the parent do all the answering. In addition, these remarks are designed to discourage an interaction set whereby the professional is the expert who will be able to solve all the family's problems. Rather, door-opening statements function to stimulate parents and family members to talk about a particular issue or situation.

Questions and comments such as "Can you tell me about how you see the matter?" "How do you feel about having a child with a disability?" "Can we talk about that?" "Tell me about that," and "That's interesting" illustrate door-opening statements. In addition, there are door-opening responses one can make to specific parent-initiated comments, such as in the following examples:

PARENT: Nothing seems to go right at home anymore.
TEACHER: Oh, tell me more.

PARENT: Parent–teacher conferences always upset me.
TEACHER: Sounds frustrating.

Clarifying Responses and Questions

Clarifying responses and questions serve to provide additional information or additional elaboration for the listener. In situations where, for whatever reason, the teacher is unable to follow or understand the parent, it is best for him or her to ask directly for clarification. Statements such as "I'm not sure exactly what you mean" and "Could you state that again?" present requests for clarification. This same strategy can also apply in situations where professionals desire feedback regarding whether they have been understood correctly. "What is your understanding of all of this?" illustrates this type of clarifying statement.

Clarifying responses perhaps most commonly can serve to prompt parents and family members to elaborate on a point. Generally, open-ended questions (as opposed to those that can be answered with a specific single word or phrase) will be the most effective way to elicit additional information, although teachers should be aware of the tone and meaning of their question and how it may be interpreted. For example, asking parents who are concerned about a class scheduling issue, "What do you want me to do about it?" may be interpreted as defensiveness or an attempt to end the discussion. Perhaps more open dialogue would be elicited by asking instead, "What do you think a good schedule for Shanti would look like this year?"

In addition to providing clarification, these responses indicate that the teacher is attentive and interested. Examples of this type of clarifying statement include "You mentioned feeling guilty about not giving as much attention to Ryan's brother. What do you mean?" and "Can you tell me more about how you felt when Ryan was diagnosed with autism?"

Paraphrasing

Listening can also be conveyed by restating or paraphrasing what was presented, and the intent of the technique is threefold. First, this process serves to demonstrate to the parent or family member that the teacher is, in fact, actively listening. Second, the process allows parents and family members an opportunity to hear themselves through the teacher. As parents may be more able to absorb and understand their own thoughts and motivations when echoed through another person, this process can prove highly beneficial.

Finally, the restatement process can help secure agreement between what is said and what is perceived. That is, content restatement allows others to hear what we believe we are hearing and thus affords them the opportunity to clarify our understanding. Consensus and understanding in the conferencing and counseling process compose a basic component without which little progress and rapport can take place. The restatement of content process frequently transpires through statements such as "You seem to be saying that you don't understand the nature of your son's special education program" and "If I understand correctly, you would like to see more emphasis put on vocational training for Jennifer."

Reflecting

Along with attention to the manifest content of a parent's message, the professional should show sensitivity to the feelings and emotions being expressed. To be in a position to accurately reflect, the listener must be able to empathically follow the parents. Empathy, as previously noted, is so integral a component of accurately responding to affect that one can legitimately undertake the process only after this basic listening condition has been achieved. The reflection process, just as with restating content, is undertaken for three reasons. First, these responses communicate to the parent or family member that the professional is listening to more than the expressed content of the message; that is, the person's feelings are also being followed and understood. This act serves to legitimize his or her feelings and to communicate that it is acceptable to have such emotions. This simple acknowledging of the acceptability of parents' feelings can serve to greatly enhance the communication and rapport-building process. Failure to acknowledge or adequately respond to the feelings of parents is frequently interpreted as an indication that emotions are not an acceptable component of the conference and that the teacher is either uninterested or unable to respond to affect. Either situation can impair the conferencing process. Although teachers may consider themselves most qualified to deal with issues unrelated to affect, the nature of the needs of many parents and families with exceptional members dictates that the professional has no alternative but to respond appropriately to emotion.

The reflection process also allows parents and family members an opportunity to hear their own feelings expressed through a concerned and involved professional. As emotions may or may not be evident to a parent or family member, this mirroring process can play an insightful role. In this way, for example, parents could respond to observations that they appear to have been "extremely hurt" by the insensitivity of the professional who provided the initial diagnosis or by their child's lack of acceptance by neighborhood peers.

Finally, reflection of feelings serves to confirm the accuracy of the teacher's perceptions. Although parents may not always acknowledge their feelings (even when correctly identified by the teacher), this process nonetheless does communicate the sensitivity and attentiveness of the professional and gives parents an opportunity to clarify the professional's perception. The mother of a child with a learning disability, for instance, was told during a conference with the teacher that she seemed very angry and frustrated. Subsequent to this response the mother revealed she was unaware of her pervasive anger, although she noted, "I knew something was going on with me." These feelings associated with her son's disability had probably been impeding previous parent–teacher progress and communication.

As suggested, the reflecting process takes the form of accurately understanding and expressing to the parent or family member those feelings that are present. The teacher plays the role of a mirror, reflecting both those feelings expressed by the parent and those observed by the professional but not directly stated.

Though conceptually valid, the reflection process has been criticized in recent years, primarily because of inappropriate and rigid use. In instances where counselors attempt to rely on this procedure in the absence of other established listening and conferencing techniques, and when the reflecting response takes on a hackneyed and routine format, its efficiency will be greatly diminished. Many individuals have encountered at least one aspiring therapeutic agent whose entire counseling repertoire consisted of an overused phrase such as "It appears that you feel . . ." or "I hear you saying you feel . . . ." In instances of following this strategy rigidly, one can expect minimal success. This is particularly true in educational settings, where parents and family members are typically not seeking therapy for themselves.

It should be apparent at this point that reflecting affect or any other single communication strategy or tool will prove inadequate and inappropriate if relied on exclusively. Relative to interactions with teachers who serve children with exceptionalities, parents and families have multiple needs; hence, it is logical that they will be inadequately served by over-reliance on any single method. Nonetheless, it is important for teachers to remember that they must have strategies for responding to affect. When emotional content is the most salient feature of a session, teachers must respond appropriately. To fail to do so will undoubtedly undermine other aspects of the parent–teacher interaction and the future goals of the relationship. Thus, the teacher must concentrate on developing an authentic and spontaneous style compatible with his or her personality but also appropriately responsive to the emotions of the parent. Examples of reflecting affect follow:

> PARENT:　It's just heartbreaking to see Tommy flounder in school and not be able to do anything to help.
> TEACHER:　It's really frustrating.

PARENT: We could have just shot the psychologist who told us our son was mentally retarded. He was so cold.

TEACHER: You feel like he wasn't very sensitive to your feelings.

Nonverbal Behaviors

Nonverbal behaviors include body positions and postures (e.g., arms folded tightly, slouching in the seat, a leg bouncing up and down), facial expressions (e.g., quivering lips, frown, flushed face), and verbal components beyond the actual words (e.g., tone, inflection, and cadence of speech). The influence of nonverbal behaviors can add to or detract from communication processes (Olsen & Fuller, 2003; Seligman, 2000; T. E. C. Smith et al., 2006). Sometimes nonverbal behavior strengthens the message, such as when a father declines an invitation to sit down and speaks loudly and rapidly while communicating displeasure with the information that his son was suspended for fighting at recess. This nonverbal behavior confirms and punctuates the teacher's interpretation that the father is emotionally upset and angry. In contrast, a mother's crossed arms and frowning expression may belie her verbal assertion that she is comfortable with the current placement decision; her nonverbal behavior is incongruent with her verbal message. Teachers should be sensitive to the nonverbal behavior of parents and the possible cues they may provide regarding the parents' communicated message or their emotional reaction to what has been said within that specific context.

Likewise, teachers should be aware of their own nonverbal behavior. A teacher who is sitting comfortably in the chair, leaning slightly forward, and nodding her head while the parent is speaking is demonstrating nonverbal indicators of active listening. If her verbal responses are given in a calm voice and supportive tone while she maintains eye contact, her verbal and nonverbal strategies are congruent in sending the message that she is interested in two-way dialogue with the parents.

Silence

Periods of silence may also serve to facilitate listening and interactive processes. Though some individuals may view the absence of conversation as wasted opportunities or times of discomfort, counseling authorities and researchers have identified silence as a valuable listening and attending tool (Friend & Cook, 2007; Seligman, 2000).

The value of silence is in part a function of the listening opportunities associated with this response. That is, during absences of conversation professionals can concentrate on listening and attending rather than talking. Silence may also communicate a willingness to listen. Thus, silence may cue parents and family members that the professional is interested in listening to and understanding them rather than expecting them always to concentrate on what he or she has to say. A silent pause after a parent's comment also indicates that the teacher is thinking about and taking time to fully comprehend the parent's message. Silence may also draw out taciturn parents and family members. That is, the psychological vacuum created by silence may sometimes serve to stimulate conversation, thus giving parents and family members opportunities to be heard and understood. Finally, silence allows professionals opportunities to attend to nonverbal signs. Thus, periods of quiet allow one time to attend to body language and other nonverbal cues as opposed to concentrating on what is said.

It should be obvious that parents and family members expect professionals to talk and interact. It is equally obvious, however, that professionals' prudent use of silence can facilitate an effective communicative environment.

Summarization

A final technique is for professionals to summarize for parents or family members, at periodic intervals, the information and affect that have been generated or observed. Summarizing statements can thus occur at points in the conference other than at the close and can be designed to respond to manifest both content and affect. Again, the intent of these comments is to communicate to parents that the professional is interested in and sensitive to what they are saying and that he or she is attempting to understand them. Summarization statements can also serve to clarify perceptions of parents and family members and to sensitize and integrate affect. Examples of these types of statements include "Can we say, then, that you felt most uncomfortable about special education placement because you didn't understand the diagnostic testing and because you felt powerless to help your son?" and "To summarize, it appears that you have identified three major concerns."

Developing the Listening Environment

Effective communication is most easily achieved within a suitable listening atmosphere, including physical space and climate that support other efforts to communicate interest and sensitivity. In addition to providing an acceptable external setting, teachers must also strive to create an acceptable interpersonal setting. This should include establishing a psychological atmosphere that will impart a sense of well-being and security for parents of children with exceptionalities. In particular, one should attempt to achieve a professional yet relaxed atmosphere. Although few would argue with the latter's importance, the mechanism for achieving it may not be readily apparent. There are, however, a variety of steps teachers may take to produce the most desirable conferencing conditions.

Ensure that the physical environment is relaxed, comfortable, and inviting (Couchenour & Chrisman, 2000). Attention to the physical setting may not always enhance the overall success of the parent–professional conference, but failure to attend to this important feature may significantly interfere. It is critical that parents feel their conversations and meetings with teachers will be private and confidential; consequently, it is important to arrange for a professional setting away from uninvolved persons and where the meeting is unlikely to be interrupted. A classroom may or may not serve this purpose.

Arrange for appropriate furniture. To create an atmosphere conducive to discussing parent–teacher matters, all parties should be provided comfortable, adult-sized seating. Not only will such physical considerations facilitate an adult-to-adult conversation but failure to attend to this factor may significantly impair the parent's and/or professional's capacity to pay attention.

Acknowledge parents' and family members' role as collaborators and active participants (Christenson, 2004). Recognition of parents' and family members' potential collaborative contributions, personal investment in their offspring, and need for involvement in the communication process will go a long way toward facilitating an appropriate listening environment. That is, professionals must recognize and believe that listening to parents facilitates collaborative relationships and the realization of mutual goals because parents know a good deal about their children that professionals have no way of knowing and because parents care about their children and have every right to be involved in program development. Such a mind-set is important because it serves to remind us that parents and families have significant contributions to make if professionals allow them to be heard.

Strive to achieve relationship parity with parents and family members (A. Turnbull et al., 2006). There is no question that professionals typically enter these relationships with more experience and training than the parents involved. Nonetheless, parents bring information and resources to these relationships that can significantly facilitate children's growth and development. Maximally capitalizing on such contributions requires that professionals view parents and family members as equals in the interaction and decision-making process. This translates into perceiving parents as partners because their input is valuable rather than because they are legally permitted to be involved.

Strive to understand the parents' frame of reference. Teachers sometimes act on assumptions regarding family structure (e.g., single parent) rather than on *who* the family is as a unique system (Christenson, 2004; Keller, 2004). An environment that supports dialogue includes a true effort on the part of professionals to understand and appreciate a family's frame of reference. This not only helps professionals remove themselves from situations and issues but also assists them in generating understanding and in clarifying parents' genuine concern for their children, which are basic components of effective conferencing.

Be prepared. No single measure will facilitate the desired psychological climate of the conference as much as solid preparation. Both parents and professionals tend to report feeling qualified, confident, and relaxed when they are well prepared for a conference. Accordingly, a thorough review of a child's folder and an assessment of progress and problems experienced, together with an outline of agenda items to be pursued, will typically aid in creating the conditions necessary for a meaningful interaction to occur.

Identify anxiety-reduction measures. Conferences scheduled back-to-back, which prohibit professionals from taking a short break, frequently serve to increase the anxiety of teachers. Though some administrators may consider breaks between sessions a luxury, their overall importance should serve to make them a mandate. Some individuals have taken the few minutes prior to a parent conference to jog in place, breathe deeply, engage in passive mental imagery (visualizing a relaxing scene), and practice deep-muscle relaxation exercises. Although the means for best achieving a relaxed state will vary from person to person, teachers must remember that these efforts will aid in creating an appropriate conferencing climate. Professionals should also keep in mind that productive interactions with parents will depend at least in part on one's capacity to put them at ease. Consequently, it is essential in preparation for the conference that teachers attempt to reduce parents' anxiety. This process will consist to some extent of reducing uncertainty for the parents. That is, parents should be informed of the time of the conference, the amount of time allotted, the location of the school and meeting room, the purpose of the session, and the information that they should be prepared to receive or share.

Maintain a natural demeanor in the conference. Rather than adopting a contrived manner simply to simulate an ideal "counselor style," the teacher is far wiser to assume as natural a posture as possible. Such a strategy will serve to put all parties at ease.

Recognize that parents of students with disabilities frequently hear negative statements or appraisals of their child. Starting every conversation with parents with a positive statement about their child or with the focus on capacities and growth and not just on deficits and failures will communicate to parents care and concern for the whole child.

Technology

There are a number of ways that teachers can communicate with parents; some are high tech, and others are quite simple. Teachers have routinely used print messages in the form of letters home, classroom newsletters, monthly bulletins, and the like to keep parents informed of the activities and current events in their classroom and to provide suggestions of home activities that can support student learning. One of the most commonly used written communication techniques is the communication journal, traveling notebook, or home–school notebook (Davern, 2004; T. E. Hall, Wolfe, & Bollig, 2003). These notebooks are carried to and from school as a vehicle for enhanced communication and thus contain entries written by both parents and teachers. The notebooks can document ongoing student progress and program implementation, serve as a tool to facilitate instructional decision making when patterns of behavior are observed between home and school, and facilitate collaboration of efforts jointly undertaken by parents and teachers such as when an academic skill taught at school can be reinforced at home (T. E. Hall et al., 2003; A. Turnbull & Turnbull, 2001). Notebooks can be particularly useful when students have limited communication skills and are unable to relay to their parents important aspects of their school experience or when their schedule requires them to spend time with a number of different teachers who can add comments to the notebook as it is routed with the student throughout the day (Davern, 2004). Entries in these notebooks should have a consistent format that is easily understandable to parents (e.g., free of jargon), should relate to current Individualized Education Program goals, include specific data or objective information whenever possible to illustrate the point being articulated, and should encourage two-way communication (T. E. Hall et al., 2003; A. Turnbull & Turnbull, 2001).

Teachers are increasingly utilizing more sophisticated technologies in communicating with families. Some teachers have substituted computer e-mail messages for the traditional phone call when families have access to home computers. This form of electronic communication can save time, particularly when teachers have computers available at their desks and can compose messages throughout the day or as their schedule allows. It is also more reliable and eliminates the frustration of phone tag and can be cost-effective for schools that have increasing capabilities to access the Internet (Jacobson, 2005). In addition, the ubiquitous nature of pagers and cell phones with text messaging options offer other quick, confidential methods of exchanges (Strom & Strom, 2002).

Strom and Strom reported on the field study of one system where high school teachers used personal digital assistants (PDAs) to record student conduct (both desirable and undesirable behaviors) and transferred these data to desktop computers in their classrooms. The reports were also conveyed to parents' pagers via phone in the teacher's classroom using a common set of codes printed on a wallet-size card. This was particularly useful for the many parents who work outside the home and are not available to take phone calls or check e-mail during the day. The pagers were set to vibrate or beeping alert and signaled for parents to check the pager display to see the message. Teachers committed to sending a report to parents each day by 5:00 P.M. so the information on behavior could be incorporated into their interaction with their child at home that evening. Parents contacted the reporting teacher's pager by entering a student identification number to acknowledge receipt of the message. Teachers (93%) reported that PDAs facilitated record keeping and that pagers were a more efficient method of communication with parents than phone. Parents (93%) indicated that the timely pager messages helped them to know when their adolescents need their instruction, advice, or discipline. More than 90% of the parents reported that pagers were easy to operate, and 87% determined that messages were simple to interpret using the common set of codes. This use of technology was supported by a partnership with the business that provided the PDAs and pagers and suggests the increasing interest in the application of technology in home–school communication.

Whatever method is chosen, it is essential that teachers involve parents in developing the communication strategies they will implement and in determining how often communication will occur. Asking parents for their preference regarding communication reflects sensitivity to the unique circumstances of their family (A. Turnbull & Turnbull, 2001; L. T. Zionts, Zionts, Harrison, & Bellinger, 2003).

Summary

Evidence is emerging that the quality of family–school partnerships is a critical factor in appropriate services for students and families. Strong partnerships reflect a collaborative approach and require effective ongoing communication between home and school. The ability to accurately listen to and communicate with parents and family members is one of the most elemental attributes of the successful collaborator and a primary basis for obtaining and disseminating information. Successful parent and family partnerships also allow for a variety of communication strategies rather than a standard, uniform prescription. The ability to create an appropriate listening environment is so germane to the parent–teacher communication network that other conferencing components will depend on the mastery of this single skill.

Exercises

1. Identify an individual (preferably a friend, relative, or classmate rather than a parent) to relate a topic of interest to you. Practice the following:
   a. putting yourself and the person with whom you are relating at ease,
   b. maintaining good eye contact,
   c. being an empathic listener, and
   d. making use of specific listening behaviors, including door-opening statements, clarifying responses and questions, paraphrasing, reflecting, nonverbal behaviors, silence, and summarization.

   Discuss with the person the reactions that you both had to the various procedures. This can be an in-class or out-of-class exercise.

2. Observe other people, including the students in your class, as they manifest different emotions and feelings. Pay particular attention to the way in which their nonverbal cues (e.g., posture, expressions, etc.) serve to communicate the way they feel.

3. Recall and analyze the feelings you have had in instances where your collaborative input was wanted and unwanted. Attempt to identify situations where you felt parents or family members

displayed these attitudes. Are there particular conditions or behaviors you can identify that resulted in these attitudes?

4. Attend to individuals whom you consider good and poor listeners. Identify the particular characteristics that lead you to categorize them as you do.

Chapter 4

Development of Trust in the Family–Professional Relationship

I've had two bad experiences, life-changing experiences, and I think the moral of that was "screw me once shame on you, screw me twice shame on me," and I mean that's the trust issue. I will always have my guard up [*she begins to tear up*]. It's the administration. Trust is the center of this. When Emily was a second grader and I signed that first IEP [Individualized Education Program], I remember leaving there thinking, that wasn't too bad—I've heard bad things about this. And then, the next week I went to a training conference, and I sat there and listened to a session on IEPs, and I sat there and she [the presenter] basically described all of these things that I had allowed to happen in the meeting, like the IEP was empty and meaningless, the goals were too low . . . and the lightbulb came on. If she met those goals—she was already half a year behind—she would end that year a full year behind. Then another session explained the research saying that if they're not reading by third grade, there's a chance they may not learn to read, and so these professionals are supposed to have my child's best interests at heart. OK, I was very naive, and so I went back and I told the teacher and the principal that I wanted another IEP meeting and this is what I was going to ask for. I say 'naive' because when we started the meeting, there was a new person in charge of the meeting, with more power, higher up in the administration, and they knew what I was going to ask them and they already knew what they were going to tell me. So there's another trust issue. If I can't talk with the people in charge of my daughter's education without . . . . Now why should I have to be discreet about that or have a strategy? Why can't I just be open and have dialogue? That was just a horrible meeting, and I went alone. Again, a trust issue I guess. Why would I need my husband? I do everything else without him [*she laughs*]. But there was no discussion. It was . . . . I had done my homework. I had my little notebook there, which I got ridiculed for. At one point I couldn't find something [in the notes], and a teacher said, "That must be on another page." I said something about a specific approach—and I understand that parents cannot dictate, I'm not sure if I knew that at the time—but I said, you know you've got to think outside the box, there are other school districts doing this, and the psychologist nudges the person in charge and says, "What box is she talking about?" Just that kind of stuff that was not professional, that blows your trust right out of the water. And as soon as I said what I wanted, they said, "We don't do that here," and I would say, but why? And they would say things like "I don't have to answer that" . . . just demeaning comments like that [*she chokes up*]. I have to get over this, but I don't think I ever will.

It was a bad situation because it was like they drew the line in the sand. I have a very strong God-given protection, and I thought, "You messed with the wrong person." It should never have been like that. I wanted my daughter to learn how to read, and that was all I could see. Truly, that was all I could see, and I could see everything standing in the way. We're going to use our home-brewed method that we use for everybody.

All of the resource teachers have been wonderful, and I have nothing but praise for them. I've had very good communication with them throughout. I could see how much Emily depended on them and got attached to them, so that helped me trust them because I felt they had a relationship with her. Emily can learn the material, but she learns differently and she has high anxiety. Give her her space and an environment she can focus in. It takes her typically half a year before she opens up to the teacher, and then she relaxes. She needs someone to help her, but I sometimes worry if she's getting too much extra help with assignments and things. I think the teachers understand what I want as a parent and that I don't want them to give her too much help, but that will always be a question. They have to know exactly how much help to give without giving too much. That would be a hard position to be in because you want her to feel successful.

She's not getting perfect test scores, but that's a trust issue as well. I want her grades and test scores to accurately tell how she's doing. I have been suspicious of the end-of-year testing. I don't want the teachers to score it so that it brings the score up. I want them to be honest, not just tell me what they think I want to hear. I want Emily to be able to function "out there." I think it goes back to honest communication.

A basic concept of effective parent and family conferencing is that the process is not something applied to parents and family members by professionals; rather, it involves joint participation. It is collaborative. The meaningful participation of parents and professionals, however, will depend largely on the latter's capacity to establish conditions conducive to a cooperative and collaborative effort. Paramount among the factors associated with the development of the environment will be the educator's skill in establishing a relationship based on trust. Without trust, the ability of parents and professionals to effectively communicate and collaborate will be significantly impaired. A. Turnbull, Turnbull, Erwin, and Soodak (2006) referred to trust as the keystone for partnerships with families. They asserted that, like the central stone of an architectural arch, other principles of partnership such as communication, advocacy, and commitment crumble without trust, the fundamental element. Others (K. S. Adams & Christenson, 2000; Blue-Banning, Summers, Frankland, Nelson, & Beegle, 2004; Frowe, 2005; Lake & Billingsley, 2000) have also identified trust as essential to any therapeutic and collaborative relationship.

Although trust in the counseling and collaborative relationship is typically thought of as an atmosphere created *for* parents and family members, it is equally important for the professional to have trust *in* parents and family members. As the teacher is not an unfeeling technician, simply programmed to disseminate and interpret information, but rather an individual who is profoundly affected by the attitudes and responses of parents and families, professionals must be able to both create and receive trust. It is simply unrealistic to attempt to establish a collaborative relationship in which parents are expected to trust the professional without a reciprocating response. Unfortunately this futile strategy has sometimes been pursued and may explain somewhat why the parent–professional relationship has not been noted for high levels of mutual trust.

The Collaborative Nature of Trust

Trust, in the context of parent–professional collaborative relationships, forms the foundation on which the conditions for achieving objectives grow. In fact, in both professional and business affairs, little can be accomplished without an acceptable level of trust. H. Gill, Boies, Finegan, and McNally (2005) referred to it as "an essential lubricant of successful working relationships" (p. 288). Even though definitions of this rather nebulous term may fail to describe its precise characteristics, professionals are in agreement as to its significance (Frowe, 2005; Goddard, Tschannen-Moran, & Hoy, 2001; A. Turnbull et al., 2006).

K. S. Adams and Christenson (2000) defined trust in the family–school relationship as "confidence that another person will act in a way to benefit or sustain the relationship, or the implicit or explicit goals of the relationship, to achieve positive outcomes for students" (p. 480). Others have identified trust as a necessary condition for change and growth to occur. In keeping with this notion, Bryk and Schneider (2002) noted that the quality of trusting relationships in schools is a significant predictor of school improvement. As teachers feel trusted and supported by parents, they are more likely to implement new ideas in their classrooms. Likewise, as parents feel trusted and valued, they are less concerned with monitoring the behavior of teachers and more likely to contribute willingly to school efforts (Miretzky, 2004; Soodak & Erwin, 2000). In the opening vignette we saw how the interactions between a parent and school personnel during a planned meeting can have a serious impact on the trusting relationship.

Although the characteristics and distinct features of trusting associations will vary from situation to situation, certain qualities typify these relationships. One particular aspect of individuals in a trusting relationship is their heightened willingness to take interpersonal risks and to reveal elements of themselves to the other people. Risk taking, in this context, is a willingness to make oneself vulnerable. That is, parents, family members, and educators involved in trusting collaborative relationships display confidence that agreed-on patterns of behavior will prevail. Although similar in some respects to gambling, trusting is more a faith in or reliance on the recurrence of previously agreed-on standards. Whereas gambling involves a situation where one ventures a small risk to possibly secure a large gain, interpersonal risk taking is more aligned with confidence in a previously identified outcome. In gambling, an individual does not expect to be consistently reinforced; by contrast, interpersonal risk taking, and the trust on which it is based, requires confidence that what one anticipates will in fact occur.

It should be apparent that collaboration will be little more than a hollow pretense without assurances from both parents and educators that mutually agreed-on roles and arrangements will occur. Thus, for example, when parents confide in a teacher, taking the risk that their confidence will be maintained, they expect (and trust) that this assurance will be upheld.

Accordingly, the willingness to venture, which is a direct manifestation of a trusting and collaborative relationship, must not be associated with uncertainty. That parents and families of children with exceptionalities are often vulnerable to uncertainties and self-doubt underscores the importance of working to establish trusting relationships.

Efforts to create a trusting relationship must begin early in the parent–teacher partnership to ensure a solid foundation for positive interactions. K. S. Adams and Christenson (2000) offered the following scenario that illustrates how the first contact may hamper effective problem solving as well as stall or hamper future interactions:

> A seventh-grade student begins a new junior high school. This student gets into a verbal disagreement with a teacher regarding a missing assignment. This disagreement escalates into a situation in which the student is suspended from school. At the re-entry conference, parents and teachers, who have not met each other prior to this conference, are searching for indicators that the other partner is worthy of their trust. However, in the emotionally charged environment of a suspension re-entry meeting, the parties engage in blaming each other for the suspension. The parents feel the teacher was being too harsh and mistreated the student, whereas the teacher feels the parent is merely coddling the student and that the student was insubordinate, which is a clearly defined infraction deserving a suspension. In this scenario, prior contact between the parties in a positive or emotionally neutral environment could have built trust and understanding. Previous positive interactions may have carried the parent and teacher beyond the immediate tension of the re-entry conference to a more effective resolution of the issue in question. (p. 481)

The trusting relationship, on which the conditions of collaboration, change, and growth are based, involves three basic components. First, professionals must create, with the aid of parents and family members, an atmosphere in which a shared feeling of safety exists. Second, the professional must provide reassurance and a model for risk taking. Finally, both the professional and the parent must reinforce one another for their risk-taking and collaborative efforts.

Creating the Conditions of Safety

One of the primary ways that educators can establish the safe, trusting, and secure atmosphere needed for collaboration is through a display of warmth for the parents with whom they work. Rogers (1962) suggested that counselors who are authentically warm and positive in this way are more likely to produce desired outcomes. Rogers termed this attitude "positive regard." Along with others (Bailey, Skinner, Rodriguez, Gut, & Correa, 1999; Friend & Cook, 2003; Swick, 2003) he convincingly articulated the need and value of establishing a supportive atmosphere for individuals involved in a collaborative relationship.

An atmosphere of safety will also be facilitated when parents and teachers are comfortable with themselves and willing to enter the collaborative relationship without a facade. Parents must feel secure in the belief that there will be no reprisals to their child for their own active, assertive challenges during collaborative processes (Soodak & Erwin, 2000). Likewise, teachers need to feel comfortable enough to be open with parents without fear of being attacked. This openness requires that teachers and parents suspend judgment and evaluation of the information and situation until they fully explore the meaning and explanation provided (File, 2001; Friend & Cook, 2003).

One mother of an adolescent with a severe behavior disorder revealed to the program staff serving her son that she was able to put her trust in them only after "doing some testing." In particular, this involved assessing the extent to which staff members were willing to follow through with her requests and with what they said they would do. Although in previous programs the mother had been promised numerous things, little follow-through was provided. After the program staff had convinced this mother that they were willing to make good on their promises, she was more willing to enter into a trusting relationship.

This example illustrates three components often associated with trust: ability, benevolence, and integrity. Tschannen-Moran and Hoy (2000) suggested that ability, or competence, is necessary to instill trust. Parents need to feel that the teacher has the skills and abilities to best serve the educational needs of their child. Hoy (2002) identified benevolence, or a sense that the teacher has the student's best interests at heart and will protect those interests or at least do no harm, as another critical element to establishing trust. Parents need to feel that teachers will treat their child with fairness, compassion, and goodwill. In addition, integrity, or the honesty of the teacher's character and authenticity and the fact that the teacher means what he or she says and can be relied on in terms of words and actions, impacts trust at its most basic level. Teachers may be able to combat low levels of trust by actions indicating ability, benevolence, and integrity (H. Gill et al., 2005).

Providing Reassurance and a Model for Interpersonal Risk Taking

In addition to developing an atmosphere of trust and safety, teachers must be willing to provide cues and reassurances for parent and family risk taking and a model for this behavior. Hence, in spite of the degree of safety and rapport developed, parents and family members must have reassurance that the teacher will maintain their trust even under vulnerable conditions. In addition, the professional must not expect parents and family members to display a willingness to enter into an interpersonal relationship until he or she has set the stage for this action.

> Trust always comes with an element of risk because we can never fully control the actions of others or fully allow for the contingencies of life. If we have absolute control over the actions of another, then there is no need to trust them because we can be assured that the behavior we desire will be forthcoming. (Frowe, 2005, p. 38)

In fact, trust represents the deliberate intention to take a risk in a relationship (H. Gill et al., 2005). Although professionals need not display vulnerability to secure a reciprocal response, they must nonetheless demonstrate a willingness to show their humanness and to suggest that they may not have all the answers. Such conditions form the basic elements of effective collaboration. For example, the mother of an elementary-age boy with a learning disability confided it was only after a teacher acknowledged she did not have all the solutions to the boy's problems that the mother felt willing to share information and collaborate. She noted, in particular, that she had been exposed to a series of professionals who gave the impression that her child's behavior could be easily managed if the right techniques were used, implying that she was not using the right approach. Only after being asked to jointly develop a cooperative and collaborative plan was she willing to candidly provide the information needed to develop the intervention strategy.

The willingness to expose oneself in a parent–educator relationship must also be based on a feeling of security and a belief in joint responsibility and solutions. Though professionals may agree that a relationship exists between an educator's attitudes and the development of security with parents, consensus regarding the methodology for identifying the precise nature of these attitudes may be much more difficult to secure.

The Risk-Taking Questionnaire shown in Figure 4.1 serves as one means for educational professionals to gain feedback relative to their capacity to create conditions of safety for parents and family members and thus to facilitate a collaborative problem-solving relationship. Use of the instrument is simple. Respondents place a check mark in the column that most accurately describes their degree of comfort for each item (i.e., very comfortable, somewhat uncomfortable, etc.). This measure also can be completed again at a later time to assess changes that have occurred. Finally, a coworker or supervisor who knows the respondent well can also complete the rating. Comparing personal perceptions with those held by colleagues can offer interesting insights.

Providing Reinforcement

An amendment to the adage "Behold the turtle, he makes progress only when he sticks his neck out" might be that he is willing to stick his neck out only because that behavior was followed by a positive consequence. Accordingly, parents, families, and professionals must be reinforced by their honesty, sincerity, willingness to share relative information, and collaborative efforts. Though a safe atmosphere in and of itself will provide the means and opportunity to secure positive internal feedback for risk taking and collaborative behavior, this willingness can be greatly augmented by appropriate positive external feedback. One parent related that a teacher's positive feedback regarding the parent's openness was of tremendous personal value. Although positive reinforcement may ordinarily be considered applicable only with children in classroom settings, one should remember that there are ample demonstrations of the efficacy of operant conditioning on adult behavior too (Skinner, 1948). Overwhelming evidence supports the contention that positive verbal feedback will facilitate the rapport-building and general communicative process (Seligman, 2000).

Development of a Trusting and Collaborative Relationship

Although one could argue that the foremost requirement for professional status is technical competence, an equally compelling argument would contend that in the area of parent and family conferencing, the professional must be equally skilled in gaining trust and establishing a collaborative relationship. Regardless of teachers' technical competence, teachers

How comfortable are you . . .	Very Comfortable	Somewhat Comfortable	Neutral	Somewhat Uncomfortable	Very Uncomfortable
1. telling parents that you don't know?	☐	☐	☐	☐	☐
2. telling parents that you made a mistake?	☐	☐	☐	☐	☐
3. suggesting to parents that another professional made an error?	☐	☐	☐	☐	☐
4. suggesting to parents that they should consider therapy for themselves?	☐	☐	☐	☐	☐
5. telling parents that there are behaviors displayed by their children that you dislike?	☐	☐	☐	☐	☐
6. displaying your emotions in a parent–educator conference?	☐	☐	☐	☐	☐
7. confronting parents with their failure to follow through on agreed-upon plans?	☐	☐	☐	☐	☐
8. talking about your own problems in a parent–educator conference?	☐	☐	☐	☐	☐
9. praising parents for things they do well?	☐	☐	☐	☐	☐
10. having parents take notes during conferences?	☐	☐	☐	☐	☐
11. allowing parents to observe in your class while you are teaching?	☐	☐	☐	☐	☐
12. allowing parents to tutor their own child at home?	☐	☐	☐	☐	☐
13. allowing parents to use behavior modification procedures with their own child at home?	☐	☐	☐	☐	☐

Figure 4.1. Risk-taking questionnaire.

(*continues*)

	Very Comfortable	Somewhat Comfortable	Neutral	Somewhat Uncomfortable	Very Uncomfortable
14. telling parents their "rights"?	☐	☐	☐	☐	☐
15. having parents assume an active role during IEP conferences?	☐	☐	☐	☐	☐
16. having parents ask you to defend your teaching strategies?	☐	☐	☐	☐	☐
17. having parents bring a friend to IEP conferences?	☐	☐	☐	☐	☐
18. having parents call you at home about a problem their child is having at school?	☐	☐	☐	☐	☐
19. having parents recommend a specific curriculum for use with their child?	☐	☐	☐	☐	☐
20. having parents review school records on their child?	☐	☐	☐	☐	☐
21. having parents collaborate on various problems and issues?	☐	☐	☐	☐	☐
22. maintaining relationship parity with parents?	☐	☐	☐	☐	☐

Figure 4.1. (*continued*)

must first be able to secure the confidence of parents and families, and only where this trust and rapport have been developed can they utilize whatever technical skills they have. Thus, the efficacy of essentially every strategy and technique of the educational professional will be intricately tied to the relationship developed with the parents. In fact, T. B. White (2005) suggested that people have more confidence in the accuracy of recommendations of benevolent providers rather than of experts when making emotionally difficult or high-stakes decisions.

Even though a great deal has been said about the erosion of trust in parent–educator relationships, it is significant to note that good and trusting relationships do exist. An analysis of factors associated with the development or dissolution of confidence, trust, and a willingness to collaborate reveals several elements that should be given close scrutiny.

Parents and teachers must be willing to give if a trusting and collaborative relationship is to develop. In the trusting relationship, both families and professionals are willing and comfortable in contributing to a common cause. One father of a child with a severe disability reported that he enjoyed contributing time and energy to community programs for children and adults with disabilities. When asked about his efforts for all individuals with disabilities, he commented that he made these contributions because doing so was personally gratifying. Likewise, educators who have successfully conducted collaborative parent-oriented programs have commented that they are willing to invest the necessary time and effort in these endeavors because they enjoy the results or recognize the ultimate benefits as worthwhile. In virtually every instance the trusting and collaborative relationship stems from a willingness to give that is not motivated by a hope for reciprocation. These individuals do not need to keep score ("If I do this for you, what will you do for me?"), and they are not motivated by a need to think of themselves as martyrs making a sacrifice. They fulfill their own needs by responding to the needs of others.

Both parents and educators must acknowledge that they have a commitment to children. It is not uncommon to hear parents say that professionals can never truly understand the plight of families because they are with the child for only a few hours daily and because they are paid for their services. Professionals, on the other hand, have been heard to say that parents fail to take responsibility for their children or that the child's problems relate directly to the parents' problems. Unfortunately, such attitudes will almost universally impede the development of a trusting and collaborative relationship. Parents and professionals must acknowledge that they are both actively committed to the child and that only through their mutual concerted efforts will progress take place.

Both parents and educators must assertively serve as advocates for children. Although cooperation and collaboration provide an obvious component of the successful parent–educator relationship, so does the need for strong advocacy. The two roles are not opposing, and in fact many indications suggest that respect and trust most likely prevail when both parties can candidly share their perceptions and positions. In the case of children and youth with exceptionalities, advocacy means that children's interests receive priority status. Although this may lead parents and family members to perceive matters differently from the way professionals do, it does not mean that they should distrust or otherwise oppose cooperating and collaborating with educators and other professionals involved. Conversely, parents should not automatically accept all recommendations without considering child and family needs as well as alternative suggestions. Parents, families, and professionals must strive for a relationship wherein all parties can voice their opinions and disagree. Such an open relationship strengthens the family–professional partnership and facilitates the growth and maintenance of a collaborative and trusting relationship. Openness and directness also promote boundary clarity, thus reducing opportunities for confusion and frustration to develop.

Following one conference, a mother revealed to a teacher that she was elated at the teacher's willingness to strongly argue a point. This mother, who had gained the reputation of being somewhat disagreeable, indicated it was a pleasure not to be patronized. She further revealed that she felt the teacher's willingness to stand up for her beliefs indicated her commitment to the child.

Cultural diversity and the difference between race and ethnicity and culture were presented in Chapter 2. Some research has suggested that parents from culturally diverse groups may bring a level of cultural mistrust into relationships with professionals (Whaley, 2001a). This may manifest in parents feeling that they must be more vigilant in watching over their child's education at the classroom level (Fields-Smith, 2005). Teachers should not interpret mistrust as a personal response to themselves when it may be a cultural response based on previous interactions (Whaley, 2001b). It will be more effective to address issues of mistrust directly and attempt to establish meaningful relationships with parents by being open to learning from them and being responsive to their needs and perspectives.

A positive outlook is essential to the development of trust and collaboration. Inevitably these relationships will undergo periods of difficulty for both parents and families and educators of children and youth with disabilities. When both parties firmly believe that the situation will improve and when they are willing to actively work together to accomplish this goal, however, the relationship will survive the ups and downs of the child. Without doubt, a willingness to collaborate and trust will grow when every change in a child's behavior or progress is not viewed as an opportunity to determine what the parents or the teacher did to create the situation.

Professionals and parents must both be willing to reinforce and confront one another. A goal for both parents and teachers of children with exceptionalities is to acknowledge that they are equally committed to their respective roles. Accordingly, neither parents nor teachers must become so immersed in the collaborative relationship that they lose their independent perspective. Only when parents, family members, and educators can independently analyze and respond to particular situations will trust and an effective collaborative relationship develop. Thus, both groups must be able and willing to selectively and appropriately praise the other for things that are done well and to confront or disagree on matters where a difference of opinion exists. Such a perspective facilitates feelings of efficacy, which promotes confidence and other protective interpersonal conditions.

Parents' and professionals' maintenance of sensitivity to the needs of one another bodes well for a sound working relationship. A fundamental component of a trusting and collaborative relationship is the ability to demonstrate sensitivity to the needs of another person. This skill requires that parents, family members, and professionals concentrate on recognizing one another's positions and feelings. For professionals, this will involve attempting to truly understand the parent and family frame of reference rather than analyzing the appropriateness or logic of their needs or positions. Furthermore, this process will involve the ability to listen and respond to the affective elements of the family's world. Thus, while assertively advocating their own position for a child, parents, family members, or professionals must also stay sensitive to the positions of the others. One important guide for teachers is the recognition that nothing is more important to parents than the well-being of their child. Teachers often report more success in engaging in collaborative interactions with parents when they place the strengths and vulnerabilities of the child at the center of the conversation and can speak about the whole child (Lawrence-Lightfoot, 2004b).

Ideally, parents and professionals must want to trust one another. Rather than waiting to be "shown," parents and teachers should actively want to trust and collaborate. Although trust must be earned, it is counterproductive to adopt an attitude of distrust until reasonable evidence to the contrary has emerged. That is, parents, family members, and professionals must avoid restricting trust only to situations in which another person has been manipulated into responding in an acceptable manner or when trust-related responses have been observed. Rather, a willingness to trust and collaborate must be pervasive and relatively contingency free.

As a further component of this concept, the educator and parent must be willing and able to understand and accept themselves. Only through the demonstration of this attitude can they expect others to trust them.

Be willing to promote parity-based relationships (Friend & Cook, 2003). In this regard, parity refers to professionals' perceptions of parents and families as equal partners in the educational and development process of children and youth with exceptionalities. Thus, in spite of differing perspectives and backgrounds, both professionals and parents must assume that both parties have important skills and knowledge related to serving children and that the contributions of both groups are valued.

Professionals and families should have opportunities for identification of goals and outcomes. Ideally, the goals and outcomes identified by parents and professionals should be shared and mutual. Yet even if this turns out not to be the case, an important element of developing a trusting and collaborative relationship involves opportunities for all parties to promote their individual perceptions of the goals and outcomes to pursue. Such conditions facilitate not only development of mutual goals but also a willingness to consider novel and innovative perspectives.

Honesty is an essential ingredient of trust and collaboration. Regardless of whatever other positive characteristics professionals may have, they must be honest if they are to earn the trust of parents and families. Although there is a difference between honesty and outspoken candor, there is no excuse for dishonesty in the parent–educator conference. If, for example, educators are not able to promise complete confidentiality, they must make that clear to the parents.

Attempt to use a solution-oriented, noncompetitive problem-solving process. Mundschenk, Foley, and Swedburg (2005) recommended that educators view most problems and issues involving parents and families of individuals with exceptionalities as having a number of possible solutions. Accordingly, they suggested that focusing on problems and alternative solutions orients professionals and parents away from less productive behaviors (e.g., blaming, challenging ideas). Furthermore, presenting ideas and solutions in a noncompetitive fashion encourages a sense of working together and thus a collaborative spirit.

Be aware of some basic dos and don'ts for parent–educator collaboration enhancement and relationship building. Although lists seldom provide a comprehensive statement of desired outcomes, they can serve to remind us of certain basic elements that should be considered. This also applies to the creation of trust and a collaborative relationship between parents and educators.

Do

1. Maintain a sense of humor.
2. Be accepting of yourself and the parents and family members with whom you work.
3. Demonstrate warmth and sensitivity.
4. Be positive.
5. Demonstrate respect for the parents and families with whom you work.
6. Be sincere.

7. Listen.
8. Use language that parents and family members can understand.
9. Attend to the emotions and body language of parents and family members.
10. Encourage and reinforce parents when it is appropriate.
11. Recognize that parents and families can be effective collaborators who are able to make unique informational and problem-solving contributions.

Don't

1. Attempt to be a sage who has all the answers.
2. Make premature judgments.
3. Be overly critical.
4. Threaten, ridicule, or blame parents and families.
5. Argue with parents and family members.
6. Use strong expressions of surprise and concern.
7. Make promises and agreements that you may not be able to keep.
8. Patronize parents and family members or personalize issues.
9. Make moralistic judgments.
10. Minimize what parents and family members have to say about their child.
11. Attempt to exclude parents in decision making regarding their child.

Confidentiality

A critical element of trust is the knowledge that school personnel will safeguard the confidentiality and privacy of students and families. The Family Educational Rights and Privacy Act (FERPA) is a federal law that protects the privacy of student educational records. Under the protections of FERPA and the Individuals with Disabilities Education Improvement Act (IDEA), parents and legal guardians (and students age 18 or older) have the right to inspect all educational records kept by the school regarding their child but not the records of other children. They have the right to question the information contained in their child's records and to challenge any information they believe to be inaccurate or misleading. They can also amend the record by including written explanations they feel clarify the information they wish to challenge (U.S. Department of Education, 2004). Parents must also be informed annually of their rights under FERPA, including the requirement that schools comply with parents' request to access records within 45 days of receipt of the request.

Educational records protected under FERPA and IDEA generally include documents such as IEPs, notes of IEP meetings, treatment or program plans, test forms or answer sheets, evaluations, transcripts of due process hearings, and correspondence between parents and school personnel. Test protocols or booklets that do not identify a student or include personally identifiable information are not considered educational records. Only those completed test protocols that include both the questions and the student's responses are considered an educational record (Rooker, 1997). Many teachers keep personal notes on their students. These notes are not considered part of the child's educational record if they are not accessible or revealed to anyone else, are not used to inform decisions made about the child, and are not kept in the permanent file (Olsen & Fuller, 2003).

FERPA requires written consent from parents prior to releasing the educational records to a third party. The school must maintain detailed records of those persons obtaining access to the student records, including the name of the person, date of access, and purpose for accessing the record (Yell, 2006).

Although it is important to guard the privacy of students and their families, it is also imperative that all teachers who work with a student have access to the information contained in the student's IEP. School personnel who have a legitimate educational interest and who are responsible for assisting in the child's education may access a student's educational record without parental consent. This in no way implies that educators may be cavalier about discussions of confidential or private information in their interactions with colleagues (Essex, 2004). Gossip and careless talk based on opinion rather than on fact is not only unprofessional but damages the trusting relationship between home and school.

Parents not only trust schools to maintain the privacy of student records but also trust them to implement the program as written. Failure to do so not only breaches a basic tenant of the relationship but may lead to due process requests and litigation against the school and individual teachers. One striking example is the case of *Doe v. Withers* (1993), where a secondary general education teacher refused to provide the testing accommodations listed on a student's IEP. Although the teacher was a general education teacher and not the primary implementer of the IEP, he had participated in the IEP meeting and had been informed by school administrators of his responsibilities to implement it as written. The teacher's failure to modify tests as required by the student's IEP resulted in the court ruling against this teacher and assessing him individually $15,000 in compensatory and punitive damages.

As discussed in Chapter 2, a significant number of families are experiencing divorce and blended families through remarriage. These diverse family configurations may pose particular challenges for teachers and schools who want to involve all parents while protecting the privacy and confidentiality of student records. Teachers may be faced with complex issues related to legal custody and living arrangements. When the school has not been notified concerning the legal arrangements of child custody related to educational decision making and access to records, we think it is best to err on the side of inclusivity to ensure effective communication and access. Teachers can ask for the address of both parents. Copies of report cards and school notices can be mailed to both parents, and joint or single-parent conferences can be scheduled in response to parental preferences. In addition, notices of school events and activities should be inclusive so that all family members feel welcomed.

Values and the Development of Trust and a Willingness to Collaborate

There is currently tremendous concern with value issues, particularly regarding those differences that exist between students and their parents and families, students and educators, and parents, family members, and professionals (A. Turnbull et al., 2006). Because values hold the very beliefs, convictions, and other persuasions through which individuals structure their lives, they are a paramount factor in establishing and maintaining a trusting and collaborative conferencing relationship. Given the salient nature of values, it is obvious that conflicts and dissonance can arise when professionals and educators are unaware of their own values or those of others or when teachers presume that their values are more acceptable than those of the parents and families with whom they work (Fiedler & Swanger, 2000). That is, failure to recognize one's own values or the importance of another's may facilitate a severe breakdown in the communication process. Although the significance of values to the communication process may be somewhat disconcerting, it is not difficult to understand. The technological advances of the past decades combined with the ever-changing divergent and contradictory values of our society serve to obscure the validity of even the most basic convictions and principles. In fact, more than ever before, individuals (including parents and educators) are questioning the existence of any universal values in our multicultural and diverse society. In addition, an individual's values are not rigidly maintained but dynamic and constantly changing. And yet, despite the tenuous and ethereal nature of values, they exist as a basic determinant of the parent–teacher conferencing relationship and thus are an aspect that must be understood and dealt with if trust and collaboration are to result.

The need for teachers to understand the nature of values comes primarily from the role of values in decision making. In particular, both parents and professionals tend to utilize their personal value systems in making educationally related decisions. In exercising judgments we draw on our experiences, but we are also influenced by the personal set of values, principles, expectations, and attitudes we hold (Frowe, 2005). That is, individuals, contrary to what they may believe or would have people think, tend to respond on the basis of their values rather than on logic or empirical facts. Values, for example, frequently form the basis for a professional's choice of one intervention approach over another. In addition, many times the teacher's goals are more an extension of his or her own professional values than of the family's needs. Finally, the efficacy of a particular strategy will often relate to the extent to which certain desired outcomes align with a particular value system. Thus, for example, a teacher may consider that a particular parent has made significant strides if the family spends additional time together, when in fact the parent's relationship with his or her child has not changed. Hence, it is undeniable that values in a parent–educator relationship become a primary factor in the communication and collaboration process.

The goal of value clarification and assessment is typically not to change individuals' values but rather to make them aware of their own patterns and the values of other people. An acknowledgment of the differences in individuals' values will conceivably make teachers more empathic and knowledgeable of the basis for parent–professional conflicts. Over the past several decades, researchers have undertaken the task of clarifying personal values and becoming sensitized to others' values, and activities have been designed for use with teachers, counselors, and parents (see, for example, Kirschenbaum, 2000). These procedures are designed not to instill a particular set of values or change a person's value system but rather to sensitize one to his or her own values and to those of others. The accomplishment of this goal will, without question, be closely tied to the development of a trusting and secure interpersonal relationship.

Summary

Trust is a fundamental element of collaborative relationships and the foundation on which effective family and professional programs are based. Strategies and procedures for establishing and maintaining trust and collaboration exist, and professionals must actively pursue them. Although trust may be considered so elementary as to defy attention, its importance to the communication and collaboration process demands it be assigned a prominent position by professionals who aspire to effectively meet the needs of parents and families. Attention must be given to establishing safe and supportive interactions within contexts that encourage both teachers and parents to take risks with each other and to recognize and respect the values each hold. Finally, teachers must safeguard the confidentiality and privacy of students and their families.

Exercises

1. Identify the characteristics of a friend or relative that you trust and find friendly to collaboration. Translate these behaviors into procedures that you can use to increase the trust level and collaborative relationships of the parents and families with whom you work.

2. Generate a list of values that you hold, trying as much as possible to be honest with yourself. Note the manner in which sensitivity to this factor can improve your relationship with parents and family members.

3. If you were the parent of a child with a disability, what specific behaviors would you look for in your child's teachers to demonstrate their ability, benevolence, and integrity? Compare your response with those of your classmates.

4. Speak with a building principal about his or her school's procedures in relation to FERPA.

PART 2

Regularly Occurring and Ongoing Conferencing and Collaboration Activities

Initial Contact and Information Exchange Conferences: Forming the Foundation for Successful Collaboration

One father shares his experience of the start of another school year:

We were really nervous about the start of this school year. They scheduled our first team meeting—where everyone from the school who works with Anthony would be there—in October. We had spoken with the principal and Anthony's third-grade teacher last year about the problems he was having in school, but most of the people were new to us. The social worker asked us a lot of questions that we answered on the form the principal sent home, so the meeting dragged on longer than it needed to. Everyone went around the room and talked about what was wrong with Anthony, then they asked if we had any questions. I wasn't sure what all they were talking about, and I could tell that my wife was upset because she didn't say anything. I know that Anthony can be a handful, but he's really a great kid if you can get him to listen to you.

We weren't sure what Anthony had been doing since school started. I know teachers don't have much time, but before the school year starts and you have your classes, sit down, take 5 minutes, call the parents or write them a note so they know you are interested. Let them know you want to know about their child and his family. Get a little background knowledge about what the child is like. Then the parent knows that you are wanting to see their kid in your class . . . instead of walking in cold and blind at the beginning of the school year knowing nothing about this child except for what you heard in the teacher's break room or from his teacher last year, which isn't always good. So, it helps the teacher, but it also sets the stage for positive relationships with the parents. I think it's a really good thing to do.

The opening vignette illustrates the anticipation parents often feel as they prepare for their first meeting with professionals. Plato's creed that "the beginning is the most important part" seems particularly well suited to describing the initial contact between parents, family members, and professionals. As this vignette illustrates, parents and families are poised at early interactions with professionals for some indication of a meaningful positive partnership. In most instances this preliminary interaction will establish the tenor for future contacts and, as such, should be considered among the most significant of all parent–school sessions. Because the nature and timing of the initial session are dictated by a number of factors, this session can take several forms. Regardless of the specific nature of the initial contact process, however, the classroom teacher should always be involved in it.

Inclusive Nature of the Initial Conference

Initial contacts between parents and professionals are rarely limited to a single meeting or a single professional. Rather, initial parent and family contacts with school and community professionals occur over a period of time, in a number of different settings, and with a variety of professionals. Consider, for example, a typical parent-contact scenario for a child believed to have a significant educational problem. Prior to involvement by special services personnel, the student's regular classroom teachers will usually have contacted his or her parents on several occasions in an effort to obtain and/or provide information and to identify problem-solving strategies (Pierangelo & Giuliani, 2006; Salend, 2008a). Much of the information gathered in this fashion, whether in written or oral report form, will influence future parent–professional communication exchanges.

If a child continues to experience significant educational problems, additional diagnostic and remedial actions are likely. An initial step may involve prereferral assessment, whereby an attempt is made to obtain informal evaluation data and apply regular classroom-setting problem-solving strategies. Prereferral assessment may involve a variety of professionals (e.g., counselors, classroom teachers, special educators, psychologists, administrators) and a number of different activities, including information exchange with parents and family members. Thus, it is common for parents and family members to have significant contact—sometimes initial contacts—with professionals prior to the identification of a student as eligible for special education services.

Additional professional–parent contacts may result from prereferral assessment recommendations for comprehensive and multidisciplinary evaluation. At this point social workers and psychologists may obtain family history, whereas physical therapists and medical personnel may inquire about the child's developmental history (Pierangelo & Giuliani, 2006). After the evaluations have taken place, these same professionals may provide parents and family members with interpretations of testing results. Thus, parents and family members have opportunities for numerous professional contacts—many of them initial type—during the evaluation period.

If the team ultimately agrees that a child needs specialized services, further parent–professional contact will occur during the Individualized Education Program (IEP) conference. In addition to developing a student's individualized program, parents and professionals may engage in other activities construed to be a part of an initial contact conference. At a later stage, concurrent with or following program implementation, parents and family members may again meet with their child's teachers and/or direct service personnel. During such conferences one would expect additional information exchanges, rapport building, and collaboration.

This overview of parent and family involvement in evaluation, planning, and service-delivery activities illustrates the comprehensive and lasting nature of initial parent–educator contacts. Thus, various elements of the initial contact conference will be carried out by various individuals at different times. The segmented nature of the initial contact conference underscores the importance of organizing and orchestrating parent and family contacts with school personnel. Parents and families must be spared from having to provide the same information to different professionals and at the same time guaranteed adequate opportunities to meet with those who can best respond to their specific questions and concerns (e.g., school psychologist, related services and support teachers, inclusion coordinator). In this regard, classroom personnel play a prominent role. Specifically, teachers and other direct service professionals often see parents and family members subsequent to prereferral assessment and evaluation, thereby being in a unique position to determine which initial contact activities must be emphasized. They also have a significant part in establishing and maintaining parent and family rapport and developing the foundation for collaboration—primary initial conference activities. Finally, teachers and other direct service persons are uniquely qualified to discuss specialized methods and procedures for the individual child, information most parents and family members find particularly useful.

Purposes of the Initial Conference

The initial conference is first and foremost designed to establish rapport and a foundation for collaboration with parents and families. In addition, this first session should solicit information and history from parents that is pertinent for accurate assessment and educational programming. A third purpose for this contact entails providing parents with information regarding their son's or daughter's exceptionality and the educational interventions and strategies to be employed. Finally, the initial conference provides educators an opportunity to evaluate and better understand parents and families. This is imperative for ensuring that the school, agency, or organization successfully orchestrates cooperative efforts between home and school. The following sections will discuss the initial conference with regard to each of these purposes.

Establishing Rapport

A fundamental reason for initial contact conferences is that they can facilitate a positive and collaborative working relationship. Positive initial contact with parents has been shown to serve not only as a vehicle for increasing the probability of success with students but also as the basis for other types of parent–school interaction. Early on, Duncan and Fitzgerald (1969) investigated the effects of establishing a positive parent–school relationship with individual parents prior to pupils' entrance into junior high school. Initial positive parent contacts caused a significant increase in parental interest in the school as well as an increase in student attendance and grade point averages; the dropout rate and number of disciplinary referrals decreased for pupils whose parents participated in the program.

Recent research on family involvement indicates that programs that engage parents and families have a positive effect on student outcomes, including higher grade point averages and scores on standardized tests, better attendance, improved behavior at home and school, and better social skills and adaptation to school (Christenson & Cleary, 1990; Henderson & Mapp, 2002). Christenson and Cleary (1990) also documented that parents who are actively involved in their children's education tend to perceive teachers as having better teaching skills than less involved parents. More important, these investigators noted that there was a positive relationship between parents' involvement and school effectiveness ratings and that parents who are most involved in their children's education have an enhanced sense of personal efficacy. This sense of increased personal efficacy has been noted not only for parents of young children but also for those of middle-school- and high-school-age children (Shumow & Lomax, 2001). Accordingly, professionals should attempt to make initial contact with the parents of each student referred for an exceptionality-related issue. Even when other professionals have had prior contact with the parents, the teacher should attempt to facilitate future positive contact and a collaborative spirit by meeting with parents and family members.

An additional argument in favor of conducting initial interviews to establish rapport is that such contact can facilitate parental and family member cooperation, participation, and collaboration in the development of their son's or daughter's IEP. This document is jointly developed by a representative of the school or agency (other than the teacher), the teacher(s), the parents or legal custodians, the student (when appropriate), and other individuals chosen at the discretion of the parents or school or agency. The enactment specifies that the IEP must be in effect prior to the time a student receives special education services.

Although the concept of an IEP represents a monumental step toward ensuring that children and youth with exceptionalities receive needed services, the participation of parents in this process is not automatically guaranteed. That is, even though parents are theoretically equal partners in the IEP development process, their initial face-to-face contact with professional staff frequently takes place at the IEP conference. Also, this conference often is the time when they receive interpretative test information and learn about the IEP process. Many parents and family members will be intimidated, emotionally upset over the diagnosis of their child as exceptional, or simply unfamiliar with the myriad professionals in attendance at IEP meetings. In such circumstances, they probably cannot serve as contributing and functioning members of the IEP team. If the goal is to secure meaningful participation and collaboration from parents in this significant conference (and other conferences as well), one must take special measures. The most efficient means of reaching this goal is to meet with and establish a working and collaborative relationship with parents and families prior to the IEP conference. Once this step has been accomplished, the process of educating a pupil has the potential to become a truly cooperative and collaborative endeavor between home and school.

Professionals should not underestimate the importance of a positive parent–educator relationship from the outset; it is the primary purpose for conducting the initial session with parents, and it sets the stage for future interactions. As noted by Christenson (2004),

Partnering with parents is an attitude and is not only an activity to be implemented. And yet, schools tend to be activity driven, despite the fact that gaining the cooperation of and collaborating with parents is not primarily a function of the activities provided. Rather, "families and schools as partners" is a way of thinking about forming connections, not about how educators can "fix" the family. (p. 95)

Obtaining Information From Parents and Families

As previously suggested, each of the reasons for conducting the initial parent conference relates to the dual supposition that parents have a significant impact on a child or adolescent's ability to function in educational settings and that parent–professional contact should not begin when problems arise (Darch, Miao, & Shippen, 2004; Walther-Thomas, Korinek, McLaughlin, & Williams, 2000). Therefore, an open and ongoing collaborative relationship between home and school is crucial. One of the most obvious reasons for obtaining background information from parents and family members early in the educational planning process is that it may lead to data not previously discovered. Historically, a high percentage of programs for students with disabilities and at risk have served children and adolescents from minority and lower socioeconomic groups. Thus, educators and related school personnel often have been the single professional group to come into contact with all school-age children identified as exceptional. For these reasons, it is apparent that to base the assessment or educational planning process on a pupil's individual history requires that the educational community secure that information necessary for maintaining a child advocacy role and for guaranteeing appropriate services. Professionals must obtain relevant information consistent with optimal educational planning and, as noted previously, it may be acquired over time by a variety of professionals.

Most educators find an interview outline beneficial when conducting the initial session. With experience, however, many find that they can obtain the needed information in an organized fashion without rigidly adhering to a set format. The format proposed in the following section focuses on information most commonly of value to the educator; however, because each initial session will have its unique emphases and purposes, users should adapt the format accordingly. For example, the interviewer should be highly sensitive to not duplicating previous efforts. With great regularity, parents report that they are irritated by multiple interviewers from the same school system or agency asking the same questions.

The following sections describe specific information to obtain as well as a format for conducting the initial session. As noted previously, the requisite information may be gathered by a variety of individuals over a period of time rather than during a single initial interview conference.

PARENTS' STATEMENT OF ISSUES

Even though the interviewer may have access to detailed diagnostic information regarding a child's school-related exceptionality, the initial interview should commence with a request for the parents to discuss their perception of the presenting problem or issues (Barclay, 2005; Salend, 2008a). This type of information is dealt with in the first session for four basic reasons. First, even though educators and other diagnosticians may have conducted a thorough multidisciplinary evaluation of a child, no one will possess more information about the child than his or her parents or guardian, so they should always be asked to supply what they know. A second reason for beginning the initial session in this manner is that it offers the most effective way of getting the parents to talk. In addition, once the parents have begun to discuss the issues, the interviewer can direct the session, based on information the parents have provided, into those areas that appear to warrant further attention. A third reason is that the interviewer can thereby determine whether parents and family members have received accurate diagnostic information and also whether they fully understand it.

Finally, requesting that the parents state the issues in their own words helps determine whether their perception of the exceptionality matches that of the professionals who have assessed the child. In cases of discrepancy, the educator will need to clarify the nature of the differences in understanding and plan a strategy for bringing about greater insight. In instances where a significant discrepancy exists, the interviewer should attempt to determine whether the parents' statement reflects inaccurate information provided during an interpretation, whether they have misinterpreted or denied information conveyed in an earlier interpretation, or whether they are presenting accurate information that should alter professionals' diagnostic information and inferences. Although the interviewer may choose to avoid dealing in depth with a discrepancy issue during the initial interview, it must be explored at some point.

DEVELOPMENTAL HISTORY

Although the developmental history of a child or a youth with an exceptionality is of significance when professionals are designing an educational program, the educational interviewer may not need to obtain that information directly. That is, if it is apparent that another professional, such as a school nurse, physician, social worker, or psychologist, has previously obtained and recorded the child's developmental history, the educator may skip this area. In situations where it is doubtful that the history has been obtained, however, such information should be sought at this session. Because school personnel are sometimes the only professionals to have sustained contact with children with exceptionalities, they must ensure that students are not denied appropriate services because of the professionals' lack of background knowledge.

A child's developmental history will consist of those significant events that have occurred since the time of conception. Consequently, the interviewer must be sensitive to unusual events during the pregnancy, birth, newborn, and childhood periods. Specifically, the following should be explored: emotional stress or unusual circumstances that occurred during the pregnancy, complications or difficulties during delivery, and complications, illnesses, or serious accidents that took place during the infant or childhood stages. Because parents tend to respond that "nothing" of significance occurred, even in describing unusual situations, one should design discussions in this area to require more than simple "yes" or "no" responses. Thus, the interviewer should ask parents to elaborate and provide specific data such as the age at which specific major developmental landmarks were reached—for example, the age at which the child talked, walked, and developed bowel and bladder control and when he or she had specific illnesses, accidents, and behavioral manifestations. When possible, a developmental history questionnaire should be sent to the parents prior to the session; then during the conference, attention can be directed at following up on areas in need of clarification. A sample developmental history form appears in Figure 5.1. This particular questionnaire serves well either when completed by parents ahead of time or when used as a format for obtaining developmental information at the time of the conference.

It must be emphasized that the information generated from a developmental history may not be directly translatable into educationally related recommendations. For that reason, educators having to solicit developmental information must be willing to make referrals to professionals who have more expertise in applying these types of data.

PARENTS' ANALYSIS OF CHILD'S ATTITUDES AND PREFERENCES

This section of the interview allows parents (or family members) to comment on their son's or daughter's attitudes toward school, home, and friends, and it provides them an opportunity to discuss the child's likes

(text continues on p. 132)

THE CHILD DEVELOPMENT UNIT
A University Affiliated Program
University of Kansas Medical Center

Name of Child _____ Date of Birth _____

Address _____

Father's Name _____ Birthdate _____

    Occupation _____ SSN _____

    Phone Number: Home _____ Work_____

    Address _____

Mother's Maiden Name _____ Birthdate _____

    Occupation_____ SSN _____

    Phone Number: Home _____ Work _____

    Address _____

Legal Relationship of Parents to Patient (please check):

    Natural Parent: Mother ☐   Father ☐
    Adoptive Parent: Mother ☐   Father ☐
    Step-Parent: Mother ☐   Father ☐
    Foster Parent: Mother ☐   Father ☐

    Relative: _____

Figure 5.1. Patient information form. Copyright 1994 by The University of Kansas. Reprinted with permission from The Child Development Unit, A University Affiliated Program, University of Kansas Medical Center.

(continues)

All persons living in the home:

Name	Age	Relation to Patient	Present School Grade or Highest Grade Completed
_____	___	_____	_____
_____	___	_____	_____
_____	___	_____	_____
_____	___	_____	_____
_____	___	_____	_____
_____	___	_____	_____

Parental Concerns

Please describe the major concerns you have in seeking help for your child. List your concerns in order of their importance to you.

1. (Most Important) _____

_____

2. _____

_____

3. _____

_____

4. _____

_____

5. _____

_____

Figure 5.1. (*continued*)

How can the Child Development Unit/University Affiliated Program help you most with these concerns? _____

_____

_____

Medical History

Pregnancy

While pregnant did child's mother have any of the following:

	Yes	No		Yes	No
German measles	☐	☐	Vaginal infection or bleeding	☐	☐
Anemia (low iron)	☐	☐	Have a high fever	☐	☐
Diabetes	☐	☐	Smoke cigarettes	☐	☐
Kidney problems	☐	☐	Use alcohol	☐	☐
High blood pressure	☐	☐	Use drugs	☐	☐
Any severe emotional problems	☐	☐			

What medications did child's mother take during pregnancy? (include vitamins and iron) _____

Birth

Was the child born: early _____ late _____ on time _____

Was child born by C-section? Yes _____ No _____ If yes, please give reason for C-section: _____

_____

About how long was mother in labor? _____

What was baby's birth weight? _____ length? _____

What was baby's condition at birth? _____

_____

Figure 5.1. (*continued*)

(*continues*)

Has child ever had the following:

	Yes	No		Yes	No
Eye or vision problems	☐	☐	Anemia	☐	☐
Ear or hearing problems	☐	☐	Vomiting spells	☐	☐
Allergies	☐	☐	Frequent diarrhea	☐	☐
Asthma	☐	☐	Frequent colds	☐	☐
Convulsions or "spells"	☐	☐	Kidney or urine problems	☐	☐
Head injury	☐	☐	Meningitis	☐	☐

Has child had any other health problems not listed above? (Describe)_____

_____

_____

_____

Does child take medication on a regular basis?　Yes _____　No _____

Please list medications taken and amount:

_____

_____

Development & School History

Development

At what age did child first:

Sit alone	_____	Feed self finger foods	_____
Crawl (hands & knees)	_____	Speak first real words	_____
Stand alone	_____	Speak first real sentences	_____
Walk well	_____	Become completely toilet trained	_____

Figure 5.1.　(*continued*)

School History

Is your child currently enrolled in a school program?   Yes _____   No _____

If yes, please answer the following:

School Name: _____

Address: _____

Grade (if applicable): _____

Has child been evaluated by school diagnostic team?   Yes _____   No _____

If yes, when was evaluation completed? _____

Please describe child's performance at school. What subjects does he or she do well in; what subjects does he or she have difficulty with?

_____

_____

_____

_____

Does child receive any special services to help him or her at school? Yes ___ No ___

If yes, please describe: _____

_____

_____

Social-Emotional Development

Does child exhibit behaviors at home or school that concern you? Yes ____ No ____

Figure 5.1. (*continued*)

(*continues*)

If yes, please describe the behaviors that concern you: _____

_____

_____

What methods are used to discipline child? _____

_____

_____

Are these methods effective?   Yes _____   No _____

What does child like to do to occupy his or her time? _____

_____

Does child have regular playmates or friends?   Yes _____   No _____

Person completing application _____

Relation to child _____   Date _____

Parent/Guardian Signature _____

Please enclose a recent picture of your child if available.

Return Form to

Patient Services Coordinator
Child Development Unit
3901 Rainbow Blvd.
Kansas City, KS 66160-7340

Figure 5.1. (*continued*)

and dislikes, hobbies, and leisure-time activities and whether there are home issues that may impact the child's learning or behavior at school (Darch et al., 2004; G. Taylor, 2000). It is also a vehicle for discussions of behavioral and social traits and tendencies. The interviewer should be sensitive to such behavioral traits as antisocial or withdrawn behavior, temper tantrums, aberrant sleeping patterns, enuresis or encopresis, hyperactivity, and destructive or overaggressive responses.

Discussions of a child's attitudes and personality not only help gather information for use in educational planning but also provide the parents an opportunity to comment on the child's areas of strengths. Because the initial parent interview often focuses on a child's problems (at least with regard to children and youth who have disabilities), it is important to encourage parents to also talk about their youngster's strengths. Indeed, if the parents are unable to provide such information, this very observation is valuable for the educator.

HISTORY OF PAST SCHOOL PERFORMANCE

Although the educational interviewer usually has access to information about the child's school-related history, it is nonetheless important that the parents and family members comment on this area. Specifically, the focus should be on parental perceptions of school success and failure and their causes, academic performance as compared to the child's peer group, and those academic and social areas in which the parents would like to see the greatest investment of effort. In addition, the parents should have a chance to discuss previous relationships they and their child have had with school personnel. This area has frequently been reported as among the most beneficial for educators to explore.

Finally, the interviewer should discuss with the parents any measures they have employed to deal with the child's problems. For example, a discussion of strategies and supports parents have implemented at home or their perception of the effectiveness of previous interventions recommended by school personnel may provide valuable insight into potential solutions to current learning and behavioral issues. In addition, it is not uncommon for parents of children with mild disabilities to have had prior contact with a number of professionals. Not only does knowledge of past evaluation results and remediation strategies aid in planning for the student in the classroom but a discussion of these procedures can function as an invitation for parents and family members to discuss issues associated with gaining an evaluation of their child.

PARENTAL GOALS AND EXPECTATIONS

Parents' and family members' goals and expectations for their child with an exceptionality, including the roles parents and educators play, will exert a significant impact on the relationship between the family and the school (Salend, 2008a; Sheldon, 2002). Consequently, this significant variable element must be carefully analyzed. First, of course, one must determine what these goals are and whether they are commensurate with the child's abilities.

Teachers should also solicit information from parents about their expectations regarding the educator, the school (or agency), and the community. For example, parents may assume that identification of a student as disabled and eligible for special education support services will result in significant curriculum modifications and immediate academic and social improvements. Although some of these expectation issues may be resolved at IEP conferences, the educator needs to obtain parents' perceptions relative to their goals if a specific strategy for reducing discrepancies is to be planned (Christenson & Sheridan, 2001).

SOCIOLOGICAL INFORMATION

Another area of significant educational interest, and thus a topic for the initial conference, concerns the ecological and sociological aspects of the child's environment. An understanding of the child's family and home and community environment will enable educators to more adequately understand and plan for the student.

Items of specific interest in this area include (a) the socioeconomic status of the family; (b) the individuals living in the home; (c) the physical and mental health of those residing in the home; (d) the ethnic, cultural, or religious backgrounds and beliefs of the family that may have an influence on the parents' attitudes toward educational planning; (e) the languages other than English spoken in the home; (f) the child-rearing practices and attitudes of the parents and family members; and (g) the type of supervision provided the child or adolescent before and after school, including whom to contact regarding implementation of out-of-school programs.

Although interviewers agree on the importance of avoiding personal questions, it is necessary to address those issues that will provide an adequate understanding of the family. It is important to ensure, however, that the information gathered is used to establish positive relationships with families and improve outcomes for students rather than to reinforce stereotypes or preconceived judgments about families (Christenson & Sheridan, 2001).

Though no simple strategy exists for securing this sometimes sensitive material, most frequently it will emerge through a positive interpersonal relationship with the parents.

Providing Parents and Families
With Information

Although some might argue that families have ample opportunity to gain information about the educational program their child with an exceptionality will receive through the various preliminary contacts that occur (i.e., meetings prior to or concurrent with assessment and diagnostic decision making), these sessions, including diagnostic feedback and IEP meetings, often fail to provide all the information in which parents and family members are interested. One obvious explanation for this lack of information is that the classroom teacher, the individual most knowledgeable about the educational program, often has only marginal involvement in these early meetings with parents and families. Likewise, those professionals who have the most involvement with the parents initially may be unable to provide basic information about the classroom operation. As noted by one father following an interpretation conference, "Those may have been smart people, but they never did tell me what time school started and ended, what supplies he would need, and how the class would be different from his other one." It is absolutely mandatory, therefore, that parents have an opportunity to meet individually with the classroom teacher—the one person most capable of satisfying families' information needs and specifically describing collaborative opportunities and expectations.

Just as educators expect parents to be able to provide basic information about their child, parents and families should be able to expect educators to inform them regarding the procedures to be employed with the child. Although this is a logical expectation, historically it has not been the norm. Rather, teachers and other educational personnel have sometimes been more concerned with obtaining information from parents than with providing information to them.

Although the specific information to disseminate depends on the unique needs of parents and family members, the condition of the pupil, and the educational program to be utilized, certain generic elements should be covered, including (a) a discussion of assessment and diagnostic procedures and findings, (b) a description of the educational program to be employed with the student, (c) a rundown of the methodology for evaluating pupil progress and the manner in which such information will be communicated, and (d) a discussion of problem-solving alternatives and other resources available to the parents and family through the school and community.

ASSESSMENT AND DIAGNOSTIC INFORMATION

The heavy emphasis on formal assessment procedures with children and adolescents who have exceptionalities has been criticized by a number of authorities (Adelizzi & Goss, 2001; Pierangelo & Giuliani, 2006; Salvia, Ysseldyke, & Bolt, 2007). Nonetheless, testing results—both formal and informal—continue to serve not only as a major means of drawing diagnostic inferences but, more important, as the basis for making educational programming decisions. Consequently, the importance of assessment in any diagnostic and remediation program must not be underestimated.

Along these lines, parents and family members frequently mention that one of their strongest and most immediate needs is for interpretative information about their son or daughter. Even in instances where interpretative data have been shared previously, many parents and family members indicate they want more information. Although the reasons for this situation may vary, there appear to be several basic considerations.

First, though parents may have been involved in the interpretation process, even one skillfully conducted, they perhaps were intellectually and emotionally detached from the conference. It is not uncommon to find that parents are overwhelmed by the quantity and sophistication of material covered in a conference or that they are in a state of emotional shock over the diagnosis and may not be in an emotional state to hear details of the disability (Gilliam & Mayes, 2005; Nissenbaum, Tollefson, & Reese, 2002; Seligman, 2000). Parents have frequently reported that they were able to hear information presented only up to the point that the term *mentally retarded, emotionally disturbed, brain damaged,* or whatever was used. Consequently, even though some parents and family members may appear attentive and involved, they may actually comprehend little of the information coming at them.

In addition, professionals' own perceptions of their role in the interpretive conference may influence their ability to communicate fully with families. One mother commented,

> The people that we went to, I think are very good at diagnosing, but I don't think that they really thought about the outcomes. They were thinking about the diagnosis right now and what the child had. . . . [They] mentioned absolutely nothing about what we could look for down the road with him and I don't even think that was on their minds at that point. (Nissenbaum et al., 2002, p. 34)

Second, many parents and family members seem more comfortable receiving information from teachers than from other professionals whose role, identity, mission, and commitment they may understand less clearly. Teachers have been the brunt of much recent criticism, yet as a group they remain among the most respected and endeared of all professionals.

Third, parents and family members frequently report that the initial interpretation of testing results was so muddled by esoteric language and terminology, acronyms, and other confusing information that they could not benefit. Although teachers are not immune to this type of error, as a group they tend to engage less in this kind of nonfunctional behavior than other professional groups. In addition, classroom teachers and other direct service providers (e.g., speech pathologists, occupational therapists) usually have more samples of behavior on which to base their inferences and are in a position to augment standardized testing results with informal measures and observations that are more closely aligned with remediation or enhancement programs.

As implied, parents of exceptional offspring frequently experience a number of concerns at the time of their child's evaluation and program alteration. Such concerns can take a number of forms, but frequently they are expressed as questions. The Institute for Community Inclusion (2005) listed a series of questions frequently asked by parents of children with mental retardation, many of which surface at the time of the initial parent–educator conference. These questions follow:

- What exactly is mental retardation?
- How is the diagnosis made?
- When is the diagnosis made?
- What causes mental retardation?
- Can a child with mental retardation have other disabilities?
- Will my child need medical tests?
- Is mental retardation the same as mental illness?
- Will medication help my child?
- Are there different types of mental retardation?
- Where will my child receive his or her needed services?
- How much help will my child need?
- What can I do to help my child?
- Where can I go for more help?

These questions and others may surface during the initial interpretation session and occur on a regular basis in ensuing contacts. The conferencer should note the questions that do arise as a reflection of the framework of current parental concerns. An understanding of that framework will facilitate meaningful communication during later interactions.

In brief, the reinterpretation process should focus on (a) offering a clarification of the purpose of the evaluation and the expectations for the assessment, (b) providing an opportunity for parents and family members to ask questions about the assessment procedures, (c) presenting the evaluation findings in summarized form, (d) encouraging parents and family members to raise questions about or discuss the findings, (e) restating the recommendations, (f) allowing an opportunity for parents and family members to raise questions about or discuss the recommendations, (g) discussing the manner in which the recommendations are to be implemented, and (h) identifying those individuals who are responsible for implementation. Though some parents and family members may need only a brief review of this information, others will require a more thorough discussion; hence, the person who conducts the meeting must adapt the following format accordingly.

Clarify the purpose and expectations for the evaluation. Although more and more professionals are acknowledging the limitations of tests, the public still attributes powers to these instruments that often outweigh their capabilities. Consequently, the purpose of the testing, the capabilities of the instruments used, and the expectations of the diagnostic team should be shared with parents.

Discuss the assessment procedures. As diagnosticians often assume either that parents understand or that they do not really need to understand the nature of the assessment procedures, there has been a tendency to provide test results without an explanation of what the tests involve. For example, if parents are informed that their son or daughter has a developmental disability, an emotional disturbance, or a learning disability, they should also be apprised of the manner in which the condition was identified. Although it is not necessary to enter into discussions regarding the validity of particular tests, it is necessary to inform parents of the nature of a particular exceptionality. In addition, parents can frequently augment specific findings once they are aware of the types of behaviors sampled. Without this discussion parents cannot be expected either to understand the evaluation process or to serve as a collaborative member of the team (Sandall, Hemmeter, Smith, & McLean, 2005; A. Turnbull, Turnbull, Erwin, & Soodak, 2006).

Summarize the findings. Assessment results should be given to parents and family members in abbreviated form, with attention turned to those areas considered most significant. Because most assessment techniques yield data in the intellectual, educational (achievement), emotional/personality, physical/sensory, or ecological areas, an interpretation summary should follow this outline. It is critical, however, that the summary provided to parents represents an integrated picture of the whole child that includes the student's strengths and capacities, rather than simply a series of disjointed clinical reports that focus only on deficits.

Allow opportunities for questions. As noted previously, parents and family members may be far more able to ask questions after the initial interpretative session. Consequently, subsequent conferences must allow parents and family members to address areas of concern or confusion. The teacher should be prepared to entertain difficult questions related to the diagnostic and placement process. Questions such as "What will happen after we're gone?" "Will he be able to marry?" "Did we cause this?" and "Will his children have the same problems?" are not uncommon. To help parents deal with these complex issues, the following guidelines may be useful: (a) have the parents and family members define what they mean by their terms (e.g., *mental, hyper*), (b) determine whether parents and families are looking for an answer or structuring an opportunity to offer their own views (frequently parents who ask this type of question are merely looking for an opportunity to talk), (c) allow the parents and family members an opportunity to discuss their feelings and perceptions, and (d) attempt to candidly answer questions when the questioner is sincerely looking for an answer. Throughout, it is important to keep in mind that "I don't know" may be the most appropriate response at times.

Restate recommendations. Not only must recommendations be reviewed, especially those specifics the teacher can best address and clarify, but the parents must have an opportunity to raise questions about the remediation strategies. Because this is probably the most frequently glossed over component in the initial interpretation (and obviously a major need for parents), the teacher should plan for it very carefully.

THE EDUCATIONAL PROGRAM TO BE EMPLOYED

Although individuals who routinely conduct interpretation and disposition conferences may be proficient at meeting many of parents' and families' basic needs, they may be unable to offer specific information about the operation and nature of the educational program and the enrichment and adaptation strategies to be provided. Consequently, even though descriptors such as *low student–teacher ratio, individualized program, structured classroom, inclusion classroom,* and so forth may suffice for indicating what type of model will be provided, this area requires further clarification for parents and families. Thus, topics that should be discussed are (a) classroom and school schedules, (b) classroom and school philosophy and administration, (c) academic adaptation and enrichment programs (goals and objectives for the student and the manner in which the school personnel and program will be able to satisfy these needs), (d) classroom management and emotional–social intervention strategies, (e) support personnel and programs to which the student will be exposed, and (f) availability of parent and family programs. Chapters 10, 11, and 12 discuss specific aspects of these topics that vary across student ages; however, the general content should be included in initial conferences.

Classroom and school schedules. Parents and family members will be interested in the educational and treatment schedule and routine their son or daughter will follow, including the bus schedule; school starting and stopping times; the child's activity schedule (including those in general and/or special programs); lunch, recess, and break periods; the school calendar (including vacations, special events, and so forth); and a listing of those activities that the student will be exposed to in a special program or the special activities that are provided as a part of an inclusion program. Both day-to-day and longer term schedules should be shared with the parents.

Classroom and school philosophy and administration. Because the philosophy of the teacher and the administration will dictate the general educational approach, the teacher must provide this information to parents and family members. For example, inclusion program philosophies and interpretations vary widely from system to system. Parents may be concerned about how those philosophies are operationalized in terms of combining educational services and supports such as how functional curriculum and community-based instruction will be integrated with a general education placement (Salend, 2008a). Furthermore, educational programs serving students with emotional and behavioral disorders can follow any one of a number of orientations, including behavioral, psychoeducational, or ecological (Kauffman, 2005). Consequently, in language they can understand, parents and family members should be oriented to the philosophy of the program.

Remediation, adaptation, and enrichment programs. As noted, individuals who interpret test information and make program recommendations for parents and family members may have limited information regarding the specific academic programs to be employed for a particular child. Thus, even though a strength or deficit area may have been identified, the precise manner in which it will be dealt with may receive little attention. Program components such as degree of structure, curricula, specific procedures and equipment, and teaching strategies should be outlined. Attention should also focus on the goals and objectives identified in the IEP as well as on any other areas that the teacher thinks need further clarification or about which parents and family members raise questions.

Classroom management and emotional–social intervention. Emotional–social intervention strategies to be applied should receive the same attention as the specifics of the academic intervention programs. This orientation will include both the manner in which IEP goals and objectives will be accomplished and overall classroom management. The teacher should give special attention to procedures that may be considered novel or controversial or that are based on reward systems or consequences. Using token economy systems and time-outs and making certain class activities are contingent on classroom productivity or behavior should be discussed.

Support personnel and related services. Related services, or those services needed by a student with an exceptionality to maximally benefit from specially designed instruction, are defined as

> transportation and such developmental, corrective, and other supportive services (including speech-language pathology and audiology services; interpreting services; psychological services; physical and occupational therapy; recreation, including therapeutic recreation; social work services; school nurse services designed to enable a child with a disability to receive a free appropriate public education as described in the individualized education program of the child; counseling services, including rehabilitation counseling; orientation and mobility services; and medical services, except that such medical services shall be for diagnostic and evaluation purposes only) as may be required to assist a child with a disability to benefit from special education, and includes the early identification and assessment of disabling conditions in children. (Individuals with Disabilities Education Improvement Act, 2004, § 1401(22))

Because related services frequently involve resources and personnel that are unfamiliar to the parents, these services will require careful explanation (Leiter & Krauss, 2004). The following example describes the role of the physical therapist in language that parents can understand. Similar descriptions may be developed for each ancillary role.

Physical therapists (PTs) are involved in the development and maintenance of motor skills, movement, and posture. They may prescribe specific exercises to help a child increase control of muscles and use specialized equipment, such as braces, effectively. Massage and prescriptive exercises are perhaps the most frequently applied procedures, but physical therapy can also include swimming, heat treatment, special positioning for feeding and toileting, and other techniques. PTs encourage children to be as motorically independent as possible, help them develop muscular function, and reduce their pain, discomfort, or long-term physical damage. They may also suggest dos and don'ts for sitting positions and activities in the classroom and may devise exercise or play programs that children with and without disabilities can enjoy together (Heward, 2006, p. 446).

Teachers should also be alert to the myriad acronyms used to discuss related services and ensure that family members understand what is being said during the meeting. One teacher of students with multiple and severe disabilities reported that some of the families he works with have difficulty remembering terms even though their children have been receiving special education and related services for several years. In an effort to put parents more at ease, he takes the initiative to interject comments such as "OT, that stands for occupational therapy and works with small muscles . . . is that right?" if the occupational therapist has not already provided such clarification.

Parent and family programs. As many special education programs involve parents and families, the teacher should review for parents the schedules, expectations, and procedures associated with their component. Individual and group conference dates, workshop schedules, and resources available to the parents and family (both in the school and in the community) should be reviewed. In addition, because some parents and family members are interested in augmenting classroom academic programs through home tutoring, the teacher should structure or provide input and material for parental teaching activities. Finally, parents and family members should be informed about procedures for visiting the classroom, general expectations for their role, materials and equipment they should supply, and other related items.

To ensure that the information deemed important for parents continues to be readily available to them, a handbook may prove to be an excellent resource, for both the parent and the teacher. As with all material presented to families, the handbook should include information presented in language that is clear, concise, succinct, attractive, inclusive, and written on a level parents can understand. With regard to the handbook's content, Barclay (2005) suggested that it serve as a vehicle for communicating the school's philosophy, mission statement, policies, and procedures as well as for conveying a strong commitment to forging partnerships with families. Part of one teacher's handbook appears in Figure 5.2.

EVALUATING STUDENT PROGRESS AND DISSEMINATING THIS INFORMATION TO FAMILIES

Assessing the progress of students and communicating such information to parents and family members form a basic and necessary element of any good educational program and provide an essential component of any collaborative effort. Accordingly, the initial conference should include a discussion of the manner in which students are evaluated, how parents

We're off to a **BRIGHT** start and are going to have a **STELLAR** year!

Figure 5.2. Sample table of contents of a program handbook.

will be kept up to date, and the type and frequency of communication the parents prefer (Matuszny, Banda, & Colemen, 2007; Moore, 2003).

The Individuals with Disabilities Education Improvement Act mandates that students' progress toward meeting annual goals described in the IEP be measured and reported to parents periodically throughout the school year. This may be accomplished through the use of quarterly report cards, but many parents prefer communication on a more frequent basis. Appropriate alternatives (in addition to parent–teacher conferences) for this purpose include telephone contacts, daily or weekly progress reports, letters and notes, and technology-based communication such as electronic mail (F. Ramirez, 2001; Salend, 2008a; G. Taylor, 2000). Evidence that parents prefer regular, informal contact (Sicley, 1993; Simpson, 1988; A. Turnbull & Turnbull, 2001) underscores the need for appropriate planning in this area. Thus, these parent–educator communication procedures should take place on a regular basis and be designed to focus on progress rather than problem areas.

Telephone contacts are most appropriate as a means of providing parents with reinforcement and feedback, scheduling conferences, providing progress reports, and obtaining information on changes in behavior or performance. Besides being convenient and time saving, the phone contacts also can serve to overcome some parents' inability or unwillingness to attend face-to-face conferences. In spite of the advantages, however, telephone contacts pose several potential problems. First, whether or not a call is scheduled at a mutually convenient time, some parents do not wish to be telephoned at home. Second, although a convenient means of communicating, telephone contacts must never be thought of as substitutes for ongoing person-to-person conferences. Finally, the telephone should typically not be used to confront parents or to discuss any sensitive material that should be dealt with in a face-to-face fashion.

Daily or weekly progress reports can be used to communicate the student's academic performance, preparedness for class, effort, behavior, peer relations, and homework completion (Barclay, 2005; Salend, 2008a). To be most effective, these reports should be sent home on a regular basis, and both the family members and the child should be able to clearly interpret the contents. Examples of reporting systems used to communicate with parents are provided in Figure 5.3.

Letters and notes to parents can also be useful communication tools and are most appropriate for reinforcing parents, family members, and/or the child as well as for facilitating routine information exchange. Just as with the telephone, however, letters and notes should not be used as a

	Reading	Math	Language Arts	Science	Social Studies	Health
Leroy had satisfactory social behavior						
Leroy completed his work independently						
Leroy participated in group activities						

U WERE THE 🍎

OF MY 👁 TODAY!

_____

HAD GOOD BEHAVIOR.

_____

TEACHER

Figure 5.3. Sample parent report.

means of sharing sensitive information, criticizing parents or children, or handling other types of communication best exchanged in person.

More and more educators today rely on communication via computer, cell phone, and other technology, and there is every reason to believe that such options will become increasingly popular in the future. For example, e-mail and cell phone text messaging allow parents and family members and professionals to exchange information conveniently and efficiently. Some professionals are even exploring the use of school videos (or DVDs) as a way to provide families with pertinent information regarding school programs and policies. This medium of communication may be a particularly innovative way to reach families who have difficulty with literacy themselves (Calabrese, 2006; Payne, 2005). As is the case with telephone and written communication, technology-based systems are best reserved for facilitating routine information exchanges such as progress reports and for disseminating information rather than for solving problems.

In addition, teachers should be aware of the range of skills families display regarding the use of technology. Some families do not have access to current technologies for reasons such as cost and lack of training, and thus, educators should make information available through multiple sources. Conversely, many families view the Internet as a viable and flexible medium for accessing information regarding their child's disability and access it frequently (Blackburn & Read, 2005; Zaidman-Zait & Jamieson, 2007). As a result, some parents come to the initial contact conference with a wealth of information—some of it accurate and some not. Educators need to be prepared to correct Internet-based misconceptions while encouraging families to learn more about their child's exceptionality in any way they can.

GROUP CONFERENCES

Although parents and family members should have an opportunity to exchange information with educators on a one-to-one basis when their child first enters a program and thereafter as required, many of their basic information needs can be satisfied effectively through group meetings. Thus, even though group sessions must not supplant individual conferences, they can serve as a vehicle for disseminating common information and discussing shared issues and for facilitating communication between parents and family members with collective concerns. In particular, sessions focusing on the nature, characteristics, etiology, and prognosis of an exceptionality; a description of the general educational program being utilized; and the manner in which pupils are evaluated are highly compatible with a group format.

Information regarding an exceptionality. One of the most common needs expressed by parents of children with exceptionalities is the need for information on the nature, characteristics, etiology, and future implications of their child's condition (Seligman & Darling, 2007; Simpson & Zionts, 2000; L. T. Zionts, Zionts, Harrison, & Bellinger, 2003). The search for this kind of information represents both an immediate reaction to an exceptionality and the ongoing concern of parents and families. Accordingly, educators should be aware that information relating to an exceptionality presents a commonly requested agenda item. In this regard parents and family members may benefit as much (if not more) from being allowed to discuss their own perceptions and to share their own information regarding an exceptionality as from facts disseminated by a professional. In addition, and perhaps most important, group interactions can be both enlightening and stimulating for the participants. In some instances parents and family members may discover other families with issues similar to their own, or in other instances they may gain the confidence necessary to apply new techniques with their children. In still other situations, group sessions may provide parents and family members a forum for discussing their perceptions and feelings about their children with a truly empathic group. As observed by Rutherford and Edgar (1979), "Group training provides support for parents who feel socially isolated from parents of normal children. In some cases, the friendships formed during these training sessions have been maintained long after the training sessions have terminated" (p. 161). When provided an opportunity to interact in the right kind of group setting, parents and families of children with exceptionalities frequently respond by becoming more actively and productively involved with their children and the educators who serve them.

The importance of addressing the characteristics, etiology, and prognosis of an exceptionality should not be underestimated. First, the complexity of these issues may make their comprehension by parents and families extremely difficult. Certainly if professionals have as much difficulty understanding the various exceptionalities as they appear to, parents and family members can be expected to share the same plight. In addition, even when families have a cognitive understanding of a condition and its related factors, they can still be expected to demonstrate emotional needs that require attention. Group interactions and the support that can come from families meeting together frequently serve to satisfy this need. Though group sessions must not take the place of individualized and in-depth interpretation, planning, and evaluation conferences, they can help clarify and facilitate understanding and acceptance by parents and families.

One teacher of children with learning disabilities held a parent group session each year on factors associated with her students' exceptionality. As a part of her discussion, she focused on definitions of learning disabilities, including an interpretation of specific factors associated with the definitions (e.g., involvement of one or more of the basic psychological processes, IQ-achievement discrepancy). Furthermore, she made available a list of common terms associated with "learning disabilities" (e.g., attention-deficit/hyperactivity disorder, poor self-concept, phonological awareness) and discussed these items with parents and family members. Finally, she employed her list of terms as a vehicle for stimulating discussions with the participants. This veteran educator revealed that when she gave parents lists of terms, she not only was supplying them with a future reference but also generating questions and stimulating lively discussions that might not otherwise have occurred.

Other means of structuring informative group sessions on characteristics and related issues include videotapes, filmstrips, guest speakers on a particular topic, and adults with disabilities commenting on their personal experiences. Regardless of the format used, however, time should always be allotted for discussions. As suggested earlier, family interaction opportunities typically are the most salient part of any group meeting.

Educational program description. When topics on the educational and related services programs and procedures to be employed are taken up in group sessions, they should support information provided in individual conferences and should present items for general discussion. Areas of discussion and information exchange will occur on topics similar to those pursued during initial parent conferences, including classroom and school schedules, policies, and orientation; academic and social intervention and enrichment programs; ancillary services and personnel available to students; and parent and family programs. Because parents and family members should have had an opportunity to pursue these matters individually at the time of the initial conference, group sessions should be designed to reacquaint families with the original information and any changes that may have taken place and to allow for discussions among the participants.

One teacher of students with mild disabilities gave parents a written description of her educational program at the time she provided an oral overview. She reported that this strategy served both to provide parents and family members with a resource for later referral and to stimulate discussion. The meeting took place in the special education resource room and was structured to accommodate questions, demonstrations, and comments, all of which aided in facilitating a discussion. The teacher discussed the classroom schedule with the parents, and because each of the students was in an inclusive classroom for a significant part of each day, she spent a considerable amount of time discussing the general education support and communication system she used. Finally, the teacher also provided a thorough description of the reinforcement and behavior management system she used in her class and the manner in which this system was coordinated with the students' general education teachers. Again, this topic was structured so as to facilitate discussion.

A number of educators address general information relating to educational programming at annual "open house" meetings. Of course parents should be invited to make individual appointments at a later time to discuss specific matters as needed.

Evaluation procedures. Group meetings can offer an appropriate vehicle for discussing the manner in which a student will be evaluated and the mode in which this information will be communicated to parents and family members. In many instances, children with exceptionalities who enter special education programs have a long history of school failure, making the topic of evaluation particularly interesting. Moreover, as the majority of children and youth with exceptionalities receive at least a portion of their education in regular classrooms, it is important to discuss the manner in which educators will coordinate evaluations across various settings and classrooms. Just as with other topical areas, information should serve as a follow-up to discussions during individual conferences and be presented in a fashion that facilitates group interaction. Accordingly, the teacher should carefully plan ways of ensuring parent and family participation. Without such prior planning, the major benefits of group conferences may go untapped.

PROBLEM-SOLVING ALTERNATIVES

Some parents and families of children with exceptionalities will have needs that require utilizing certain community agencies or school district support services. Accordingly, the teacher should be able to provide information on how and where to secure the necessary services, including those for the parents or family as well as for the child with an exceptionality. The educator should be familiar with available social and welfare services; respite care programs; babysitting services for children and youth with exceptionalities; psychiatric, psychological, and counseling services; social agencies; and so forth. Finally, the educational conferencer should be aware of crisis intervention programs that serve the immediate needs of parents and families. Though many will not need this type of information, those who do should be assured that educators can make appropriate referrals to assist them in meeting their needs (J. L. Epstein, 1992; Matuszny et al., 2007).

Evaluating Parents and Families

A fourth major purpose for conducting the initial conference is to identify the characteristics, including strengths and weaknesses, of parents and families. This process stems from the supposition that for an educator to collaborate and effectively make use of the resources within parents and families, these resources must first be understood. Both popular and professional literature reflect abundant interest in the influence of parents and families on the development of their offspring (Christenson, 2004; Spann, Kohler, & Soenksen, 2003; A. Turnbull et al., 2006), and as empirically illustrated, parents and families can exert a profound influence on children's development and school-related performance. However, whereas attention in this area focused at one time almost totally on parental influence as the cause of certain problems, today more and more consideration goes to procedures for collaborating and enlisting the aid of parents and families in accomplishing specified goals, responding to family needs, and better understanding the impact of the family on the pupil. Thus, rather than being held responsible for certain types of educationally related problems, parents and family members are viewed instead as partners in the educational process. Although the process in general has been demonstrated as logical and efficacious, the strengths and weaknesses of parents and families—including their needs and participation preferences (see Chapter 1 for a discussion of this issue)—must be carefully evaluated to ensure an effective parent–educator program. In the same manner that a teacher implements an educational program only after determining a student's abilities and needs, he or she must also take careful stock of parent and family strengths, weaknesses, and needs.

Each of us constantly evaluates the individuals and families with whom we work using criteria that are consistent with our own values and needs. Parent and family assessment methods, however, must be tempered by the use of more objective criteria, including (a) parents' strengths and weaknesses, (b) family structure, (c) family interactions, (d) family functions, and (e) family life cycles.

PARENTS' STRENGTHS AND WEAKNESSES

However intimidating as it may sound, the task of evaluating strengths and weaknesses is carried out very effectively by many educators. Particular areas of attention include parents' cognitive, educational, and personality and emotional characteristics as well as their personality and health (Carlisle, Stanley, & Kemple, 2005). Some educators may not consider themselves qualified to estimate the cognitive capabilities of another person, especially in the absence of formal testing. Still, it is possible to make reasonably accurate general estimates of intelligence based exclusively on verbal interactions, at least to the point of understanding whether an individual is functioning at or near an average intellectual level. Anything beyond that is not valid or useful. On the basis of the information the parent provides, however, especially as it relates to occupation and education, as well as his or her verbal fluency, memory, and demeanor, educators can frequently draw reasonably accurate intellectual inferences. The rationale for undertaking this analysis is simply that different parents will need different programs; it cannot serve as a basis of etiology for a student's exceptionality or as a discriminator for services. Moreover, because racial, ethnic, language, and other diversity-related factors may influence one individual's perceptions of another, educators must be extremely cautious in making inferences.

Parents' educational level is also significant when considering needs and appropriate levels of participation. Sometimes parents will volunteer the extent to which they have been formally educated, and at other times such information can be inferred from their occupation, vocation, or behavior. Just as when making intellectual judgments, educators have the intent here simply to determine whether the parents are literate and, if so, the extent to which they will be capable of utilizing self-directed programs, participating as tutors with their own child, and so forth. Although this process may appear to be an invasion of privacy, the success of many collaborative programs is founded on such information. Consequently, the teacher would be remiss by neglecting this area.

Physical and health considerations include the age of the parents and family members, plus their health, physical limitations, sensory deficits, and other related factors. Although a particular program might be effective under normal circumstances, modifications may be needed for a parent or family member with a physical or health-related disability.

Personality factors are probably the most significant variables in determining the success or failure of collaborative and home-school programs, yet they are also the most elusive. Although educators frequently report that they feel unprepared to analyze the personality of another adult, simple observations of the parents' style and strategies often help teachers arrive at estimates of personality. Of course educators need to closely monitor their own values and biases in this area, but information relating to parents' personality and attitudes can be extremely helpful to educators.

One mother, for example, repeatedly referred to herself in a conference as highly dependent on other individuals for providing care for her son with mental retardation. She revealed that she relied heavily on friends and relatives for making even minor parenting decisions and reported feeling overwhelmed at the prospect of making independent decisions and assuming total responsibility for the child's care. Though the educational conferencer identified independent functioning as a goal for this mother, she also wisely adopted the strategy of initially collaborating with the mother in conjunction with someone from her circle of support.

Although information regarding parents' characteristics is important, it is usually not formally recorded. In fact, because such information stems from subjective judgments, the teacher is advised not to make a written record of it (e.g., parents' estimated intellectual abilities, emotional stability).

FAMILY STRUCTURE

As discussed in Chapter 2, family structure is increasingly varied, and these variations must be considered when evaluating parents and families. In particular, one should assess a family's membership characteristics, cultural style, and ideology (Christian, 2006; Lambie & Daniels-Mohring, 1993; Olsen & Fuller, 2003; Rock, 2000; Simpson & Fiedler, 1989; A. Turnbull & Turnbull, 2001).

Family membership characteristics include the family's size, individual member factors, and extrafamilial support. Membership characteristics, in turn, determine the needs and resources of a given family. For example, the needs of a divorced mother with six children will likely differ from those of a two-parent family. Furthermore, extrafamilial support, such as close friends or relatives, can have a significant impact on the availability of parents to participate in school meetings and other education-related activities.

Families are also influenced by cultural and ideological factors, which affect their values and their perceptions of the needs of their child with an exceptionality. Thus, parents and family members react differently to the stress of coping with a child with an exceptionality. Some become immersed in their child's education and development, whereas others may distance themselves from the school program. Obviously these factors must be evaluated and accommodated on an individual basis.

A family's socioeconomic status should also be assessed as a part of determining their educational involvement. For instance, perhaps a family experiencing financial strain cannot afford to become actively involved in their child's treatment or education.

FAMILY INTERACTIONS

An analysis of family interactions involves consideration of the interplay among individual family members. For example, a family may have four subsystems: (a) adult–adult (partner interactions), (b) parental (parent–child interactions), (c) sibling (child–child interactions), and (d) extended family (family members and close friends) (L. J. Johnson, Pugach, & Hawkins, 2004). Families will experience a variety of interactions, and all family members feel those interactions that affect any of the four subsystems. For example, in discussing the proposition that parents should assist in teaching their children at home, A. P. Turnbull, Summers, and Brotherson (1983) described the following:

> Consider the example of a mother who has agreed to work on a home training program in the area of feeding with her severely retarded child. Allowing her child to feed himself triples the time involved in each meal. While the mother is working with the child on feeding, her dinner conversation with her husband and other children is substantially limited. After the other family members finish dinner, the father cleans the kitchen and the siblings proceed to their homework all feeling that some of their needs have been overlooked. Meanwhile, the mother is feeling isolated from the rest of her family and frustrated over all the tasks to which she must attend before midnight. (p. 5)

According to Olsen and Fuller (2003) and other investigators (L. J. Johnson et al., 2004; Lambie & Daniels-Mohring, 1993), the interaction between the four family subsystems is based on cohesion, adaptability, and communication. Knowledge of these factors will assist educators in effectively meeting the needs of all family members and in selecting an appropriate level for their participation in the educational program of the child with an exceptionality.

FAMILY FUNCTIONS

A. Turnbull et al. (2006) noted that families serve the needs of their members through the following eight categories of family functions: affection, self-esteem, spirituality, economics, daily care, socialization, recreation, and education. It is important to note that education is but one of the functions with which a family must be concerned. Overemphasis in one area may reduce the family's ability to effectively respond to needs in others (Parette & Petch-Hogan, 2000). Educators should understand family functioning to secure appropriate levels of parent and family involvement and collaboration and to plan in accordance with prevailing needs and capabilities.

FAMILY LIFE CYCLES

In many ways families are organized in terms of life cycle developments such as the birth of the child, school entry, puberty, graduation, marriage, and so on (Kapinus & Johnson, 2003). Families of students with disabilities may experience stages that are protracted, shortened, or never occur

(Demarle & le Roux, 2001). For many reasons educators should be aware of the life cycle events that affect families of children and youth with exceptionalities (Seligman & Darling, 2007; T. E. C. Smith, Gartin, Murdick, & Hilton, 2006; A. Turnbull et al., 2006). First, life cycle events clarify the changing nature of a family's needs and characteristics. For instance, a recently widowed parent might have less time and energy to be involved in his or her child's education. Second, awareness of a family's life cycle events heightens educators' sensitivity to the sources of stress that affect the family. Again, parents experiencing stressful times will undoubtedly expend their personal resources in the area(s) causing them the most stress. Finally, with the proper support, the challenges families experience at each stage may facilitate their development or acquisition of new skills.

A significant family life cycle issue to which educators should be particularly sensitive relates to developmental changes. Such changes include a family's progression from one stage to another, including couples without children, families with preschool children, families with school-age children, families with youth, families with adults and their children who reenter families, postparental families, and aging families. Movement from one stage to another is frequently accompanied by stress. This stress may be multiplied when a child or adolescent with an exceptionality does not meet the family's hope for successful transition. For example, parents may need support and help in planning for adequate care of their child with an exceptionality once they themselves are no longer capable of doing so (e.g., through death, aging, or disability). Awareness of such factors has obvious implications for understanding, collaborating on, and planning for parent and family needs.

Summary

Initial contacts between parents and professionals must be considered a basic and essential component of an effective parent–educator relationship. The four major elements of this conference—establishing rapport and a collaborative relationship, obtaining information, providing information, and evaluating parents and families—can facilitate the pupil's educational process as well as the positive working relationship between parents and professionals.

Exercises

1. Conduct a simulation conference using the role-playing materials in Appendix A. Materials are provided for two major groups of exceptionalities: students with high-incidence disabilities and students with more severe disabilities. The role-playing materials for the high-incidence grouping fall within the exceptionalities of behavior disorders and giftedness. The more severe disability role-playing materials are in the areas of autism and mental retardation. Use those materials most closely aligned with the students you are associated with or plan to educate.

   In conducting the simulation exercise, one individual should assume the part of the parent, using the materials labeled "Parent Perceptions." Another person, taking the part of the teacher, should structure his or her responses around the teacher materials. A third individual should assume the role of the evaluator, using the evaluation form provided.

   In disseminating the information about your program to the person playing the part of the parent, talk about an actual program you would employ with this student.

   Change roles after completing the exercise.

2. Conduct an analysis of a parent and family with whom you have contact. In particular, comment on the parents' strengths and challenges and the family's structure, interactions, functions, and life cycles. Note the specific questions you would like to ask the family.

Chapter 6

Expanding Interventions: Parents as Treatment and Intervention Agents

The first parent training I went to was about special education services, adult issues, transition plans, and things like that. There were about 30 people there, and the presenter had a child on the [autism] spectrum, so I thought it would be good. She gave a lot of information, but she just kept talking and talking; it was all one sided, and I didn't like that. Besides, Jake was only 3, and, oh my goodness, it was way over my head! Later, I went to a training session for parents on IEP [Individualized Education Program] meetings. It was more appropriate for my situation, and I learned a lot. I guess I had never thought about helping to write goals because they're usually written when I get there. It is so important; parents need to know what the law allows. Schools won't always give what they should. That's what we faced with getting a one-on-one aide for our son. It was about the money.

I went to another session with about 10 parents and some teachers and school officials. The presenter really knew what she was talking about, and I learned a lot, but it was relaxed. If you had a question, you could just ask it, and the discussion went back and forth between parents and the presenter. It was great. I didn't want it to end!

The staff from the autism center came to our home to show us how to use a token board with Jake. It was hands-on. She [therapist] explains, and she makes you do it. You're the parent and it's your house, so you should be doing it. She showed us how to reward Jake for good behavior like when he sits at the table and to ignore his screaming and crying—not even to look at him. We also talked about things we wanted to add to his treatment plan, like hand-holding. Jake won't hold hands; he bolts, especially in the parking lot or the grocery store. They worked on it first at the center, and then we carried it [the plan] over at home.

Schools really need to partner with parents. Patience is huge on both sides. We need to learn to take advice from each other. That was a big issue for us last year. Jake's teacher thought she knew it all, but parents really do know their child and have something to offer.

The process of helping the parents and families of children and youth with exceptionalities to effectively serve their own children requires instruction in basic behavioral change strategies and home tutoring methods. Such an approach allows parents to effect planned behavioral and academic changes in the natural environment, thereby extending the influence of professionals beyond the classroom setting. Target behaviors include those occurring exclusively in the home setting and problem behaviors occurring in both the home and the school environments. Such home–school collaboration is a significant means of involving parents and family members in the management of behavior concerns as well as in academic remediation or acceleration programs.

Historical Perspective and Overview of Issues

Ample empirical documentation exists to show that the parent–child relationship affects behavior (Kauffman & Landrum, 2009; G. R. Patterson, 1982; Sanders, Mazzucchelli, & Studman, 2004; Webster-Stratton, Reid, & Hammond, 2001; Westling & Fox, 2009). Consequently, it is not surprising that professionals have attempted to influence the social and academic behavior of children through work with parents and families. To fully reap the benefits of parental involvement, however, professionals must move beyond the more traditional mechanisms such as parent conferences when report cards are distributed and parent–teacher associations to empower parents and families to take a more active role in the educational progress of their child. This requires a shift in perception from the idea that parents are a source of their child's problems to a belief that parents can join directly with school professionals in shaping their child's academic and social behavior. Although at one time parents and family members were perceived as passive recipients of professional services, they are now viewed as critical resources that can augment school-applied procedures. With increasing regularity, parents and family members are being trained to use problem-solving procedures with their own children in natural environments.

We need to be aware of the differing ways that parents and families may choose to become part of their child's intervention program. Some parents are open to specific suggestions and training methods regarding ways to encourage their child to complete homework, improve math computational skills, or pick up toys. Others may be looking for more generalized or ongoing assistance in how to alter the noncompliance of their child or manage the child's difficult interactions with siblings at home and peers at school. It is therefore incumbent on the professional to determine what kinds of outcomes are foremost in parents' minds before suggesting they become involved in training.

Use of Behavioral Intervention Strategies by Parents and Families

One of the most prominent and effective problem-solving alternatives available to parents and family members derives from behavior analysis technology. This behavioral model is based on fundamental principles about the way in which children learn and the relationship between students' behavior and the variables that affect it. It assumes that parents and family members should have an opportunity to take active roles in the intervention programs implemented with their children rather than being passive onlookers.

The procedures associated with behavioral interventions are designed to focus on observable and measurable behaviors. In the model, *behavior* refers to any observable and measurable action, and behavioral interventions assume that children's responses can be modified through systematic application of learning principles (Alberto & Troutman, 2009). Furthermore, because the model assumes that behavioral principles can be taught to parents and family members and that "problem behaviors" represent inadequate or incorrect learning (rather than underlying pathology on the part of the parent or child), parents and family members can be taught ways of teaching their children to make more appropriate and developmentally mature responses. Thus, the behavioral model, in the present context, assumes that parents and family members will function in a systematically designed training role with their own children.

Behavior management techniques are designed to modify the frequency, rate, duration, or intensity of a specific behavior through the systematic application of learning theory principles. The selection of appropriate observable and overt behaviors is a basic concept in behavior modification. For example, "asking to be excused from the dinner table" is an observable and measurable behavior that parents can be taught to count as reliable. On the other hand, "exercising good manners," a general set of polite and socially acceptable behaviors (J. O. Cooper, Heron, & Heward, 2007), would be difficult to measure in a clear, concise, and accurate way. If parents are to employ behavioral techniques to increase or strengthen their son's or daughter's appropriate behavior, specific observable behaviors must be the focus of intervention efforts in order to obtain agreement among independent observers on the frequency, rate, intensity, or duration of the behavior and also on the effectiveness of any intervention procedure applied.

Behavioral approaches assume that the observable environmental events that precede and follow a response are the agents responsible for a given behavior and that systematic manipulation of these factors will be associated with predictable changes in behavior. Therefore, the procedures associated with a behavioral approach are such that parents and other laypersons can learn how to apply them, thereby extending the treatment process to the natural home setting and the range of family activities that involve the child. Nonbehavioral approaches, on the other hand, focus on more unobservable variables and intervention techniques that, in addition to being difficult to evaluate, cannot easily be transmitted and applied by parents and families, who have extensive contact with the child in the natural environment.

Parents have successfully participated in the design and implementation of behavioral intervention programs and have also trained others to implement the techniques (Symon, 2005). Moes and Frea (2000, 2002) reported significant reduction in challenging behavior and increase in compliance when family members were supported in implementing specific behavioral strategies during family routines identified by the family as important contexts for treatment. Reid, Webster-Stratton, and Baydar (2004) evaluated an intervention program that included a parent training component and observed increases in prosocial behavior and decreases in child conduct problems at home. Parents have also been trained to use a behaviorally oriented instructional method during daily activities at home wherein they give their children explicit commands and a model demonstration of the directive (mand-model procedure) to teach and increase verbal language skills (Mobayed, Collins, Strangis, Schuster, & Hemmeter, 2000).

One additional benefit of the behavioral approach is its wide applicability. Even though up to about 15% of all children and youth may be considered exceptional, this does not mean the remainder of children and youth do not have intervention needs or problems. Obviously, the parents of a typically developing child would acknowledge that management, structuring, and tutoring techniques are needed from time to time. Consequently, because of the complexity of child development and child rearing, parents and family members at some point will be faced with tasks for which they have little or no preparation. The techniques associated with applied behavior analysis and behavioral interventions are appealing and rewarding to parents and families because of their effectiveness and relative ease of use. In addition, behavioral interventions do not automatically assume abnormality; therefore, avoid labeling individuals with whom the techniques are used. Because behavioral principles assume that the same laws that govern adaptive behaviors govern all maladaptive behaviors, no attempt is made to differentiate between "normality" and "abnormality." Rather, behaviors are evaluated relative to their own unique adaptiveness, and techniques are differentially developed to decrease maladaptive behaviors while increasing adaptive behaviors.

Parent- and Family-Applied Tutoring Programs

Evidence continues to mount showing that parents and family members can promote and augment specific academic skill development with exceptional children, thereby underscoring the importance of their involvement in their children's educational programs (Baker, 2003; Rosenzweig, 2001). An underlying assumption for such involvement is that active student responses (e.g., writing, task participation, oral reading) are more functional than passive ones (e.g., listening to a lecture). As a result, providing numerous opportunities to respond in a variety of settings (i.e., home, school) becomes critical for mastery of academic and behavioral skills. Parent and family member application of home tutoring programs is an effective means of increasing children's opportunities to practice and learn. In fact, the increased attention parents are able to provide during instructional activities in the home may in and of itself increase active academic participation even without specific parent training (Duvall, Delquadri, & Ward, 2004).

Instructional systems designed to increase active academic participation not only give students higher rates of academic responding via direct ecobehavioral assessment but also correlate with higher academic achievement on criterion-referenced and standardized measures (Becker & Gersten, 2001; Duvall, Ward, Delquadri, & Greenwood, 1997; Simonsen & Gunter, 2001; Tucci, Hursh, & Laitinen, 2004).

As previously noted, individualized parent and family involvement programs tend to be most effective. Not every parent or family member of a child or adolescent with an exceptionality is interested or effective in conducting a home tutoring program, but when they do have the interest and aptitude, tutoring programs are invaluable. Erion (2006) completed a synthesis of research in which parents or family members provided tutoring in a basic academic skill such as reading, spelling, and math. Although most of the studies reviewed involved reading and primary-age students, the results "provide support for parent tutoring as an effective procedure for improving the academic skills of children" (p. 95). Valleley, Evans, and Allen (2002) demonstrated that parents can be trained to reliably implement a reading fluency intervention with overcorrection procedures for errors and a motivational system for accuracy to improve their child's reading skills. Similarly, Persampieri, Gortmaker, Daly, Sheridan, and McCurdy (2006) observed that a combination of instructional and motivational strategies implemented by parents lead to increases in oral reading fluency. Koegel, Symon, and Koegel (2002) reported that parents who received specialized training in motivational techniques (i.e., pivotal response training) to elicit expressive verbal language "increased their teaching opportunities during daily routines, which resulted in higher levels of their child's communication" (p. 101). Finally, the generalization benefits of parent-implemented programs also have been noted (Charlop-Christy & Carpenter, 2000; Dillenburger, Keenan, Gallagher, & McElhinney, 2004; Hoagwood, 2005; Kaiser & Hancock, 2003; Lafasakis & Sturmey, 2007).

Williams (1959) was among the first to report parents' use of a simple extinction procedure to eliminate bedtime tantrums by a 21-month-old child in a relatively short period of time, and the problem behavior did not reappear. Although not extraordinary in its methodology or results, this study demonstrated that parents could be taught to effectively utilize behavior modification procedures in a natural environment. In essence, it initiated an era of parent and family participation in the training of their own children. Since Williams's study, innumerable other research reports have unequivocally demonstrated the efficacy of employing parents and family members as behavioral change agents (e.g., Anderson & McMillan, 2001; Charlop-Christy & Carpenter, 2000; Kuhn, Lerman, & Vorndran, 2003; Najdowski, Wallace, Doney, & Ghezzi, 2003; Symon, 2005).

Even though behavior and academic change principles are empirically derived and highly effective, their ultimate success rests on the skill of the individuals using them. Thus, even the most efficient and well-planned parent and family program must be implemented correctly to produce change (Persampieri et al., 2006; Ruiz-Primo, 2006; Sterling-Turner, Watson, Wildmon, Watkins, & Little, 2001). As a means of isolating factors that may be correlated with successful parent- and family-applied programs, several researchers have evaluated the characteristics of those involved. Using a direct teaching format rather than a lecture or reading approach, Mira (1970) failed to find a relationship between parents' intellectual abilities, education, and socioeconomic status and their ability to employ behavior modification procedures. Others (Lundahl, Risser, & Lovejoy, 2006) have suggested that economically disadvantaged families did not benefit from parent training as much as their nondisadvantaged counterparts; however, these families benefited significantly more from individually delivered behavioral parent training compared to group delivered training. Likewise, poorly functioning families, those lacking in cooperation, and individuals evidencing psychopathology have proved poorer candidates for the role of change agent than parents and families without such problems (Engels & Andries, 2007; Reyno & McGrath, 2006).

Data suggest that when appropriately trained, motivated parents and family members can be effective in the role of change agent (Devlin & Harber, 2004; Sarafino, 2001; Webber, Simpson, & Bentley, 2000). Furthermore, academic progress can be facilitated when parents, family members, and educators work in concert to achieve specific school goals (Baker, 2003). Finally, when parents and family members are trained to manage maladaptive behavior in the environment in which the response is manifested, the greatest degree of success and generalization will be realized (Dunlap & Fox, 2007; Gentry & Luiselli, 2008; Peterson, Carta, & Greenwood, 2005). As suggested by McDonough and colleagues (2005),

> Two important things happen when parents are taught to apply behavioral principles and techniques with their children. The training of new behaviors occurs in the natural environment, and parents' methods of training become in sync with those used at school, creating stimuli common to both settings. (p. 201)

A word of caution: Where a problem is manifested and where the intervention is applied relate directly to problem ownership and the level of anticipated parent and family and educator involvement. That is, some parents and family members may have limited motivation to participate in solving an academic problem that occurs exclusively in the classroom. Likewise, educators may be uninterested in serving as a resource for behavior problems that take place at a babysitter's or at Sunday school. As a result, the primary responsibility for problems and their solutions must be determined. Until the ownership for a problem has been identified, proposed problem-solving strategies will prove ineffective. Thus, until the parents and educators can agree on the nature of a given problem and the person most responsible for its occurrence and solution, interventions cannot be expected to show progress.

Thus, because the success of any change program is a function of both the skill with which the various components are implemented and the motivation of the participants, the anticipated levels of motivation and responsibility on the part of the individuals involved must be considered carefully. In particular, the models presented in the sections that follow are most appropriate for problems that occur in home environments or settings where parents and family members are most apt to be responsible or motivated to bring about changes; therefore, these procedures should be applied only when parents and family members will assume at least partial problem ownership and intervention responsibility.

Parents and Families as Behavioral Change Agents

As noted in the procedural flow depicted in Table 6.1, a successful behavior management program cannot be developed and implemented in a single conference session. The model is time sequenced for procedural objectives and activities. In addition, the process assumes that individuals who utilize these procedures have a basic working knowledge of operant conditioning and applied behavior analysis procedures. Individuals who do not meet this basic criterion are encouraged to supplement this outline with basic behavioral information.

Session 1 Procedures

Identify and operationally define a behavior of concern. An initial step in establishing a parent- or family-coordinated behavior management program consists of soliciting a statement of concern from parents and family members specifically related to those behaviors they consider most in need of change. This basic step is contingent on parent and/or family motivation and at least partial acceptance of ownership for the problem. Accordingly, the educational conferencer cannot expect parents and families to identify problem behaviors they do not perceive as problems in the home setting or to accept ownership of problems that occur exclusively in the classroom.

TABLE 6.1.
Parent- and Family-Applied Behavioral Intervention Training Procedures

Procedural Steps	Specific Activities
Session 1	
Identify and operationally define a behavior of concern.	• List and operationally define the parents' and family members' concerns about specific problem behaviors shown by the child. • Prioritize parent and family concerns. • Identify the child's adaptive, positive, and desirable behaviors. • Select one problem behavior for modification, choosing a behavior for which success is probable.
Identify environments and situations where the target behavior occurs, and conduct a functional assessment of factors that may affect or control the target behavior.	• Determine the individuals, situations, times, and circumstances surrounding the occurrence of the problem behavior, and identify possible variables and factors that may be affecting or controlling the behavior.
Identify factors that may be operating to support the target behavior.	• Determine the responses of the parents, family members, and others in the environment following the emission of the target response.
Train parents and family members to identify, observe, and record the target behavior.	• Identify and demonstrate simple observation and recording procedures to the parents and family members. • Aid the parents and family members in applying these systems in order to evaluate the target behavior in the home environment. • Train parents and family members in procedures to establish reliability. • Make adjustments in the observation and recording systems based on feedback from the parents and family members.
Session 2	
Train parents and family members to chart and analyze the behavioral data.	• Train parents and family members to use simple visual displays to chart the target behavior. • Train parents and family members to record daily observations on the chart. • Train parents and family members to inspect the baseline data for variability and trend.

(continues)

TABLE 6.1. (*continued*)

Procedural Steps	Specific Activities
Establish and implement intervention procedures and performance goals.	• Select with the parents and family members appropriate consequences for modifying the target behavior. Intervention procedures should be positive (if possible), practical, economical, simple, and realistic. • Establish appropriate outcomes. • Train parents and family members to apply the intervention program in the home, employing the behavioral principles of consistency, constancy, and immediacy. • Train parents and family members to continue observing, recording, charting, and analyzing the target behavior after the intervention procedures have been applied.
Session 3 and Subsequent Meetings	
Show parents and family members methods of analyzing and interpreting data relative to the target behavior.	• Aid parents and family members in inspecting and analyzing the data with respect to desired outcomes.
Make changes in recording, charting, and intervention procedures, as needed.	• Implement program modifications, as needed.
Encourage parents and family members to maintain contact with the behavioral conferencer and to apply the same model with other behaviors.	• Adopt a follow-up schedule for parents and family members to use in reporting the success of the home-based program. • Encourage parents and family members to apply the general model techniques with other problems.

Even though applied behavior analysis principles are characterized by versatility and adaptiveness, they are most effective when observable and measurable responses can be pinpointed. Furthermore, the response selected for modification must be defined in such a fashion that it allows the individuals involved with the child to perceive the behavior in an identical manner. For example, hyperactivity to one parent may consist of crying, screaming, and distractibility, whereas to another it may mean primarily failing to complete homework assignments. Consequently, it is essential to the success of any applied behavior analysis program that each participant be trained to observe the target behavior in the same way.

Applied behavioral analysis and intervention techniques are designed for use with responses that contain movement. Therefore, persons employing a behavioral strategy should determine, through either interviewing or direct observation, whether the proposed target behavior contains movement. For example, parents can be trained to see a child wash the dinner dishes or hit a sibling. In contrast, behaviors with minimal movements are difficult to analyze. Daydreaming, for example, would typically not be as acceptable a choice of target behavior as a response containing more visible movement.

An additional consideration relative to selecting an appropriate target behavior concerns whether the response selected for modification is repeatable. Although the family of a child who engages in severe temper tantrums may wish to modify this response, it is a poor choice for a formal applied behavior analysis program if the behavior occurs only once per month.

Prior to developing a parent-applied behavioral intervention program, the conferencer should also determine whether the response selected for change has a definite starting and stopping point. For most efficient management, a target behavior should have a definitive cycle of repeatable movement. For parents and families to accurately measure a behavior, the behavior should consist of a relatively short cycle with clear starting and stopping points, such as completing an assigned task or throwing objects. Sleeping, on the other hand, has relatively obscure starting and stopping points. In addition, it involves a cycle far too long for most parents and family members to measure accurately.

A major task of the parent and family counselor consists of translating into operational definitions the concerns parents and family members have about their child's behavior, thus establishing targets for modification. Typically, parents and family members find it reasonably easy to list these behaviors if the task has been adequately explained and if they are motivated to effect change. The educational counselor may discover that some parents and family members can identify only one behavior in need of change. When this is the case and if the response appears appropriate for modification via an applied behavioral analysis and intervention approach, the single target behavior will suffice. This limiting process makes the establishment of priorities for change an easy matter. Even when a number of problem responses are generated, parents and families will often have fixed in their own minds a priority problem most in need of modification.

In situations where a problem response occurs exclusively in a school environment but parents and families are involved in the management process (e.g., home reinforcement for acceptable school behavior), the conferencer is responsible for operationally defining the behavior. The procedures defined for aiding parents and families in identifying a behavior are follows.

The importance of asking parents and families to focus on their child's positive or adaptive behaviors cannot be overemphasized. This tactic can provide a perspective to the family members regarding their child's overall behavior pattern. For example, it is not unusual for a single behavioral excess or deficit to generalize in the minds of the parents to the extent that they perceive the youngster as demonstrating virtually no positive qualities. Statements such as "He always causes problems at home—he just can't seem to do anything right" are common. The process of pinpointing a behavioral excess or deficit for modification coupled with an analysis of a child's strengths, however, places the complaint in proper perspective. Identifying a child's strengths may be the one positively oriented component of an otherwise problem-oriented model, and this makes it an extremely significant program feature and one that should not be underestimated.

In addition to careful consideration of the motivation and interests of parents and family members in selecting a target behavior for modification, care must be taken in selecting a response with which success is a possibility. Especially in programs designed for children with exceptionalities, professionals should not initially select behaviors that have been highly resistant to other treatments. Although professionals must be responsive to the goals of parents and families in applying the technology, they must also be aware that when success is forthcoming, it tends to bolster the implementer's confidence and makes it possible to successfully intervene with other more difficult problems. Thus, even though the parents of a 10-year-old nonverbal child with autism might want their son to talk, this outcome would probably be a poor choice for an initial target behavior. Instead, selecting an initial behavior likely to be achieved such as signing the word *more* may be appropriate. After the counselor has established his or her personal validity and the validity of the proposed procedures, and after the parents have determined their own ability for successful intervention, more difficult problem responses can be considered.

Identify environments and situations where the target behavior occurs, and conduct a functional assessment of factors that may affect or control the target behavior. In addition to identifying an appropriate target behavior for change, the behavioral conferencer must seek information about the environments and circumstances surrounding the occurrence of the response. Although the relationship of the environment to the response is frequently overlooked, it is crucial to gain an understanding of it, including whether the response is generalized across settings or is environmentally specific. As noted by J. O. Cooper et al. (2007), "Evidence from decades of research indicates that both desirable and undesirable behaviors, whether washing hands or screaming and tantrumming, are learned and maintained through interaction with the social and physical environment" (p. 501).

The behavioral conferencer must also determine which individuals are most frequently in contact with the child when the problem response appears. In just a few instances will the response pattern be independent of the individuals involved, hence the importance of understanding this factor. As observed by Bandura (1969), "Under naturalistic conditions behavior is generally regulated by the characteristics of persons toward whom responses are directed, the social setting, temporal factors, and a host of verbal and symbolic cues that signify predictable response consequences" (p. 25).

Environmental and situational factors also aid in determining the appropriateness of a behavior management strategy (Zirpoli, 2008). That is, in the course of obtaining information about the environments and situations surrounding the problem, the conferencer may conclude that a given behavioral strategy is not appropriate and that other solutions should be considered. For example, a student's mother requested an appointment with his classroom teacher to discuss problems she was having at home in controlling his behavior. Discussing the circumstances surrounding the situations revealed that the problem (antisocial behavior) occurred only when the child was at the sitter's during a 2-hour period in the late afternoon. Further discussion revealed that the sitter frequently abandoned the child during the time he should have been under her care and that the "antisocial" act consisted of "wandering around" an adjacent neighborhood. On the basis of this information, the teacher suggested engaging another babysitter instead of developing a behavior modification program.

Behavioral engineers are increasingly recognizing the importance of conducting a functional assessment of problem behaviors (Chandler & Dahlquist, 2006; Cihak, Alberto, & Fredrick, 2007; Dunlap, Newton, Fox, Benito, & Vaughn, 2001), and the significance of this preintervention component of the behavioral model must not be minimized. As suggested by Reese, Richman, Zarcone, and Zarcone (2003), "Functional assessment is an empirically validated approach for matching individual treatment recommendations to variables that contribute to maintenance of challenging behavior . . . treatment components can be selected that focus on modifying the environment and teaching appropriate behaviors that serve the same function as the individual's challenging behavior" (p. 87). Although there is controversy regarding the specific methods that define a functional assessment (e.g., Alter, Conroy, Mancil, & Haydon, 2008; Drasgow & Yell, 2001; Gresham, 2003; Sasso, Conroy, Stichter, & Fox, 2001), several components should be included to identify the contextual variables that trigger and reinforce the challenging behavior so that interventions can be designed to bring about meaningful behavior change.

Identify factors that may be operating to support the target behavior. Both adaptive and maladaptive behaviors are controlled by environmental conditions (J. O. Cooper et al., 2007). Consequently, a problem behavior occurring in or around the home environment is a function of existing stimulus conditions or related factors located there. A preintervention functional assessment should include gaining an understanding of those variables associated with the maintenance of the problem response or understanding the results of a child engaging in a particular undesired response. For example, a youth with a severe disability may engage in a particular aberrant behavior because he lacks a way of communicating his needs.

Although there is no easy strategy for interpreting and understanding the effects of behavior, an attempt should be made to identify significant variables correlated with the occurrence of a target response. Specifically, the major factors of concern include (a) the environmental circumstances that trigger a particular response, (b) the response itself, (c) the reinforcing or consequent stimulus, and (d) the function the behavior serves for the child (i.e., to gain something positive, avoid or escape something unpleasant, or increase or decrease sensory stimulation [Chandler & Dahlquist, 2006]). In this paradigm, and in the successful construction of a parent-applied behavioral intervention program, behaviors are a function of their consequences or communicative intent. Therefore, understanding and modifying variables that control behaviors—as well as implementing proactive programs based on these findings—is essential.

As behavioral interventions may involve manipulation of consequences and antecedent conditions, the goal here is to solicit information from parents and family members about what happens prior to and immediately after the occurrence of the target behavior. The following types of questions are useful in this respect: "What happens right before he tantrums?" "What happens right after the tantrum starts and ends?" "How do others in the family respond to the tantruming?" and "What does she get from her tantrum?" Bersoff and Grieger (1971) also suggested that conferencers focus on the interactions that take place between the parents and child, the parents' perception of these interactions, the punishment tactics employed by the parents, and the manner in which expectations, praise, and punishment are presented to the child by his or her parents.

Train parents and family members to identify, observe, and record the target behavior. In keeping with standard behavior management procedures, parents and families should be instructed to employ simple measurement and evaluation procedures. Even though some parents and family members may appear threatened and overwhelmed by this seemingly difficult task, the conferencer should be able to quell such anxiety. He or she can inform parents and others of the importance of accurate behavioral measurements, pointing out that this feature is an integral and basic element of successfully employing behavioral supports and interventions and that a system feasible and flexible enough for parents to utilize can be identified (Maurice & Taylor, 2005; Shapiro & Clemens, 2005). One can typically persuade parents and family members being counseled in the use of behavior management to participate in the measurement process by stressing that only through measurement can a thorough analysis of the behavioral excess or deficit and its antecedent and consequent events be gained. Besides, without such exact observation and recording activities, the team cannot determine whether the contingencies being manipulated are having the desired results.

The second prerequisite for achieving measurement compliance relates to ensuring that participating parents and family members are knowledgeable about the measurement process to be used. Thus, carefully considered explanations, programming, and modeling must accompany each set of procedures. Only when parents and family members have received proper instruction can competence be assumed. Because the remaining components of the model hinge on successful measurement, it is essential that appropriate attention be given to this aspect of the overall methodology.

Parents and others can be trained to employ several observational recording techniques including continuous, event, duration, interval, and time sample recordings.

Continuous measurements (anecdotal records) involve recording the various responses manifested by a child over a given period of time. Although this procedure allows the parents and family members an opportunity to record a variety of behaviors, it lacks reliability and requires a great investment of resources that may not be available to families. Besides, this recording technique would rarely be the most useful alternative for parents and families being counseled in the use of behavior management methodology.

Event-recording techniques, on the other hand, are typically very functional for parent and family use. These procedures consist of making a cumulative account of specific behavioral events. For example, parents can use an event-recording system to note the number of times a child follows commands or the frequency of one child kicking another. In addition to being relatively easy for parents and family members to understand, event-recording systems are highly adaptable to a variety of target behaviors.

Duration recording, another observational system appropriate for parent and family use, involves calculating the amount of time a child engages in a particular behavior. This alternative is most preferable when the length of time a given behavior occurs is considered the most significant response descriptor. For example, the amount of time children engage in tantruming is often a far more accurate descriptor of their behavior than the frequency with which the behavior occurs.

Interval-recording systems involve dividing a predetermined observation period into equal time segments. Parents and families who use this procedure should be advised to record whether the target response occurs during each interval. Although this recording technique requires the undivided attention of the observer, it offers the advantages of allowing the person to observe more than a single target behavior.

Time sampling, although similar to interval recording, offers the advantage of not requiring continuous observations. Parents and family members are trained to determine whether the child being observed is engaging in the target behavior at the end of a specific time interval. For example, a child's study behavior might be observed by his parents for 1 hour, with recordings made at the end of each 5-minute period. Every 5 minutes the parent or family member would observe whether the child was studying. This procedure is efficient, as it generates a significant amount of data while allowing the parents to carry on other activities.

Regardless of which measurement alternative the behavioral counselor selects, it is essential that parents and families have collaborative input regarding its selection and a thorough working knowledge of its use. Thus, rather than advising parents and family members to "record the number of times John refuses to comply with a request you make," parents and family members must be provided precise instruction, including a statement of the specific time period during the day when the measurement will occur, and the specific procedure (tally sheet, golf counter, kitchen timer, stopwatch, etc.) for measuring and recording. Furthermore, parents should be instrumental in determining which measurement approach would be easiest for them to integrate into their lifestyle. This collaborative process should result in clear and concise agreed-on procedures, including a written product for the parents or others to use as a reference.

During this initial conference, the behavioral engineer should also provide the parents and families with a form or format for recording the target behavior. Because graphing and charting procedures should be pursued during the second conference, this format can, and should, be as simple as possible. (A sample form appears in Figure 6.1.) The baseline observation should be structured so that it can be completed within 5 to 7 days. Fewer observation days will provide a less than adequate picture of the response, whereas longer baselines may endanger parents' willingness to participate in the program.

For example, Sheridan and McCurdy (2005) provided a case example of a mother who reported that starting homework and completing it in a timely manner was problematic for her daughter, Jenny, and often resulted in arguments and negative discussions between the two. Prior to implementing an intervention plan, the mother recorded how long it took Jenny

Child's Name _____

Observer's Name _____

_____

Target Behavior _____

Operational Definition of Behavior _____

_____

_____

Time of Observation _____

Date	Frequency or Duration	Comments

Figure 6.1. Sample recording form.

to begin working on homework following the first prompt and how long it took for her to complete all assigned work. During the weeklong baseline period, Jenny's mother recorded an average of 40 minutes elapsed time between instructing Jenny to begin and the actual initiation of work (p. 57).

Although reliability procedures offer an excellent addition to the behavioral system, this component is not as imperative. That is, if obtaining reliability data appears to present a problem, it may be eliminated. Even though a major advantage of the reliability process is allowing for the active participation of more than one family member, it should not become a deterrent to overall program participation.

Finally, during the baseline period, parents and family members should be able to consult freely with the behavioral engineer. At a minimum, the conferencer should make at least one phone contact. In addition, parents and family members must feel free to contact the educator if problems or questions arise.

Each of the steps involved in developing a successful parent- and family-applied behavior management program is critical; however, the importance of a successful first session is paramount. Specifically, the majority of failures can be traced to procedural problems in the initial planning session. If the behavioral engineer can successfully establish his or her own validity and the validity of the program; select an appropriate target behavior for management; accurately analyze the environments, situations, and variables surrounding the response; and obtain measurement data from the parents and family members, the overall success of the program is greatly enhanced. Again, one essential ingredient in the process consists of persuading the parents and family members to follow through with each component of the program.

Session 2 Procedures

Train parents and family members to chart and analyze the behavioral data. One of the initial tasks in the second session of the behavioral intervention training sequence will be to demonstrate graphing and charting procedures. Prior to meeting with the parents and family members, the educator should construct a demonstration graph similar to the one shown in Figure 6.2. As illustrated, all components should be labeled and completed, except the actual data points.

By using a form similar to the one shown, the behavioral engineer can demonstrate how data points are inserted and connected. The same training format can be used to train the charting procedures for the remainder

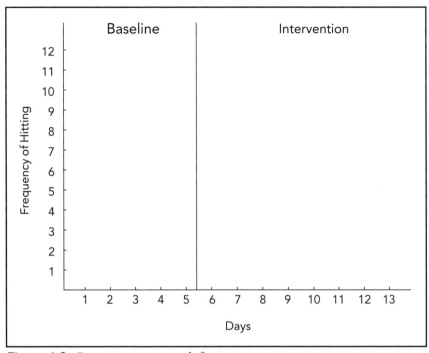

Figure 6.2. Demonstration graph form.

of the program. The use of modeling and tangible products makes charting and graphing relatively simple to teach.

During the same training session, the behavioral engineer should acquaint parents and family members with the information derived from the baseline data and how these data will be compared with subsequent measures. Finally, the behavioral engineer should apprise the parents and family members of concepts related to baseline trend and variability. The extent to which this information is conveyed is, in large measure, a function of the interest and abilities of parents and family members.

Establish and implement intervention procedures and performance goals. Parents and families involved in applied behavior analysis programs with their own children are confronted with target behaviors that can be classified as either behavioral excesses or deficits. That is, parents and family members may consider their offspring lacking in a particular response, such as completing homework assignments or engaging in desirable social interactions with neighborhood children, or they may consider him or her excessive on some dimension of behavior. For example, parents may think that their child cries or quarrels too often or manifests an unnecessary level of some other behavior. Because of the nature of the model and the manner in which problem responses are operationally defined, behavioral programs are designed to either increase or decrease the occurrence of a specific behavior under specific conditions. This goal is accomplished via systematic manipulation of antecedent variables and consequences.

Operationally, a reinforcer is an environmental event that strengthens the behavior it follows (J. O. Cooper et al., 2007). A punisher, on the other hand, weakens the behavior it follows (Alberto & Troutman, 2009). Hence, parents and family members must recognize that if an environmental event fails to change a behavior, it does not operationally qualify as a meaningful consequence, regardless of whether they perceive it to be effective. The only valid method of judging whether a stimulus event is effective consists of observing its influence on the behavior it follows. For that reason conferencers should remind parents and families to continue the measurement procedures throughout the program as a means of determining the influence of a given consequence.

The selection of an effective consequence or antecedent condition is not an easy task. Through functional assessment of the target behavior, however, including observing children and assessing their preferences, potentially motivating reinforcers may be designed (Cannella, O'Reilly, & Lancioni, 2005; Logan & Gast, 2001; Sarafino, 2001). For example, Miltenberger (2004, p. 314) posed a series of questions that might be asked of the child and parents: What does the child like? What does she enjoy doing? How does she spend her free time? What would she buy if she had money? What does she find rewarding? Often parents can identify a number of potentially effective home reinforcers such as preparing dinner with a parent, operating the dishwasher or other appliance, having money to purchase a desired item, playing computer games, receiving attention from a parent, or getting additional play time (J. E. Walker & Shea, 1999). In other cases a reinforcement menu, or a listing of possible reinforcers from which a child can choose, is an excellent way to make available a variety of positive consequences (Alberto & Troutman, 2009; Salend, 2008a).

Even though punishers and negative consequences may have some appeal, parents and family members should be encouraged to utilize positive strategies whenever possible. A number of researchers have demonstrated that parents and family members can be effective in modifying the behavior of their own children through reliance on positive reinforcement programs. Risley and Wolf (1966), for example, used shaping and reinforcement procedures to train an institutionalized child with severe emotional disturbance to engage in adaptive behaviors. After successful results had been achieved in a laboratory setting, the child was returned to the home environment, where the mother was instructed in applying the same behavioral techniques. This transfer of the intervention procedure to the home resulted in a significant increase in adaptive behavior. McKenzie, Clark, Wolf, Kothera, and Benson (1968) reported a significant increase in children's academic behaviors when parents agreed to base weekly allowances on weekly grade reports.

More recent literature presents empirical examples of successful home–school partnerships that were designed to address the challenging behavior of children in home and community environments (Lucyshyn, Horner, Dunlap, Albin, & Ben, 2002). Jason and Fries (2004) reported that parents were able to reduce television viewing by using a simple token exchange system where the children earned tokens by engaging in school-, play-, or housework-related activities or by purchasing viewing time by cashing in tokens provided at the start of each week. Peterson et al. (2005) taught parents in their home to use normally occurring situations and the child's interests to facilitate language learning. Increases were noted in children's verbal comments, correct responding to parent questions, and the mean length of utterance of the comments. Wade, Ortiz, and Gorman (2007) observed that parents' implementation of graduated extinction procedures were effective in improving bedtime compliance.

Selection of an appropriate behavior intervention should hinge not only on an evaluation of the child but also on the needs and characteristics of the parents and family. That is, the intervention selected should be compatible with the parents' and family's values, resources, and needs based on collaborative parent and family input (Koegel, Symon, & Koegel, 2002). In particular, interventions that are realistic, feasible, economical, and practical tend to be more effective. For instance, a couple had become extremely concerned about their 9-year-old son's nocturnal enuresis. The child, according to his parents, wet the bed at least 5 or 6 nights a week. During an informal conference the parents asked the boy's learning disabilities teacher for assistance, and she recommended they purchase a urine alarm system, a monitoring device designed to awaken youngsters when they begin to urinate. Unfortunately the device, which cost $58.00, was beyond the financial means of the family.

As suggested in this example, the acceptability to parents of the proposed intervention should be determined: "Parents must not only be willing to allow their child to participate in treatment; they must also be willing to participate actively in the treatment themselves" (J. R. Pemberton & Borrego, 2007, p. 29). Thus, the treatment must be acceptable to the parents to increase the probability they will implement the intervention as designed, resulting in a successful outcome. The acceptability of any treatment will hinge, in part, on the parents' perceptions of the anticipated positive outcomes for the child in particular and the impact on the family as a whole (Dillenburger et al., 2004; Simpson, 2005; Simpson, McKee, Teeter, & Beytien, 2007).

The agreed-on experimental procedures should be communicated to parents and families in both oral and written form. That is, rather than simply explaining to parents and families what to do, the educator should provide them with a plan sheet that details the procedures to follow. Parent training can include a variety of components such as explaining and modeling the procedure, discussing video vignettes, engaging in role-playing and practice, and providing feedback on parents' use of the procedure (Charlop-Christy & Carpenter, 2000; Powell-Smith, Stoner, Shinn, & Good, 2000; Webster-Stratton, 2005). If parents or family members later forget or do not clearly understand particular segments of the intervention, they will have access to a written procedural plan. An example of such a procedural plan sheet appears in Figure 6.3.

The first column, "Description of Program," is reserved for a general statement of the objectives of the project, including who will be responsible for carrying out the procedures, what times (hours) of the day the program will be in effect, where the program will be implemented (home, neighborhood, store, etc.), and the procedures that will be involved. The "Description of Target Behavior" column provides an operational definition of the target behavior. This description should be stated in such a fashion that the parents and family members can easily comprehend it. In addition, the strategy to be used in measuring the target behavior should be briefly described here.

In the third column, "Procedures Prior to Observation of Target Behavior," any pertinent responses and structuring procedures can be described, particularly those based on a functional analysis of the behavior. For example, if a parent-applied behavior management program is designed to decrease tantruming at bedtime, parents should receive specific instructions on how to structure conditions related to the target behavior. For instance, the parents should tell their child to prepare for bed at a certain time each evening. To be consistent with the intervention program, these instructions should be delivered in a systematic fashion. Likewise, if a program were established to increase compliance behavior, the conferencer should instruct parents in when and how to deliver commands. Although professionals are encouraged to be collaborative in their approach, they

	Child's Name	Chuck Downs
	Parent's Name	Ms. Lois Topps
	Date Started	September, 2009

Description of Program	Description of Target Behavior	Procedures Prior to Observation of Target Behavior	Procedures Following Observation of Target Behavior
The program is designed to reduce Chuck's tantruming. The program will be implemented at home on a daily basis at bedtime (8:30 p.m.). Chuck's mother and father will carry out all procedures.	Tantruming consists of severe crying, screaming, hand and leg flailing, and other out-of-control behavior, including jerky extensions of the body. Target behaviors will be observed daily at bedtime, at home, from 8:30 p.m. until 7:00 a.m. the following morning.	At 8:00 p.m. daily, Chuck will be told that he has to start getting ready for bed. Specifically, his mother will assist him in washing, brushing his teeth, and changing his clothes. She will also inform him that she will read to him until 8:30 p.m. after he has gotten into bed. At 8:30 p.m. the mother will inform Chuck that it is time for him to go to sleep, and then she will leave the room, closing his door as she departs.	Chuck's mother, along with other members of his family, will refrain from entering his bedroom (except for emergencies) after 8:30 p.m. Thus, regardless of Chuck's behavior, he will not be allowed to receive visitors, leave his room, or otherwise interact with family between 8:30 p.m. and 7:00 a.m. the following morning. The subsequent evenings during which Chuck does not tantrum, he will be provided special reinforcement by his mother and other family members (e.g., "I liked the way you quietly went to bed last night").

Figure 6.3. Procedural plan sheet.

must also recognize that the technical aspects of most behavioral intervention programs will require direct instruction.

The fourth column, "Procedures Following Observation of Target Behavior," allows for a description, in specific and sequential fashion, of the consequences or procedures to apply when the target behavior occurs. This information must be communicated to parents and family members in an easy-to-follow manner. Because the plan sheet is intended for the benefit of parents and family members, appropriate language should be used throughout.

The importance of preparing a written plan sheet for use by parents and family members cannot be overemphasized. This procedure provides a basic way to reduce parents' and family members' uncertainty while increasing their faith and ability to collaborate in following the program, thus increasing the overall probability of success. Modeling, demonstration, and monitoring techniques should also be utilized to aid participants in implementing agreed-on procedures. Hence, as a means of augmenting the verbal and written program instructions and avoiding misunderstandings, actual demonstration or modeling should be used.

The importance of this step was illustrated in the implementation of a parent-applied behavior management program with a 6-year-old boy with mental retardation. An intervention program had been designed to reduce the child's negativism. In particular, both parents had experienced difficulty in getting the child to obey their requests or commands, and hence they described him as "headstrong" and "set in his ways." Although expressive language was not his primary mode of communication, the youngster frequently did use phrases such as "no-no," "I won't," and "I can't."

In this case negative behavior was operationally defined as a refusal, either verbal or nonverbal, to obey a parental request or command. An event-recording procedure was employed to measure oppositional behavior daily between the hours of 2:00 P.M. to 4:00 P.M. and 6:30 P.M. to 8:30 P.M. Both observation and experimental procedures were carried out in the child's home. Baseline data indicated that the boy displayed an average of 21.85 specific instances of negative behavior per day (median 23). This measure was found to be fairly stable, although slightly ascending, during the 7 days of baseline.

Following baseline procedures, learning theory principles and procedures that had proved effective with other children in decreasing oppositional episodes were discussed with the parents. A two-prong intervention program was agreed on, with the goal of diminishing oppositional behavior: the parents agreed to eliminate attention for oppositional behavior, while introducing attention and social praise for cooperative behavior, and they agreed to place the child on a chair in a corner for 3 minutes immediately following each instance of oppositional behavior.

During the initial phases of the experimental procedures, the professional who collaborated with the parents in designing the program received several anxious phone calls from the mother. With each contact the mother appeared more upset and less sure of her ability to carry out the prescribed program. Supportive efforts proved only marginally successful. The child was described as "uncontrollable" when attempts were made to implement the time-out procedures. In addition, he was said to "kick the wall and me [mother]," "chew on his chair," and "scream" when placed in the corner. The mother also stated that only by physically holding her son could the procedure be implemented.

The child and his mother returned to the behavioral engineer's office for further instruction. Because specific instructions obviously were needed, a tele-coaching system was devised whereby the mother could follow verbal instructions that the child could not hear via a radio and earplug. The behavioral engineer stood on one side of a one-way mirror and made suggestions to the mother regarding what to say and do—when to reinforce, when to ignore, and when to implement time-out procedures. Comments included "Tell him that was very good," "Ignore that," and "Take him to the time-out chair now." After a single instruction period, the mother commented that she felt much more knowledgeable of the intervention procedures.

Following this training session the number of negative episodes decreased significantly. Specifically, the mean number of oppositional incidents was reduced to 3 (median = 2). According to parental comments, the child became "much easier to live with." They also reported that he had begun to use expressive language more, arguing against requests rather than totally refusing. Although they considered this tactic to still be negative, it was more sophisticated than a mere "no."

Even though these procedures were time-consuming, the benefits were obvious. Although many parents and family members do not require such explicit training, most can benefit from behavioral demonstrations and modeling procedures. In all instances, the conferencer must ensure that parents and families are familiar with the procedures to be followed.

The conferencer must also play an active role in helping parents and families establish acceptable program goals and outcomes. Goal setting involves writing down the criterion level of the target behavior and the time frame within which it will be achieved (Miltenberger, 2004). The behavioral goal should be acceptable to parents as well as to professionals such that it is deemed to be fair, appropriate, and reasonable (Sarafino,

2001). Is the outcome of the proposed intervention program likely to make any real difference in the life of the child and the family? As an important component in a home intervention program, the goal should be included on the procedural plan sheet.

Session 3 and Subsequent Meetings

Follow-up meetings are primarily designed (a) to assess the influence of program procedures, (b) to establish and modify performance goals, and (c) to make program changes. Although parents and families must have access to the behavioral engineer at other than established follow-up meeting times, most modifications will be made at these sessions.

The conferencer must be cautious when suggesting or supporting program changes. That is, consequences and antecedent modifications must be given ample opportunity for success. Though amendments should be made in instances where intervention programs lack efficacy, it is important that the process not involve capricious changes.

Finally, subsequent sessions must be structured so as to provide reinforcement for parent and family efforts. Because parents will be instrumental in determining the success of any program, and their behavior, like that of their child, is effected by consequences, positive feedback must be offered. This often neglected element is frequently the basis for successful program results (Donley & Williams, 1997; Turbiville, Umbarger, & Guthrie, 2000).

Parents and Families as Academic Tutors

In this discussion and procedural outline of parent and family tutoring procedures, the term *academic* refers to more than traditional academics (e.g., reading, math, spelling). Within this section the term will refer to a variety of school-related activities, including prereadiness, readiness, independent living, self-help, prevocational, and so on. As with the application of behavioral intervention procedures, the proposed model here assumes that individuals utilizing it possess a working knowledge of applied behavior methods. Not every parent or family member of a child or adolescent with an exceptionality will make an acceptable tutor. Because of interest, time, motivation, temperament, skills, or other factors, some parents and family members will not—or should not—serve as tutors. Thus, professionals must not aggressively pursue home tutoring as an option for all families. Instead, on the basis of a collaborative partnership format, conferencers should carefully consider this option for those parents and family members who demonstrate appropriate interest, skills, and resources. As with other aspects of parent and family participation and partnerships, tutoring should be based on parent and family choice, not on professionals' coercion. The procedures for family tutoring appear in Table 6.2.

Session 1 Procedures

Identify and operationally define an academic subject for tutoring. As with parent and family behavioral intervention programs, identifying an appropriate subject for remediation, practice, or acceleration forms the initial step in establishing a parent and family tutoring program. This basic step is a collaborative effort, and thus it hinges on parent and family interest, concern, skill, temperament, and at least partial problem ownership. When these factors are not evident, or when other evidence suggests that parents or family members would not make satisfactory tutors (e.g., poor academic skills, temperament problems, limited child rapport), training should be deferred to others, including private tutors.

Though collaborative in nature, decisions relating to tutoring programs and materials should reflect a strong professional influence. Accordingly, educators should solicit parent and family academic concerns, assist them in ranking their concerns, and then ultimately guide them in the selection of tutoring subjects and areas. Thus, after considering parent and family input, the educator assists parents in selecting an appropriate tutoring area and then writes an operational definition of a behavior for tutoring intervention (see the preceding section's discussion of how to write target behavior definitions). Tutoring targets must be congruent with the child's needs and abilities, parent and family skills and resources, and overall school program. Drill-and-practice activities (e.g., color identification, math facts, word identification, etc.) are particularly appropriate and responsive for many parent and family tutoring programs.

Identify appropriate tutoring materials. As suggested, a professional should primarily select tutoring materials. Thus, as part of this process, educators must consider a student's strengths and weaknesses, including IEP goals and objectives, as well as parent and family strengths and resources. As noted, for many parents preference should be given to drill-and-practice activities. Educators should provide parent and family tutors with all materials required for successful implementation of a given program. For example, rather than telling parents that multiplication flash cards will be needed, the flash cards are provided to the parents. Almost without exception, educators should select parent and family tutoring activities from

TABLE 6.2.
Parent- and Family-Applied Tutoring Procedures

Procedural Steps	Specific Activities
Session 1	
Identify and operationally define an academic subject for tutoring.	• List and define professionals' and parents' and family members' academic skill concerns. • Prioritize teacher, parent, and family concerns. • Identify student's academic strengths. • Select and define one subject or area for tutoring.
Identify appropriate tutoring materials.	• Select tutoring materials for parent and family use.
Train parents and family members to use tutoring materials and methods.	• Train parents and family members to use instructional materials. • Train parents and family members to use instructional procedures.
Train tutors to observe and record children's responses.	• Identify and demonstrate simple observation and recording procedures for parents and family members. • Aid parents and family members in applying an observation system to evaluate the target response in the home setting.
Session 2	
Amend tutoring methods and materials.	• Make adjustments in tutoring materials and methods based on data and feedback from parents and family members. • Make adjustments in the observation and recording systems based on feedback from the parents and family members.
Train parents and family members to chart and inspect tutoring data.	• Train parents and family members to use simple visual displays to record and chart academic data.
Establish performance goals and outcomes.	• Establish appropriate performance goals, expectations, and outcomes.
Session 3 and Subsequent Meetings	
Show parents and family members methods of analyzing, interpreting, and sharing data with educators.	• Instruct parents and family members in methods of inspecting and analyzing data relative to previously established goals and outcomes and in sharing tutoring data, results, and issues with educators.
Make changes in materials, procedures, recording, and charting, as needed.	

subjects with which the child and his or her teacher(s) are familiar and which reinforce and enhance basic classroom skill development.

Train parents and family members to use tutoring materials and methods. As with behavioral intervention programs, parents and family members should receive specific tutoring instructions. Instructions should include the following oral and written information:

1. A specific time should be designated for tutoring. Tutors should start and stop on schedule, as agreed on with the teacher. Although the duration of tutoring sessions will vary with a child's age, exceptionality, and so forth, most sessions should be limited to approximately 30 minutes daily, 5 days per week.
2. As much as possible, tutors should conduct all tutoring sessions in the same place at a table or desk. In addition, the site should be quiet (e.g., free from TV or stereo noises).
3. Tutors should strive for consistency. When different family members act as tutors, they should attempt to maintain the same conditions and setting, including an appropriate atmosphere.
4. Tutors must recognize the importance of following directions agreed on in program development, especially those specified by the teacher. Deviations from this protocol, such as introducing new materials, procedures, or activities, should be avoided.

New tutoring materials and methods are best introduced via demonstration. That is, procedures and materials should be both explained and demonstrated to parents and family members. This activity should include opportunities for parents and family members to apply tutoring procedures under simulation conditions (i.e., with the teacher role-playing the part of the child demonstrating typical behaviors).

Specific tutoring procedures will vary according to the materials, the children to be trained, the target, and a host of other factors. Yet several common methods should be followed. First, tutors should be trained to present materials, instructions, or tasks only when the child is quietly attending to the tutor or the task. Second, tutors should be advised of cues appropriate for prompting the desired responses. In the case of word recognition, for example, tutors must know when (e.g., after a specified duration, after an incorrect response) and how (e.g., sounding out the first syllable) to prompt a child who is encountering difficulty. This process may also involve training in such techniques as modeling, fading, shaping, and chaining. Finally, tutors should be trained to respond to children's responses, including dispensing appropriate reinforcers and other consequences for a given behavior. In particular, parents and family members should be advised to provide reinforcement for correct responses immediately following the desired response and in a consistent and clear manner. (Positive consequences appropriate for use by parent and family member tutors are discussed in an earlier section of this chapter.)

Train tutors to observe and record children's responses. As with parent- and family-administered behavioral intervention programs, tutors should be trained to observe, record, and monitor children's progress. Without such data, neither parents nor educators will have a basis for interpreting students' gains and the effectiveness of tutoring programs. Event recording, discussed earlier in this chapter, typically affords the most appropriate and effective means of parent and family data collection. For monitoring purposes, data are often recorded as frequencies or percentages. Thus, tutors may record the number or percentage of correctly identified math facts or the number or percentage of correctly identified word cards.

Session 2 Procedures

Amend tutoring methods and materials. On the basis of parent and family member feedback and observational daily data, educators must make the necessary adjustments in the original tutoring program. If, for example, a child fails to make the expected progress, the educator, in collaboration with the parents, must determine modifications necessary for success. To be effective, teachers should be familiar with the curricula being tutored and thereby with anticipated response patterns. That is, teachers should have classroom baseline data for the children being tutored to determine whether they are progressing in accordance with the rate shown in the classroom.

Train parents and family members to chart and inspect tutoring data. In a manner similar to charting and inspecting behavioral data, tutors should maintain daily progress profiles on the children they work with. Typically, parents and family members who conduct tutoring sessions do not conduct baseline assessments; however, they must chart children's progress over training sessions. These data form the basis for subsequent curriculum modifications and adjustments and thereby play a significant role in any home tutoring program.

Establish performance goals and outcomes. In accordance with a collaborative model, educators and parents involved in home tutoring programs should jointly recommend performance goals and outcomes. Because this is often a professional task based on a variety of factors, however, educators typically should take a leadership role in this regard. It is important to identify goals consistent with IEP objectives, classroom instructional goals and outcomes, and students' needs and abilities. For example, if an IEP objective requires that the child be able to identify 25 specific words, home tutoring in this area should be geared toward accomplishing this goal. Such coordination facilitates not only appropriate parent and family tutoring expectations but also development of a partnership between home and school.

Session 3 and Subsequent Meetings

The third session and subsequent meetings between family tutors and educators will focus mainly on student progress and/or tutoring problems. Educators should maintain regular contact with parent and family tutors, making adjustments and introducing new methods and materials as required. Many of these contacts may be informal, as opposed to face-to-face meetings.

Summary

As noted throughout this chapter, behavioral and educational principles often can be effectively applied in natural environments by the parents and families of children and youth with exceptionalities. The success of the proposed model depends on both the effective use of a collaborative strategy and the conferencer's ability to translate technical tenets into functional procedures. Accordingly, the conferencer must recognize parent- and family-implemented behavioral intervention and tutoring as tools that can be effectively applied only through a partnership process in combination with effective conferencing skills. Without attending, listening, rapport, and other fundamental conferencing elements, it is unlikely that these approaches will be effective.

Exercises

1. Conduct a behavioral intervention simulation conference using the materials in Appendix B. Descriptions are provided for the cases previously presented for the initial interview role-play exercise (i.e., Teddy and Terri). Use those materials most aligned

with your career goals or experiences or those you have used in the previous role-playing exercise.

In conducting the simulation exercise, one individual should assume the part of the parent, using the additional information provided in this appendix. The conference should be parent initiated; that is, assume that the parent in the exercise contacted the educator to obtain some assistance for a home-based problem.

No materials are designated for the person playing the role of the conferencer. Background information on each case, however, can be obtained from the descriptions provided for the earlier simulation conference. A third individual, who plays the role of evaluator, is to use the evaluation forms provided in Appendix B.

The behavioral conference should be separated into two separate sessions. The first should cover those elements identified in Table 6.1 as "Procedural Steps" in Session 1. At the completion of this session, individuals playing the part of the parent should generate baseline data on the identified target behavior. This information should be written on a form similar to the one in Figure 6.1 (sample recording form).

A third individual should assume the role of the evaluator, using the evaluation form provided for Session 1.

Following the first segment, individuals assuming educator roles should prepare a graph similar to the one shown in Figure 6.2 to demonstrate how baseline data are transferred to a chart. Those in educator roles should also develop a list of consequences or intervention procedures to discuss with parents and a procedural plan sheet as shown in Figure 6.3. (The plan sheet is not to be completed until Session 2.)

The second phase of the simulation conference should adhere to the "Procedural Steps" in Session 2. As noted previously, this session will make use of the data generated by parents following the first conference, the graph for translating the parent-generated data, the possible consequences generated by the educator, and the educator-developed plan sheet. Because the text provides only basic information regarding appropriate reinforcers, extinction methods, punishers, and antecedent programs, individuals unfamiliar with fundamental behavioral intervention methods are advised to review a text specifically devoted to this topic.

The second phase of the simulation conference should be evaluated using the evaluation form provided for Session 2.

Individuals should change roles after completing both phases of the conference.

2. Conduct a tutoring simulation conference for a child and family described in Appendix A and Appendix B. Use those materials most aligned with your area or those you have used in previous role-playing exercises. In conducting the simulation exercise, one person should assume the role of parent, and another should assume that of teacher. The conference should be parent initiated; that is, assume that the parent in the exercise contacted the educator regarding establishing a home tutoring program.

No materials have been developed either for the individual playing the role of the conferencer or for the person who plays the part of the parent. Thus, specific parent and teacher academic concerns and tutoring materials must be developed by participants, based on descriptions provided in Appendix A and Appendix B.

The conference should be divided into two separate meetings: The first should comprise those elements identified in Table 6.2 as "Procedural Steps" in Session 1 and the second should follow the "Procedural Steps" in Session 2. This session will require a week's worth of tutoring-progress data so that charting may be demonstrated to tutors. Thus, persons playing parent roles must manufacture percentage or frequency data for educators to use in demonstrating charting procedures.

Individuals should change roles after completing Session 1 and Session 2 procedural steps.

Chapter 7

Progress Monitoring Conferences

We've had a really good year so far. The first week of school we had a conference with Mrs. McNeil, our daughter Leah's teacher. Mrs. McNeil went over the school handbook—policies, procedures, and stuff like that. Then she explained how she would be working on the goals on her [Leah's] IEP [Individualized Education Program] and what kinds of things we should expect to see in terms of Leah's progress until report card time, particularly in reading. Then we'd meet again and see if any changes needed to be made. She told us about the FISH folder that would be an ongoing part of parent involvement this year. Each night, Leah brings home her FISH folder for us to review—a pocket folder that Leah had decorated with brightly colored pictures of tropical fish. In small type below the FISH label they'd printed Family Involvement Starts Here. In the pocket on the left is completed work from that day in all her subjects and any announcements or newsletters for us. In the pocket on the right are any homework assignments or activities Leah needs to complete or particular skills or concepts we might work with her on that week during the course of family activities. In the three-ring section in the middle there's always a graph or chart showing Leah's daily or weekly progress on one of her individual goals. Even though she's in third grade, Leah really struggles with reading, and one of her goals focuses on that. It has been great to actually see her improve on the number of words she reads correctly and the [comprehension] questions that she answers, and she gets so excited when she tells us, "My line is going up!" Mrs. McNeil also uses a point system in her class so that Leah can earn points for being prepared for class, raising her hand,

and doing her work. The point chart comes home in her folder, so we can see how her day has been and talk with her about special activities or privileges she's working for. There's also a place for us to write any comments or questions we have for any of her teachers, and we usually get the answer the next day in her folder, or we get a call from the teacher. We talk with Leah about what she did in school that day, what she'll be doing tomorrow, and then we sign the FISH ticket, and Leah takes it back to school the next day with her FISH folder. The signed FISH ticket goes into a big fish bowl for a drawing at the end of the month for a special reward.

We know every night to ask to see her FISH folder. It's great! We really feel like we know what's going on with Leah this year. We know what to talk about at parent conferences because we see the progress that she's making, and we know that her teacher wants us to be involved in her education on a daily basis.

Monitoring students' progress has always been one of the hallmarks of the educational process (Wallace, Espin, McMaster, Deno, & Foegen, 2007). Individual parent–educator conferences that focus on students' school progress are among the most common and significant of all parent–professional interactions. These sessions allow for the clarification of information exchanged via non-face-to-face means (e.g., notes and report cards) and for the direct dissemination of information relevant to a student's education. In addition, progress report conferences allow for evaluation of IEP goals and objectives and serve as a mechanism for maintaining contact among parents, family members, and professionals.

Although there may be disagreement regarding the most appropriate timing for the progress report conference, research maintains that these sessions should be held on a regular basis (Black, 2005; Flaugher, 2006; Kroth & Edge, 2007; Mathur & Smith, 2003). Most schools plan these meetings to coincide with report card or grade reporting schedules, although such conferences also should be held to meet the individual needs of parents and students. Black (2005) suggested that they not be held exclusively at times of crisis. In fact, when educators discuss issues with parents on a regular basis, parents report feeling positive anticipation of conferences, in part because of their confidence that there will be no real surprises (Minke & Anderson, 2003).

Just as students with exceptionalities receive individualized programs and schedules that correspond to their unique needs, so too must their parents have individually scheduled feedback conferences (Garriott, Wandry, & Snyder, 2000; L. J. Johnson, Pugach, & Hawkins, 2004; G. Taylor, 2000). These important conferences play a unique role in the parent–school relationship. In a study of parent participation in an inner-city school, Flaugher (2006) found that positive interactions with school personnel on an ongoing basis is not strongly associated with parental participation in evening programs (e.g., PTA meetings, Family Fun Night, sports activities) because parents perceive these events to have different purposes. Specifically, parents who meet frequently with teachers do so to ensure their children's school success and to learn about their classroom experiences. They distinguish these types of contacts from all other programs that do not have this specific focus.

Parents who are involved in their child's education want specific information regarding their child's performance and functioning compared to expectations for their age or grade, and they want to know whether their current placement and program plan is closing the gap between the child's functional level and those expectations. Specifically, they want to see evidence of progress made since the previous conference or assessment of their child.

Even though the professional's preparation for and skill in the progress report conference will be significant, the most crucial factor related to a favorable conference outcome will be the success of previous parent–educator contacts. In particular, it is typically unrealistic to expect a completely satisfactory progress reporting session if prior positive contacts have not occurred. In such instances parents most likely will lack the rapport, trust, and/or prior information required for effective participation and collaboration. Consequently, professionals must recognize that parent–educator interactions are cumulative, and regardless of one's skill in conducting the conference, success will depend on prior positive contact.

Discussing Student Progress With Parents and Family

A variety of factors will dictate the specific agenda for each progress report conference, including the nature and extent of a student's exceptionality and the needs of parents and families. Several common areas, however, should be examined as a part of each session, including a cursory review of factors associated with the diagnosis and intervention procedures along with academic growth and performance, social and behavioral factors, and educationally related physical variables.

Parents should receive prior notice (written or spoken) of both the nature and purpose of the conference and the areas that will be reviewed. Stevens and Tollafield (2003) recommended that invitations be extended to all of a student's family members (extended, blended, and estranged) to show that the teacher values the contributions they each make to the student's life. In addition, this prior notice should inform parents and family members that they will be allowed to discuss any concerns they have related to their child's program. Thus, the conferencer should be able to structure the session without giving the impression that all aspects have been predetermined; otherwise, parents and family members either may assume that they have no input into the direction of the conference or may attempt to discuss matters that would be more appropriately dealt with in other types of conferences.

Especially with parents and family members who may be relatively unfamiliar with special education and their child's specific educational or treatment program, the educator should provide an overview of the events that led to the student's diagnosis and program and of the current status of the program. Although the degree of attention given to this phase of the conference will depend largely on participants' familiarity with the pertinent information, each conference should include this material. The cursory review of presenting issues should be followed by a brief recap of diagnostic findings, the student's IEP, the educational and intervention program being used, and a summary evaluative statement. The intent of this overview (albeit brief in some instances) is to remind the parents of the somewhat complicated process that led to the diagnosis and programming or placement of their child and then to bring them up to date on the nature and efficacy of the resulting intervention program. In addition, parents and family members should have an opportunity to raise issues or ask questions about any of these factors.

Providing Feedback on Academic Progress

Independent of exceptionality, parents are concerned with the academic progress of their child and ought to be involved in decision making about the child's academic plan. E. J. Martin and Hagan-Burke (2002) pointed out, "In today's schools, the relationship between educators and parents is becoming one in which both professionals and families have mutual power and influence regarding a child's educational experience" (p. 62). Hence, even in instances where a program modification was implemented for other than learning issues, parents still want information on their child's academic performance. *Academic*, in this context, refers not only to traditional school-related subjects and skills but also to self-help, prevocational, vocational, and similar areas.

The format for discussing academic information with parents and family members resembles that used in a general progress report overview, with content relating specifically to academic and academically related performance. Accordingly, parents and family members should first hear a brief review of the academic issues existing prior to the program modification and the diagnostic findings relative to this exceptionality. This process is designed to establish a historical basis for the intervention program and to aid the parents and family members in more adequately understanding the nature of the exceptionality. A conferencer may invest relatively little time in this topic with parents and family members who have had recent opportunities to discuss the diagnosis and its implications. Thus, it is essential to gauge the needs of parents and family members in this area accurately, taking care to provide sufficient information to answer their questions without excessively reviewing materials with which they are familiar.

When sharing academic information with parents, educators must ensure that the information creates an accurate picture of ongoing student progress, helps parents understand curriculum and individual student goals and objectives, assists parents in understanding what occurs in the classroom, and helps parents form an accurate picture of their child's strengths and needs (L. D. Adams, 1999–2000; Pogoloff, 2004; Raver, 2004). Communicating academic progress to parents can be a tool to strengthen the parent–educator relationship if done effectively. J. B. Pemberton (2003) noted that individual progress assessment reporting can fail if the information conveyed is not easily understood, is communicated in way that is not meaningful to stakeholders, or is communicated too late to impact student learning.

One aspect of progress reporting is an explanation of the tests and procedures employed in the diagnostic and intervention processes. Because these procedures may in part consist of formal, standardized tests administered by other professionals, the classroom teacher, if he or she is to conduct the conference, should be familiar with the measures and the manner in which they were used in the evaluation process.

The ability to review test data and interpret diagnostic findings to parents and family members (especially standardized assessment measure data) will necessitate having a thorough knowledge of the instruments being discussed (Stevens & Tollafield, 2003). As standardized procedures are designed to compare a child's performance with normative data, it is imperative to the accurate interpretation of the data at hand that the professional be thoroughly familiar with these procedures, including having knowledge of the standardization samples and the reliability, validity, and adaptability of the procedure for children and youth with exceptionalities. Only with this information should the conferencer attempt to interpret test data to parents and family members. Individuals lacking this background should request assistance from those with specific expertise in this area.

In addition to standardized tests and other such measures, informal assessment results, trial teaching findings, and other criterion-referenced assessment data are an important part of progress monitoring and reporting. In fact, these assessment procedures and the resultant data may not only be more easily disseminated by teachers but also be far more meaningful to parents and family members (L. D. Adams, 1999–2000; Deno, 2003; J. B. Pemberton, 2003). With one informal assessment strategy, curriculum-based measurement (CBM), teachers collect frequent but brief samples of important student behavior, such as the number of words the student reads correctly during 1-minute probes, and record results on a graph to visually present a record of student progress (Lewis & Doorlag, 2006). Because CBM monitors progress through direct, continuous assessment, and the measures are sensitive to small changes in skill level, these data may provide indicators of an effective instructional program or suggest the need for modification of the existing intervention. CBMs may also be used to set growth standards for students with and without disabilities and may assist parents and teachers in setting more ambitious academic goals for students within effective intervention programs, particularly in the area of reading (Deno, Fuchs, Marston, & Shin, 2001). An example of a CBM graph is illustrated in Figure 7.1.

In addition to CBM, Salend (2005) and Lewis and Doorlag (2006) noted several informal procedures such as checklists and inventories, direct observation, portfolios of student work samples, and classroom tests that also strengthen the process of disseminating information to parents and family members. Advantages of these procedures include the similarity of the assessment items to the student's annual goals and the skills under development in the classroom, the involvement of the classroom teacher in the assessment procedure, the relative ease of administering and interpreting informal techniques, and the wide range of skills that can be evaluated. The reliance on informal measures, including a review of the "Present Levels of Educational Performance" section of the IEP, should also aid the conferencer in minimizing the use of esoteric diagnostic findings and in facilitating the dissemination of functional information. In addition, it is important to note that the Individuals with Disabilities Education Improvement Act (2004, § 1414(d)(1)(A)) requires that each IEP include a statement of how the child's progress toward annual goals will

Student: __Leah_____   Teacher: __Mrs. McNeil_____

Goal Area: __Reading_____   Grade: __3rd_____

Present Level of Performance (provide a summary of baseline data of the student's performance in authentic activities):

> Leah is correctly reading 44 words per minute when reading third-grade material.

Annual goal:

> Given a third-grade reading probe, Leah will read 100 words correct per minute for three consecutive assessments by May.

How will student's progress/growth be monitored?

> Curriculum-Based Measurement probes, third-grade level

Who will collect/record these data?

> Teacher

What is the schedule for monitoring progress?

> Weekly

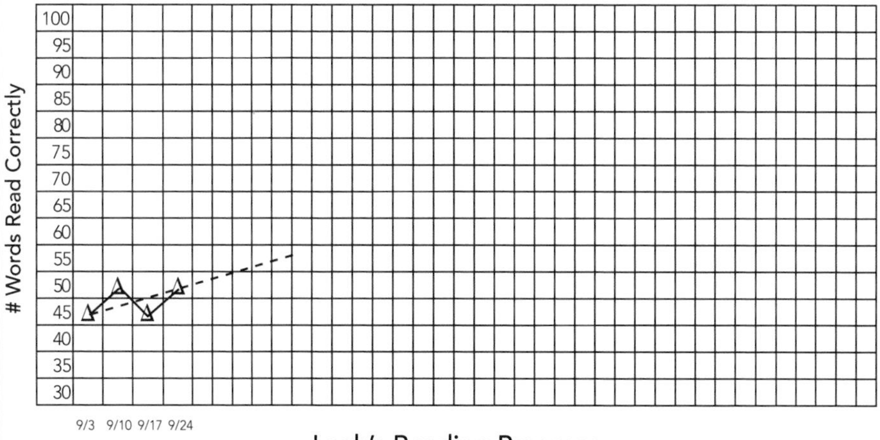

Leah's Reading Progress

Parent Participation/Comments:

Figure 7.1. Progress monitoring chart.

be monitored and reported to parents. More specific information regarding the development of the IEP is presented in Chapter 11.

Although the progress reporting conference is not exclusively designed to serve as an IEP evaluation session, one can facilitate an interpretation of academic progress by following the format established on the IEP. That is, each annual goal should be presented to the parents and family members for review and discussion, followed by a statement of the means of accomplishing each goal. For those students with IEPs that include short-term objectives, the discussion should also include the strategies employed to reach these targets. Finally, the conferencer should discuss with the parents and family members the effectiveness of the curriculum or academic remediation program in achieving the desired goals. This model for disseminating information appears in Figure 7.2.

Though in certain situations academic progress reports may unfold independent of a student's IEP, in many instances information on student progress can be disseminated effectively through adherence to the IEP model. This process has the major advantage of utilizing a document about which parents and family members should have had prior input. In addition, this strategy allows for interpretation of progress made on a previously agreed-on approach. In particular, this can serve as a demonstration that the teacher is truly following a joint parent–educator collaborative plan. Though this message is frequently given to parents and family members, the present strategy represents one means for actually demonstrating the authenticity of the message.

Providing Feedback on Social Progress

In addition to requiring information on their child's academic performance, parents are also interested in their child's social development and functioning. Parents want information regarding their child's daily social interactions, such as with whom they socialize, who their friends are, and how they are perceived by others (Davern, 2004). The format for providing this information resembles that used for disseminating academic progress. That is, the conference should involve a discussion of the child's school social history and any particular behavioral or social issues associated with the referral for program modification. A discussion then should follow the assessment findings relative to these issues, the intervention procedures employed to manage these concerns, and an evaluation of these procedures. Just as with academic functioning, this communication process can be facilitated, at least in part, through an interpretation of IEP annual social goals.

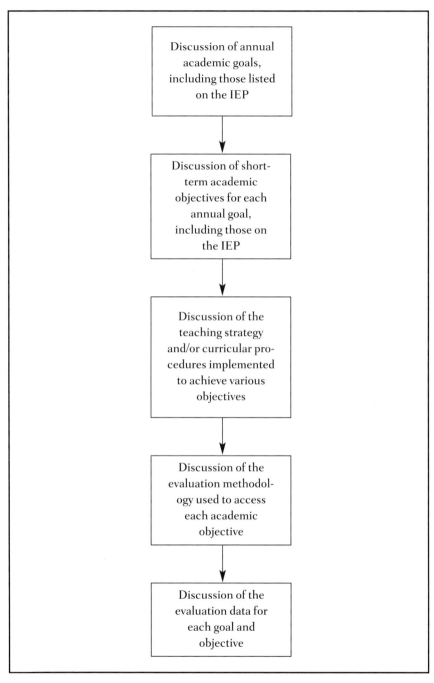

Figure 7.2. Model for disseminating academic progress information to parents.

The conferencer should also be able to comment on social or behavioral problems that have developed since the time of referral or placement. Patterns of conduct disturbance, shyness and social interaction difficulty, immaturity, or social withdrawal, particularly when representative of a marked change in behavior, should become items for discussion. Although educators should discuss these social patterns with parents when first observed rather than hold them as agenda items for a scheduled progress conference, they frequently are also dealt with at such sessions. Particular social and behavioral patterns that the conferencer will want to note include the following items:

- Rejection by peers
- Shyness
- Preoccupation
- Excessive daydreaming
- Social withdrawal
- Excessive anxiety
- Depression
- Inability or unwillingness to sustain effort and complete tasks
- Confusion
- Rigid patterns of behavior
- Extreme sensitivity
- Patterns of regression
- Truant or chronic tardiness
- Impulsiveness
- Physical aggression and violent tendencies
- Defiance
- Responses suggesting that rules and regulations apply only to others
- Disruptiveness
- Difficulty in responding to authority figures
- Hostility

Although this list is in no way complete, it does suggest those general patterns of behavior to which educators should be sensitive and on which appropriate attention should focus in parent–educator conferences. In discussing this information the educational conferencer should not attempt to place the responsibility for a school social problem with parents. It is appropriate, of course, to apprise parents of a classroom social behavior and to solicit their thoughts on its nature and cause, but it is essential that the conferencer also provide a possible solution or intervention strategy. Educators should be brief, specific, and calm when delivering negative messages to parents, conveying a sense of confidence that the problem can be solved (Minke & Anderson, 2003; Montgomery, 2005). It is imperative that teachers be prepared to respond to parents who become upset by the information without becoming reactive and defensive themselves. Babcock and Backlund (2001) provided examples of prompts that teachers might use to demonstrate empathy toward the parents, capitalize on parents' expertise, affirm the helpfulness of parents' contributions, and encourage open dialogue: "I can see that you are as frustrated as I am with Todd's behavior. . . . Can you share any information with me that might help me understand what causes Todd to be disruptive? Tell me more!" (p. 35).

The conferencer may justifiably suggest ways in which the parents can be involved in the progress reporting, but it is inappropriate to identify a school-based social problem without a possible solution or to attempt to make the parents independently responsible for arriving at a solution to the problem. It is also important to present social and behavioral excesses, deficits, or other issues discussed in the progress reporting conference in an empirical fashion. That is, rather than relating to parents and family members that a child is "defiant," "withdrawn," "hyperactive," or "inattentive" without an adequate explanation of the nature and extent of the problem, the conferencer should offer a more scientifically and objectively based analysis of the situation. This may take, for example, the form of a line or bar graph that illustrates the nature and significance of a particular social behavior. The important element is that parents and family members be able to understand the nature of the problem and be convinced that the professionals have thoroughly analyzed the situation. In addition, the data presented must demonstrate that the child's behavior represents a change and/or that the pattern falls outside the classroom norm. This probably can be achieved best by offering a comparison of the child's behavior with that of his or her peers. Finally, this process can serve as the basis for entering into a discussion of the present intervention strategy and later as a means of evaluating the procedure. The following example illustrates how this empirically based interpretation process was employed.

A 9-year-old fourth grader presented a concern to his teacher because of his chronic failure to hand in written assignments. She noted that this child was a disruptive element in the classroom but that he "had good potential." In preparation for a progress reporting conference, the teacher began keeping a record of the daily English, spelling, social studies, and writing papers the boy completed and handed in within the appropriate class periods on the day assigned. The measure did not include homework assignments or impose quality criteria for the material submitted.

The teacher found that the child's mean rate of assignment completion was 31.2%, whereas that of the other class members was 88%. She noted, however, that differences occurred in his rate of assignment completion as a function of his becoming aware that he was being observed. In particular, his mean rate of performance prior to awareness of being observed was 21%, but this rate increased to 55.6% after he determined that his behavior was under scrutiny.

During a regularly scheduled conference, the teacher shared this information with the parents, along with a proposed strategy for managing the problem. She explained to the parents that the child would be exposed to a three-point reinforcement program to increase the number of completed assignments. The program would involve (a) social reinforcement immediately following his submission of papers, (b) a self-charting program, and (c) the privilege of being the "teacher's errand boy" on days when at least 90% of his assignments were completed. At a follow-up conference, the teacher shared the results of this program with the parents in the format shown in Figure 7.3.

Videotapes and other forms of technology can also be used to communicate a student's progress to parents and families. A teacher of students with severe and multiple disabilities sent a text message to one student's parents informing them that their son had independently eaten lunch with a fork that day. Another teacher of high school students with mild disabilities used the video function of her cell phone to capture an example of a student appropriately completing written assignments during his study hall period and then sent the video clip to his mother. Technology can assist educators in illustrating small increments of growth on IEP objectives not measurable on standardized assessment instruments and in providing parents with a better understanding of the issues and behaviors discussed at conferences (Hundt, 2002).

Alberto, Mechling, Taber, and Thompson (1995) reported that 48% of the parents they surveyed preferred videotapes as a progress reporting option. Indeed, educators can use videotapes to communicate a student's progress at face-to-face progress report meetings, and Alberto et al. (1995) noted that many parents "indicated that it is much easier for them to take a tape home than to schedule meetings and arrange childcare" (p. 18). Though videotapes can be used to communicate students' academic progress, visual products of social and behavioral problems and issues have obvious advantages.

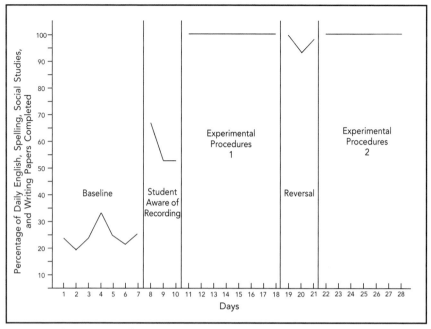

Figure 7.3. Results of program to increase the completion of written assignments.

Providing Feedback on Physical Progress

Parents and family members of children and youth with a physical exceptionality will be interested, of course, in receiving feedback in this domain. In such cases, a format similar to that employed in the academic and social and behavioral areas will serve. That is, the educational impact of the physical exceptionality and the diagnostic findings relative to the disability should be discussed with parents, followed by a discussion of the intervention and curriculum strategies being employed to deal with the problem and the efficacy of these strategies.

Although the majority of children and youth with exceptionalities will receive services for problems other than physical ones, it is nonetheless important for the education conferencer to include this category of information. Indeed, even in situations where a child's exceptionality is of a cognitive or social nature, the conferencer should consider the physical domain in preparing for the parent feedback conference. For instance, Prevent Blindness America (2005) identified signs that may indicate vision problems. These include the following:

Appearance of the eyes

- Eyes crossed
- Red-rimmed, encrusted, or swollen eyes
- Inflamed or watering eyes
- Drooping lids
- Recurring infections

Complaints

- Headaches, nausea, or dizziness
- Blurred or double vision
- Burning or itching of eyes

Behavior indicative of possible vision difficulty

- Rubs eyes, squints, or frowns
- Has trouble reading or holds objects close to eyes
- Thrusts head forward or backward, or holds head at unusual angles

The educator should be equally sensitive to indications of possible hearing impairment. Signs such as language delay, atypical speech patterns, inattentiveness, erratic school performance, apparent inability to follow verbal directions, confusion, and lack of attention to environmental sounds present potentially significant information and should be both discussed with the parents and professionally evaluated.

In preparation for the progress reporting conference, the educator should also be aware of other physically related symptoms, signs, and patterns that may require further investigation. Indications of substance abuse or dependence, illnesses, frequent school absence or tardiness, signs of extreme fatigue, poor gross and/or fine motor coordination, and enuresis and encopresis may be potentially significant and thus become necessary items for discussion with parents. Educators may simply request information from parents and family members regarding these patterns, or they should be ready to suggest a method for acquiring further data or an intervention strategy for dealing with the problem.

In addition, some of the information on students' physical progress may come from related services professionals such as occupational and physical therapists (Friend, 2005; T. E. Hall, Wolf, & Bollig, 2003). Therefore, conferencers should be prepared to discuss the variety of progress monitoring measures with parents, the situations in which the progress was monitored, and how that progress impacts student learning.

Staging the Progress Report Conference

In addition to having a set dissemination format for providing parents and family members with information, the educational conferencer should have an appropriate style, guidelines, and methods for structuring and transmitting data. These skills should allow for both the effective transmission of information and the successful disposition of problems and issues that may arise in the course of a session.

Satisfying Information Needs Through Collaborative Discussion

Progress reporting conferences are designed to give parents and educators an opportunity to discuss a child's school behavior and academic performance. Although these conferences should facilitate sharing, the progress report conference has been typified by a one-way flow of information (Garriott et al., 2000; Rock, 2000). Consequently, the conferencer must ensure that the session represents a collaborative discussion process. That is, though some individuals may consider parents solely the receivers of educational data, a progress conference can be successful only when it involves educators and parents discussing and sharing information, attitudes, concerns, and positions (Garriott et al., 2000; Kroth & Edge, 2007; Swick, 2003). Effective communication requires interaction. It is essential then that the educational conferencer not lose sight of this basic fact and that, regardless of time constraints and the amount of information to be dispensed, he or she discuss information with parents and family members rather than lecture. In particular, this will involve (a) being sensitive to the emotions and feelings of parents and family members and to the goal of achieving a satisfactory understanding, (b) being attentive to questions presented by the parents, and (c) making them collaborators in the progress report rather than exclusively receivers.

Notifying Parents and Family Members of the Progress Report Conference

Lack of parental attendance is a major challenge confronting educational conferencers. Because face-to-face progress conferences obviously cannot proceed without parents and family members present, educators must identify procedures for securing their attendance at the meetings.

First, educators must recognize that parents and family members will be motivated to attend parent–educator conferences only after having been exposed to prior reinforcing experiences with school professionals.

Therefore, successfully conducted initial conferences, IEP planning sessions, problem-solving meetings, and other collaborative contacts will all serve to promote the attendance and participation of parents and family members in progress report conferences. As part of American Education Week, one school district in Idaho organized a "Substitute Student Day." This involved having parents attend school for one day in place of their sons and daughters. This or similar programs should serve to sensitize parents to their child's educational program and should facilitate the development of rapport on which attendance and participation in parent–educator conferences can be based.

For formal meetings such as annual reviews or IEP meetings, educators should send parents an invitation at least 2 weeks prior to the meeting (Rock, 2000) and may attach a personal note to help explain the purpose of the invitation and put parents at ease (Pogoloff, 2004). Educators should ensure that any notice sent to parents is nonthreatening and relieves parents' anxiety by providing clear information about the purpose, logistics (meeting location, beginning and projected ending times, parking information, etc.), topics to be discussed, and ways that parents can prepare for the conference (Dabkowski, 2004; L. J. Johnson et al., 2004; Minke & Anderson, 2003).

Other considerations can also help promote the attendance of parents:

- Provide sufficient notice of the scheduled conference for parents and families to plan accordingly. This may involve announcing the schedule for progress conferences early in the school year and then following up at a later time with a letter regarding the specific date of each conference.
- Ask parents for input into scheduling the time of the conference. Schools should consider schedules that allow for evening and daytime meetings and be sensitive to parent's work schedules.
- Employ whatever means necessary to ensure that parents and family members know how to reach the conference site. Maps, guides, or well-planned directions should be provided if needed.
- Identify community resources that can facilitate the participation of parents and family members in conferences. Agencies providing transportation and babysitting, for example, are particularly important, or schools can provide these services directly.
- Be willing to conduct the session in the parents' home or a community building nearby if necessary.

Allotting the Correct Amount of Time for the Conference

Ideally, the conferencer should be able to individualize the time requirements of each session to best meet the needs of parents, families, and students. Administrative personnel, however, frequently schedule progress conferences, including time allotments, for entire buildings or districts; consequently, one may not have a major role in determining the time available for each conference. At a minimum, no less than 30 minutes should be scheduled. In addition, it is often advisable to set a time limit for the session. This frequently will serve to keep both parents and professionals "on task" and to facilitate growth and reduce irrelevant discussions. Parents and family members should be advised, of course, that changes may occur as needed and as schedules permit and that additional time can be provided at a later date if required. Indeed, the limited time available for most progress report conferences may require that follow-up sessions be scheduled to deal with special problems or other agenda items that the parent or conferencer may wish to discuss.

Preconference Planning

The success of the parent–educator progress report conference will correlate highly with preconference planning efforts (Kroth & Edge, 2007; E. J. Martin & Hagan-Burke, 2002; Minke & Anderson, 2003; Rock, 2000). These planning efforts should involve attention to the following:

- The child's records, including the IEP and previous parent–educator conference notes, should be reviewed carefully.
- An outline of those items to be discussed should be prepared.
- The conferencer should review standardized test data and informal assessment information so that he or she has a clear understanding of the student's progress. These data should include the student's strengths and needs.
- A careful selection of papers and work samples should be made in preparation for the conference. These portfolio samples should be representative and illustrative of particular concepts and should be dated and sequentially arranged for comparative purposes.
- Parents should be provided a portfolio folder of their child's work to take with them after the conference. This work sample should be representative of their child's performance and

consistent with feedback provided by the conferencer. Evaluative comments should appear on the papers to aid parents and family members in understanding the concepts being illustrated.

- Educators should plan for an acceptable environment for the session, including a professional and confidential setting. In addition, the conferencer should make arrangements for adult-sized furniture for all participants that allow parents to be seated next to educators, such as at a round table, rather than across a desk from them. Pads and pencils for note taking should also be available.
- Parents and family members should be prepared to participate in the conference. (This important component is addressed in depth later in this chapter.)
- The educator should prepare each student for the conference by apprising him or her of the purpose and nature of the session and the materials to be reviewed. The student also should be offered an opportunity for input into the agenda. Finally, one should consider the possibility of the student's participation in the session. In instances in which such involvement is appropriate, the student should receive training (e.g., information, discussion opportunities, and role-playing) for participating in the conference.

These preliminary efforts can aid in reducing the anxiety of both the student and the family members.

Conducting the Conference

Pogoloff (2004) pointed out that for conferences to be effective, educators must first develop personal relationships with parents through ongoing individual interactions. To set the tone for positive individual interactions, conferencers should demonstrate effective communication strategies such as listening carefully, conveying respect, and maintaining openness to the other's perspective and ideas (Davern, 2004; Salend, 2005; Soodak & Erwin, 2000; L. T. Zionts, Zionts, Harrison, & Bellinger, 2003). Consequently, as an integral component of the conferencing process, the educator should be able to establish and maintain rapport and a collaborative relationship with parents and families. Conferencers can initiate this relationship by means of a warm greeting, a positive lead, and a willingness to work together.

The conferencer should attempt to create as informal and relaxed an atmosphere as possible. It is important, in addition to communicating aspects of a child's progress, that the conferencer also listen to parents and family members. As noted previously, providing parents and families exposure to a good listener is frequently the most effective relationship builder.

BEING CLEAR AND SPECIFIC

Other preliminary procedures include reviewing the purpose of the conference with parents and family members and clarifying the role of the conferencer or other individuals involved in the session. That is, the sophisticated nature of educational service-delivery systems and their related personnel may require some explanation for parents and families. For example, it is important for parents to recognize the role of a resource or consulting teacher or the function of an inclusion specialist, as well as the manner in which these individuals form part of the service-delivery team and affect students and their families. It is also helpful for the conferencer to remind parents and family members of any time limitations for the session and that the agenda items not covered in the time allotted or not related specifically to the progress conference can be dealt with at a later time. Finally, in initiating the meeting, the conferencer should encourage parents and family members to participate in the session by asking questions or commenting on the educator's observations or related matters and by collaborating on decisions and interventions.

The conferencer should always begin the discussion by addressing areas of growth and progress. That is, in reviewing the academic, social, and physical areas, educators should provide specific statements and examples of success and growth before attending to less positive components. The conferencer must specifically detail and document the nature of the gains shown for this information to be most meaningful. Typically, one can accomplish this by showing parents and family members curriculum and portfolio samples of work completed by the student. As suggested previously, these materials should be given to parents to take home following the conference.

Following the review of areas of growth, parents and family members should be apprised of areas in which additional improvement is needed. The educator should transmit this information, just as with growth feedback, in clear and empirical terms. Especially with regard to social problems, the conferencer must be able to clearly explain and document the nature of a problem. For example, the educator could share a graph or show a videotape of the times a child is out of his or her seat without permission as opposed to telling parents that their child is "hyperactive" or "noncompliant." In addition, it is essential that the educator provide possible solutions to any weaknesses that are identified. This process should also allow parents and family members an opportunity to discuss the nature of the problem and to collaborate on solutions. This will take the form of discussing what the educator suggests doing to remediate the problem (e.g., "Jerry will work 20 minutes extra per day with the class paraprofessional on his math flash cards") as well as what parents and families might do to aid in solving the problem (e.g., using a home–school notebook system that will allow parents to praise a child daily for good social behavior at school). The educator should also build in a time and mechanism for providing parents and family members feedback on the effectiveness of the agreed-on intervention strategy.

MAINTAINING A PROFESSIONAL ATTITUDE

Although the conferencer will want to establish a warm, accepting, and collaborative atmosphere where parents and family members can feel free in expressing their concerns, it is important to maintain professional ethics and decorum. In particular, parents and family members should have an opportunity to share concerns about their child and the individuals who work with him or her without creating a forum for criticizing other educators, agencies, or school policy. The conferencer must be able to offer parents and families an airing of matters related to their child's education without promoting griping and gossiping about issues only tangential to the true issues being discussed. In instances where parents and family members focus on complaining about other teachers or educational personnel, the conferencer may need to direct the discussion to more appropriate areas, perhaps simply by reminding everyone of the limited amount of time available for discussing the student and suggesting they should attempt to focus on that task.

Conversely, it is also important to note that parents and families must have an opportunity to be heard, even if the subject of their discussion is not specifically related to their child's school progress. The conferencer must not be too quick to direct the attention of parents and family members away from a topic they consider worthy of discussion—such a strategy would run counter to collaboration. Consequently, only in instances where an unproductive focus dominates the session or when the intensity of the content raises ethical issues should the discussion be redirected. In some cases, the conferencer can listen to the concerns of parents and family members without agreeing, can refer parents and family members to the individual most able to effect some type of appropriate change (e.g., principal, school board members, hospital administrator), and can employ subtle redirection techniques (reinforcing, attending to content more directly related to the session) as alternatives to direct confrontations about the appropriateness of content.

CONCLUDING THE CONFERENCE

The conference should wrap up with a verbal summary of the discussions that occurred, including a brief review of the high points of the student's progress and a restatement of those activities that will be implemented to deal with identified weaknesses and problems. In particular, the summary should include individual responsibilities for the various programs to be followed, methodologies for monitoring progress and evaluating success, and the manner and dates for exchanging this information.

The conference should be concluded on a positive note. In particular, the conferencer should reinforce parents and family members for their participation, extend an invitation for them to stay in touch when they experience a problem or require further information (this may involve scheduling a follow-up conference on the spot to discuss agenda items not covered or items not specifically related to the progress conference), and encourage them to maintain their interest, participation, and collaborative spirit. One important goal of the progress reporting conference should be to have all participants leave the conference feeling "more connected, optimistic, respected, and empowered than they did before the encounter" (Minke & Anderson, 2003, p. 50).

After the Conference

It is important to remember that responsibilities do not end with the conference meeting. Rather, the conferencer should attend to the following tasks: (a) record results, (b) provide feedback to other appropriate school or agency professionals, (c) perform activities agreed on in the conference and promptly provide feedback to parents regarding the results of these efforts, (d) review the progress report conference with the student, and (e) evaluate the conference.

RECORD RESULTS

Making an accurate and meaningful record of the progress report conference is a basic professional duty, integral not only to that particular conference but also to future interactions. Because it is not at all unusual to exchange significant and elaborate information and to devise cooperative intervention programs during parent–professional conferences, the proceedings must be captured in written form. In these written reports the reader should find an integrated summary of discussions that ensued, including academic, emotional and social, and physical information exchanged. The conferencer should take care to present this information in a fashion that captures the interactions that occurred between the parent and family and professional participants, as opposed to providing only a summary of the student's progress.

The summary report should also make reference to recommendations that emerged and the manner in which these recommendations will be collaboratively implemented. Included should be items for later discussion at the annual IEP review meeting. Finally, the report should identify the individual(s) responsible for carrying out each agreed-on recommendation, activity, and evaluation procedure.

Conferencers should record the discussions that take place in progress report conferences in as accurate a fashion as possible. Because professionals must be able to validate the accuracy of their reports and inferences, it is essential that extreme care guide the preparation of parent conference reports. As observed by Kroth and Simpson (1977), "Some school records may contain potentially libelous material, and not only can parents challenge the accuracy of information contained in their child's records, but they also have legal recourse in situations where the recorded information provides an unsupported or damaging picture of the student" (p. 118). Conference reports must provide clear and functional summary information that is free of damaging data and inferences. The use of a laptop computer or carbonless duplicate paper to record the conversations during the conference (rather than at a later time) might help to ensure the accuracy of the report, particularly if participants have an opportunity to review it prior to leaving the meeting. Copies of the written summary that includes the parents' and family members' input can then be distributed to all participants as a tool to enhance continuity of communication and accountability (Pogoloff, 2004; Stevens & Tollafield, 2003). The conferencer or a member of the program planning team may want to follow up with parents the next day and address any questions or concerns they may have (L. J. Johnson et al., 2004; E. J. Martin & Hagan-Burke, 2002).

PROVIDE DIRECT FEEDBACK TO OTHER PROFESSIONALS

In addition to preparing a written report of the conference, the educator may wish to disseminate information to some individuals directly. This should occur especially when the information may directly result in curriculum, attitude, or procedural modification and when questions persist regarding the degree to which information will be seen if available only in written form.

For example, a junior-high-level learning disabilities resource room teacher learned from one of her student's parents during a progress report conference that their son had recently started taking antihistamines for hay fever. She had noted that the child seemed extremely lethargic and distractible for the past several weeks during the 2 hours he was in her resource program. Although this teacher was not aware that similar problems were occurring in the student's general education classes, she made individual visits to his other teachers following the conference to apprise them of his medical condition.

Even in the best of programs, reports may go unseen by those individuals who most need the information. As a result, highly significant data should be disseminated face-to-face to ensure that in fact it is shared.

PERFORM AGREED-ON DUTIES

Although rapport and trust can take hold through the use of basic interpersonal skills, parents' ultimate satisfaction and belief in an educator and a program will come only with the performance of agreed-on tasks and the communication of results. In the final analysis, delivery on promises is the fundamental determinant of rapport and collaborative success.

REVIEW RESULTS OF THE CONFERENCE WITH THE STUDENT

In instances where a student is not a part of his or her own progress report conference, the teacher and/or parents should provide feedback. This process should consist of an overview of the items discussed, the progress results noted, and the various recommendations made. As much as appropriate, the student should be exposed to the same collaborative format and information as the parents. He or she should have an opportunity to raise questions, to be part of any problem-solving efforts, and to have input regarding the various recommendations. Among the most significant components in this process is the need to stress that the purpose of the conference is to apprise parents and family members of the student's progress (an effort that will be of direct benefit to him or her) and that progress report conferences are routinely scheduled for all parents and family members.

EVALUATE THE CONFERENCE

The evaluation of efforts is needed in all areas of education, including parent and family involvement. School and agency personnel, along with almost every other professional, should be able to demonstrate the efficacy of their efforts. Conferencers, therefore, need to engage in ongoing self-reflection and analysis of all aspects of the conference to identify areas requiring change to promote active parent participation (Dabkowski, 2004). Information should be obtained by all participants to analyze the effectiveness of the meeting and participant satisfaction (Minke & Anderson, 2003; Rock, 2000). It is imperative, however, that any evaluation tool used (such as a survey, checklist, or questionnaire) yields information directly associated with the desired goals and objectives of the meeting. This need for evaluative feedback is further highlighted by noting that personal satisfaction with a conference may not always indicate true success. For example, a teacher who talks incessantly during a conference may conclude that the session went well, but in spite of this personal feeling of satisfaction, she may have given others few opportunities to voice an opinion or collaborate and may have actually failed to provide certain basic information. Consequently, the conferencer should, as a regular practice, conduct an evaluation of the session.

One suggested procedure for obtaining this feedback appears in Figure 7.4. This instrument can serve as a self-evaluation measure or as a means of allowing one's colleagues (or the parents) to provide feedback. The questions can also become a preconference checklist for remembering the specific components to address.

Responding to Questions From Parents and Family Members

Parents and family members of children with exceptionalities will have questions regarding their child and the future long after an initial diagnosis has been made and special educational provisions delivered. Consequently, the conferencer should expect that questions will arise in the course of the progress reporting conference that may or may not relate directly to the agenda. It is important, of course, to make the discussions collaborative and to keep them related to the task at hand, but it is also important to address the issues and questions that parents and family members raise. As a result, the professional must be able to contain the session within certain parameters without being so rigid as to extinguish items not associated with the preconference agenda. Making this discrimination while at the same time providing appropriate feedback to parents, all within a somewhat unrealistic period of time, is in no way an easy task.

Pupil's Name: _____ Date: _____

Conferencer: _____

Person Completing Evaluation: _____

			Needs
I. Preconference Evaluation	Yes	No	Improvement
1. Was the conferencer familiar with the pupil's and family's background and related information, including the IEP?	☐	☐	☐
2. Was an agenda developed and followed?	☐	☐	☐
3. Was a review of previous test data and informal assessments conducted such that a reinterpretation of results could be conducted if necessary?	☐	☐	☐
4. Was a portfolio of the pupil's representative work prepared for the parents?	☐	☐	☐
5. Was an adequate environment prepared for the conference?	☐	☐	☐
6. Was the pupil prepared for the conference?	☐	☐	☐
7. Were the parents prepared to participate and collaborate in the conference?	☐	☐	☐
8. Was sufficient time allotted for the session?	☐	☐	☐
9. Were the parents appropriately notified of the conference?	☐	☐	☐
II. General Conferencing Evaluation			
1. Were the parents appropriately informed of the purpose of the conference?	☐	☐	☐
2. Was the session conducted in a systematic and sequential manner?	☐	☐	☐
3. Was the conferencer able to keep the interview flowing and on course?	☐	☐	☐

Figure 7.4. Progress report conference evaluation procedure. *(continues)*

	Yes	No	Needs Improvement
4. Did the conferencer provide the parent with an opportunity to ask questions?	☐	☐	☐
5. Was the conferencer able to attend to the parent rather than to notes?	☐	☐	☐
6. Was the conferencer able to include the parents as collaborative participants?	☐	☐	☐
7. Did the conferencer appropriately rephrase when necessary?	☐	☐	☐
8. Did the conferencer summarize the session?	☐	☐	☐

III. Evaluation of Specific Conference Content

	Yes	No	Needs Improvement
1. Was the conferencer able to provide a general progress report to the parents?	☐	☐	☐
2. Was the conferencer able to provide an adequate report of academic progress?	☐	☐	☐
3. Was the conferencer able to interpret previously administered tests/evaluation procedures?	☐	☐	☐
4. Was the conferencer able to clearly explain the pupil's academic program (remediation strategy) to the parents?	☐	☐	☐
5. Was the conferencer able to interpret the pupil's success as a function of the academic program (remediation or acceleration strategy)?	☐	☐	☐
6. Was the conferencer able to interpret to the parents the future outcomes, progressions, and expectations for the pupil?	☐	☐	☐
7. Was the conferencer able to provide an adequate report of social/emotional progress?	☐	☐	☐
8. Was the conferencer able to provide the parents with a remediation plan if a social/emotional problem was targeted?	☐	☐	☐

Figure 7.4. (*continued*)

	Yes	No	Needs Improvement
9. Was the conferencer able to provide an adequate report of physical progress?	☐	☐	☐
10. Was the conferencer able to solicit and respond to questions raised by the parents?	☐	☐	☐
11. Was the conferencer able to identify information that would later be used to amend the pupil's IEP?	☐	☐	☐

IV. Additional comments:

_____

_____

Figure 7.4. (*continued*)

One of the most important points to remember is that parents and family members may raise a question for which they are not seeking a response but which will provide them an opportunity to redirect the session. For example, a parent who asks, "Why is our child retarded?" may simply wish to offer his or her perceptions. On one occasion when this very question was raised, the conferencer noted that it was a difficult question with many possibilities and asked the parent for her thoughts. The mother stated that she believed it was related to her heavy cigarette smoking during pregnancy. She revealed that her in-laws had chided her for smoking while pregnant and specifically warned her that such behavior could produce mental retardation, poor health, or small stature in children. Although the mother had been told previously that her smoking had not caused her son's disability and thus did not need another professional to repeat the message, she did feel a strong urge to talk about the situation. As this example shows, the conferencer should attempt to determine when parents and family members desire information and when they just need someone to listen. As noted by Benjamin (1969), "Not every question calls for an answer, but every question demands respectful listening and usually a personal reaction on our part" (p. 74).

Frequently conferencers observe that they are asked to respond to difficult or sensitive questions only after having had several prior meetings with parents and families. That is, only after rapport, trust, and a collaborative relationship have been satisfactorily established will parents and family members feel sufficiently comfortable in sharing this type of information. Thus, the conferencer should regard these difficult questions, many of which have no answers, as a sign of rapport and a request for the professional to listen and collaborate.

It is critical to the collaborative relationship that parents not only be allowed but also encouraged to ask questions to gain a better understanding of their child's progress. If parents do not spontaneously do so during or after the progress reporting conference, educators should prompt parents by asking if they have any questions (Dabkowski, 2004). Conferencers' responses should be formulated in language easily understood by parents and family members and should include examples and anecdotes to clarify their response (E. J. Martin & Hagen-Burke, 2002; Stevens & Tollafield, 2003).

In their study of collaborative partnerships, Blue-Banning, Summers, Frankland, Nelson, and Beegle (2004) reported parents prefer that educators respond to their questions with clear, open, and honest communication that does not candy coat unwelcome news or information. In fact, the proper handling of questions not only has a dramatic impact on parent–educator relationships (Swick, 2003) but helps define a competent educator, "someone who is not afraid to admit when he or she does not know something, but—an important caveat—is willing to find out" (Blue-Banning et al., 2004, p. 178). It is always better to tell family members that you do not have the information readily at hand but will get back to them as soon as possible rather than attempt to bluff a response (L. J. Johnson et al., 2004).

Preparing Parents and Family Members to Participate

With ever-increasing frequency parents and families are being asked and expected to participate actively and productively with professionals in developing and maintaining appropriate educational services for their children (Simpson & Zurkowski, 2000). As a result of the work of parent groups, advocates, legislators, and other forces, parents have been accorded the rights and privileges commensurate with a colleague relationship. Some researchers, such as McAfee and Vergason (1979), have focused on more immediate and practical issues. In particular, they suggested, "The issue is not whether parents should be involved, nor the extent of involvement, but rather how the situation can be structured to best utilize parents in efforts to maximize the educational achievement of children" (p. 4).

With respect to progress reporting conference participation, this approach suggests the need to prepare parents and family members to engage in planning and participate in the various activities associated with their child's educational program. This should include information on being a legitimate collaborative member of the parent–educator progress report conference. In pursuit of this goal, educators should equip parents and family members with questions to think about prior to the session, including the skills parents are most interested in the student developing, the strengths and weaknesses of the student, any work samples produced at home, and other related issues.

Without doubt, parents and family members can be trained to engage in conference activities that will facilitate their participation. The following are suggestions to offer parents and family members to aid them in becoming more functional conference participants.[1]

- Arrange your schedule so that you can arrive on time. If you are not familiar with the school or neighborhood, ask for directions or secure a map of the area.
- Arrange for a sitter for your other children. If you are unable to do so, ask the school if arrangements can be made to have someone (perhaps an older student volunteer) attend to the children during the conference. It is disruptive to a conference to have children distract the educator and parents and family members.
- Determine how much time has been allotted for the session and stay within that time frame. If all of your concerns and questions are not addressed within that period, you can make another appointment.
- Discuss the upcoming conference with family members and the student. Ask for input from these individuals, especially if they will not attend the meeting with you. If you feel com-

---

1. As this list may appear somewhat self-serving for professionals, the information will be most effective when disseminated by someone other than the teacher—a parent advocate or support group, a school administrator, and so forth.

fortable with the idea, discuss with the educator the possibility of including your child in the conference. A number of educators recommend including students in their own conferences. This strategy may demonstrate to students that the responsibility for an education is theirs, and it eliminates the problems associated with disseminating secondhand information to students.

- Do not gossip about other teachers, students, or families. Be candid, however, in relating information that may be beneficial to professionals.
- Review any notes and school documents (including the child's IEP) that you have prior to the conference.
- Bring a written list of questions and items that you want to discuss with the teacher. Do not rely on your memory. Included should be information related to academic, social and emotional, and physical areas. Specific questions such as "Is he reading at grade level?" "What is his reading level compared with children his age who are in the general education classroom?" "Do you have disciplinary problems with Sue?" and "How do you discipline Hector?" can all be useful in eliciting specific feedback.
- Do not come to the conference looking for a fight or an apology from the teacher for your child's school-related problems. Rather, arrive ready to work and collaborate for the child's benefit. If you feel, however, that the professional is in error or does not understand the entire situation, share information that you have. Whatever the situation, you should constantly be looking for ways to resolve conflicts and to solve problems associated with your child's educational program.
- Make a list of information you believe should be shared with the student's teacher and other professionals. Include the child's particular likes, dislikes, and attitudes, as well as specific information that may aid the teacher in better understanding the student's particular situation.
- Consider taking notes during the conference, or ask someone to come with you to do so. After the conference attempt to summarize the important points and happenings that took place.
- Praise the teacher and educational system for things they do well.

- If the conferencer uses a term or concept that you are unfamiliar with, ask for an explanation.
- Accept responsibility for problems that are yours. Likewise, follow through with any plans or activities that you agree to.
- Do not expect the conferencer to solve your personal problems or those of your family. The person conducting the progress report conference will most likely be a teacher. Although educators may be able to make referrals, they are not therapists.

This list, of course, is far from comprehensive. Above all, the educator must remember that the maximum growth of a child will be facilitated by parents, family members, and educators collaboratively working together. For parents and family members to be most productive in conferences, however, they must receive appropriate training. As suggested by a number of authorities, parents who are educated in school-related matters will be more satisfied with the system, because they will have been involved in the establishment of its design (Friend & Cook, 2003; Rock, 2000; Salend, 2005; Soodak & Erwin, 2000).

Summary

Progress report conferences remain among the most common of all parent–educator interactions and, consequently, are among the most significant. These meetings afford the opportunity for parents, family members, and teachers to exchange information and develop and expand a collaborative relationship. In addition, these meetings provide an opportunity for significant information to be exchanged for the benefit of children and youth. In spite of the potential significance of these meetings, however, one must remember that the success of the parent and family and professional progress report conference will closely align with the establishment of rapport, trust, and a cooperative relationship and with the participation training parents and family members have received. Thus, the educator cannot realistically expect the progress report conference to be effective in the absence of prior positive associations. When parents, family members, and educators who have well-established collaborative relationships make use of the progress report conference as one means of sharing information, however, the results can be highly facilitative of the goals and desired outcomes of everyone involved.

Exercises

1. Interview parents regarding their preferences for receiving progress reports on their child, including the types of information they would like to receive on a regular basis, the frequency of the reports (e.g., daily, weekly, monthly), the format of the reports (e.g., home note or checklist), and their expectations for their role (e.g., do parents want to reply to each teacher-initiated progress report, and in what manner?).

2. Design a progress monitoring system that you would use to communicate to parents the progress their child is making in your program. Include items and sections such as the following:
   - stated goals for each appropriate domain,
   - a graphic format to display the progress data,
   - the student's strengths or particular area of growth,
   - identified areas where improvement is needed,
   - a section to record parent's questions and concerns,
   - suggestions for ways parents can support the student's progress at home, and
   - samples of the student's work.

3. Conduct a progress report conference with parents. Following the session, ask the parents, a colleague, or both to evaluate your performance using the instrument shown in Figure 7.4. Compare the ratings you gave yourself with those assigned by the others. On the basis of the feedback, develop a list of procedures that will enable you to function more effectively in your conference.

Chapter 8

Unplanned Conferences

Vignette

April, a special education teacher, has worked for 5 years with children with a range of mild disabilities in first through third grades. One year Tanya, the mother of one of her students, served as a parent volunteer in the school. Although Tanya was asked to help with the kindergarten classes, she frequently stopped by April's classroom to check on her son, Brian. Several times a day she would walk into the classroom to ask April for a quick "update" or walk to Brian's desk to ask him directly to report on his day if April was occupied with another student. April was accustomed to Tanya's keen interest in all aspects of Brian's educational program. In fact, because they lived in the same neighborhood, it was not unusual to have an impromptu conference with Tanya in the produce isle of the local supermarket. April was pleased to have a parent who was so involved and supportive of what she was doing, but she began to feel that Tanya's visits were intrusive, and she dreaded seeing her at the classroom door.

It is becoming increasingly apparent that for parent–teacher conferences to be successful, educators must become trained and prepared for a variety of encounters and situations (Friend & Cook, 2007; Kampwirth, 2003; Seligman, 2000; Simpson & Simpson, 1994; Tingley, 2006). In particular, good conferencers are

- aware of the various factors impacting and influencing families of children with exceptionalities;
- competent in establishing and maintaining collaborative relationships;

- knowledgeable of basic communication skills;
- competent in sharing information with parents and families;
- skillful in apprising parents of legislation relating to children with disabilities, helping them become advocates for their own children and more effective consumers of educational services;
- effective in training parents and family members to function as change agents within the natural environment;
- competent in solving problems and resolving conflicts with parents and families;
- skillful in conducting a variety of individual and group conferences; and
- adroit in helping parents and families more effectively accommodate and integrate their children with exceptionalities into family units.

In addition to acquiring skill and competence in these areas, educators must be prepared to contend and interact with parents and family members at times other than during scheduled sessions. As any educator will attest, numerous situations can arise in which parents expect to see or talk with their child's teacher or other educational personnel during nonscheduled times and without first having called for an appointment. In fact, because some schools require that teachers be in their classrooms before and after school to talk with parents who want to drop in, many parents and families likely will assume that conferences can and should occur at their discretion (including in the checkout line of the neighborhood supermarket or over the telephone). Finally, as a number of educators have discovered, it is during unscheduled meetings that parents may be most apt to manifest intense emotions and sentiments, including anger, sorrow, guilt, and despair.

Thus, educators must be equipped with suitable attitudes and skills to deal with parents and family members on these occasions. Although unscheduled conferences have received far less attention from researchers and writers than more traditional parent–educator meetings, they are nonetheless important.

Developing Attitudes and Strategies for Unplanned Conferences

Although educators might understandably prefer scheduled and structured meetings, they must acknowledge that at least some of their contacts with parents and family members will be unplanned. Teachers must not only accept the inevitability of these contacts but also develop appropriate attitudes and strategies for enhancing their success (Trumbull, Rothstein-Fisch, Greenfield, & Quiroz, 2001). In the opening vignette, April needed to communicate directly with Tanya her sense of appreciation for her active involvement, particularly her willingness to volunteer at school, while establishing guidelines for when it was appropriate to stop by the classroom to inquire about her son.

Educators must be able to understand themselves and their behavior as related to unscheduled parent and family meetings. That is, they must be able to acknowledge their honest feelings about parents' and family members' calling on them unexpectedly, telephoning them at home to talk about students with special needs, and attempting to conduct conferences in noneducational settings. When professionals become cognizant of their own anxieties, fears, and resentments at being unprepared to deal with certain issues, values, and educational philosophies regarding unplanned interactions with parents and families, they will usually be more adept at handling these situations. Moreover, this self-understanding can assist them in structuring situations to meet needs more effectively.

Educators must accept all types of parent and family involvement as a basic component of program success. Two premises basic to the effective collaborative involvement of parents, families, and educators are that (a) parents and families must be perceived as integral and legitimate components of any educational or treatment program for children, and (b) a variety of options for serving the needs of parents and families must be made available, including unscheduled interaction opportunities. Unless educators accept this position, little can be gained from the implementation of parent and family programs. Both families and educators must be able to perceive the other party as having a justifiable role in facilitating a child's growth and development and as being worthy of cooperative and collaborative involvement for a child's benefit. In particular, both planned and unplanned conferencing opportunities must be extended to parents and family members as a means of facilitating both the development of children and the enhancement of parent–professional communication.

Educators must have confidence that planned change can occur with and through collaborative parent and family involvement programs. Educational conferencers must believe in their capacity to positively influence the behavior of parents and families and the capacity of parents and family members to facilitate the growth and development of their children. Thus, educators must accept the premise that children with exceptionalities and their families can positively change when exposed to appropriate conditions and contingencies and that educators can engineer and effect such changes. For parents and family members to achieve desired change, however, they must receive a variety of interaction and communication opportunities with educational personnel, including both planned and unplanned meetings. The acceptance both of families' ability to change and of educators' ability to facilitate this process through planned and unplanned interactions is basic to the successful implementation of many parent and family programs.

Educators need to be assertive in unplanned conferences. As noted, some meetings with parents and family members of children with exceptionalities will be unplanned but also necessary and productive. Educators, however, must also recognize that circumstances surrounding these conferences are characterized by varying levels of acceptability. For example, one teacher became concerned because a student's mother who had never attended a planned conference routinely called her at home after 10:00 P.M. to discuss her child's school progress. Another teacher reported that the grandmother of one of her students who was actively involved in her granddaughter's educational program called at 7:00 A.M. Christmas morning to ask for advice on how to handle the child's apparent jealous tantrum over the gifts her sister had received. That these and similar situations regularly occur can be attested to by anyone who has ever worked in an educational setting; therefore, educators must be able to exercise appropriate assertiveness in structuring unscheduled conferences. Though the educational conferencer must be tolerant and accepting of unplanned meetings, he or she must also be explicit about the circumstances surrounding these sessions.

Assertiveness can reduce an educator's vulnerability during unplanned parent meetings and direct interactions into more productive areas. It can aid conferencers in expressing their rights without infringing on the interests of others (Dettmer, Thurston, Knackendoffel, & Dyck, 2009; Ivey, Ivey, & Simek-Downing, 1987; Lambie & Daniels-Mohring, 1993) and can help conferencers articulate positions in a positive and productive manner. Though educators must be appropriately accommodating of parents' and family members' requests for unplanned meetings, they must also recognize the need to offer structure and guidance regarding these requests. In particular, educators must know when to say "no," how to express emotions and perceptions truthfully, and when to continue, reschedule, and terminate meetings with parents and family members. Failure to act assertively in conferencing will facilitate neither the parent–professional relationship nor a child's school progress; in fact it likely will restrict the development of collaborative relationships.

Educators need to provide structure and guidelines for unplanned conferences. Informing parents and family members of guidelines, protocol, and rules of conduct for unscheduled conferences offers one essential means of enhancing the productivity of these meetings and avoiding misunderstandings. Although such information may be shared during a conversation, it should also be disseminated in written form. Some educators describe such ground rules during initial conferences and then follow up with a written reference (and an additional explanation) at open house meetings. The information should include an explanation of when an unscheduled conference is appropriate, the hours available for such meetings, the situations that may be inappropriate for a drop-in session, and the conditions and times during which an educator will accept calls from parents and family members at school and at home.

It is essential that administration staff aid in establishing and implementing such guidelines to ensure district or school endorsement and some consistency across programs. Information regarding unplanned conferences also should be considered for dissemination through other modes, such as meetings of the parent–teacher association, local newspapers, parent-coordinated service organizations, school newsletters, and school policy and procedure handbooks.

Parents and family members likely will need and appreciate information regarding their participation in unscheduled meetings. Therefore, just as parents must learn to be functional participants in conferences about Individualized Education Programs and other school-related sessions, they also must become aware of the variables and procedures associated with unscheduled meetings. Such structure is necessary to make unplanned conferences an appropriate and maximally beneficial form of parent–educator communication.

Educators need to have effective communication skills. As suggested earlier, parents or family members who arrive at unscheduled times for conferences with educational personnel will frequently have a particular concern or need. In conjunction with these absorbing and acute needs, educators may encounter atypical emotional manifestations. That is, parents who appear without first scheduling an appointment are likely to be concerned about a specific incident at home or school, overwrought with a particular feeling, or in some other way agitated and upset. Thus, teachers can expect to encounter a greater proportion of angry, frustrated, and upset parents and family members at unscheduled conferences.

Educators must be prepared, therefore, to apply appropriate communication skills. Although good communication is an integral component of any parent–teacher conference, special attention to the characteristics associated with maximizing interactions should be considered at unplanned encounters. In particular, educators should strive to (a) attend to parents' and family members' messages, both verbal and nonverbal; (b) recognize and value parents' and family members' perceptions and concerns (even if one does not agree with them), accepting rather than interpreting what is being shared; and (c) address the conflict directly. Consideration of these and similar factors may enable conferencers to convert potentially unhealthy situations into collaborative problem-solving sessions.

Educators need to prepare for unscheduled conferences. Though by their very nature unplanned meetings between families and educators preclude comprehensive planning, conferencers can anticipate and prepare for many unscheduled encounters. For instance, educators should consider maintaining well-organized and up-to-date files on each student; having lists of names, addresses, and telephone numbers of school and community agencies available for families; having written guidelines available for parents to use in structuring their child's home-study schedule; and being familiar with the use of conflict resolution strategies. Even though educators may be unfamiliar with the specific types of unplanned meetings they will have with parents and families, they can anticipate and make general arrangements for most of the sessions they will encounter.

Specific Types of Unplanned Meetings

Although a variety of unscheduled encounters with parents and family members can be expected, educational conferencers are most likely to contend with several recurring types of meetings: telephone conferences, e-mail messages, meetings in noneducational settings, and encounters with angry parents, emotionally overwrought individuals, garrulous parents, family members who are seeking counseling or therapy for their own problems, and parents who insist on observing their child or talking with an educator during class time.

Telephone Conferences

Just as no businessperson could hope to be successful without making appropriate use of the telephone, neither can educators. Telephone communication affords the professional an easy and personalized means of interacting with parents and family members. Furthermore, it reduces the problems of misinterpretation and message delay that are common when notes are sent home. Yet in spite of the numerous advantages, telephone interactions present a variety of concerns. First, the telephone should typically be considered a less-than-equal alternative to face-to-face meetings. Telephone conversations not only deny the educator full access to an individual and his or her nonverbal responses and demeanor but can also limit a conferencer's capacity to provide clear and meaningful feedback. That is, the conferencer will not be able to rely on or produce visual displays, examples of academic work, or other permanent products. Accordingly, telephone interactions are totally dependent on the ability of parents, family members, and conferencers to send and receive verbal messages effectively, a capacity that cannot always be counted on (Al-Hassan & Gardner, 2002; Correa, Jones, Thomas, & Morsink, 2005; A. Turnbull & Turnbull, 2001). The telephone is often a weak mode of communication in attempting to resolve conflicts, reach joint solutions to problems, or respond to emotions. Although conferencers may be required to respond to the initial needs of parents and families on the telephone, they are advised to follow such initial interactions with face-to-face meetings during problematic situations.

Educators are also well advised to structure their telephone interactions with parents and family members early in a relationship. This structure can be offered at initial conferences or open house meetings in the form of suggestions as to when parents should call, matters that are appropriate for telephone communication, and under what conditions parents and family members should telephone educators at home or on their cell phones (L. J. Johnson, Pugach, & Hawkins, 2004; A. Turnbull & Turnbull, 2001). In a similar manner, conferencers should obtain permission from parents to call them at home or work as well as to inquire about convenient times for their conversations. The telephone can be a particularly effective tool when used by conferencers to reinforce children, family members, and parents; to maintain open lines of communication; and to provide ongoing feedback. Parents can also facilitate communication with educators by relying on the telephone primarily as an information exchange device. Beneficial use of telephones by parents and family members, however, can be anticipated only with appropriate structuring.

A teacher of adolescents with learning disabilities provided a specific time when parents could call her at school to discuss matters of concern. She arranged with the secretary in her school to take messages and to remind parents who called at other times that she would receive nonemergency telephone calls only at specific times (previously negotiated with the parents). This same teacher routinely requested that parents telephone to alert her of changes occurring in their home or with their child's behavior, to clarify notes sent home, or to discuss other matters of their choice.

E-mail Messages

Like telephone contacts, e-mail messages provide a quick and efficient means of conveying information between educators and parents. Most educators have access to a school or personal e-mail account and can compose messages at one time or across several sessions as their time allows. Unlike the immediacy of phone contacts, e-mail enables educators to be more thoughtful in constructing their response to ensure clarity and completeness in a format that may be more feasible than a written letter or note. Even with the use of "emoticons" such as smiley faces that can be included in messages, however, e-mail messages are less personal than phone calls. This disadvantage may be offset by the benefit of the written record that is created when either party uses the "reply" button and keeps an electronic copy of the exchange.

There are caveats, however, to the use of e-mail. As e-mail is an "immediate" technology, correspondents have a tendency to expect an instant response to a sent message. In addition, the simplicity of use may prompt some parents and family members to send multiple messages. One teacher of students with multiple and severe disabilities commented that he received a barrage of e-mail messages almost daily from a mother who expected responses to her instant messaging. He explained that he was not able to access e-mail throughout the day and would attempt to reply once at the end of the school day.

As mentioned in Chapter 5, parents and families are becoming more skilled and comfortable with the use of technology. Conferencers should provide families with the necessary guidelines so that they can take advantage of any technology that facilitates ongoing communication with families and supports collaborative efforts.

Noneducational Settings

One teacher of children with learning disabilities confided that she had transferred her church membership to another community so that she would not have to contend with the parents of her students on Sundays. Other educators have noted that they are apprehensive about meeting their students' parents and families in public or nonschool settings because of similar experiences. Hence, educators who are uncomfortable talking with parents in out-of-school settings must insist on conducting their conferences only at particular times and places. When approached by parents and family members outside the classroom, these educators must politely, yet assertively, instruct parents and family members about the appropriate manner for setting up a conference. Just as physicians and dentists are reluctant to discuss professional matters with their patients at ball games and restaurants, educators must be equally resistant.

Some professionals might assume that the protocol associated with this matter is so universally understood that it does not require further attention. Nevertheless, parents and family members should be informed early on of educators' preferences regarding unplanned meetings; only then can a mutually understood expectation exist.

One special education teacher who was new to a small rural community found that she was constantly being approached in a variety of settings outside of school by parents wishing to discuss their children. As one means of contending with this situation, she began carrying cards printed with her name and school telephone number. When approached by parents wanting an on-the-spot conference, the teacher would give them a card along with instructions for setting up an appointment. She made clear that this arrangement would ensure that she would have the necessary time and access to materials to serve their informational needs adequately.

Meetings With Angry Parents and Family Members

For many educators there is no situation quite as intimidating as the prospect of an angry parent or family member arriving without prior notice. Yet as unfortunate as these situations may be, they do occasionally occur. Even good relationships between families and professionals can sometimes involve conflict. Hence, even in situations where conferencers have invested time and effort establishing rapport and a spirit of collaboration with parents and families, serious disagreements and misunderstandings may develop. Furthermore, the frustrations experienced by parents and families of children with exceptionalities may result in periodic displays of anger toward a child's teacher or other educational personnel independent of these individuals' behaviors.

Recognition of these basic factors may enable the conferencer to maintain a suitable frame of reference and a willingness to involve parents and families in joint problem solving. In fact, a major problem associated with these conflict situations is their potential impact on future relationships. Failure to effectively contend with parent and family anger can result in reduced cooperation and willingness to collaborate, exacerbated suspicion, and the eventual destruction of good communication. On the other hand, conferencers who contend with anger effectively and convert these situations into opportunities for joint problem solving can enhance feelings of trust and value in families and a willingness to cooperatively seek solutions to problems.

Rule number one is that conferencers' communication skills (discussed previously in Chapter 3) will determine their success in unplanned meetings with angry parents and family members. In particular, an effective conferencer must be able to listen accurately and creatively without becoming defensive, recognize and appropriately respond to emotions, maintain a willingness to collaboratively solve problems rather than to patronize or retaliate against aggressive individuals, communicate to parents and family members that it is acceptable for them to have values and opinions that differ from educators', maintain an adult-to-adult relationship rather than a superior–subordinate attitude, and offer explanations and information without being sanctimonious.

In addition, conferencers may wish to consider the following when interacting with angry parents and family members:

- Allow parents and family members to talk about their concerns without interruption. Rather than attempting to respond as issues are raised, the conferencer should allow persons to fully explain the issue.
- Attempt to record the concerns voiced by parents and family members; however, first consideration should be given to maintaining an acceptable listening environment.
- Be aware that some of the issues raised by angry parents and family members may not actually be significant concerns to them. In their anger parents and family members may comment on issues that are obviously not relevant, and thus educators must be able to help irate persons focus their concerns.
- Be aware of your own body language and the nonverbal responses of parents and family members during these exchanges. Concentrate on keeping your voice low, relaxing, and avoiding defensive or intimidating gestures.
- Avoid attempts at discounting problems or parents' feelings regarding issues (e.g., "Now let's not overreact" or "You couldn't possibly feel that way").
- Avoid arguing with parents and family members.
- Respond to feelings without putting parents and family members on the defensive (e.g., "You are very angry" or "I see a great deal of hostility in you today") and without using clichés (e.g., "I feel that you are saying to me . . ." or "Now just calm down, honey").

- Avoid strong emotional reactions and insensitive responses, including sarcasm, disbelief, hurt, and anger.
- Request clarification from parents and family members on points you do not understand, but avoid constantly interrupting, asking two questions at once, or using leading questions.
- Attempt to keep angry persons on topic without eliminating the opportunity for them to voice additional concerns.
- Avoid attempts to engage parents and family members in collaborative problem solving before they have had an opportunity to express fully their concerns and to vent their anger.
- Be sensitive and sympathetic to parent and family problems without assuming responsibility or ownership.
- As much as possible, avoid responding to wrongful and generalized allegations (e.g., "If you were a decent teacher, this wouldn't have happened") or threats (e.g., "You can expect to hear from my lawyer" or "I plan to call the superintendent of schools").
- When confronted by parents and family members with a confirmed history of being physically or verbally abusive toward professionals, ask that a colleague sit in on the session.
- Recognize that most anger is motivation that can be translated into collaborative problem-solving efforts.

The teacher of a group of intermediate-grade children with severe disabilities was surprised one day after school by an irate parent. This individual, whom the teacher had known for several years, accused her and her colleagues of several wrongdoings, including a lack of concern over the well-being and future of their students. By simply allowing the parent to talk about her concerns and by not responding defensively, the educator was able to determine that her family had recently been under severe emotional stress and that this situation had been aggravated by a note from the teacher outlining a new inclusion program. After the parent had an opportunity to vent her feelings and concerns, a discussion of the new program ensued. In addition, the educator was able to suggest several alternatives for alleviating the stress factors in the home.

Meetings With Parents and Families Who Are Emotionally Overwrought

Although many parents and families experience positive outcomes of having a child with a disability (e.g., Poyadue, 1993; Scorgie & Sobsey, 2000;

Taunt & Hastings, 2002; Tsai, 2000), conferencers can also expect parents and families to have a number of strong emotional reactions to their children's conditions (Ferguson, 2002; T. Hall, 2000; Hornby, 1994; Nissenbaum, Tollefson, & Reese, 2002; Paul & Simeonsson, 1993; Simpson & Carter, 1993). Accordingly, educators can anticipate periodically interacting with emotionally upset parents and family members.

Although the process of effectively responding to overwrought parents and families consists of a number of components, the conferencer should keep two basic points in mind. The first relates to the need to validate emotions and to indicate that it is acceptable for parents and family members to have certain feelings such as anger, frustration, and disappointment. Furthermore, educators should be willing and able to communicate that they are comfortable and capable of helping parents and families contend with such feelings. More than anything else, conferencers must assure parents and families that their emotional responses are both acceptable and understandable.

Second, responding to the emotional reactions of parents and family members must take precedence over other agenda items. For example, parents who become emotionally upset during an unscheduled conference ostensibly initiated to deal with other matters should be dealt with as if their emotional response were the single most salient issue rather than a concern that must be eliminated so that attention can refocus on the initial topic. Frequently when parents arrive at unscheduled times for meetings with educators and subsequently manifest strong emotions, their major concern is associated with their own feelings rather than with the stated issue.

Conferencers should consider the following points during interactions with emotionally upset parents and family members:

- Listen. Avoid attempts at talking parents and family members out of their feelings or aiding them in denying their responses.
- Become aware of your own reactions when confronted with emotionally overwrought persons. Such self-examination will help educators recognize how they manifest their anxieties, including avoidance of eye contact, shifts in body posture, and body movements.
- Recognize that emotionally overwrought persons are in a highly vulnerable position. Therefore, conferencers must be able to verbally support parents and family members (e.g., "It's OK for you to cry"), physically offer assurance (e.g.,

touch an arm, offer tissues), and psychologically communicate a sense of understanding. At all costs, conferencers should avoid being critical (e.g., "Come on, pull yourself together") or intolerant of emotional responses (e.g., "My job as teacher allows me to talk with you only about your daughter's performance in school, not that other stuff").

- Avoid offering quick solutions; frequently the best strategy for dealing with emotionally upset parents and family members is to allow them to talk without interruption.
- Avoid patronizing remarks and clichés.
- Do not discount or refute the descriptions of feelings or events offered by emotionally upset parents and family members; rather, let the emphasis rest on understanding these perceptions.

During one unscheduled conference initiated by a parent seemingly to discuss her daughter's school progress, it quickly became obvious that the mother's major concern was not her child's academic development. This parent had been traumatized by a severe accident that had befallen her daughter, and although she had begun to recognize her child's need for special school services, she continued to experience a number of strong feelings associated with the accident and its effects. As a result, the educator redirected the focus of the conference toward the mother's feelings and emotional concerns. This session was later followed by a scheduled progress report meeting.

Meetings With Garrulous Parents and Family Members

Parents and family members who chronically show up for unscheduled conferences without any more serious purpose than an interest in chatting can be exasperating. Conferencers may hold open portions of each day or week for unplanned meetings but with the intent of using such opportunities to discuss relevant items. When a talkative parent or family member fails to make appropriate use of this time resource, conferencers must firmly and positively structure the situation. Failure to do so can result in a waste of professional time, interference with parents who actually require legitimate attention, and deterioration in parent–educator relationships.

Educators confronted with talkative persons may wish to consider the following ideas:

- Inform parents and family members early in the school year that although unscheduled meetings can be held, these sessions should occur on an irregular basis and are not designed for casual visitations.
- Confront parents and family members who consistently arrive for unplanned conferences without a purpose or agenda. Such a straightforward strategy is typically more profitable than devising more roundabout measures for ending or avoiding these meetings.
- Consider setting a time limit for all unplanned conferences. Although conferencers must be willing to make adjustments according to the needs of individuals, this strategy can serve to reduce time spent in insignificant areas.

After having tried a number of more subtle approaches, one teacher finally confronted a parent of one of her students who routinely showed up in her classroom after school without an appointment. When confronted, the parent explained that she enjoyed seeing the teacher and hearing about her child's progress, albeit in an indirect fashion. After being made aware of her behavior and the restrictions it placed on the teacher and other parents, the mother became more appropriate and collaborative in her conferencing behavior.

Meetings With Parents and Families Who Are Seeking Counseling for Themselves

Occasionally conferencers find that parents and family members who frequently call on them to discuss their children are actually seeking counseling for themselves. This may be the case when parents arrive without prior notice and the focus of each session revolves around the family or the difficulties experienced by that parent. In such instances, it is extremely important that educators distinguish individuals who simply want to chat from those needing psychological counseling. In situations where parents and family members require psychological counseling, the conferencer should refer them to other professionals better qualified to serve their needs. Hence, teachers must be cautious not to dismiss a parent who chronically drops by as someone who simply wants to pass the time of day when the individual may indeed be seeking professional services.

Although educational conferencers must be aware of their role and recognize their professional limitations, they must also know their obligations. That is, they must not simply terminate a relationship with a parent or family member because that individual needs in-depth counseling. Rather, educators must rely on their relationship with a parent or family member and on their clinical skills to reach a point where they can be assured the person will not be threatened by referral to another person or agency. Failure to act in this manner may result in the family member's both rejecting referrals for counseling and discontinuing relationships with educators that may be needed for their child's continued growth and development. The following is an example of an appropriate response:

> I get the feeling that you are asking me to help you with a problem for which I am not trained. I am really flattered that you trust me enough to confide in me, but because I can't really be of help to you, I'd like to suggest a few possibilities where you can get assistance from a trained professional. In any event, I'd like us to continue to schedule our parent conferences to discuss Joan's progress in school. (Seligman, 2000, p. 244)

A response such as this, delivered in a sensitive and caring manner after a trusting, collaborative relationship has been developed, may help parents access needed professional assistance without jeopardizing future interactions with the teacher.

Meetings With Parents During Class Time

Occasionally educators may be confronted by parents who either wish to observe their children without having made prior arrangements or wish to engage in a teacher conference during class time. Obviously these situations can be both troublesome for educators and disruptive to pupils.

One way to clarify procedures for parents who wish to observe their children or meet with educators during class time is to inform them of the protocol surrounding these activities. This information should be given to parents when their children are placed in a program and during periodic updates dictated by changes and individual needs. These guidelines may be provided verbally but should also be disseminated to parents and family members in written form for later reference.

Educators may determine that allowing a parent to observe a class without prior arrangements does not constitute a problem. In such instances, however, some educators may request that the parent wait in an office area until the teacher or another educator can determine if they have a particular concern and what they want to observe. This procedure also gives the educator a chance to remind the parent of guidelines and rules

for classroom observation. Taking the time to attend to these considerations can often convert a potentially distressing situation into a good collaborative learning experience. Conversely, in instances where parents have
not made prior arrangements to observe a class and when doing so would
disrupt a scheduled activity, the educator must courteously, yet firmly, insist that the parent arrange to visit on another occasion.

Educators confronted with parents and family members desiring an
immediate meeting must be able to determine whether the circumstances
warrant an on-the-spot conference. School psychologists, counselors, and
some itinerant and consulting personnel may be able to see persons under
these conditions with only minor difficulties; however, classroom teachers
face a much more difficult situation.

One particular policy that can eliminate problems in this area is assertive adherence to the requirement that all visitors to a school or agency
check in at the central office and sign a visitors book. This policy, followed
by virtually every school and most agencies, allows an administrator, counselor, or another person to make judgments regarding the needs of a parent
or family member and decide whether a teacher's presence is required in
a conference or whether the parent may proceed to the classroom. When
warranted, these professionals can make arrangements for a teacher's class
to be covered by someone else or for the meeting to take place during a
free period.

After receiving a note from his child's teacher describing a behavior
problem, one father of a boy with an emotional and behavioral disorder
arrived at school the following day just as classes were starting with the
intent of meeting with his son's teacher. This individual was allowed to
confer with the school counselor until the teacher's planning period. At
that time, the counselor, parent, and teacher were able to meet regarding
the incident. This session led to more adequate evaluation systems and a
more regularly scheduled series of conferences.

Undoubtedly, parents and family members who arrive at their child's
school during class hours demanding to hold a conference will not be particularly welcome. Nonetheless, educators must not be so rigid and insensitive as to deny parents access to professional services. Rather, efforts
should be made to negotiate a time when pertinent parties can be brought
together. In addition, when a parent or family member wishes to see an individual who is not available at the moment, arrangements should be made
to have the person meet with someone else whenever possible. After all,
when parents or family members have concerns that are so pressing that
they arrive at a school without prior notice, they should receive immediate
attention. Failure to do so can lead to unfavorable outcomes.

Summary

Even though educators may prefer to hold conferences with parents and family members at scheduled times, unplanned meetings will occur. Consequently, educators can and must be prepared for these encounters to work successfully with parents and families.

Exercises

1. Draft a list of expectations and rules for family visits to your program that afford meaningful access while protecting against unnecessary disruptions. For example, may parents proceed directly to the child's classroom, or must they first check in at the office? Are visits permitted on all days or only those specified on the school calendar? How might those rules and expectations differ for visits in a preschool or early childhood center, elementary school, middle school, and high school?

2. Conduct unplanned role-play conferences with another individual. Your sessions should be structured around the following:
   - a parent-initiated telephone conference
   - attempts by a parent or family member to conduct a conference in a noneducational setting
   - a meeting with an angry parent or family member
   - a meeting with an emotionally upset parent or family member
   - a meeting with a garrulous parent or family member
   - a meeting with a parent or family member seeking personal professional help
   - a meeting with a parent who insists on observing a child or conferring with a teacher during class time

   In conducting the exercise, one individual should assume the part of a parent or family member, another the part of the educator, and a third the role of an observer and discussant. Following each session the observer should discuss with the participants those procedures that were employed to deal with the situation and the strategies that might have been more appropriate.

   Each member in the group of three should assume each role in the exercise.

Chapter 9

Resolving Conflicts

Mr. and Mrs. Jackson agreed to come to school at 7:30 the following morning. We could have 15 minutes together. I asked them to bring Todd [their 14-year-old son] with them. When they arrived, we spent a few minutes with small-talk rapport building and then got into our mutual interests. When I talked about the concerns [refusal to follow directions, verbally provoking others, talking back to teachers] of both [teachers], Mrs. Jackson nodded a lot, and Mr. Jackson looked very unhappy, glancing first at me and then at Todd. I also revealed the latest turnaround that the [teachers] had reported, emphasizing Todd's prosocial actions. This gained a smile from everyone except, unfortunately, Mr. Jackson. Deciding to focus on the negative only, he pinned Todd down with an angry look and told him he won't have that sort of behavior and this is the last time he wants to hear of it. (Wouldn't it be nice if that's all it took, I thought!) Mr. Jackson didn't comment on the prosocial part. Todd's response was that he was doing fine in all other classes; these two were just boring. To my surprise, Mrs. Jackson said that was true; couldn't Todd be moved out of those classes? I thought all of these comments were telling in regard to the family dynamics: Mr. Jackson gives an order and focuses on the negative, and Mrs. Jackson makes an excuse and seeks an escape route for Todd. I respond by saying that Todd and I were discussing his behavior in social studies and English. I felt that we had made some progress over the past week and that we should continue to try to have Todd meet his responsibilities in all his classes since I felt confident that he could. I asked Todd what he thought, and he said, "Yeah, maybe." I thought that answer kept him OK in the sight of both parents: he's passively promising to behave to satisfy his father, and he's leaving the door open for continued complaints about these boring classes in case he needs to use this ploy again with his mother (Kampwirth, 2006, p. 311).

When we think of conflict with parents, we may conjure up images of confrontations and angry words spoken with intense emotions. Certainly that type of scenario provokes anxiety and apprehension for most educators. It is important, however, to view conflict from a broader perspective so that we understand the factors that contribute to conflict and identify how those factors may be mitigated. In the opening vignette, although we don't see direct confrontation, we do see myriad factors that must be addressed to avoid home–school relationships defined by varying degrees of conflict.

First, we have a situation where the educator has asked to meet with parents to discuss a serious behavioral concern but can allocate only 15 minutes to the interaction. Second, the mother and father represent a family dynamic where parents have different perspectives and possibly different goals related to their son's educational program. In addition, they appear to have disparate styles of responding to Todd's inappropriate behaviors. Finally, although the presence of the student may sometimes be appropriate (this is discussed further in Chapter 12), Todd may have been included in the interaction at a point prior to the establishment of a collaborative relationship with the parents. All of these factors may precipitate conflict in home–school interactions unless addressed adequately.

In many respects the ideal parent–educator relationship is considered one that embodies harmony, unity, understanding, and a collaborative attitude. Some have even suggested this relationship should be free from conflict, which, although understandable, is inaccurate. Much attention has been focused on the need to establish and maintain rapport and trust and to be sensitive to values, both educators' values and those of families with whom they relate. This does not mean that educators need to establish and maintain a working relationship without conflict and disagreements. In fact, differences in goals and opinions should be encouraged to facilitate collaborative problem solving and interpersonal growth.

Although one cannot deny the need for an acceptable working relationship and atmosphere, it is important not to confuse this with an association in which conflicts are totally absent. Interactions between individuals with diverse goals, backgrounds, and motivations will periodically involve differences and conflict. Accordingly, it is necessary that this normal and healthy product of human interaction not be perceived incorrectly. To totally preclude conflicts, collaborators would need to either avoid situations that could potentially breed differences of opinion or fail to recognize their own feelings and needs. In instances where differences of opinion and conflict are totally absent, so too is effective communication. In fact, "constructive conflicts encourage open discussion and allow full exploration of each party's needs, concerns, values, and interests—the essential ingredients of authentic communication" (Cheldelin & Lucas, 2004, p. 7). It is important, then, that educators develop tools to identify sources of conflict and articulate them as identified problems that can be solved collaboratively. In this way, conflict can help clarify issues, increase involvement, and promote growth, as well as strengthen relationships, when the issues are resolved (Dettmer, Dyck, & Thurston, 2005; Duquette, Ragin, & Stewart, 2000; Jehn & Chatman, 2000).

Factors Associated With the Development of Unhealthy Conflict

In the course of developing and implementing educational and training programs for children and youth with exceptionalities, collaborators will be faced with opportunities to make a multitude of decisions. Each of these decisions will reflect the values, training, experiences, and goals of the individuals involved in the process, and thus each will potentially be the source of differences and conflicts. In situations characterized by free and open communication, the expression of different opinions and the resulting resolutions can enhance the interpersonal relationship between family members and professionals and subsequently the appropriateness of the services provided to children (Covey, 1989; Fisher, 1994; O'Sullivan & Russell, 2006).

There are, however, other conditions associated with the development of conflict that are not products of open communication and are more difficult to resolve. These situations cannot be considered healthy and do not reflect differences of opinion based on free and open communication. Rather, these conflicts develop as a reaction to situations that lack effective avenues of communication. Solutions to these problems usually come not through the use of standard conflict resolution models but rather through the development of acceptable family–professional relationships and communication strategies. Ways in which unhealthy conflict situations can develop are discussed next.

Conflict expressed as anger, hostility, or fear may become the sole form of self-expression. The capacity to express differences of opinion and position exists as a necessary and vital means of maintaining an open and effective collaborative relationship. If there is no opportunity to openly express differences, parents and family members are deprived of a primary avenue of appropriate communication, which often results in the expression of strong emotion, such as anger or sorrow. Such emotional outbursts are usually employed to gain attention or to release a buildup of minor frustrations that could have been dealt with through effective communication.

There may be insufficient opportunity for parents, family members, and professionals to exchange information. In the absence of an adequate information exchange system, both families and educators are more likely to misunderstand and to blame the other for the development of problems. There are a number of challenges to ongoing communication opportunities, such as transportation issues, child care, work schedules, and simply finding time (Peña, 2000); however, when parents and family members are not a part of the decision-making process and when information does not flow between parents and professionals (such that the basis for decisions and changes is not clearly understood), one can anticipate conflicts.

Professionals may fail to offer viable models and direction for problem-solving collaboration and conflict resolution. Although differences of opinion may be a normal by-product of a healthy adult-to-adult relationship, the professional must set the tone and provide directions and a model for managing problems and conflict. In particular, the conferencer must be able to clearly communicate that it is appropriate for parents and family members to have opinions different from those of the professional and that strategies exist for reconciling differences such that the needs of children will still be met most effectively. This message must be supported by actual demonstrations of problem-solving and conflict resolution behavior.

Professionals and parents and family members may lack a shared language and knowledge of established protocol. Conferencers can expect anger, despair, or withdrawal when parents and family members are exposed to language and procedures that they fail to comprehend (Harry, Allen, & McLaughlin, 1995; Henderson, Mapp, Johnson, & Davies, 2007; Peña, 2000). Seligman (2000) and T. E. C. Smith, Gartin, Murdick, and Hilton (2006) advised that educators use language appropriate for each parent's social, cultural, and ethnic background, without appearing to be talking down to them. Al-Hassan and Gardner (2002) elaborated on the elements of collaborative programs that engage parents from cultural and linguistic backgrounds different from the educators', including tactics to inform parents about the procedures utilized in identification, referral, and intervention processes. These authorities have recognized the necessity of making parents an active part of the communication process and underscored the potential for unhealthy interpersonal discord in the absence of common language and shared information.

There may be an absence of trust and acceptance of value differences. The creation of an effective environment in which communication can occur necessitates a basic measure of trust and an acceptance of one's own values and those of others (Cormier & Nurius, 2003; Mapp, 2002; Mundschenk & Foley, 1997). Here again, language is crucial. For example, after an educator conferences with parents about the importance of daily work completion, his or her asking parents whether their son does his homework may imply mistrust of parental supervision. Asking parents to talk about their son's homework routine, however, elicits the necessary information without offering an unintentional challenge.

J. L. Epstein and Sanders (2000) observed that teachers and parents often have little understanding of each others' interests in children and schools. Teachers are unaware of parents' goals for their children, and parents are unaware of the specifics of educational programs and teachers' expectations. Without this basic ingredient of effective communication, parents, family members, and professionals will lack the basis for both collaboration and healthy conflict resolution. When conferencers employ effective communication strategies that honor families' values and goals, they may lessen or mitigate the disappointment and frustration that often accompany conflict while strengthening efforts to form collaborative relationships with families.

Parents and family members may lack appropriate methods for influencing their child's educational system. For parents and professionals to communicate and arbitrate their differences in an effective and functional manner, they must have acceptable modes of influencing the child's educational program (Carkhuff, 1985; Ramos, 1995). Without this option, families have no alternative but to withdraw from interactions with the school, bitterly accept the situation, or create conflicts.

Conflicts resulting from one of these or related deficiencies or policies can be effectively resolved only by addressing the underlying issues. Though crisis intervention and short-term solutions are possible, ultimate and lasting success will come only from the development of mutually satisfying responses to underlying problems.

The Communication Process: An Analysis

In the final analysis, the capacity to resolve conflicts effectively or to create conditions in which productive conflict resolution strategies can be applied is a function of the quality of the communication process. The essential components of this process, according to Trenholm (2005), are the sender, who encodes a message; the message itself; and the receiver, who must correctly decode the message. For effective communication to occur, all components must be coordinated and functional.

The *encoder* (sender) must be able to transmit information in such a fashion that another individual will be motivated to attend and respond. The success of this endeavor will relate directly to the sender's communication skills, conversational style, attitudes, socioeconomic status, and technical knowledge. In addition, the encoder's nonverbal messages will also play a significant part of the communication process. Gestures, posture, facial expression, body language, and voice tone are only a few of the ways in which nonverbal communication occurs (Cooley & Triemer, 2002; Dettmer et al., 2005; Robinson & Fine, 1995).

The *channel* is the medium through which the communication is sent. Most messages in human communication are either seen or heard, thus the visual and auditory channels are used most frequently (Friend & Cook, 2007). In face-to-face interactions, verbal, nonverbal, and paralanguage (e.g., cadence, pitch, tone of voice) codes are employed. In written communication, telephone contacts, e-mail, or other systems where input is limited by the channel, however, there is a greater chance of communication breakdown (Hamilton, 2001) and, therefore, potential for conflict. Conferencers should be attentive to selecting the most appropriate channel through which to communicate with parents.

Another aspect to consider is the *congruence* of the message. Congruence occurs when the various aspects of the message such as facial expression, verbal components, and nonverbal components are communicating essentially the same thing (Pugach & Johnson, 2002). Conversely, if there are discrepancies between words and actions, mixed or incongruent messages may promote confusion, and subsequent conflict may result (Cormier & Nurius, 2003). For example, this excerpt from Friend and Cook (2007) illustrates a congruent message:

> The community liaison talked quietly with several parents while others freshened their coffee. When everyone returned to the seating area, he smiled and said, "If we're ready to continue I'd like to describe the role of the Community Liaison Office." He paused

and, smiling slightly, looked around the room as people took their seats in the semicircle of chairs. "We are here to talk things over with you. Whenever you have questions or want more information about your child's program, we will be here to discuss your concerns and try to answer questions." He paused, smiled slightly, and looked slowly around the room again. When he made eye contact with a group member, he maintained it long enough to give the member the opportunity to raise a question or offer a comment. "As parents we all have concerns," he continued, moving a chair into the semicircle to sit between Diane Long and Jerome Jackson. Putting his hand on the arm of Diane's chair and looking at her, he interrupted himself. "Diane, do you remember when my son started talking about getting a job and I ran checks on the business through the employee relations department at your office?" Smiling shyly and laughing, Diane said, "I surely do! That was one long week in our neighborhood." The community liaison laughed while still looking at Diane, then he leaned forward in his chair, put his elbows on his knees, and let his clasped hands fall between them. He glanced down for a silent second. Then, looking up, he said slowly, "Yes, as parents we all have concerns about the decisions our children make and the challenges they must face. We know we have to let go if we want our kids to grow into independent, productive, adult living. But it's hard—especially because we know their special needs." Quickening his pace slightly, he looked directly at each group member and said decidedly, "That's where the Community Liaison Office comes in. We have information about community opportunities, hazards, and supports; and we know your sons and daughters." (pp. 223–224)

This speaker's use of physical space (joining the group) and verbal (speaking softly and decidedly, laughing) and nonverbal behaviors (smiling, pausing for comments or questions, making eye contact) presented a consistent, congruent message that communicated clearly.

The communication process also depends on the accurate *decoding* of the sender's messages. This capacity relates directly to the receiver's attitudes, communication skills, background, experiences, and ability and willingness to collaborate. In addition, the accurate reception of messages relates to the receiver's ability to solicit feedback regarding assumptions made and the exactness of information decoded. In particular, this involves asking for clarification or examples to verify understanding of a message. In fact, given the many nuances of language, conferencers should ask more and assume less (File, 2001). Helpful strategies to obtain critical feedback, as discussed in Chapter 3, include clarification, paraphrasing, reflection, and summarization (Cormier & Nurius, 2003; Ivey & Ivey, 2003; Okum, 2002).

A related skill is the ability to provide feedback to senders. Although it is important to avoid making moral or value judgments, the receiver must be able to generate appropriate feedback. Without this mechanism the sender has no way of determining whether the message has been accurately received.

Finally, receivers, especially educators, must be sensitive to emotional and verbal cues. That is, in addition to the manifest content of the sender's message, receivers must also be able to focus and respond to affect. Numerous researchers and practitioners (Ivey & Ivey, 2003; Lambie, 2000a; Tillett & French, 2006; P. Zionts & Simpson, 1988) have concluded that the emotional content of a message may be the most salient feature, and thus the listening and responding process must consider this feature.

Communication:
The Key to Conflict Resolution

Though talking and exchanging information are typical, everyday functions, the process of really communicating and collaborating with another individual is different and often more difficult. True communication and collaboration, whether between parents and professionals, friends, or lovers, requires mutual acceptance, attentiveness, trust, and an atmosphere of good feelings. In these situations the participants assert an interest in and an understanding of another person as well as the information this individual attempts to impart.

Even though this propitious level of communication is ideal, it also lies within the bounds of many parent–educator conferences. One would be naive, of course, to expect this level of involvement in the absence of prior parental contact and rapport or with every parent; however, without at least a basic atmosphere of effective communication, a fruitful interpersonal relationship will remain unattainable. Interestingly, although both parents and educators have revealed the need and desire to communicate (Friend & Cook, 2007; Mundschenk, Foley, & Swedburg, 2005; Sicley, 1993), a high level of dissatisfaction persists regarding communication and collaboration opportunities. Without question, effective resolution of conflicts will be possible only in a suitable interpersonal atmosphere. In addition, such an atmosphere will aid in preventing irreconcilable disunion and conflict between parents and professionals.

Variables Associated With Conflict Resolution

A variety of factors will affect any interpersonal conflict and the approach selected for resolving the dissonance, including the nature of the conflict and its importance to the individuals involved in the discord, the time and resources required to gain resolution, the willingness of the participants to compromise and allow for concession, and the relationship and rapport that existed prior to the conflict. These factors influence not only the conflict resolution strategy chosen but also the potential for resolution. In situations involving cooperation, conflict resolution is likely; likewise, it is unrealistic to expect that any strategy will be effective when one or both parties are unwilling to collaborate and make adjustments. An illustration of this potential for resolution appears in Figure 9.1.

The Nature of the Conflict and Its Perceived Importance

The nature of the conflict and its perceived importance to parents, family members, and professionals present a major variable influencing any reconciliation. A situation perceived as significant will more frequently be associated with a position of inflexibility and steadfastness than one considered less consequential. When parents, family members, and educators

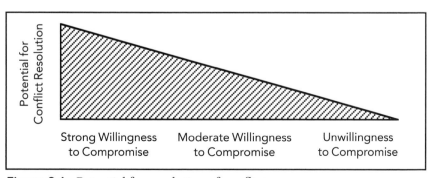

Figure 9.1. Potential for resolution of conflict.

all regard an issue as highly important, the conflict resolution process becomes even more intricate and difficult.

One set of parents, for example, had worked for several years to establish an association for children with exceptionalities in their community, and they considered their efforts directly responsible for the services their 12-year-old with a learning disability was receiving. When the recommendation was made to fully include their son, these parents openly and firmly resisted, noting that the boy had been unsuccessfully "mainstreamed" for several years prior to the development of what they considered an appropriate educational program. The child's teacher felt equally strongly that this student would benefit from an inclusion program, observing that he had made significant progress and was capable of functioning in a regular class setting. The strength with which the parents and teacher assumed their respective positions made the negotiation of a mutually satisfying outcome much more difficult than if such strong stands had not been taken.

Time and Resources Required for Resolution

Although resolution is possible in a majority of conflict situations, the success of the process will be associated with the amount of effort and the number of resources required to reach a solution. Because most educators (particularly classroom teachers) and families have time and resource limitations, the resolution of conflicts becomes possible only when the process operates within the means of the participants.

One classroom teacher involved in a curriculum conflict with the parents of an adolescent with retardation was unable to invest the time necessary to resolve the issue satisfactorily. Although the teacher felt that progress was being made, the amount of time required to work with the parents became unreasonable. The teacher ultimately referred the parents to a district administrator. Although not as well versed in knowledge of curriculum as the teacher, the administrator had more time to spend with the parents in negotiating a resolution.

Willingness of the Participants to "Lose"

Unfortunately, the conflict resolution process can sometimes take on an atmosphere in which the involved individuals perceive the inability to prevail as a failure. Especially when polarization occurs, or when extreme positions are adopted and strong affect is present, the resolution process—regardless of how strongly based on reason—can take on a "win–lose" flavor.

It is mandatory that the conferencer dissolve this atmosphere if successful conflict resolution is to occur.

Prior Relationship and Rapport

Perhaps the single most significant factor in resolving conflict between parents and educators is the nature of their preconflict relationship. It is not surprising that when parents and educators have a sound collaborative perspective based on mutual respect and effective communication, the resolution process will be much easier to achieve. Covey (1989) referred to this relationship as "an emotional bank account" (p. 18), a metaphor for the trust that has been developed between two individuals. In this regard, he noted that trust in a relationship develops in accordance with factors such as honesty, courtesy, kindness, and keeping commitments. Similarly, when individuals make withdrawals from their emotional bank accounts, because of failing to listen, betraying trust, overreacting, and so forth, they erode the amount of trust in a relationship and thus may be vulnerable to overdrawing their account. Without question, a sound relationship based on mutual respect and trust bodes well for parents and educators to effectively work out their differences.

Approaches to Conflict Resolution

Just as with any problem-solving strategy, a variety of ways emerge in which conflicts can be expressed and dissipated. Some are by nature more effective and appropriate than others, plus different conflict situations will create a need for different resolution approaches.

Avoidance

Individuals in conflict situations can either avoid the issues involved (and with it the disunion) or deal with them directly. Avoiding conflicts is an obvious option but by far the least acceptable. Not only is it difficult to avoid conflicts, but doing so can severely limit the growth potential of any collaborative relationship. As suggested by a number of researchers and practitioners, open, effective communication occurs only when participants feel confident in expressing their thoughts and feelings (Bradley, Brown, & Mack, 2000; Lambie, 2000b; A. Turnbull, Turnbull, Erwin, & Soodak, 2006).

Accommodation

Although a conciliatory and accommodating attitude is a necessary component of the effective conflict negotiation process, it is counterproductive as the sole means of resolving issues. Individuals may avoid conflicts and stress in their relationships simply by always accepting another individual's position, but this strategy has at least two major limitations. First, it is virtually impossible to be accommodating in all situations, particularly with individuals who are quite demanding or who request conditions that are inappropriate or unachievable. Second, this approach will almost always cause frustration and anger, thus serving to strain rather than support a collaborative relationship. Although an accommodating attitude is a basic requisite for effective conflict resolution, it offers neither an end in itself nor an adequate strategy for resolving conflicts.

Competition

The competitive style is characterized by a desire to satisfy personal concerns and goals at the expense of others (Bradley et al., 2000; Isenhart & Spangle, 2000; Rudawsky, Lundgren, & Grasha, 1999). The goal of the interaction often is to win, and so power struggles are common. There is a greater likelihood of suspicion and a hostile attitude toward the other party, and as a result the relationship may be damaged by competitive interactions.

Collaborative Problem Solving

An alternative to avoidance, accommodation, and competition is collaborative problem solving. This strategy has the distinct advantage of providing a means for meeting parents', families', and educators' needs while serving the best interests of the child. These circumstances, according to a number of authorities, lead to win–win situations (Covey, 1989; Friend & Cook, 2007; Isenhart & Spangle, 2000).

Successful problem solving depends on a variety of factors, including awareness that conflict resolution requires effective use of negotiation skills. Although some may consider negotiation alien to education, in fact educational conflict resolution resembles negotiations in business and politics. In particular, negotiation success is associated with these major factors: (a) availability of factual information surrounding an issue, (b) appropriate use of power, (c) institutional support, (d) effective communication skills, and (e) constructive openness.

AVAILABILITY OF PERTINENT FACTS

Availability of factual information surrounding the issue is a sine qua non of conflict resolution. Educators cannot resolve conflicts by means of facts alone, and they cannot enter into meaningful problem solving without background information and facts. Accordingly, those attempting to resolve conflicts with parents and families must have accurate information, such as student files, professional records, knowledge of pertinent protocol and policies, reports from other professionals, and so forth.

A teacher of a child with mild mental retardation discovered the importance of accurate information when attempting to resolve a conflict that involved withholding lunch from the student as a consequence of failure to complete assignments. The teacher was unaware that the student was diabetic and hence needed to follow a rigid eating schedule. Availability of such information could have prevented the conflict.

APPROPRIATE USE OF POWER

The power of each member presents another critical element in the negotiation process. *Power* here refers to one's capacity and willingness to take action and create change. The importance of such power in conflict resolution lies in the fact that individuals who lack the desire or capacity to make change when appropriate, or who fail to take suitable action, cannot engage in conflict resolution. When parents or family members believe that professionals are unable to take necessary action, their capacity to engage in problem solving becomes severely limited.

One element of power involves acknowledging one's capacity to create change. Educators often consider themselves relatively powerless, commenting that administrators, legislators, and other agencies hold the power and that they themselves have little decision-making authority. Yet educators have tremendous potential to implement change and thus to engage in problem solving and conflict resolution with parents and families. One of the first orders of business for educators wishing to enter into conflict resolution, therefore, is to acknowledge their capacity to produce change. Although not all conflict resolution and problem solving involves making changes, the potential for creating such conditions must exist.

Another element of power involves the willingness to take risks. Educators must be willing to admit when they or their program is in error and to acknowledge there are times when their program or policy must be maintained in spite of pressure to the contrary or when popular decisions are not the most appropriate. Furthermore, risk taking requires conceptualizing problems in a creative manner and selecting novel solutions and strategies. Obviously, the backing of administrators and colleagues is a major consideration in one's willingness to take risks.

A third element of power within the context of conflict resolution involves the ability and willingness to follow through on decisions and agreements. Nothing undermines families' confidence in professionals more than their failure to carry out what was agreed on. In an analysis of data on more than 6,000 individualized family service plans (IFSPs), Perry, Greer, Goldhammer, and Mackey-Andrews (2001) reported that on average only half of the service hours on the IFSPs were actually delivered to children and families. Likewise, Leiter and Krauss (2004) reported that although a small percentage of parents request additional related services for their children, 80% of parents who do request services reported problems in obtaining those services and were much more likely to be dissatisfied with their child's educational services. Educators must not only follow through on commitments and agreements but also ensure that others in the system (e.g., administrators, colleagues) do so as well.

Finally, educators sometimes face parents who appear to be demanding, legalistic, or unreasonable in their requests, acting as though they hold greater power in the relationship. Most demanding parents have experienced prior incidents that have left them with deep-seated mistrust of educators and the educational system in general (Lambie, 2000b; Miretzky, 2004; Soodak & Erwin, 2000). They may feel demeaned and as though they have been treated with condescension (McEwan, 2005) and may attempt to become an authority on interventions, service-delivery options, or instructional methodologies so that they can demand a specific course of action in order to be taken seriously by school personnel. It is important to remember that in a truly collaborative relationship, "expert power" works both ways; parents also have power (D. Brown, Pryzwansky, & Schulte, 2001). In fact, parents and families are uniquely qualified as authorities on their child; they know the child more intimately than any professional does. They should not be made to feel that they must acquire the professional skills and competencies of educators to be full collaborators with the school and to secure appropriate services for their child. Conferencers should demonstrate respect for the opinions and perspectives of parents by orchestrating opportunities for meaningful input and using effective communication strategies when differences arise. An appropriate response, for example, is "Although I do not see it that way, I do understand your belief and thus the feelings you have about this situation" (Lambie, 2000b, p. 7).

In addition, when individual interventions are not successful or programmatic changes need to be made, educators can avoid making parents feel defensive by simply providing the rationale and proposed goal of an intervention, which might promote a paradigm shift from problem-focused blame to solution-focused cooperation (O'Sullivan & Russell, 2006). In summary, productive conflict resolution may ultimately depend on professionals' skills in identifying and using appropriate power.

INSTITUTIONAL SUPPORT

Institutional support, as related to conflict resolution, involves obtaining support from administrators and others. This process entails making administrators and others aware of pertinent situations and, when necessary, including them in decision making. Thus, one teacher who anticipated a parental conflict over a decision to exclude an adolescent with a mild disability from the school bus for 3 days because of unacceptable behavior shared relevant facts and perceptions with his building principal and the director of special education. These individuals' attention to the matter resulted in support for the bus-exclusion decision during the resulting conflict with the youth's parents.

EFFECTIVE COMMUNICATION SKILLS

Effective problem solving also requires effective communication and interaction techniques, including an awareness of the needs and emotions of the parents, family members, and professionals involved in the conflict. Above all else, successful problem solving relies on good communication skills.

As previously noted, a basic feature of effective communication is the use of responsive listening skills (Cormier & Nurius, 2003), that is, attention to both the manifest and the emotional content of messages. Related to this listening process is the ability to respond empathically. This feedback mechanism presents a primary means by which educators can communicate interest and understanding, including acceptance of parents' feelings. This acceptance will in no way detract from the ability of the conferencer to negotiate; it will, in fact, produce the opposite effect. Although educators may not agree with parents and family members on particular issues, they must be able to understand the latter's position before attempting to resolve a conflict. Conferencers who can listen effectively provide a supportive environment for parents and family members where they can be heard without fear of blame. This atmosphere increases the parents' feelings of safety and their willingness to engage in collaborative problem solving, which can occur only when threatening conditions are removed. For example, Ruth's parents were upset that she had participated in a classroom birthday party, and they confronted her teacher, accusing her of acting recklessly because of Ruth's allergy to peanuts. The teacher listened calmly as Ruth's parents spoke and then assured them that she had made sure that all of the snacks were safe for Ruth because she knew how serious the condition was. Ruth's parents were immediately relieved, realized they had overreacted out of worry, and felt greater confidence in the teacher's understanding and commitment to Ruth.

The listening and responding process is also designed to provide feedback. This clarification and perception-checking mechanism serves to assure the person talking that the message is being received accurately and that the receiver is truly interested and listening. Listening does not require the conferencer to agree with the position taken by parents or family members; rather, it simply means communicating interest and understanding. The listener may also find it beneficial to acknowledge particular components of a person's message. By attending to and acknowledging the validity of portions of the person's position, and looking for areas of mutual agreement, the conferencer maintains an atmosphere conducive to problem solving while establishing a basis for inquiring, questioning, and negotiating on areas of disagreement. Such a procedure is far superior to attempts at arguing without this rapport-building mechanism.

CONSTRUCTIVE OPENNESS

Mutual problem solving also requires an atmosphere of constructive openness. Although one might assume that withholding feelings and opinions may reduce the chance of hurting, angering, or alienating parents and family members, it seldom accomplishes that goal. In instances where the conferencer is not open, the parent or family member is denied access to the feedback needed to build and maintain a relationship and to engage in collaborative problem solving. Constructive openness is not the same as undifferentiated candor but limited to responses that facilitate the relationship and problem-solving process. That is, confrontation and openness that are ends in themselves and that lack the potential to improve the relationship or solve the conflict should be avoided.

Constructive openness does make use of confrontation. Although confrontation may generate an image of anxiety and open dissension and thus be perceived as a detractor to the conflict resolution process, it can form an essential part of the negotiation process. To be effective, however, confrontation must be accompanied by other problem-solving tools and communication facilitators; it is a counterproductive process when employed independently of other basic communication and negotiating procedures. Conferencers should note that the intensity of any confrontation should be only as strong as the parent–educator relationship and should thus avoid strong and frequent confrontation in new and weakly formed collaborations.

Constructive confrontation allows for the opportunity to authentically identify one's feelings and frustrations. That is, it can serve as one primary avenue for expressing anger, emotion, or concern without producing additional conflict or stress. In particular, "I" messages (e.g., "I am concerned," "I am upset by . . .") have been identified as useful for this purpose (Cormier & Nurius, 2003; Ivey & Ivey, 2003; Kampwirth, 2006). These responses tend to be safer and more appropriate than "you" statements (e.g., "You are not doing what we agreed on," "You don't seem to be as concerned as you should be").

Constructive confrontation also tends to be most functional when employed in descriptive form. That is, the conferencer should report what is seen (e.g., "I have observed that James has not had his daily report card signed for 2 weeks"), what is felt (e.g., "I am concerned," "I am uncomfortable"), and what is desired or expected (e.g., "I would like to see us arrive at a mutually agreed-on plan"). Above all, the confrontation process must focus on the situation or behavior of concern rather than become an attack on the parents or family. Personal attacks simply do not facilitate the goal of improving communication or interpersonal openness.

Constructive confrontation is not an easy tool to use, but it offers a way of voicing concern while creating an atmosphere of openness and effective communication. It must thus be maintained as one possible strategy in the conferencer's repertoire.

A Model Conflict Resolution Process

Educators called on to resolve conflicts with parents and family members should adopt a strategy based on collaborative problem solving, active listening, mutual respect, shared decision making, and active negotiation. Moreover, the model used should be designed to produce win–win outcomes, as opposed to creating one winner and one loser. Such a strategy is described next.

Step 1: Set the Conditions for Collaborative Conflict Resolution

Nonjudgmental, or active, listening is the single most important tool in handling conflict effectively (Cheldelin & Lucas, 2004). That is, the parties involved in the conflict should each demonstrate a willingness to understand the position of the other without challenging, interrupting, or otherwise interfering with an individual's ability to communicate. Because professionals will likely have little control over parents' willingness to listen reciprocally, they should take a leadership position in this regard by indicating the advisability of this process (e.g., "I would like to recommend that each of us listen to the other person so that we can understand one another and see where we agree and disagree") and by setting a good example for active listening, including attempts at understanding the emotions that accompany a message. Though these steps will guarantee neither an understanding of the differing perceptions and positions involved in a dispute nor an effective problem-solving atmosphere, they will obviously go a long way toward achieving these goals.

A second element associated with this process involves professionals' attempts to separate their perceptions and feelings toward the individual(s) with whom they are disagreeing from the substantive issues of the conflict. In all too many cases, individuals become so entangled with the personal variables in a conflict that they lose sight of the end goals. As a case in point, the parents of a young child were asking the school district to make substantial curricular and procedural classroom changes to accommodate their child. Their approach, however, was extremely adversarial, threatening, and demanding, and eventually the district personnel involved in the conflict began losing sight of the substantive issues associated with the case (i.e., the merits of what the parents were asking for). That is, rather than focusing on the requests and concerns, the district representatives reacted primarily to the parents' attacks, criticisms, and threatening demeanor. Such a reaction is, of course, understandable and natural, but educators must remind themselves that their positive or negative feelings about parents should be kept separate from their attempts to resolve substantive issues. Because neither professionals nor parents will be immune to personal attacks and criticism, and because such variables will likely generate emotions that may interfere with problem solving, techniques such as using cognitive self-prompting (e.g., reminding oneself to concentrate on the issues) and constructive confrontation and delaying problem-solving attempts until both parties are more in control of their emotions are advisable.

The initial intent for resolving conflicts should be to learn by working together (Dettmer et al., 2005). Such an approach sets a tone that facilitates creative reconciliation of differences, encourages reciprocal responses on the part of parents (thereby furthering a productive collaborative climate), and helps both parents and educators concentrate on salient points of agreement and difference. Dettmer and colleagues reminded educators of the rule they teach children for crossing the street, but they applied it to developing rapport and dealing with conflict and emotions:

Stop talking, judging, and giving advice;
Look at the long-term outcome of good communication; and
Listen to parents, colleagues, and others who work in collaboration for children with special needs.

Setting the conditions for collaborative conflict resolution also involves identifying the problem, its owners, and the individuals associated with the conflict. Pugach and Johnson (2002) noted that problems may be child centered, curriculum centered, teacher centered, or an issue of the larger school community. Friend and Cook (2007) observed that the most difficult step in problem solving is identifying and defining the problem and that successful interactions will be possible only if the problem is accurately delineated: "Phrasing problems as questions conveys to participants that 'answers' are possible and lends a constructive tone to collaborative problem solving" (p. 35).

One way for conferencers to begin the conflict resolution process is to assertively state the idea or position about a particular problem, describing the impact on themselves using "I" statements such as "I feel let down" and demonstrating concern for other individuals who have joint ownership in the issue with statements such as "I realize that . . ." (Dettmer et al., 2005). Active listening, whereby the individual commencing the process attempts to understand the other individual's position and perception, should follow this initiating response. This component of the process requires that a relationship appropriate for conflict resolution exists, that the parents be able to engage in verbal interactions, and that sufficient time be allotted for the process. Finally, the process requires that both parties be willing to work toward a solution to the problem.

Step 2: Identify and Evaluate Possible Solutions for Resolving the Conflict

On the basis of the aforementioned effective communication principles and subsequent to an agreement by the parents and professionals to try to solve the problem, parents and professionals should attempt to jointly and collaboratively generate possible solutions to the identified problem. Friend and Cook (2007) recommended that all persons affiliated with the issue participate in the process, that individuals involved in the process be encouraged to be creative in their problem solving, and that each suggestion be given serious consideration. This requires first brainstorming all possible solutions then identifying feasible solutions to the identified problem. As part of the win–win approach, Covey (1989) suggested participants make a list of the results that they would consider a fully acceptable solution and look for new options to obtain those results. Accordingly, the next step is for participants to collaboratively select and implement the problem-solving strategy with the most apparent utility and acceptability to the participants. Only after individuals have had ample opportunity to generate possible solutions should evaluations of alternatives proceed. Again, this process should be structured such that both the parents and family members and the conferencer have equal opportunities to evaluate alternatives.

Step 3: Implement a Mutually Agreed-On Problem-Solving Strategy

Participants should recognize at this point in the problem-solving process that substantial resolution progress has been made. That is, important interpersonal and communication factors have been addressed, and conditions for conflict resolution have been set in motion. Moreover, the individuals involved have had opportunities to recommend possible solutions to the problem as well as to evaluate each solution suggested. Participants must then decide on an action plan and the specifics of what can be done to ensure that the solution to the identified problem becomes a reality (Hamilton, 2001; McEwan, 2005). As was noted earlier, the success of this component of the resolution process will depend on the participants' willingness to contribute their efforts to the program, to collaborate and compromise, and to seek win–win solutions.

Step 4: Evaluate the Mutually Agreed-On Problem-Solving Strategy and Make Modifications as Needed

This final, equally important, stage of conflict resolution consists of evaluating the solution outcomes (Friend & Cook, 2007; Taylor, 2000), the fidelity with which the solution was implemented (E. J. Martin & Hagan-Burke, 2002), and the participants' satisfaction with the selection (Friend & Cook, 2007; Kroth & Edge, 2007). In instances where success or consensus is not within reach, the conflict resolution process may be reinitiated or other problem-solving steps may be taken.

Use of the recommended collaborative conflict resolution process is illustrated in the case of a dispute involving the parents of a student with a learning disability. In this example, the parents were notified by their son's former learning disability teacher that the child, who had been included in a general education classroom for several months, was having problems in this setting. The child's general education teacher questioned his appropriateness for a general education classroom, but his parents were strongly committed to their son being in an inclusive setting. The special education teacher, who was serving as a consultant to teachers of children in inclusion programs in the district, requested a conference to discuss the problem. At this meeting, attended by the parents, the general education classroom teacher, and the special educator, the parents were informed that although their son's academic performance was satisfactory, he had recently developed a number of behavioral problems. The parents were shown behavioral charts that indicated excessive vocalizations and non-compliance. Both teachers revealed concern over the behavior and suggested that a strategy for managing the problem be selected. The educators acknowledged that the problem was in their domain and thus was their responsibility (and that they were willing to take total charge of the problem); however, they indicated a desire to include the parents in the solution. This approach was taken in part because on several occasions in the past the parents had complained that school personnel had not included them in their planning efforts or kept them informed.

The parents, when informed of the problem, responded that they had not experienced an increase in behavioral problems at home. They did, however, accept partial ownership of the problem and voiced a willingness to be involved in the intervention process. The parents and educators subsequently discussed alternatives for managing the problem. Options included additional individualized classroom attention, periodic visitations to the school counselor, medication, various reinforcement and punishment contingencies, and a cooperative home–school communication program. Once presented, the advantages and disadvantages of each alternative were discussed.

These discussions resulted in the selection of a home–school communication program as the best option. Specifically, the program consisted of the teacher issuing 10 behavioral evaluations to the child over the course of each day. Each evaluation, reported as "satisfactory" or "needs improvement," was recorded on an index card and given to the child immediately after it was made. The child was required to bring home at least seven satisfactory cards per day to receive a reward of his choosing. Following the initial conference between the parents and teachers, the program was discussed with the child and subsequently implemented. The educators and parents remained in close contact throughout the course of the program to judge its effectiveness and make necessary adjustments.

Analyzing Your Conflict Resolution Style

If educators were to honestly analyze their style in interacting and resolving conflicts with parents and family members, they would probably discover they have some characteristics that are far more facilitative than others. Therefore, it important for conferencers to be aware of how conflicts arise, the ways in which their manner contributes to conflicts, and the options that are available for resolution.

Figure 9.2, "Analyzing Your Style," provides educators a simple method for examining the manner in which they interact with parents and family members. Respondents should be honest, of course, in completing the form. After responding to the survey, educators might find it helpful to ask a colleague or parent to complete it as observers of their style. Analyzing and discussing with others how that style affects relationships and conflict resolution approaches with parents and family members can help educators get a better picture of themselves in these interactions. Although this survey does not purport to make quantitative comparisons or predictions, it does offer a revealing means of looking at problem-solving styles.

Problem-solving and conflict resolution skills must be a reliable part of each conferencer's repertoire. In addition, it is important to realize that an individual's style, personality, attitude, and demeanor will affect the resolution process. Even more significant than the conflict resolution model or the problem-solving approach ultimately selected are the participants' interpersonal characteristics. Thus, educational conferencers must not only work to develop their listening, negotiation, and other communication skills but also find ways of becoming aware of their own interpersonal style. Without such awareness, the most salient component of problem solving will remain an enigma.

Due Process Safeguards

Sometimes even the best efforts to resolve conflicts in a collaborative and constructive manner are not successful. Probably no single phrase in edu-

Are you . . .	Always	Frequently	Sometimes	Never
1. Able to stay informed about the parents with whom you relate and their family situation?	☐	☐	☐	☐
2. Irritated by parents who offer alternatives for managing the classroom behavior of their children?	☐	☐	☐	☐
3. Willing to let parents tutor their own children at home?	☐	☐	☐	☐
4. Honest with parents?	☐	☐	☐	☐
5. Able to confront parents?	☐	☐	☐	☐
6. Prone to arguments with parents?	☐	☐	☐	☐
7. Aware of how your emotions are communicated through your body language?	☐	☐	☐	☐
8. Willing to "take risks" with parents?	☐	☐	☐	☐
9. Prone to active listening with parents?	☐	☐	☐	☐
10. Annoyed by parents who suggest curriculum ideas?	☐	☐	☐	☐
11. Threatened by parents who initiate a conference?	☐	☐	☐	☐
12. Threatened by parents who request access to school records and data?	☐	☐	☐	☐
13. Willing to engage in joint problem solving with parents?	☐	☐	☐	☐
14. Uneasy about admitting to parents that you don't have all the answers?	☐	☐	☐	☐
15. Threatened by aggressive parents?	☐	☐	☐	☐
16. Uncomfortable with parents who display emotional behavior?	☐	☐	☐	☐
17. Prone to make assumptions about the parents with whom you interact?	☐	☐	☐	☐
18. Creative in problem-solving strategies?	☐	☐	☐	☐
19. Reluctant to make changes in the ways you deal with parents?	☐	☐	☐	☐
20. Troubled by what you wish you had said but did not say in conferences with parents?	☐	☐	☐	☐

Figure 9.2. Analyzing your style. *Note.* Although reference is made to "parents," items also refer to family members.

cation produces a more visceral response than "due process." Both parents and educators seem to associate it with legal involvement, conflict, and proceedings more aligned with a courtroom than an educational setting. The provisions of procedural due process, however, as specified in the Individuals with Disabilities Education Improvement Act (IDEA, 2004) to govern the assessment, educational placement, transfer, and rights of children and youth with exceptionalities, essentially comprise the parents', student's, or school district's right to challenge a recommended course of action.

The basic concepts associated with educational due process were initially articulated in *Pennsylvania Association for Retarded Children (PARC) v. Commonwealth of Pennsylvania* (1972). In the decision, the court stipulated that no child with mental retardation can be assigned or reassigned to either regular or special education status or kept from receiving a public education without a prior recorded hearing before a special hearing officer. The court decision was also accompanied by a series of steps detailing the operational elements of due process, much of which is currently, at least in concept, a part of the procedural protections contained in IDEA. The procedural protections afforded parents and children under IDEA fall under several broad categories, including parental access to records, independent evaluations, surrogate parents, parental notice, and right to file a due process complaint (see 20 U.S.C. § 1412–1415).

Parents or legal guardians have access to all records and data pertaining to the identification, assessment, and program planning of their child. This component accentuates the need not only for a complete and thorough evaluation but also for an accurate and professional report of the findings and recommendations to parents.

Parents and legal guardians are also entitled to obtain an evaluation of their son or daughter at public expense from qualified (licensed or certified) examiners not affiliated with the district or agency recommending the action if they can demonstrate in a hearing that the evaluation conducted was deficient or biased or that the district or agency did not have available qualified examiners. Parents may also secure an independent evaluation at their own expense if they are dissatisfied with the school's evaluation, and that evaluation must be considered by individuals charged with making disposition recommendations.

The importance of initial rapport and an adequate multidisciplinary and comprehensive evaluation cannot be overemphasized. As dissatisfaction is frequently associated with a lack of parental input or involvement, diagnostic and assessment teams should be able to both support their findings and provide parents with the opportunity for input into the analysis of the issues and intervention strategies.

In instances where a child or adolescent is a ward of the state or the parents are unavailable or unknown, the appointment of a surrogate parent must take place. Surrogate parents are commissioned to represent the child in all matters pertaining to evaluation and program planning. Like biological parents or legal guardians, surrogates must be provided written notice of any proposed changes in the identification, evaluation, or educational placement of the child or of the school's decision not to make such changes. In addition, the school district must provide parents, guardians, or surrogates a copy of all of the procedural safeguards available to them each school year and in the following situations:

- at initial referral or if a parent requests an evaluation,
- upon receipt of the first state complaint or first due process complaint in a school year,
- as required under the discipline procedures, and
- if a parent requests a copy (IDEA, 2004).

Parents also have the right to reimbursement of their attorney's fees if they prevail in a due process hearing or judicial proceeding. Conversely, the court may also award attorney's fees to school districts for frivolous or unfounded complaints brought by parents.

These procedures are in place to protect eligible students and their families and to ensure the child receives a free appropriate public education. If the procedural or substantive requirements of IDEA are absent or misapplied, serious conflict situations may result that trigger filing a due process complaint.

Due Process Complaint

Parents and legal guardians must have a formal opportunity to present complaints on any matter relating to the identification, evaluation, programming, or educational placement of their child (IDEA, 2004). This process is designed to afford parents, schools, and agencies the chance for an objective and structured hearing, the outcome of which will lead to an appropriate educational program in the least restrictive environment for the child. The complaint process includes three components: mediation, resolution process, and due process hearing.

MEDIATION

Each state is required to have a mediation process by which a neutral third party assists parents and school districts in arriving at a mutually satisfactory decision (IDEA, 2004). Mediation is voluntary and may not be used to delay a parent's right to a hearing. It allows for less formal discussions facilitating resolution early in the complaint process and may nurture rather than destroy the trust and cooperation between home and school. Mediation can produce excellent outcomes, but only if both parents and school personnel are willing to move from their intractable position to one of compromise through a process of effective communication and problem solving (Margolis, 1999; Mills & Duff-Mallams, 2000). The formalized written mediation agreement, signed by parents and the school district representative, is legally binding and enforceable in state or federal court.

RESOLUTION PROCESS

IDEA requires the school district to call a resolution session within 15 calendar days of receipt of the parent's due process complaint (2004). The purpose of the session is to provide parents and relevant members of the IEP (Individualized Education Program) team who have specific knowledge of the facts identified in the complaint an opportunity to discuss the basis of the complaint so that the issue might be resolved. Both the parents and the school district may agree in writing to waive this resolution session or to substitute the IDEA mediation process. If the issue is resolved, a legally binding settlement agreement is signed that is enforceable in state or federal court and that may be voided by either party within 3 business days of its execution. If the complaint is not resolved within 30 calendar days of its receipt, a due process hearing may occur. The resolution session is another step toward attempting to resolve disagreements in a less adversarial setting than a due process hearing (Mandlawitz, 2007).

DUE PROCESS HEARING

When a due process complaint is received, the parents or school district involved has an opportunity for an impartial hearing (IDEA, 2004). Hearings can be held by the state, intermediate, or local educational agency, depending on the situations and state regulations. School districts and agencies must apprise parents of their due process rights under IDEA. These rights include the following:

- The right to a fair and impartial hearing that parents may choose to open to the public. This right specifically affords the disputing parties the opportunity for an orderly hearing coordinated by a qualified and objective hearing officer who has neither a professional nor personal interest in the outcome of the hearing. Hearing officers thus cannot be employees of the school or agency involved in the action.

- The right of the parents to have both their child and the counsel of their choice present at the hearing. Those who function as counsel can be professionals (e.g., attorney, educator, or psychologist) or another parent or advocate whom the parents or legal custodian considers appropriate to represent their interests and those of the child. Both the parents and their counsel are guaranteed access to information and data employed by the school or agency in recommending the disputed action. The parents and their counsel also have authority to present expert witnesses and testimony (e.g., educational, medical, or psychological) in support of their position and to cross-examine individuals presenting information on behalf of the agency or school. Only evidence that is disclosed at least 5 days prior to the hearing can be presented.

- The right of the parents to a verbatim recording of the hearing. This record must be made by a mechanical recording device or an official court reporter. Unless the involved parties agree to an extension, the hearing must be held and a final decision rendered by the hearing officer within 45 days after the resolution session or joint agreement to waive the session. The parents must be provided a copy, at no cost, of the decision report.

- The right of both parents and school districts to appeal the decision of the hearing officer. Generally, the first level of appeal is to the state education office. Further appeals, however, can be made through the traditional court system. From the time of the request for a due process hearing through the appeal process, the child remains in the setting he or she was assigned to prior to the recommended action unless school officials and parents agree to another arrangement, the hearing officer orders a change, or a judicial decree orders a new placement (Osborne & Russo, 2006).

Although due process complaint procedures exist as a necessary and essential safeguard, they should not serve as a routine mode for arbitrating differences. Individuals with experience in formal due process hearings are quick to point out that they are adversarial by their nature and rarely lead to mutually satisfying decisions. Accordingly, both educators and parents must develop other means for resolving differences and gaining appropriate services for children. Indeed, more and more school districts and agencies are relying on a variety of conflict resolution measures to avoid a formal due process hearing whenever possible.

Summary

Planning for children and youth with exceptionalities and coordinating the viewpoints and goals of the parents and professional educators involved will periodically result in conflicts. Although at times formidable, the process of negotiating mutually satisfying alternatives can provide a powerful growth experience for both parents and educators and can lead to creative planning for students. When parents and educators are open and willing to engage in problem-solving and conflict resolution processes, most issues can be dealt with satisfactorily. Although conflict may appear to be an area to avoid, its pervasive and salient nature in the parent–educator relationship mandates appropriate strategies for its eventual occurrence and resolution.

Exercises

1. Complete Figure 9.2, "Analyzing Your Style." Discuss characteristics of parents and professionals that can facilitate and detract from a desirable conflict resolution atmosphere.

2. Conduct a conflict resolution simulation conference using the materials in Appendix C. Descriptions are provided for the cases previously presented for other role-play exercises (i.e., Teddy and Terri). Consequently, you should use those materials most aligned with your area or those that you have used in previous role-playing.

   In conducting the simulation exercise, one individual should assume the part of the parent, using those materials labeled "Parent Information." Another person, taking the part of the teacher, should structure his or her responses around the "Educator/Professional Information." A third individual should take the role of the evaluator, using the evaluation form provided.

   Participants should assume that the conference is parent initiated; that is, the parent in the exercise contacted the educator regarding the described issue. Individuals should change roles after completing the exercise.

PART 3

Addressing the Issues and Needs of Families Across the Years

Chapter 10

Parents and Families of Young Children With Exceptionalities

Alan is very cheerful. He pretty much does his own thing, marches to the beat of his own drum. Although he's going on 3 years old, he still really doesn't play with other children. When his older brothers, ages 6 and 4, come into the room, he will sometimes leave and go play somewhere else, but if they are running around the house or wrestling, he'll join in the running or wrestling or those really active type of games. He loves interacting with adults. He's very loving. He hates elevators, and he doesn't like loud noises. He loves playing in water and doesn't like having shoes or socks or anything on his feet. As soon as we enter a building, it doesn't matter if it's home or not, he wants those shoes and socks to come off. He's really good at letter and number recognition. He really likes that and wants other people to draw them. He'll say 'number 4' or 'H.' He also responds really well to music. You don't have to sing a song too many times for him to know the words and sing along. He loves wooden puzzles.

Some of his weaknesses are his expressive and receptive language. He's behind there. His dad and I think he has the words. Getting him to use them is hard. Getting him to follow directions is hard. Sometimes he can follow one-step directions that he has done several times before, but to ask him to do something he hasn't done . . . sometimes it's hard to get him to focus in on you so you can tell him the direction. He also has trouble with anything that's not in his routine or that he doesn't want to do at the present time.

At this point Alan is considered 'at risk.' He is scheduled for a diagnostic evaluation in 2 weeks. For Alan, his teachers would be more like therapists. We see his therapists on a weekly basis, and because he falls in the category of 'birth to 3,' either his father or I am in all of his therapy sessions. Alan has speech therapy twice a week and developmental therapy once a week, and he is about to start occupational therapy for some sensory issues. There is a 6-month review of what Alan has accomplished on his IFSP [Individualized Family Service Plan] and what his next goals are, and it's a team effort between the therapist and us parents. I'd like for him to be able to have more direction and more self-help skills where he doesn't need guidance all the time. We all have input on what we've seen, and the therapists have things that they suggest. Of course, we as parents have our say as to what we want to do as far as following up on those suggestions, and I think we always do, and we usually are in agreement concerning Alan. We communicate by talking on a weekly basis face-to-face.

We just had our 6-month review for Alan. They were very informative, the therapists and case manager. Because Alan is turning 3 in March, there were some things to go over as far as transitions going from the birth to 3 program to the programs offered once the child is 3. They were very helpful as far as giving me information as to what our rights are and other types of services that Alan could receive.

Our family is pretty close—we live close and have close relationships. Family members, of course, usually try to help out as best they can, especially his grandmother who lives close by. She also helps out when there is something special going on with Alan that we need to do, like if we need child care, she offers it. There is support at the university; there's an organization called Southern Regional Early Childhood Programs. It offers programs for families, and actually being involved in those programs has helped me find the resources for Alan as far as speech evaluation, knowing if there were developmental delays, and how to contact Child and Family Connections for children from birth to 3. Child and Family Connections has resources, too, and you get to meet other families—it's a good support.

Professionals have long recognized that a family member's age is a salient factor in parent and family conferencing because the needs of parents and families vary according to the stages of a child's development (Dunst, 2000; Friend, 2006; Hallahan & Kauffman, 2003; Odom & Wolery, 2003). There is, of course, strong evidence that parents and families play a prominent role in a child's development and consequently must constitute a significant component of any educational program (Bailey et al., 1998; Dunst, Hambry, Trivette, Raab, & Bruder, 2000; Lucyshyn, Dunlap, & Albin, 2002; McWilliam, Wolery, & Odom, 2001; Wacharasin, Barnard, &

Spieker, 2003). As observed by Bronfenbrenner (1974), evidence indicates that the family is the most effective and economical system for fostering and sustaining the development of the child. The evidence indicates further that the involvement of the child's family as an active participant is critical to the success of any intervention program. (p. 55)

The growing attention to involving parents of young children results in large measure from legislative advances that have taken place that focus on early intervention. Recognizing the inadequacy of services for young children with disabilities, Congress included provisions in the 1986 amendments (PL 99-457) to what is now the Individuals with Disabilities Education Improvement Act (IDEA, 2004), which mandated comprehensive services for infants and toddlers and their families. Part B of the act requires that a free appropriate public education be provided to children with disabilities ages 3 to 21 and to articulate the components of the education in an Individualized Education Program (IEP). Section 619 of that act also authorizes funds in the form of grants for children ages 3 to 5. Part C provides all states with grants to serve children from birth to age 3 to meet the needs outlined in the Individualized Family Service Plan (IFSP) (Heward, 2006; Yell, 2006). Because of efforts to comply with these regulations, the availability of parent programs and family involvement opportunities has increased significantly.

Parents' and professionals' changing expectations regarding the need for parent and family involvement have also brought about expanded services. Because parents and professionals are becoming more accustomed to working together, the former are demanding and the latter are acknowledging that parents of children and youth with exceptionalities should become a part of their child's program. There is also increased awareness that a child's age, to some extent, determines parental and family needs and, subsequently, the services to be rendered. Parents of preschool children, for example, need information on normal child growth and development and appropriate future expectations for their child and should be made aware of home- and community-based resources, programs, and training methods. Parents and families of young children with disabilities may also require emotional support and information that are different from those needs of parents of an older child on how to interact with their child.

Eligibility for Services

What is now Part C of IDEA requires states to develop and implement interagency programs of early intervention services for children from birth to age 3 who are experiencing developmental delays or have a diagnosed physical or mental condition (Yell, 2006). Some children have special needs that were identified at a very early age such as autism, physical disability, or visual impairment (Scarborough et al., 2004). Because, however, of the inherent difficulties in identifying young children correctly, funding and service delivery under Part C is noncategorical. This means that children are not required to be eligible for services under a specific category of disability but may be eligible under the rubric of "developmentally delayed" (Friend, 2006; T. E. C. Smith, Gartin, Murdick, & Hilton, 2006), and many children, such as Alan in the opening vignette, may be classified as "at risk" for developmental delays.

IDEA broadly defines developmental delay as a documented delay in one or more of the cognitive, communicative, physical, social and emotional, or adaptive behavior domains, and each state determines the specific criteria for delay (Scarborough, Hebbeler, & Spiker, 2006). For example, a 25% delay or 2 standard deviations below the mean on a standardized measure in one of the domains or a 20% delay in two or more domains has been used as a criterion for services in many states (Shackelford, 2004). Data from the National Early Intervention Longitudinal Study, commissioned by the U.S. Department of Education, indicate that of the children receiving early intervention services, 62% who began prior to 31 months of age were eligible because of developmental delay, 22% were eligible because of a diagnosed condition, and 17% were eligible because they were determined to be at risk for developmental delay (Scarborough et al., 2006). These data indicate considerable variability in the infants and toddlers who enter early intervention services and suggest that there is no typical child in early intervention (Scarborough et al., 2004).

Children from ages 3 to 5 are served under Part B of the act, usually in early childhood special education programs, Head Start, or other center programs (Odom et al., 2000). The requirements for these programs are similar to those governing services for school-age children with the exception that in addition to determining eligibility based on an identified disability (e.g., mental retardation, hearing impairments, orthopedic impairments), states and local education agencies may also, at their discretion, serve children ages 3 to 9 who are experiencing developmental delays (Hanson & Lynch, 2004).

Family-Centered Services

One key to successful early intervention and early childhood special education programs is the commitment to and development of collaborative home–school relationships that treat families with respect and empower them to participate in shared decision making. The educator's role in these programs is to work collaboratively with families to identify their priorities, to obtain needed supports and services, and to capitalize on existing family strengths and capacities (Morrison, 2004; Trivette & Dunst, 2005; R. Turnbull, Turnbull, Shank, & Smith, 2004). Such collaboration will strengthen the family's ability to provide the child with appropriate learning opportunities and increase positive outcomes for the family.

Recognition of this fact has contributed to the emergence of a philosophy of service delivery that moves intervention efforts from an agency-oriented approach to a family-oriented approach (Guralnick, 2005; McLean & Shaeffer, 2003). In fact, family-centered services are recommended as "best practice" in both early intervention and early childhood education (National Association for the Education of Young Children, 2005). Many different terms have been used to describe this philosophy such as *family centered* (McLean & Shaeffer, 2003; R. Turnbull, Huerta, & Stowe, 2006), *family focused*, and *family based* (Hanson & Lynch, 2004), but each focuses efforts on the child *within the context of the family*, not simply on the child alone.

Trivette and Dunst (2005) identified the key elements of family-based practices:

> Family-based practices provide or mediate the provision of resources and supports necessary for families to have the time, energy, knowledge, and skills to provide their children learning opportunities and experiences that promote child competence and development. Resources and supports provided as part of early intervention/early childhood special education are done in a family-centered manner so family-based practices will have child, parent and family strengthening and competency-enhancing consequences. (p. 107)

According to Dunst and Trivette (1996), family-centered practices contain two critical components: relational and participatory. The relational component includes practices associated with good clinical skills (e.g., active listening, compassion, empathy, respect) and professional beliefs and attitudes about families, especially related to parenting competencies. The participatory component includes practices that are responsive to family concerns and priorities and provide families with opportunities to be actively involved in making decisions. The inclusion of both of these components is what distinguishes the family-centered approach from other approaches to working with families (Dunst & Trivette, 1996). For example, parents may identify as a family priority the interactions involving their young child with disabilities and his or her siblings and may request assistance in facilitating appropriate play activities between the children, or they may ask for suggestions for helping siblings understand the disability (P. A. Gallagher & Rhodes, 2004). In a family-centered approach, the professionals would not only utilize effective communication strategies but also respond to the family's priority by providing parents with information to capitalize on their existing strengths and to learn new skills to facilitate positive interactions within the family.

It is important that teachers acquire the full range of knowledge and skills necessary to implement family-centered practices including communication, teamwork, and family systems models (Rupiper & Marvin, 2004). When more attention is paid to *how they interact* with families rather than to *how they include them as collaborative partners* in program planning, early childhood professionals may be stronger in their relational practices than in their participatory practices. As a consequence, programs may not be as family centered as is often claimed (Dunst, 2002; Mandell & Murray, 2005; Rush, Shelden, & Hanft, 2003). Educators must be attuned to including both relational and participatory components in their professional practices serving young children with disabilities as well as in the written program plans for early intervention, the IFSP.

The Individualized Family Service Plan

Under Part C of IDEA (34 CFR § 303.12), infants, toddlers, and their families have the right to an IFSP that specifies which services will be provided to the child and family. Examples of such services include assistive technology, family training, counseling and home visits, physical therapy, occupational therapy, psychological services, social work services, speech and language services, vision services, transportation, and special instruction. Although some of these services focus exclusively on the child and some focus on the family, all benefit both the child and the family (R. Turnbull et al., 2006). IDEA also allows states to give families the option of continuing early intervention services beyond age 3, thereby delaying entrance into preschool programs and continuing to use the IFSP. The families, however, may be required to pay for some services (D. D. Smith, 2007).

A multidisciplinary and interagency team including parents, a service coordinator, and other personnel qualified to deliver the services articulated in the IFSP, such as a speech and language therapist, develops the IFSP. The IFSP must be written and contain the following:

- a statement of the infant's or toddler's present level of physical development, cognitive development, communication development, social or emotional development, and adaptive development, based on objective criteria;
- a statement of the family's resources, priorities, and concerns relating to enhancing the development of the family's infant or toddler with a disability;
- a statement of the major outcomes expected to be achieved for the infant or toddler and the family and the criteria, procedures, and timelines used to determine the degree to which progress toward achieving the outcomes is being made and whether modifications or revisions of the outcomes or services are necessary;
- a statement of specific early intervention services necessary to meet the unique needs of the infant or toddler and the family, including frequency, intensity, and method of delivering services;
- a statement of the natural environments in which early intervention services shall appropriately be provided, including a justification of the extent, if any, to which the services will not be provided in a natural environment;
- the projected dates for initiation of services and the anticipated duration of the services;
- the identification of the service coordinator from the profession most immediately relevant to the infant's or toddler's or family's needs who will be responsible for the implementation of the plan and coordination with other agencies and persons; and
- the steps to be taken to support the transition of the toddler with a disability to preschool or other appropriate services (IDEA, 20 U.S.C. § 1436 (d)).

Parent participation in the development of the IFSP is an essential component of family-centered services and is a hallmark of early intervention programming (Spann, Kohler, & Soenksen, 2003; Unger, Jones, Park, & Tressell, 2001; C. Zhang & Bennett, 2003). In the IFSP process, decisions are made by the team, not by individuals, and families may decline all or some of the recommended services without jeopardizing their receipt of other, mutually agreed-on services (Perry, Greer, Goldhammer, & Mackey-Andrews, 2001).

In the IFSP, identified outcomes should directly relate to one or more of the family's priorities or concerns. Professionals need to recognize that the hopes and goals that parents have for their child are influenced by the values, beliefs, and cultural context of the family. An understanding of this cultural context is necessary to identify realistic and socially valid child and family outcomes (Harry, 2002; C. Zhang & Bennett, 2003). Once the goals or outcomes are identified and operationally defined, the IFSP needs to include an evaluation component that systematically measures outcomes for both the child and the family (Bruder, 2005; Harbin, Rous, & McLean, 2005; Jung, Gomez, & Baird, 2004; Park et al., 2003). For example, an outcome for the child might be to communicate more effectively, whereas an outcome for the family might be to participate more fully in community recreational activities. In evaluating family-centered services on behalf of young children, professionals need to determine whether (a) they are providing the legally required services for families, (b) those services are consistent with the current philosophy of recommended practices, and (c) they are achieving desirable outcomes for families (Bailey, 2001; Bailey et al., 1998).

Thus, the development of the IFSP represents a family-centered and culturally responsive model where the full and active participation of parents and family members is encouraged and outcomes are evaluated (Hanson & Lynch, 2004; R. Turnbull et al., 2006).

Program Types

A variety of published research has supported the efficacy of early intervention with children with disabilities and disadvantaged children (Bailey et al., 2005; Bock, Stoner, Beck, Hanley, & Prochnow, 2005; Morrison, 2004; Odom & Strain, 2002; B. J. Smith et al., 2002; Wolery & Bailey, 2002) and serves as the basis for early childhood programs. Because parents present the major source of information, stimulation, and social influence for young children, their involvement is indispensable.

Hospital-Based Programs

Some families begin receiving early intervention services for their newborn in the neonatal intensive care unit (NICU) of the hospital because of low birth weight or other high-risk conditions or for health care needs (Barry & Singer, 2001). These services may be provided by a variety of professionals such as neonatologists who provide medical care, nurses who provide on-going care, social workers who assist families with emotional and financial concerns, and psychologists or developmental therapists who promote positive interactions between the infant and parents (Heward, 2006; Lovett & Haring, 2003).

Home-Based Programs

Birth to 3 programs are typically offered in the child's home or child care center, or a combination of the two, whereas preschool services are generally delivered within a school setting such a Head Start program, community preschool, or public school classroom (Hadden, 2004). Home-based programs typically include an early childhood interventionist who consults with families in their home and models appropriate strategies for working directly with the child. The emphasis is on supporting families in ways to foster the child's development and learning and to build parents' confidence in working with their child (Dunst & Bruder, 2002). There are several advantages to home-based programs, including the following:

- Parents have ready access to the professionals and typically communicate regularly with these providers.
- The services are implemented in the child's home environment and are more likely to be natural and appropriate.
- Other family members such as siblings and grandparents can observe and participate in the activities and provide additional support for the child's learning.
- Home-based programs may be more convenient for families, especially working single parents.
- Parents involved directly in the services may feel more empowered and confident in their abilities to meet the needs of their child.

There are also disadvantages, such as the difficulty in scheduling services for children who reside in more than one household because of divorce or families who struggle with daily stresses and add the demands of home-based services because they cannot or will not assume these responsibilities. Some parents may also feel uneasy about balancing their role of primary service provider with that of nurturing parent. In addition, children in a home-based program may not have sufficient opportunities for social interactions with peers (Hallahan & Kaufman, 2003; Heward, 2006; O'Shea, O'Shea, Algozzine, & Hammitte, 2001; A. Turnbull, Turnbull, Erwin, & Soodak, 2006).

Center-Based Programs

Preschool programs may include settings as diverse as private programs (e.g., church or corporate affiliated), child care programs, public school preschool special education or pre-K programs, or Head Start (Harbin et al., 2005), and a child may cross multiple settings in the course of the day when transitioning from Head Start in the morning to child care in the afternoon. Center staff provide direct teaching in domains such as fine and gross motor skills and language development, and parents are involved in observation and play activities with their child (T. E. C. Smith et al., 2006). Most center-based programs encourage social interaction and often include students with disabilities and typically developing children (Heward, 2006).

Head Start, a federally supported project initially funded in 1965, is one of the first and most comprehensive early childhood models. This program, designed to provide comprehensive educational, health, and social services to low-income families, has from its inception focused on parental involvement as an integral and basic component. A subsequent amendment requires that at least 10% of the enrollments in Head Start be children with disabilities and that their specialized services be provided in these programs (Hanson & Lynch, 2004). This includes Head Start in the range of service options for young children with disabilities in inclusive environments. In addition, family involvement continues to be pervasive, with parents routinely a part of developing and operating all components of the program. In particular, parents work in cooperation with Head Start staff to select curricula, carry out daily activities, and recruit and hire staff (McLean & Schaeffer, 2003).

Another example is the Programming for Early Education of Children With Handicaps (PEECH) project, which combines child-initiated and teacher-directed activities for children ages 3 to 5 with moderate disabilities. The primary goals of the program are to enhance language and communication skills, increase social competence, and provide access to the least restrictive environment. The program has been implemented in over 200 sites in 36 states. Children with disabilities and typically developing children receive classroom instruction together in large- and small-group activities. PEECH utilizes a team approach where team members (i.e., parents, teacher, paraprofessional, speech–language pathologist, social worker) meet regularly to discuss the child's program and the roles and responsibilities of each team member. Parents are an integral part of the team and are involved in planning, implementing, and evaluating family services based on specific characteristics of each family. Families also have access to over 1,200 activities that they can implement at home to foster skill development (Karnes & Beauchamp, 1993).

A number of advantages to center-based programs have been identified:

- The center staff can see more children.
- The center staff may have more influence over the interactions between child and parents.
- As more parents work, their children are in child care settings.
- There is increased opportunity for specialists from allied fields (e.g., occupational therapy, physical therapy, education) to observe each child and cooperate in assessment and intervention.
- Children may have greater access to peers.
- Parents may establish contact and find support from other parents at the center.

Disadvantages of center-based programs include the cost of transportation, the cost of maintaining the center facility, and the potential for less family involvement than in home-based programs (Heward, 2006; O'Shea et al., 2001).

Combined Programs

Some early intervention programs combine home services with center-based services. School services can average 10 hours per week, whereas home-based services generally provide fewer hours of direct service (Lovett & Haring, 2003). For some children who require more intervention than can be provided in a few hours per week, intensive center-based programs delivered by a variety of professionals may be combined with the continuous attention and care of parents at home. The combination of the two programs provides the positive aspects of both while negating some of the disadvantages (Heward, 2006).

Natural Environments

One key element of early intervention and early childhood special education programs is the emphasis on providing needed services in the child's natural environment. IDEA (2004) defined *natural environments* as settings that are natural or normal for same-age peers without disabilities. These settings include the child's home and community and provide real-life contexts within which to promote acquisition of competence that is culturally rooted and functional and makes it possible for the child to participate more fully and independently in those settings (Dunst et al., 2000). Children have opportunities to learn throughout the day through teachable moments embedded in naturally occurring activities. The benefits of early intervention and early childhood services will be enhanced when the child has learning opportunities throughout the day in multiple contexts. Professionals can assist parents in identifying natural learning opportunities or settings to maximize multiple learning opportunities in daily routines within contexts that are meaningful (Dunst et al., 2000; Jung et al., 2004; Odom & Wolery, 2003; Woods & Goldstein, 2003).

Language development is one area where naturalistic or milieu teaching by parents may be particularly helpful. Parents can be trained to arrange the home environment by having a selection of preferred toys available, to form a conversational interaction style with their child, and to use strategies such as modeling verbal behavior for the child or expanding on what the child says to increase the child's verbal behavior (Peterson, Carta, & Greenwood, 2005). Adults can help children expand their skills by including explanations about the purpose or function of objects during the natural course of activities across the day. For example, as the child is getting ready to draw a picture, the parent might say, "Let's find the green crayon, so you can draw a picture of the grass. Where is the yellow crayon so you can draw the sun?" (D. D. Smith, 2007, p. 142). A child who is working on fine motor skills can practice by buttoning his jacket before he walks to the park with his family. Educators can help families identify home and community activities and experiences that might serve as sources of learning opportunities such as caring for pets, visiting with neighbors, preparing the daily meals and holiday dinners, establishing bedtime routines, visiting playgrounds, or working on hobbies as outlets for activities to address child and family outcomes (Dunst et al., 2000; Jung et al., 2004). In fact, in a national survey of parents of infants, toddlers, and preschoolers, Dunst et al. (2000) identified more than 20 categories of activities in home, family, and community settings. It is important, however, to remember that parents may not always agree that incorporating learning activities into specific family routines is feasible or even desirable. It must be emphasized that the program will be planned jointly, with the parent guiding the process, and that the professionals will be sensitive to the events that transpire in the life of the family (Vacca & Feinberg, 2000).

Although certain basic generic skills underlie any successful parent conference, such as openness, tolerance, and the ability to listen, these skills must be applied in an individualized fashion, in accordance with a child's developmental stage. Efforts to involve and serve parents and families with young children must grow from the premise that a variety of individuals and needs must be served (Dunst, 2002; P. A. Gallagher & Rhodes, 2004; A. Turnbull et al., 2006). Nonetheless, in spite of the heterogeneous nature of families and the concomitant demand for individualization, needs tend to cluster in three general areas: emotional support, information exchange opportunities, and strategies for securing and utilizing services for the child and family. Though these types of needs exist in every family with young children, they are most dramatic in families of children with exceptionalities.

Need for Emotional Support

The birth of a child with a disability or the later identification of exceptionality will almost universally have a significant impact on both the parents and the ecology of the family. Considered a less-than-perfect reflection of the family, a child with a disability not only is typically associated with anxiety and strong emotion but may also make family members more vulnerable to otherwise normal pressures and frustrations (Bruce & Schultz, 2002; Hanson & Lynch, 2004; Hooste & Maes, 2003). For children first identified in the hospital, the time spent in the NICU has been described as highly emotionally charged, and many mothers express feelings of guilt over what has happened to their infant (Barry & Singer, 2001). The normal demands of life can take a toll on the family's ability to cope. Fox, Vaughn, Wyatte, and Dunlap (2002) interviewed a culturally diverse group of 20 families regarding their child's problem behavior and the ways it related to the family's lifestyle. One mother shared these reflections about her preschoolers:

> It was nuts. And it was a real strain on the family. . . . I can remember just putting them all in their car seats and driving and crying while driving down the street. Just thinking . . . well at least they're all in their car seats, and they can't go anywhere. And maybe some-

one would fall asleep. And I would just drive. And I can remember seeing my girlfriend and told her, I thought I felt like Jekyll and Hyde . . . and she said, "Kathy you're always so happy and loving." And I'm like, "And I'm dying inside." (p. 446)

Often professionals can most effectively meet the need for emotional support in parents and families with young children with disabilities by providing them an opportunity to express their perceptions, ideas, feelings, hopes, and concerns to an interested and nonjudgmental listener. This is particularly important within the framework of family-centered planning where parents are involved in decision making, the consequences of which will affect not only the young child with disabilities but also the entire family. When parents struggle to balance time or economic demands or feel uncertain about the information they need to make the best decision for their family, emotional support from a professional may help reduce family stress (Kaufman, 2001; Shannon, Grinde, & Cox, 2003). In their analysis of the interaction patterns of professional–family talk, Brady, Peters, Gamel-McCormick, and Venuto (2004) observed that professionals following a family member's expression of feeling tended to react to the content of the message rather than to the expression of feelings. For example, one mother with tears in her eyes stated, while nervously biting her nails, "Oh God, I really want her to be able to walk, you know? And, it's like she's not even sitting up yet." The professional responded, "Let's get her on the sofa and work on sitting" (p. 155).

In this interaction the professional was rushing to find a solution to fix the problem rather than simply listening to the mother's concern and accepting her feelings, thereby validating those feelings and encouraging further dialogue.

In addition, Brady et al. (2004) reported that when professionals used more indirect verbalizations, particularly when they praised, encouraged, and accepted families' ideas, families were more actively involved in the interaction than when professionals simply gave information. Validating emotions, not judging, and respecting personal impressions can help professionals build collaborative relationships with families.

Professionals are so familiar with their knowledge base that they will sometimes *underestimate* the emotional impact of the information they deliver to parents and at the same time *overestimate* what the parent actually understands (Bruce & Schultz, 2002). Following an interview about his child, one father commented, "I just wanted to get out of there. I just wanted him to stop" (p. 12).

Professionals can also provide support by helping parents and families comprehend their own reactions while adjusting to and accepting their child with exceptionalities. Families often struggle with accepting the diagnosis; resolving emotional reactions such as grief, anger, or feelings of confusion; and dealing with concerns about the impact on other family members and the overall family quality of life (B. Freeman, Dieterich, & Rak, 2002; Jackson & Turnbull, 2004; Nissenbaum, Tollefson, & Reese, 2002). Turnbull and Turnbull (2001) identified stages of the family life cycle that represent a family-systems approach that may be helpful for professionals to understand and respond appropriately to the current needs of the family. Families in the first stage (early childhood) are most concerned with obtaining an accurate diagnosis, informing family and friends about the child's disability, locating necessary services, and establishing helpful relationships with professionals. Individual parents experience different feelings at different times, in part because of individual coping skills and strengths. Families react differently as a function of socioeconomic status, their physician's attitude, the presence of other siblings in the house, cultural values, the level of family functioning, and availability of social supports (Kieff & Wellhousen, 2000; T. E. C. Smith et al., 2006; C. Zhang & Bennett, 2003). It is important, therefore, to recognize that parents and families will have different needs for support.

It is also crucial for professionals to avoid a simplistic understanding of parental reaction to their child's disability by relying on labels such as guilt, anger, or denial or by focusing primarily on the stress it produces for families (D. J. Sands, Kozleski, & French, 2000). There is increasing recognition and growing research that parents of children with disabilities report numerous benefits and positive outcomes for their family such as increased coping skills, family harmony, spiritual growth, shared parenting roles, and communication (Cho, Singer, & Brenner, 2000; Ferguson, 2002). For example, it would be inappropriate to misinterpret parents' difficulty understanding information being presented to them or disagreeing with what professionals say as a form of denial of the disability (P. A. Gallagher, Fialka, Rhodes, & Arceneaux, 2004).

Nonetheless, educators should be attentive to the stress of families and should not pile on programs, services appointments, and so on based on their view of what the family needs but rather support the family in identifying priorities and concerns (Hanson & Lynch, 2004). In a study of low-income, African American single parents, Unger et al. (2001) reported that when professionals recognized the stress these parents were under to meet their family's needs and reached out to them with respect and confidence in their ability, the parents' level of involvement was more likely to increase.

Although the need for emotional support of parents and families of young children with disabilities will vary, most parents and family members will have this need to some degree. Accordingly, professionals must be willing and able to develop appropriate strategies and alternatives for serving parents and families in this significant area. These strategies should assist families in identifying and building informal and formal networks and provide the social and emotional support that may be necessary to reduce family stress, promote parental confidence, and facilitate a mutually satisfying parent–child relationship (Dunst, 2000; Freund, Boone, Barlow, & Lim, 2005; P. A. Gallagher, Rhodes, & Darling, 2004; Hanson & Lynch, 2004).

Need for Information Exchange Opportunities

Probably the most common and generic need experienced by parents and families of young children with exceptionalities is for information and effective communication opportunities. Of particular significance to many parents of young children with disabilities are opportunities to discuss the nature and etiology of their child's exceptionality. Many parents of young children with disabilities first become concerned about their child's developmental differences in the months following birth (Bailey, Hebbeler, Scarborough, Spiker, & Mallik, 2004). Of particular concern to parents are delays in motor and language development (Stoner et al., 2005; Tsai, 2000). In a series of interviews of professionals and parents, Nissenbaum et al. (2002) reported on the interactions surrounding the diagnosis of autism. Some parents in these interviews observed difficulties on the part of professionals to speak openly and honestly with them. They suspected that professionals feel a hesitancy or fear to give a diagnosis. Parents preferred that professionals use clear, nontechnical language and encourage them to ask questions. Most parents recalled that professionals sent positive nonverbal messages (such as listening well), had relaxed body language, and showed humor, empathy, compassion, and a genuine interest in the family. These factors helped parents feel comfortable when hearing the diagnosis. Likewise, professionals acknowledged that they considered the families' emotions and how much information they felt the families could handle. They also felt it was important to begin and end the meeting by pointing out the child's strengths in order to establish a connection with parents and ensure that the family left on a positive note (Nissenbaum et al., 2002).

Most parents of young children who have suspicions about their child's development make their first professional contact with a physician. In contrast, for parents with older offspring, the most frequent contacts on their child's behalf tend to occur with school and other nonmedical professionals. It is not surprising that physicians more than any other professionals have been criticized for their demeanor and communication style toward parents with young children who have special needs (Nissenbaum et al., 2002; Stoner et al., 2005). Some parents reported that their concerns about their child were dismissed or ignored by their pediatrician, and as a result they felt the need to repeatedly pressure these physicians for referrals for additional evaluations or services (Stoner et al., 2005).

The nature of a child's condition, age at onset, and subsequent problems will at least partly determine the type and specificity of the information to disseminate to parents and families. For example, an ongoing exchange of information is especially critical when the child has communication problems thereby limiting the information the child can share with his or her parents (Stoner et al., 2005). Likewise, one can assume that parents whose children have not yet received a definitive diagnosis will require added attention, including an opportunity to exchange information. These parents, unlike parents of children with Down syndrome or another diagnosed disability, cannot yet search the Internet or directories of support groups for helpful information. Thus, parents and families of children with undiagnosed disabilities or unspecified developmental lags, including those at risk for school failure, may suffer through a relatively lengthy period of anxiety and uncertainty unless given adequate chances to communicate (Diamond & Kontos, 2004; Fleischmann, 2004; Stoner et al., 2005). Of particular help is information about the child's medical condition and development, parenting and caregiving information, and available community resources and services (Freund et al., 2005; Odom & Wolery, 2003; A. Turnbull et al., 2006). Although information exchange opportunities may not eliminate the concerns of family members, the process typically will help them deal more effectively with their youngster who has an exceptionality. Opportunities to share information that are extended to all family members such as siblings, grandparents, and stepparents are also important components of comprehensive programs associated with early intervention and early childhood special education (Kieff & Wellhousen, 2000; Parette, Brotherson, & Huer, 2000; Schwartz & Rodriguez, 2001).

Parents and families of young children with exceptionalities are often interested in discussing future expectations for their child's independent functioning, the available treatment and educational opportunities, and their child's performance in an intervention program. In a study conducted to examine parents' involvement with, and perceptions of, special education services, Spann and colleagues (2003) found that most parents talked or shared notes with educators at least weekly, and 91% of parents reported that the nature of the shared information related to their child's progress or behavior at school. Some parents, however, also reported that they felt they were the person primarily responsible for initiating communication.

Parents also are interested in discussing their child's progress in the program, the teaching and intervention strategies being employed, and the educational objectives associated with future public school placement (Hallahan & Kauffman, 2003; Hanson & Lynch, 2004; A. Turnbull et al., 2006). One area where families may need considerable information and training is the use of assistive technology (AT). Because many young children in early intervention have communication disorders, physical challenges, or severe disabilities, AT devices are frequently recommended (Parette et al., 2000). IDEA defined an *AT device* as "any item, piece of equipment, or product system, whether acquired or commercially off the shelf, modified, or customized, that is used to increase, maintain, or improve functional capabilities of individuals with disabilities" (20 U.S.C. 1402 § 602(1)), including low-tech devices such as switch-activated toys, adapted spoons, and notebooks as well as high-tech devices such as electronic augmentative and alternative communication devices that produce digitized speech output (Parette, Huer, & Wyatt, 2002; Wilds, 2001). High-tech devices are typically more difficult to learn to use. In fact, not all educators will be familiar with the AT devices prescribed for their students. If there is open and honest communication, educators will convey to parents their own need for training thereby reinforcing the home–school partnership where all adults work together (Parette et al., 2000).

Families may become frustrated with professional recommendations for AT devices that appear to be based on short-term contact with the child versus the lifetime contact of the family (Parette et al., 2000). In particular, if the commitment of family time required for implementation of the AT device and the possible impact on family routines are not discussed with the family before the device is selected and implemented, an inappropriate device may be selected, the device may not be utilized effectively, or the device may be abandoned or discarded (Judge, 2002; Parette et al., 2002). In addition, families from diverse linguistic and cultural backgrounds may hold different perspectives on the use of AT devices. For example, the family may feel that an AT device will call attention to the child in public and be unduly stigmatizing, or the family may not share the assumption that the independence the AT device can provide is valuable (Parette & Brotherson, 2004). Central to collaborative partnerships with families is the ongoing exchange of information and inclusion of families in the decision-making process for all aspects of the young child's program in a way that reflects respect for individual family values, concerns, and priorities.

Standards for Practice

The National Association for the Education of Young Children has established standards for professional practice in working with parents and families of young children. One of the standards relates to working collaboratively with families to foster children's development in all settings and includes criteria indicative of quality early childhood programs, such as the following:

1. As part of orientation and ongoing staff development, new and existing program staff members develop skills and knowledge to work effectively with diverse families.
2. Staff members use a variety of formal and informal strategies (including conversations) to become acquainted with and learn from families about their family structure, their preferred child-rearing practices, and the information they wish to share about their socioeconomic, linguistic, racial, religious, and cultural backgrounds.
3. Staff members actively use information about families to adapt the program environment, curriculum, and teaching methods to the families they serve.
4. Staff members establish intentional practices designed to foster strong reciprocal relationships with families from the first contact and maintain them over time.
5. Staff members ensure that all families are included in all aspects of the program and consider each family's interests and skills (National Association for the Education of Young Children, 2005).

These standards should provide helpful guidelines in designing and evaluating programs for young children and their families.

Transitions

Although one required component of an IFSP is a transition plan to ensure smooth transfer to a preschool program, there are several possible transition points for young children with disabilities and their families. These include transitioning from the NICU of the hospital to a home-based program, from a home-based program to early intervention services provided by agencies, from early intervention services to an inclusive or special education preschool program, and from a preschool program to a kindergarten or traditional school classroom (Odom & Wolery, 2003). In a qualitative study including parents and care providers of 48 infants and toddlers who had been identified at birth or shortly thereafter as eligible for early intervention services, Lovett and Haring (2003) examined the families' perspectives regarding three major transitions: transporting the baby to the NICU after birth, from the NICU to their home, and from early intervention services to preschool. Semistructured interviews generated several themes, including (a) families going through a birth crisis may have difficulty understanding the information they are provided, (b) some parents may not feel comfortable in their abilities to care for their children as they transition from the hospital to home, and (c) the transition from home-based early intervention to center-based preschool may cause much anxiety for some parents (p. 376).

Each of these transitions creates new demands and opportunities for the child and family. A critical component in creating smooth transitions involves preparing the child for the expected changes (T. E. C. Smith et al., 2006). Characteristics, routines, and demands of each setting will differ, so preparation for these specific transitions with necessary information and supports will help ensure optimum learning opportunities for the child in the next setting. Teachers should work collaboratively with parents to ensure as smooth a transition as possible to create a seamless service system with minimal disruptions for the child (Sainato & Morrison, 2001). Although parent participation in planning will not guarantee smooth transitions, it certainly will facilitate them for both the family and the child (T. E. C. Smith et al., 2006).

A second critical component in creating smooth transitions is preparation of the parents and teachers who will be working with the child (T. E. C. Smith et al., 2006). Parents of children who have experienced a health crisis during or shortly after birth may need to learn to provide CPR or to use and maintain medical technology such as a gastronomy feeding tube for children with health issues when they return home from the hospital (Lovett & Haring, 2003). Parents of young children with disabilities may need information and support as they inform family members and others about the child's disability and work through alterations in daily routines of the child and family (Hammitte & Nelson, 2001). As the child transitions to intervention services, parents need to learn about the new program or school and its rules, routines, demands, and expectations and to develop an understanding of the skills their child will need to be successful in this new environment. They must be prepared to meet new teachers and staff and establish new relationships (T. E. C. Smith et al., 2006). Teachers may need to be informed of environmental arrangements, scheduling considerations, and specific evidence-based strategies to support acquisition, generalization, and maintenance of skills (W. H. Brown, Odom, & Conroy, 2001; Fox, Dunlap, & Cushing, 2002; Heflin & Simpson, 2002; Odom & Wolery, 2003; Simpson, 2005; Strain & Joseph, 2004) as well as family preferences for involvement.

As Lovett and Haring (2003) noted, "Transition for families does not mean only changes in placement or services received but also can mean changes in emotional states or their perceptions of their children's and their own situation" (p. 377). Teachers will be more effective in collaboration and communication with parents if they are sensitive to these changes.

When the child reaches the age of 3, the transition from early intervention services (Part C programs) to preschool services (Part B programs) may be particularly stressful for some families. Transition to school programs typically includes higher child-to-staff ratios, increased use of large-group instruction, more structured teacher expectations, and changes in the physical and social structure of the classroom (Hadden, 2004; LaParo, Pianta, & Cox, 2000). In addition, this move not only signals a critical developmental stage for their child but also corresponds with a shift in focus as the IFSP is replaced with an IEP. Under the IFSP both the child and the family are at the center of early intervention services, whereas the IEP is child centered or school centered with the focus primarily on interventions for the child (Fox, Dunlap, et al., 2002; R. Turnbull et al., 2006). This shift includes a change in the role of parents from primary consumers of services to team members. Parents may feel pushed aside or feel less confident in actively participating in program planning than they did in early intervention services. Families of children between the ages of 3 and 5 may elect to have their program developed using an IFSP rather than an IEP and continue to receive services under Part C until the child enters kindergarten (T. E. C. Smith et al., 2006).

Parents express mixed emotions when their child enters preschool. Parents may be pleased that continuing services will avoid regression in skills (Lovett & Haring, 2003; Seery, Davis, & Johnson, 2000), and preschool environments can provide important access to peers without disabilities (Morrison, 2004; Rafferty & Griffin, 2005; Seery et al., 2000). This shift in service delivery, however, may signal a decrease in communication. Many young children ride a bus or van to and from school, and as a result families may lose the face-to-face time with teachers they were accustomed to having when service providers came directly into their home. Even when parents transport their child, the frenzied activity of arrival and dismissal times can severely limit opportunities for meaningful conversation between parents and teachers. As one mother stated,

> I don't know about his transition, but mine was really rough. He rode a big bus that pulled up outside and it swallowed him whole and he disappeared. As far as him being there, at first it tired him out, but now he loves being around the other kids. (Lovett & Haring, 2003, p. 376)

Making home visits is an excellent way to maintain communication with parents of preschool children, particularly during the first few months of the program. Many parents whose child received home-based services not only are familiar with this method of contact but appreciate access to the professionals (T. E. C. Smith et al., 2006). In fact, parents may feel abandoned by the early intervention staff they had come to rely on (Lovett & Haring, 2003), and contact with preschool teachers can help to allay their anxiety. In addition, teachers should encourage families to visit the program to meet staff and ask questions about the activities and services provided as well as to discuss preferred methods, schedules, and expectations for ongoing communication.

One strategy to facilitate a positive alliance with the family is to obtain helpful information from parents through a structured questionnaire or interview. Table 10.1 provides an example of questions that might be posed to parents in person or on a form sent home.

Other ways to help families feel more comfortable with their child's transition to preschool include helping parents prepare for the transition by informing them about what to expect in the new setting, helping them to arrange for meetings with school staff, involving them in decision making, and giving alternative choices (Lovett & Haring, 2003).

As emphasized, parents of young children require adequate opportunities for communicating with professionals, and such opportunities most likely will form the basis of other successful parent-related program efforts.

Service and Advocacy Needs

A variety of services have been identified as necessary for satisfying the needs of young children with exceptionalities and their families. These

TABLE 10.1.
Getting to Know Your Child

Date: _____

Name of person providing the information: _____

Your relationship to the child: _____

Child's full name: _____

Does your child have a nickname? _____

Child's primary language: _____

Other languages spoken in the home: _____

How does your child interact with adults he or she doesn't know?_____

_____

How does your child get along with other children? _____

_____

Describe how your child recovers emotional balance (slowly, quickly, sulkily, etc.). _____

What kinds of rewards work best with your child? _____

_____

What kind of help does your child need during routine activities (eating, toileting, changing activities, etc.)? _____

_____

What activities and toys does your child enjoy at home (books, music, outdoor play, etc.)? _____

What activities do you do with your child outside of the home? _____

_____

Please describe any recent changes in your child's life. _____

_____

Does your child have any health concerns that may limit him or her? _____

_____

Is your child on any medications? If so, please list name and reason for medication. _____

_____

(continues)

TABLE 10.1. (*continued*)

Describe your child's physical energy (child has abundance, tires easily, etc.).

_____

_____

Does your child have any food allergies or food restrictions? _____

_____

Do you have any concerns about your child's starting preschool? _____

_____

Is there any other information you would like us to know about your child? ___

_____

_____

Please check any of the following agencies with which your family has been involved:

☐ Private child care   ☐ Birth to 3 program

☐ Head Start   ☐ Special education

☐ Adult education   ☐ WIC

☐ Public housing   ☐ Department of Human Services

☐ DCFS   ☐ County health services

☐ Shelter   ☐ Other: _____

include helping parents find, train, and use babysitting and respite care; locate physicians and dentists who understand the child's needs as well as interpreters to accompany parents to medical appointments if necessary; and find GED and parent education programs (Bailey et al., 2005; Bailey & Simeonsson, 1998; Odom & Wolery, 2003; Rosenkoetter & Squires, 2004). Educators can maintain an up-to-date list of responsive community agencies with their addresses and phone numbers as well as the agency contact person to help link families with needed resources (Kaufman, 2001).

Professionals can expect a small percentage of parents and families of young children with exceptionalities to require counseling and therapy, and hence such services must be available. Parents who have unmet mental health needs, such as depression, are more likely to have difficulty learning or recalling information, and their ability to respond effectively to their child's needs may be compromised (Barry & Singer, 2001; Vacca, 2001). Mental health problems may also manifest in challenging behaviors that interfere with the educators' efforts to establish collaborative partnerships with the parents on behalf of their child (Tomlin, 2002). Therefore, in addition to making referrals for adult mental health services, educators should avail themselves of staff development activities to develop and refine their skills in working with family members who have mental health disorders (Vacca & Feinberg, 2000).

A number of parents and families will need training in the use of both behavioral and educational methods applicable in the natural environment. In these areas, parents have proved to be valuable resources and a means of extending professionally monitored intervention programs into a variety of settings (W. H. Brown et al., 2001; Fox, Dunlap, et al., 2002; Odom & Wolery, 2003). For example, Buschbacher, Fox, and Clarke (2004) worked with family members to implement functional assessment and positive behavioral support to reduce challenging behavior and increase engagement in three family-chosen home activities. Parent implementation of these procedures resulted in (a) a reduction in challenging behavior, (b) an increase in the child's engagement, (c) an increase in positive parent–child interactions, (d) a decrease in negative parent–child interactions, and (e) an increase in the number of days the child slept through the night.

In a study by Moes and Frea (2002), professionals worked collaboratively with parents to individualize the manner in which functional communication training procedures to address challenging behavior were taught and implemented in order to be contextually relevant. Adaptations to the intervention were generated that responded to the caregiving demands, family support, and social interactions that characterized the family routines. As a result, not only did problem behavior decrease and functional communication increase but consideration of the family context improved parents' perceptions of functional communication training and their ability to continue the intervention. Involvement of parents in this fashion has the added advantages of establishing appropriate child advocacy expectations and training parents in strategies they can use with children at other times in their life.

As primary advocates for their children, parents need information regarding their rights in early intervention and early childhood programs (Horn, Ostrosky, & Jones, 2003; LaRocco & Bruns, 2005; C. Zhang & Bennett, 2003), and they need to be supported in their efforts to become active collaborators. In addition to knowing their rights and responsibilities, families may have to be taught how to participate in family-centered services, particularly if they come from culturally diverse groups (Walker-Dalhouse & Dalhouse, 2001; C. Zhang & Bennett, 2003), and what to do if they feel that needed services are not being provided. Educators can facilitate parents' ability to advocate by fostering a sense of family empowerment.

Empowerment is a complex construct that incorporates a number of factors such as a sense of control over important aspects of life events, self-efficacy, participation and collaboration, and the ability to access necessary resources (Dempsey & Dunst, 2004; A. Turnbull et al., 2006). Parents report taking pride in the personal growth they experience as a result of the challenges they have effectively met and continue to meet (Hanson & Lynch, 2004). Hence, professionals should work to strengthen parents' current capacities and encourage them to develop new knowledge and skills utilizing a strengths-based approach.

A growing body of research has suggested that there is an important relationship between the manner in which professionals interact with and provide assistance to families and the families' sense of empowerment (Dempsey & Dunst, 2004). In family-centered approaches, professionals operate under the assumption that families are capable of making informed decisions that will lead to improvements for themselves (Dempsey & Dunst, 2004; Trivette & Dunst, 2005). This approach, as stated earlier, includes relational and participatory practices, and both are important aspects of effectively giving help. It should be noted, however, that although good relational skills are important in family-centered services, it is the participatory components utilized in collaborative partnerships that are the critical feature in facilitating family empowerment (Dempsey & Dunst, 2004; Dunst & Trivette, 1996; Dunst, Trivette, & Snyder, 2000).

Parents may also gain a sense of empowerment by attending legislative advocacy workshops that show them they can make a difference (Kaufman, 2001), and their attendance at such workshops should therefore be encouraged. In addition, educators can offer specific suggestions and strategies for parents to advocate at the local, state, and national levels (LaRocco & Bruns, 2005).

The diversity of family needs and the complex nature of family functioning can pose particular challenges for educators working with young children with disabilities and their families. If, however, constructive home–school partnerships that lead to meaningful and durable outcomes for children and families are in place during the early critical years of intervention for young children with disabilities, positive experiences during the elementary and secondary school years are greatly enhanced (Brody, Dorsey, Forehand, & Armistead, 2002; Fox, Dunlap, et al., 2002; Morrison, 2004).

Summary

Educators and other professionals increasingly are acknowledging that parents and families exert the most significant impact on the life of young children. Accordingly, concerted efforts have been made to serve the needs of families of children with exceptionalities utilizing a family-centered approach. This approach views the child within the context of the family and incorporates services and supports into existing routines and activities to capitalize on existing strengths and capacities and to extend learning opportunities for the child. With the increased emphasis on serving the needs of a broader spectrum of parents and families has come the realization that a child's age correlates closely with the needs of families and the types of services to be rendered. Although all families will experience such general needs as emotional support, information, and service options, their particular needs and requirements for service delivery will vary with the age of their family member. Hence, educators must be able to offer services that are consistent with various age and family considerations.

Exercises

1. Compare the needs of the families with whom you are most involved with the needs of those whose children are older or younger. Note areas of similarity and difference.

2. Conduct a survey of the parents and family members of students in an early intervention or early childhood program to identify their needs for emotional support, information, service, and advocacy. Next, identify resources within your school, agency, or community for most effectively serving these needs. Finally, compare your information with that of other individuals who are involved with students of different ages.

3. Discuss how teachers can ensure that natural supports and family strengths play an active and central role in program planning for young children with disabilities.

Chapter 11

Parents and Families of Elementary-Age Children With Exceptionalities

Vignette

My daughter, Mandy, has what is called Sturge-Weber syndrome. It's a neurological disease. When you meet her at first you'd think she really doesn't have anything wrong, except for the birthmark on her face [port-wine stain] that goes through to the brain instead of just being on the surface. There's an increase in blood flow and capillaries and a decrease in drainage that leads to migraines that lead to strokes and seizures that lead to. . . . She has glaucoma and visual problems and sometimes auditory processing problems depending on which half of her brain is working. Different learning disabilities are showing up more as she's getting older, as are behavior problems: obsessive-compulsive disorder, impulsive disorder, and anything that can go along with that. Yeah, anything that can go along with that. . . .

She's very strong willed, which can be a negative, but she doesn't seem to let a whole lot of things get to her. She can adapt to anything. If something happens to her the night before, she can have a stroke, and she's up and going the next day.

The first IEP [Individualized Education Program] conference in first grade was very frustrating for me. Usually I don't have any problem at all after so many IFSP [Individualized Family Service Plan] and IEP meetings, but that year I was questioned about her skills and her abilities. Everything I would say, someone would challenge . . . everything that I would come out with, even though everyone in the meeting has known me. It didn't matter what happened; there was a question following anything that was said. So starting out it was more tense than normal.

We always have a lot [of people] at our meetings. The superintendent, principal, and special education coordinator were there, so we had a lot of administrators. Then the school nurse, my mother, a school social worker, a psychologist, a physical therapist, an occupational therapist, and I were there. It seemed like this whole meeting was an escalation of everyone's tempers. I've never raised my voice in an IEP meeting, and I raised my voice and I cried. I don't do that. I don't ever do that in public. I was just so frustrated because I knew the changes in Mandy and no one was listening. They were all sitting, making their little notes, writing what they had to do. Typing up the IEP before I even got into the room, which we all know has happened, but that is not supposed to happen. Not just writing . . . this was writing up everything they felt needed to be done before even discussing what had happened over the summer. Well, it was like I wasn't involved all of a sudden.

She was fully included in the general education first grade, but as the year went on, we had more meetings, and we had to gradually decrease the amount of time she was included because the work became too difficult for her to keep up. At first she was coming home with 10 worksheets a night and a full story to read, and she can't read. It would take 2 hours to get four math problems done, and then there would be nine extra pages that she would be behind that she was supposed to make up when she went back to school. First grade was hard! We tried accommodations, but they weren't enough.

The teachers have been really good about communicating. If I ask for something or send a note, that same day a reply comes back or I have a phone call. I always know what's going on. I always get an answer, whether it's what I wanted to hear or not. There's a journal that gets sent back and forth, which has worked really well. I will know if this didn't get done or if something happens or if she was sick or what the plans are for the next day. I know it's not always possible, but if I do know ahead of time, I can prepare her for what they're going to be doing the next day. I write in it [journal] every morning before it goes back to let them know how her evening went and how the morning went instead of calling them or going in like some parents do every morning and try to take 10 minutes out of the teacher's time by talking to them. They don't have time for that every morning. I know that.

At our last IEP meeting, it was like starting over. 'What does she need? Is this OK? What can we do? What suggestions do you have?' It was completely opposite of what it was like at the beginning of first grade, where they were asking what I would recommend and what I see is needed for her. It was getting me involved. I wish they would do that with every parent. At the beginning I had to push to get involved, and at the end they were offering.

The transition from preschool programs to elementary school can signal a significant change for the child as well as for the family. In comparison to early intervention programs, typical elementary schools have a higher student-to-adult ratio, instruction is frequently provided in whole-group formats, and expectations for the social, behavioral, and academic functioning of the children increase (LaParo, Pianta, & Cox, 2000). In addition, unlike the adult-initiated play dates and social activities common during the preschool years, friendships and social networks are established and developed by elementary-age children independently from their parents, and peer relationships become an important part of the child's school experience.

Of course, parents of children with exceptionalities want what all parents want for their children of this age: to be happy, to have friends, to function independently, and to experience success. Parents and families can play a critical role in helping to achieve these goals if they are assisted and supported in their participation. Although parents have their own elementary school experience to guide them, negotiating the special education service-delivery system may be unfamiliar to them and thus intimidating. The needs of parents with elementary-age children are as varied and individualized as those of parents with preschoolers, yet they tend to fall within the same basic areas: emotional support and understanding, information exchange opportunities, and mechanisms for identifying, implementing, and evaluating needed services.

Emotional Support and Understanding

Identification of an elementary-age child as exceptional has a significant impact on the entire family structure but especially on parents. In some instances, identification and diagnosis confirm the family's previously undefined concerns; in other cases, the process comes as a shock. Although exceptionalities identified subsequent to infancy and preschool tend to be less severe and obvious than those found in preschoolers, their impact may well be no less significant. For students with mild disabilities, elementary school may be the first time families learn about the exceptionalities of the child, and although they want the individualized assistance the school can provide, they may have concerns about the negative implications of a special education label. Parents wrestling with their own reactions often seek an explanation for their child's difficulties and may prefer a label that does not suggest that they are somehow responsible through either genetic endowment or parental negligence (Florian et al., 2006). This is true even though parents often become aware that the disability label is the essential passport necessary to secure services and supports (McLaughlin et al., 2006; Wedell, 2003).

Although categorical eligibility may ensure that professionals are appropriately trained and specific interventions can be designed to meet the needs of the child, labels in and of themselves are not a guarantee of appropriate service delivery. It is important to stress to parents that special education programming should be based on the specific characteristics, strengths, and needs of their child.

Helping parents and families to understand their own emotional experiences and concerns is therefore crucial, even if it is not a simple matter. Parents who have observed differences in their child's development or behavior in comparison to that of other siblings or peers may, nonetheless, continue to hope that their observations are incorrect and that the child will outgrow any difficulties (Bos & Vaughn, 2006; Seligman & Darling, 2007). Professionals can assist families in processing their emotions by providing opportunities to discuss affective issues and by understanding reactions such as shock, denial, fear, guilt, bereavement, anger, and depression. The mother of a recently diagnosed child with a disability reported that even though she had read and heard of the strong reactions parents sometimes experience upon hearing of their child's exceptionality, she was surprised at her own intense feelings of anger and frustration. She did note, however, that having an opportunity to discuss these feelings with her child's teachers was beneficial.

Information Exchange Needs

Parents of elementary-age children frequently observe that one of their most prominent needs relates to meeting and exchanging information with the individuals assigned the task of educating their sons and daughters. This need seems particularly acute at the time when a child is initially identified as exceptional and assigned to a special program (Clark & Fiedler, 2003; Dunst, 2002; Stoner et al., 2005). Even though parents may have received an interpretation following their child's assessment, they frequently will benefit from discussing this information with the child's teacher after having some time to ruminate over it.

Parents should also receive information about their child's educational program and have a chance to discuss it. Specifically, they should be informed about the procedures and curriculum that will be implemented, the related services and supports that will be rendered, and the manner in which their child will be evaluated. Any additional school and community resources that may be required should also be discussed. Finally, as discussed in Chapter 7, parents should receive progress report information from school personnel at regularly scheduled intervals. Such sessions should not only consist of a review of a child's academic, social, behavioral, and physical progress but also offer an opportunity for parents to ask specific questions, discuss problems, and suggest agenda items.

A number of professionals have highlighted the importance of providing adequate opportunities for the exchange of information between parents and educators, particularly when working with culturally or linguistically diverse families (Chrispeels & Rivero, 2001; Hughes, Valle-Riestra, & Arguelles, 2002; Mundschenk & Foley, 2000; Parette & Petch-Hogan, 2000; J. E. Walker & Shea, 1999), yet, to date, criticism of standard procedures is frequently voiced. In addition, when the nature or severity of the child's disability limits his or her communication skills, effective two-way information exchanges between school and home become even more critical. Stoner and colleagues (2005) surveyed parents of children with autism spectrum disorder regarding their interactions with education professionals. One parent expressed his frustration this way:

> I don't know, I always feel—and it is more my outlook—but I never feel like I know enough about what's going on. And I think that goes from the fact that Pete can't tell me what is going on. You know? I mean I can ask him, but he is not going to tell me. Not specifically. And that is the frustrating part for me. (p. 46)

Thus, it is imperative that professionals create an atmosphere that encourages free discussion and develop structures to establish ongoing information exchange. Only such conditions will meet parents' information needs.

The Individuals With Disabilities Education Improvement Act

Without argument, the most comprehensive and significant legislation yet proposed and enacted for meeting the educational needs of children and youth with exceptionalities has been the Individuals with Disabilities Education Improvement Act (IDEA, 2004). Although the statute has been reauthorized several times since it was first passed, the basic principles have remained. These include provision of the following: (a) free and appropriate education (FAPE), including identification of and provision of service to all children; (b) individualized and nondiscriminatory assessment; (c) procedural safeguards, which protect children and youth from erroneous classification and denial of equal education and protection; (d) IEPs, which ensure an appropriate education; (e) parental opportunity for involvement in their children's education; and (f) placement of students with exceptionalities in the least restrictive educational environment.

As previously suggested, the participation of parents in the various activities associated with the identification of and programming for children and youth with exceptionalities is extremely significant. Thus, parents and family members must have the necessary information to participate fully as collaborative partners, and a crucial piece of this information is the legal basis for special education service delivery. Although reference in this chapter will be made only to parents, the reader will remember that the same principles apply to other legal guardians as well.

FREE AND APPROPRIATE EDUCATION

This fundamental element of IDEA ensures that all eligible children and youth receive specially designed instruction at public expense. Accordingly, special education for a student with an identified educational disability is to be provided at no cost to the student or the family. Moreover, special education services must be appropriate; that is, individualized for the unique needs of each student and in conformity with the written IEP.

As an important element of FAPE, children and youth with exceptionalities are entitled to appropriate related services, or support measures, such as transportation, speech-language pathology, assistive technology, occupational therapy, physical therapy, psychological and counseling services, recreation services, certain types of medical services, and similar types of resources. These supplementary aids and services should be designed and implemented so as to afford students with disabilities opportunity to participate with their peers without disabilities in extracurricular and nonacademic settings. Thus, IDEA includes provisions for related services and support resources that will permit students to benefit from their special education programs. Such measures are used to support students in both integrated and more restrictive settings.

INDIVIDUALIZED AND NONDISCRIMINATORY ASSESSMENT

IDEA requires that the assessment materials and procedures utilized for evaluation and program planning be selected and administered so as to avoid racial, cultural, or other forms of discrimination. Whenever feasible, evaluation instruments, materials, and procedures should be compatible with and administered in the child's native language or mode of communication (e.g., nonverbal for a child with a severe hearing loss), and no single procedure can become the sole criterion for determining an appropriate educational program. Identification and diagnostic procedures are given a good deal of attention in IDEA because accurate adherence to effective evaluation methodology is essential to gather relevant functional, developmental, and academic information, including information from parents, which in turn ensures that students with exceptionalities receive appropriate services. That is, without an accurate, meaningful, and complete assessment of all areas of concern, students with educational exceptionalities will probably not be exposed to appropriate intervention strategies and programs.

Historically, evaluation efforts have accentuated procedures associated with screening, classifying, and placing children and youth with disabilities in special education programs (Deno, 2005). This emphasis, however, has occurred at the expense of generating information that will serve to formulate an appropriate individualized teaching strategy. This pattern has specifically been characterized by an overreliance on a limited number of procedures with dubious levels of utility and by evaluations conducted by individuals with somewhat narrow perceptions of the needs of children and youth with exceptionalities. These evaluative shortcomings have been addressed, at least to some extent, by the critical part evaluation plays in the process that leads to the development and guarantee of FAPE. That is, the goals of a student's educational program, the special education and related supports and services he or she will receive, and the monitoring of the student's progress are all based on evaluation data (Yell, 2006). A comprehensive and multidisciplinary evaluation, just as the concepts suggest, involves a complete assessment prior to the initiation of any program modification. For an evaluation to meet the spirit of comprehensiveness, it should involve not only a consideration of the child's scores on standardized and teacher-made instruments but also an analysis of relevant home, school, and community variables that appear to exert an impact on his or her current ability to function. Consequently, the evaluation should address the concerns that led to the referral, the nature of the suspected problem, the characteristics of the individual student, and the student's learning and behavior patterns (Reschly, 2000). To support the conclusions drawn and the recommendations made, the process should provide data related to all suspected areas of need, including, if appropriate, the physical, sensory, social, emotional, communicative, and educational status of each student being evaluated.

Finally, these evaluations must be made by a team of qualified professionals and the parents as opposed to being made by a single diagnostician. That is, in addition to informal assessment procedures, direct observations, and related techniques commonly employed by classroom teachers, the input of individuals representing other disciplines must also be considered. Even though the roles of the individuals involved will vary with the diagnostic questions under consideration, the team will commonly represent the disciplines of school psychology, social work, physical and occupational therapy, speech pathology, audiology, medicine, nursing, counseling, and school administration. Input from these professional groups will, of course, be considered along with that provided by the parents.

Given the fact that interpretation and feedback contacts that take place between parents and school personnel often set the tone for future interactions, it is crucial that both the evaluation process and the interpretation of results be done in such a way as to maximize the probability of future positive contacts. Because parental permission must be obtained prior to placing, reassigning, transferring, or otherwise altering a child's program, it is essential that supporting data and attitudes assure the parents that their child is receiving the most appropriate education possible.

Obtaining permission of parents. The role of parents in the evaluation process is so significant that the procedures hinge on the ability of the evaluation team to secure permission to conduct them in the first place. Specifically, parents of children or youth who have been referred for further evaluation must be notified and apprised of the need for evaluation prior to the initiation of any assessment procedures. The notification, which can and should be given orally but that must also appear in written form, should provide a rationale for the proposed evaluation and a description of the tests and procedures to be employed and should be presented in a fashion that parents can understand.

Upon receipt of the request for permission to evaluate, parents can give one of three possible responses. First, they can grant permission for the child to be evaluated. Once permission is extended, the evaluation can commence immediately. Second, parents can choose to deny permission to have their son or daughter evaluated. In fact, they must be informed of their right to deny permission for their child to be assessed. In the event that parents choose to exercise their denial privileges, and school district or agency personnel are not successful in convincing them of the need for the assessment, the district or agency personnel can either accept the parents' position or, if they believe the child's best interests demand the evaluation, seek permission to conduct the assessment via a due process hearing. (Due process procedures will be discussed in a later section.) Finally, parents can choose not to respond to the request to permit an initial evaluation. If follow-up contacts do not produce a response from the parents, the district or agency must interpret the failure to reply as an indication that they oppose the initial evaluation. Accordingly, the same procedures applicable to a "no" response apply to a failure to respond.

The following example illustrates the rationale behind possible parental refusal. A mother and father were both angry and frightened when they received a request from the school district to conduct an initial evaluation on their first-grade daughter. The notice from the school and a follow-up conversation with the child's teacher indicated that their daughter was having "difficulty keeping up with the rest of the class." Although the district's school psychologist attempted to assure the parents that the evaluation would be routine and would not necessarily lead to special education placement (but rather to "a better understanding so that more appropriate educational provisions can be made"), they remained suspicious. Their 14-year-old nephew had been tested and subsequently placed in a special education class when he was 8, which, according to his parents, produced "nothing but problems." The mother's sister and brother-in-law had, on numerous occasions, expressed the belief that their son began to have problems only after being placed in special education. After learning that these parents had received a request for permission to evaluate, their relatives strongly recommended that they fight.

Fortunately, however, a single session with the school psychologist and classroom teacher convinced these parents that the best interests of their daughter would be served by allowing the evaluation to take place. In addition, the parents learned that their prior approval would be required before any change in their child's educational program could be initiated. As a result, consent was forthcoming.

If parents fail to respond to a request for a reevaluation of their child who is already receiving special education (required at least once every 3 years), parental consent need not be obtained if the school can demonstrate that it had taken reasonable measures to obtain parent permission (20 U.S.C. § 1414(c)(3)).

Requests by parents for assessment. Requests for evaluation can come from parents as well as from schools. The former, in fact, can request an evaluation or reevaluation of their child at any time they deem appropriate. The school district, however, has the choice of conducting or not conducting the evaluation. In the event the district concedes to the request for an evaluation, it must still obtain written permission from the parents prior to actually conducting the assessment. If the district takes the position that an evaluation is not needed, it must notify the parents, in writing, of this decision. The notice must also inform the parents that if they desire, they can request a due process hearing to arbitrate differences of opinion between the school and themselves regarding the need for an evaluation.

One mother believed strongly that her 12-year-old son was learning disabled and should be provided special programming assistance. Even though he already had been evaluated twice in 6 years by the school district's diagnostic team and once by an educational psychologist in private practice at her request, and in spite of the fact that each of the evaluations failed to indicate learning or behavior problems, she requested an additional assessment session. Because classroom reports and observations did not justify the need for another evaluation, the request was denied. Although the mother initially filed for a due process hearing, she later decided to move to a neighboring district to obtain "the right program."

Parents may also request an independent educational evaluation of their son or daughter from qualified (licensed or certified) examiners not affiliated with the district or agency recommending the action. Again, the importance of initial rapport and an adequate multidisciplinary and comprehensive evaluation cannot be overemphasized, because parents are entitled to present data from an alternate source in instances in which they question or are dissatisfied with the findings and recommendations presented them. As dissatisfaction is frequently associated with a lack of parental input or involvement, evaluation teams should be able to both support their findings and provide parents with the opportunity for input into the analysis of the issues and intervention strategies.

PROCEDURAL SAFEGUARDS

The primary procedural protections afforded parents and children under IDEA include parental access to records, surrogate parents, parental notice, and conflict resolution processes including a due process hearing (described in Chapter 9) regarding the identification, evaluation, and educational placement of the child or the provision of FAPE (20 U.S.C. § 1415(b)). In addition to the parental notice and consent requirements related to evaluation, parents must provide written informed consent prior to their child's initial placement in a special education program.

Parents have access to all records and data pertaining to the identification, assessment, and programming of their child. As noted in the assessment section, this component accentuates the need not only for a complete and thorough evaluation but also for an accurate and professional report of the findings and recommendations to parents. In addition, no information regarding their child will be shared with persons not directly involved in the child's educational program without parent permission, and a record must be kept of all persons who access the child's records. Parents may also challenge information contained in their child's records that they deem inaccurate.

INDIVIDUALIZED EDUCATION PROGRAMS

Although each of the major components of IDEA has received significant attention by parents and educators, the section that many contend has the most direct impact on students' outcomes, curricula, services, placements, and overall programs has been the requirement that an IEP be developed and monitored for each child or adolescent with an exceptionality.

The IEP is developed by a multidisciplinary team including parents, at least one general education teacher (if the child is or may be participating in general education), a special education teacher, a representative of the local educational agency or an intermediate educational unit who is qualified to provide or supervise special education services, an individual who can interpret the instructional implications of evaluation results, and, at the discretion of the parent or school, other individuals who have knowledge or special expertise regarding the child. Whenever appropriate, the child should also be present (20 U.S.C. § 1414(d)(1)(B)).

The IEP is a written document, and although the format can vary between states, school districts, and agencies, certain basic components must be included:

1. a statement of the child's present levels of academic achievement and functional performance including how the child's disability affects her or his involvement in the general education curriculum;
2. a statement of measurable annual goals, including academic and functional goals (and short-term objectives or benchmarks for students taking alternate assessment) designed to meet the individual needs of the child to enable her or him to make progress in the general education curriculum;
3. a description of how the child's progress toward meeting annual goals will be measured and reported to parents;
4. a statement of the special education and related services and supplementary aids and services to be provided to the child, as well as necessary program modifications or supports for school personnel;
5. an explanation of the extent to which the child will not participate with peers without disabilities in the general education class and in nonacademic or extracurricular activities;

6. a statement of accommodations necessary to measure academic achievement and functional performance on statewide and districtwide assessments;

7. the projected date for the initiation and anticipated frequency, location, and duration of such services; and

8. a transition plan including postsecondary goals that go into effect when the child is 16 (20 U.S.C. § 1414(d)(A)). Transition plans are discussed in Chapter 12.

Parent participation in the development of the IEP is an essential element of both procedural requirements, including meeting(s) of parents and professionals wherein joint decisions are made regarding students' educational programs, and substantive requirements related to construction of the IEP document. The IEP meeting serves as a communication vehicle between parents and school personnel and enables parents, as equal participants, to jointly decide what the child's needs are, what services will be provided to meet those needs, and what the anticipated outcomes may be. The IEP sets forth in writing a commitment of resources necessary to enable a child with a disability to receive appropriate special education and related services. Although the IEP is not intended as a legally binding contract whereby districts and agencies must demonstrate that progress specified in the annual goals and objectives has been made, it does serve to solidify the cooperative involvement of parents and educators.

There is no set length for IEP meetings as long as there is sufficient time for decision making, development of the IEP document, and meaningful parent participation. Some parents have expressed frustration that the IEP seems to have already been written when they arrive at the meeting (for example, Mandy's mother in the opening vignette) and that their input is elicited in a pro forma way by their being asked "Do you have any questions?" as the forms are circulated for every participant to add her or his signature indicating agreement. It is understandable that given the time constraints school professionals face in scheduling and conducting IEP meetings, they try to minimize the length of meetings and maximize the time that they do have. In consideration of these restraints, agency staff may come to the IEP meeting with proposed recommendations or a draft of the contents of the IEP, but in such instances it must be made clear to parents that these are only recommendations. Parents should be encouraged to ask questions, provide input, and propose their own recommendations before the IEP is finalized. Indicators of effective IEP meetings are listed in Table 11.1.

TABLE 11.1.
Indicators of Effective Individualized Education Program (IEP) Meetings

1. The meeting was held in a private, comfortable location conducive to collaborative dialogue and scheduled at a time convenient for parents.

2. Sufficient time was allowed for discussion.

3. All IEP team members were present at the meeting: parents, student's general and special education teachers, representative of the local education agency, person who could interpret the educational implications of assessment, student (if appropriate), and others at the discretion of the parents or school.

4. Parent consent was obtained for the absence of a team member, and written input from that team member was made available for the meeting.

5. Educational jargon was minimized. An interpreter was provided (if appropriate).

6. The meeting began with introductions of all team members and a brief overview of the goals and intended outcomes of the meeting.

7. The discussion opened with an overview of the student's strengths and current levels of academic and functional performance.

8. The current IEP was reviewed, and multiple sources of data were considered in designing the program plan, including information and observations from the parents.

9. All applicable special factors were considered in developing the IEP: technology, language, communication, sensory impairments, behavioral issues, and so on.

10. The annual goals (and short-term objective or benchmarks, if appropriate) written were observable, measurable, and meaningful for the student.

11. The goals (and objectives or benchmarks) were linked to the appropriate curriculum standards and designed to enable the student to access and progress in the general curriculum.

12. Behavior goals or a behavior plan was included to address behavior that interferes with the student's (or other students') learning.

13. Special education and related services included in the plan were clearly described to the parents.

(continues)

TABLE 11.1. (*continued*)

14. A schedule was determined for monitoring the student's progress to-ward achieving the annual goals and reporting that progress to the parents (at least as often as progress is reported to the parents of students without disabilities).

15. The special education and related services and supplementary aids written into the IEP are "based on peer-reviewed research to the extent practicable."

16. Determination was made regarding how the student would participate in district and/or state assessments, and any necessary modifications or accommodations were written into the IEP.

17. Transition services were written for the student turning 16 (or earlier if appropriate).

18. After the annual goals were written, placement options and necessary supports were discussed.

19. The placement determination reflected requirements for the least restrictive environment.

20. Determination was made regarding who would inform the other professionals not present at the meeting of their responsibilities for the IEP.

21. The parents were given a copy of the IEP.

22. The procedural safeguards were explained to the parents, and a written copy was provided.

Although teachers and other educational personnel may understand the components and protocol required in developing an IEP, the standards adopted by school districts or agencies may be in direct conflict with those requirements. District policy, though unwritten, may specify that only services readily available in the district are to be noted on the IEP, regardless of a student's needs. Other policies may require authors of IEPs to word components of the document in an intentionally vague or difficult-to-interpret fashion, as in writing annual goals, for example, in terms such as "demonstrating indications of improvements" rather than in more empirical and easily evaluated ways. The unfortunate thing about these practices is that they unceremoniously thrust educational personnel into the awkward position of demonstrating allegiance either to their employer or to the children they serve, and choosing either option cannot serve to accomplish the goals originally intended.

Because parents are considered such an integral part of the IEP conference, provisions exist for guaranteeing their participation. Specifically, parents must receive advance notice of the conference, including the purpose, time, location, and names and positions of those who will be in attendance. When the purpose of the meeting is to consider transition issues, parents must be so notified. They also must be informed of the agencies that will be sending a representative to the meeting, and they must be told that the school or agency would like the student to attend the meeting. Districts and agencies must also guarantee that IEP meetings are held at times and places mutually convenient to the parents and educators. Those individuals coordinating the conference must also ensure that parents can comprehend and have input into the session (e.g., interpreters must be provided for parents who are deaf or do not speak English) or, in the event that they cannot attend, that the school uses other methods to allow their participation (e.g., conference telephone calls). Although IEP conferences can take place without parental representation, the district or agency must be able to document that parents were provided an opportunity to participate. This documentation must include accounts and results of telephone calls made or attempted, copies of letters and responses to letters sent, and reports of the results of home and employment visits. Though this information is not required for every case in which parents are not involved in an IEP conference, it must be available in situations in which parents claim that they have been excluded from the conference.

IDEA requires that progress toward annual IEP goals be monitored and reported to parents of students with disabilities at least as often as it is to parents of students without disabilities. This requires the development of annual goals that are not only legally correct but also educationally useful (Bateman & Linden, 2006; Courtade-Little & Browder, 2005; Drasgow, Yell, & Robinson, 2001). Parents will want to know the specifics of what their child can do now, what progress they have made since the previous meeting, what he or she will be able to do as a result of implementation of the proposed IEP, how the team will know that the program is working, and how that expected level of progress compares with the child's peers without disabilities. Specific strategies for reporting progress to parents are described in Chapter 7.

The IEP must be reviewed or revised at least annually. Furthermore, although some delays may occur because of vacations or transportation arrangements, services identified on the IEP must be provided as soon as possible after the meeting. If a student with a disability transfers from one school district to another, the new district need not develop a new IEP if the current one is available, the parents are satisfied with it, and the new district considers the plan appropriate. Suggestions for parental participation in IEP meetings are found in Table 11.2.

PARENTAL PARTICIPATION

Even though the efforts involved in scheduling and conducting a collaborative IEP conference are extensive and time-consuming, it should be obvious that such a process has enormous benefits. Simply complying with minimum federal requirements may do little to ensure parental cooperation (Fiedler & Swanger, 2000). Family members need to be included in all discussions and decisions regarding their child's education. In fact, Lechtenberger and Mullins (2004) suggested that professionals should not lose sight of the fact that they are working with someone's child and should remember the motto "Not about us without us" when working with parents to develop meaningful educational plans beyond minimal compliance with the law (p. 19). Although not an easy task, several procedures, when correctly identified and planned for, will help the educator to include the parents more effectively in the IEP process.

The need for trust. Throughout this text readers have encountered the message that the true intent of the IEP conference can be realized only under conditions of integrity, honesty, and shared confidence between professionals and parents. Although many have advocated this position (Bateman & Linden, 2006; Dabkowski, 2004; Fidler, Lawson, & Hodapp, 2003; C. Zhang & Bennett, 2003), and thus it should be an acknowledged principle, its importance must not be underestimated. Schools and parents all too often have had an adversarial relationship, making the development of trust and a collaborative interaction difficult, but without these basic ingredients, even the most precise adherence to mandated requirements will not produce the desired results.

The staff of a federally supported public school demonstration program for students with severe emotional disorders thought it somewhat peculiar when the mother of an adolescent who was being considered for placement in the program presented two rather strong demands. The first demand was that the initial parent–teacher interview, conducted as one component of the evaluation, be held in the home, and the second demand was that a former teacher, residing in a community some distance away, be contacted regarding the boy's past performance. Both requests were honored. After the IEP conference, at which she actively participated, this mother revealed that she had been testing the staff. She indicated that although she had received a number of promises over the years from school

TABLE 11.2.
Considerations for Parent Involvement in the Individualized Education Program (IEP), by Level of Involvement and Phase of Participation

Pre-IEP conference[a]	During IEP conference	Post-IEP conference
Attendance and Approval		
Plan for meeting: (a) determine the site of the conference, (b) plan to arrive on time, (c) identify a babysitter to avoid your having to bring young children to the meeting, (d) determine how much time has been allotted for the conference, (e) attempt to identify who will attend the meeting.	Maintain a positive attitude during the conference.	Be willing to attend future meetings and to offer support and approval.
Consider bringing a friend or relative to the meeting if you are uncomfortable attending alone.	Maintain a businesslike demeanor: (a) dress in a businesslike manner, (b) bring writing materials, (c) avoid isolation via the seating arrangement, (d) listen carefully, (e) introduce yourself and request that others at the meeting do the same, including specifying their role.	
Develop a positive attitude regarding the meeting as opposed to assuming an adversarial position.	Be willing to accept responsibility for problems that are outside school. Similarly, do not expect school personnel to solve your personal or family problems. However, you may seek referrals from school personnel for such services.	
Familiarize yourself with legal and legislative special education mandates. In particular, review handbooks and pamphlets relating to IDEA.		

(continues)

TABLE 11.2. (continued)

Pre-IEP conference[a]	During IEP conference	Post-IEP conference
Sharing Information		
Maintain and organize developmental, school, and clinical records on your children and review these records (including previous IEPs).	Bring writing materials, background information, and other information that you may wish to share at the conference.	Obtain and file a copy of the IEP and any other information needed for future reference.
Develop a list of information and other data you wish to share at IEP conferences. Write this information down, because you may not remember it at conference time.		Provide conference information to family members, including the child about whom the meeting was held (if appropriate).
Suggesting Goals		
Identify with family members' (including the child about whom the conference will be held) prioritized goals for the child.	Assertively maintain a participatory status during the conference. Ask for clarification about items and concepts that you fail to understand and that are not explained, solicit input and feedback from individuals who might not otherwise share information, make suggestions you consider important, request a copy of the completed IEP, and request additional meeting time if the allotted schedule is insufficient for completing the IEP.	Prepare notes about the meeting. These notes should reflect happenings during the conference and should be filed with the student's IEP.
		Contact the appropriate personnel if clarification or additional information is required.
	Present to IEP participants the parent and family goals for the child.	Reinforce educators for their work, for example, through letters and phone calls.

TABLE 11.2. (*continued*)

Pre-IEP conference[a]	During IEP conference	Post-IEP conference
Negotiating Goals		
Consider enrolling in assertiveness training and problem-solving workshops.	Positively and assertively work with educators. Present and advocate priority goals. However, avoid arguing over minor details or attempting to dominate the meeting.	
Monitoring Implementation		
Consider enrolling in workshops on child and program assessment and evaluation.	Establish the manner in which goals and objectives will be monitored and how this information will be communicated to educators.	Maintain an ongoing record of IEP progress and skill development.
Engaging in Joint Programming		
Familiarize yourself with teaching strategies and behavior management techniques.	Establish the manner in which goals and objectives will be jointly monitored and how this information will be communicated.	
Engaging in Independent Programming		
Develop proficiency in independently carrying out teaching strategies and behavior management procedures.	Establish the conditions under which goals and objectives will be independently pursued by parents and the manner in which this information will be communicated.	

Note. Adapted from *The Second Handbook on Parent Education*, pp. 167–169, by R. Simpson and C. Fiedler, 1989, New York: Academic Press. Copyright 1989 by Academic Press. Reprinted with permission.

[a] Activities at each level of involvement are cumulative (e.g., activities at the second level include those of the first level).

personnel regarding the services to be provided her son, few had been honored. She confided that if the school personnel who contacted her were willing to come to her house and to contact a teacher whom she personally respected, "then they probably had Calvin's best interests in mind." She also reported that this demonstration convinced her that her input into the development of her son's IEP would be considered worthwhile.

Another issue related to trust is the confidence parents must have that the IEP will be implemented as written and that the individual needs of their child will be addressed. When parents feel that there is a gap between their perception of the needs of their child and the adequacy of services that are provided to the child (e.g., providing accommodations indicated on the IEP), the trust that may have previously developed will evaporate, and parents may become increasingly watchful and diligent in their efforts to secure adequate and necessary services (Spann, Kohler, & Soenksen, 2003; Starr, Foy, Cramer, & Singh, 2006; Stoner et al., 2005).

The issue of language. For parents and educators to collaboratively develop an individualized program for a student with an exceptionality, they must share a common language and vocabulary. Educators become so accustomed to using educational and medical terms and concepts that they frequently assume other people, including parents, understand their jargon. Parents may be somewhat reluctant to reveal their lack of understanding (Childre & Chambers, 2005) and, in some instances, may actually employ terms and phrases for which they have little comprehension. It is essential that the importance of a shared language not be underestimated. The selection of appropriate words and phrases, as free from jargon as possible, will ensure that parents feel more like contributing members of the IEP team.

It is also important during IEP meetings to remember the significant contribution nonverbal language plays in the communication process. Parents will naturally be ill at ease if they are faced with professionals who sit across from them, leaning back in their chair, arms crossed in front, except when they periodically glance at their watch. Conferencers should be aware of their nonverbal signals and must recognize that most parents would interact more effectively with someone who is leaning forward in interest, smiling, and maintaining eye contact (Lytle & Bordin, 2001).

The problem of intimidation. The IEP meeting may be particularly difficult for some parents whose child was previously served under an IFSP, because whereas the focus is on the family in the development of an IFSP, the focus of the IEP is on the student with the disability, with parents and families serving as collaborative partners. In other cases, there are difficulties because the development of a student's IEP requires representation from diverse fields (e.g., speech and language, social work), and parents and family members often end up in a planning conference with a number of other individuals, most of whom are professionals. Although the participation of these professionals presents a number of advantages, it has the obvious disadvantage of intimidating many parents. Because the majority of parents will have had little or no prior contact with either the other IEP participants or the guidelines of these meetings and because prior to the initial conference they may very well just be coming to grips with having a child with an exceptionality, it should come as no surprise that many have reported a great deal of apprehension and discomfort at these sessions. Lack of familiarity, understanding, and experience with the IEP process may result in parents' holding views regarding the planning meeting that are less favorable than the views held by the school professionals (Simon, 2006). After all, school professionals have participated in many IEP meetings, whereas for most parents the meetings for their child represent their only experience. In addition, a number of parents say they feel somewhat ill equipped to make a realistic contribution. For example, it is common practice to indicate the number of minutes of special education and related services and to refer to assistive technology devices (e.g., 90 minutes per week of special education, 20 minutes twice a week of speech therapy) without describing the actual services being delivered. Parents may be unfamiliar with the scope and nature of the recommended services. Hence, specificity in describing the services can help parents make meaningful contributions to the program plan (Bateman & Herr, 2006; Marino, Marino, & Shaw, 2006; Seligman & Darling, 2007). Finally, after completion of an IEP meeting, conferencers may wish to have another member of the IEP team give them feedback on the collaborative skills they displayed during the meeting. A sample IEP conference evaluation is presented in Figure 11.1.

Because parents do represent a significant resource in the IEP conference, the others must encourage them to be contributing members of the IEP team. Even though this is not an easy task to accomplish, certain procedures will facilitate the process:

- No more participants than necessary should be allowed in the meeting. Although no one should be denied admission whose contribution may be of benefit, marginally involved persons should not compromise the effective composition of the group.

IEP Conference Evaluation

Date _____ Name of child _____

Name of person observed _____

Observer(s) _____

Circle the response that most closely describes the skills demonstrated for each of the items below. Following evaluation, you should provide verbal feedback to the individual in the role of conferencer for each of the items.

1. Ability of the conferencer to inform parents of the purpose of the conference

1	2	3	4	5
Poor	Below Average	Average	Above Average	Excellent

2. Ability of the conferencer to establish an environment that promotes respect and trust

1	2	3	4	5
Poor	Below Average	Average	Above Average	Excellent

3. Ability of the conferencer to conduct the session in a systematic and sequential manner

1	2	3	4	5
Poor	Below Average	Average	Above Average	Excellent

4. Ability of the conferencer to keep the session flowing and on course

1	2	3	4	5
Poor	Below Average	Average	Above Average	Excellent

Figure 11.1. Individualized Education Program (IEP) conference evaluation form.

5. Ability of the conferencer to use language that is appropriate and understandable to a parent audience

1	2	3	4	5
Poor	Below Average	Average	Above Average	Excellent

6. Ability of the conferencer to solicit and respond to parent questions

1	2	3	4	5
Poor	Below Average	Average	Above Average	Excellent

7. Ability of the conferencer to address parents in a welcoming, nonintimidating fashion

1	2	3	4	5
Poor	Below Average	Average	Above Average	Excellent

8. Ability of the conferencer to rephrase questions in an attempt to acknowledge the contributions of parents or family members

1	2	3	4	5
Poor	Below Average	Average	Above Average	Excellent

9. Ability of the conferencer to justify the type of educational placement or program that is recommended for the pupil

1	2	3	4	5
Poor	Below Average	Average	Above Average	Excellent

10. Ability of the conferencer to summarize the conference

1	2	3	4	5
Poor	Below Average	Average	Above Average	Excellent

Figure 11.1. (*continued*)

- An informal and friendly conference style can effectively create an atmosphere of warmth for parents and a willingness to form partnerships.
- Parents should be encouraged to bring a friend or confidant to the conference, particularly someone who is familiar with the IEP process.
- Parents should have at least one professional at the conference with whom they are familiar and to whom they can relate. It is simply unrealistic to assume that parents can enter a group of professional strangers without the benefit of at least one previously established relationship and function as a contributing and collaborative member of an IEP team.

The mother of a child recently identified with mental retardation described being particularly overwhelmed at "entering a roomful of strangers who knew more about Arnie than I did." Although she acknowledged that periodically someone would ask for her opinion, she reported feeling too intimidated to respond, "even though later on I wish I had since I knew some things they didn't." The mother added, "If I had just known someone at the meeting or if I had someone to go with me, I wouldn't have felt so scared."

LEAST RESTRICTIVE ENVIRONMENT AND INCLUSION

According to this provision of IDEA, children and youth with disabilities must be educated to the maximum extent appropriate alongside typically developing and achieving students. Indeed, children and youth with disabilities may receive a placement outside the regular classroom environment only when the severity or nature of their disability demands a more restrictive setting. The specific policy of this important component of IDEA reads as follows:

> To the maximum extent appropriate, children with disabilities, including children in public or private institutions or other care facilities, are educated with children who are not disabled, and that special classes, separate schooling, or other removal of children with disabilities from the regular education environment occurs only when the nature or severity of the disability is such that education in regular classes with the use of supplementary aids and services cannot be achieved satisfactorily. (20 U.S.C. § 1412 (a)(5)(A))

Years ago, the National Association for Retarded Citizens (1973) emphasized the concept of normalization and contact with peers, noting that persons with disabilities should be aided in achieving "an existence as close to the normal as possible, making available to them patterns and conditions of everyday life . . . close to the norms and patterns of society" (p. 72). The least restrictive environment component of IDEA derives directly from this theme. In this regard, restrictiveness refers to (a) the physical setting of the educational facility, including its proximity to the student's home; (b) the degree to which the educational program is normalized (i.e., the student population, the curriculum and materials used in the program, the instructional methods used); and (c) the structure and rules of the program (i.e., the degree to which students are permitted the same choices and freedoms as other students in other schools).

On the basis of the notion of the "criterion of ultimate functioning" first articulated by L. Brown, Nietupski, and Hamre-Nietupski (1976), professionals advocated for teaching functional skills to individuals with disabilities in natural environments. Brown and his colleagues argued that if professionals and parents wanted students to be independent and competent, they needed to be taught specific skills, not behaviors representative of those skills. Their position set the tone for parents and professionals to advocate for maximally normalized settings for students with disabilities, including opportunities for contact with normally developing and achieving peers.

Subsequent work has demonstrated the positive influence of integration experiences on the behavior and skill development of students with disabilities (S. H. Freeman & Alkin, 2000; Hunt, Soto, Maier, & Doering, 2003; Owen-DeSchryver, Carr, Cale, & Blakeley-Smith, 2008; Rea, McLaughlin, & Walther-Thomas, 2002) and showed that holding all students to the same standards present in general education settings may positively impact the student's level of independent functioning after leaving school (Sun, 2007). Increasingly strong arguments are being made that integrated settings best serve the needs of children and youth with disabilities.

It is important to recognize that in spite of least restrictive environment policies that support the regular classroom as the desired arena for instruction, children and youth whose needs cannot be met in that setting must be afforded other placement options. Thus, the concept of the least restrictive environment has roots in the assumption that children and youth with exceptionalities should be educated along with their peers without disabilities to the maximum extent appropriate. IDEA specifies that this educational placement decision process begin with a consideration of the student in a general education classroom. In the event the team determines that a student with a disability cannot be satisfactorily educated in a general education classroom, he or she may be placed in an alternative setting (e.g., self-contained special education classroom). This alternative setting, however, must provide for contact and interactions with peers without disabilities to the maximum extent appropriate for the student with a disability. The identification of the least restrictive environment, which is reviewed and determined at least annually, must be based on each student's ability and performance, as translated through the IEP. As parents are major participants in this decision, school or agency personnel cannot make such a disposition independent of parent input.

Simpson and Sasso (1992) criticized the underpinning of much of the full-inclusion movement, noting that it is often based on references to "'the moral and just thing to do' rather than scientifically established benefits" (p. 3). They added,

> The full inclusion debate has too often been reduced to superficial arguments over who is right, who is moral and ethical, and who is a true advocate for children. Much of this simplistic posturing obscures the real issue (i.e., what is best for children) via claims of moral and ethical "high ground" and denouncements of "nonbelievers" as not knowing what is best and not caring about children and youth with disabilities. While perhaps effective in the short term, this process can lead to results that are directly opposite of those intended, including impediments to maximally effective programs for children and youth. We are of the opinion that full inclusion . . . is the right thing to do only if it benefits students with disabilities, their normally developing peers, or (ideally) if it is beneficial for both groups. That is, "the right thing to do," in our estimation, is that which provides the most benefits, not something that someone or some group deems appropriate because it fits their value system, is congruent with a fashionable trend, or appears to be a suitable, albeit unsupported alternative. (p. 4)

Obviously, there are parents and professionals who disagree with this and who strongly advocate for full inclusion, believing it a logical step in the advancement of services and programs for students with disabilities (D. J. Gallagher, 2001; Kluth, Villa, & Thousand, 2002; Sailor, 1991; Stainback & Stainback, 1992; Walther-Thomas, Korinek, McLaughlin, & Williams, 2000). Others take a middle path and point out that it is imprudent to place all students with disabilities in general education, particularly without careful attention to the necessary supports and services (Hallahan, Kauffman, & Pullen, 2009; Holloway, 2001; Kauffman & Hallahan, 2005;

Kavale & Forness, 2000; Mundschenk, Foley, & Swedburg, 2005; Praisner, 2003; Simpson, Myles, Simpson, & Ganz, 2005; Zigmond, 2003).

Although the controversy over inclusion is complex and multifaceted, this appears at least in part to be a function of variable terminology. That is, professionals and parents often use terms related to inclusion in different ways. As noted earlier, the least restrictive environment component of IDEA requires that students with disabilities be educated along with students who do not have disabilities to the maximum extent appropriate. Placement decisions relating to students with disabilities must begin with a consideration of educating them in regular classrooms. If it is determined that a student with a disability cannot learn satisfactorily in a regular classroom, an alternative setting may be recommended, with the stipulation that these alternatives allow for contact with peers without disabilities to the maximum extent appropriate. Thus, although the least restrictive environment concept is based first and foremost on the availability of a range of services and educational placement alternatives capable of meeting individual students' needs, placement still must be deemed *appropriate* on a case-by-case basis.

It should be pointed out that *integration, mainstreaming,* and *inclusion* are not synonymous terms. *Integration,* as related to the least restrictive environment and inclusion, generally refers to placement of students with disabilities in settings attended by their classmates without disabilities. Integration frequently refers to contact between students with disabilities and their peers without disabilities in other than shared classroom activities. For instance, integration may refer to common experiences between general education and special education students in a hallway or cafeteria. *Mainstreaming* refers to the selective placement of children and youth with disabilities in one or more regular education classes. An underlying assumption of mainstreaming is that students with disabilities should have the necessary basic knowledge and skills to benefit from a general education curriculum. That is, students who are mainstreamed are considered capable of making progress with their peers without disabilities in regular classroom settings when provided appropriate support, curricular and instructional adaptation and assistance, and individualization.

Inclusion refers to a commitment to educate students with disabilities in regular education classrooms to the maximum extent possible. Inclusion involves making support services available in general classrooms as opposed to pulling students out for services. Unlike mainstreaming, inclusion requires only that students profit from being in a general education classroom (e.g., social benefits occur), not that they successfully compete with their peers without disabilities. Inclusion can be full or selective.

The practice of full inclusion stems from basic principles that are important for both parents and professionals to recognize. First, full inclusion is a "zero reject" model; that is, it is designed to accommodate, without exception, all students with disabilities in general education classrooms. Second, students in full-inclusion programs receive their education at the same neighborhood schools or attendance centers as other same-age students who live in their area. Third, children and youth with disabilities are placed in general education classrooms at a rate consistent with disability prevalence statistics. In accordance with this provision, no more than three students with disabilities would be assigned to typical general education classrooms. Fourth, children and youth with disabilities receive their education along with same-age peers as opposed to taking classes with younger or older normally developing and achieving students. Fifth, general classroom teachers and other regular education personnel assume primary responsibility for educating students with disabilities, with the assistance and support of special education teachers and related services staff. Finally, general education classroom experiences are designed to develop and enhance students' peer relationships and social development, regardless of students' overall functioning and ability.

Just as the name suggests, selective inclusion refers to regular class placement of some students with disabilities some of the time. This moderate-inclusion perspective stems from the assumption that not all children and youth with disabilities are appropriate for full-time regular class placement. Moreover, selective inclusion (a) requires availability of a continuum of service options, (b) may be unavailable at certain schools, (c) involves some students with disabilities to receive at least a portion of their instructional services from special education and related services personnel, and (d) requires that IEP teams determine the appropriateness of general education placement for individual students with disabilities.

There is no question that the problems associated with selecting the least restrictive environment for students with disabilities are due at least partially to confusion over the various terms that relate to this process. Accordingly, professionals should help parents and other professionals deal with this difficult issue through careful clarification of terminology, including analysis of the theoretical and procedural underpinnings of various options. Knowledge of such elements should assist parents and professionals in reaching informed decisions about the least restrictive environment for a particular student, including the advisability of inclusionary placement. It should also be obvious that placement of students with disabilities in inclusive settings will necessitate availability and usage of suitable support resources, including adequate teacher planning time, a pool of trained paraprofessionals and support staff, appropriate staff development, reduced class size, appropriate outside consultants, supportive attitudes and a positive school climate, and knowledge of basic general education classroom management tools and instructional methods (Simpson, de Boer-Ott, & Smith-Myles, 2003).

Given the controversial nature of inclusion, integration, and mainstreaming and the interpretation of the least restrictive setting, it is imperative that professionals work particularly closely with parents in establishing this component of a student's program. The following should be considered:

- In determining the least restrictive environment, the educator should remember that the parent is not an opponent but rather someone who shares a common goal. Pursuant to that end, the focus should be on the student; that is, the least restrictive environment should be determined by each student's needs and the educators' and parents' interpretation of those needs rather than by the services available in the district.
- As suggested previously, parents can be expected to be active participants in gaining an appropriate education for their child only when the proper interpersonal conditions exist. The conferencer must be able to establish conditions of trust and rapport to reach consensus on significant educational decisions, including the least restrictive environment.
- Educators should not be overly anxious to transfer students with disabilities into general education classes when special classes or settings are producing desirable results. Evidence shows that many parents favorably view special class placement. If a more structured setting offers an appropriate environment and is supported by the parents, educators and parents should carefully evaluate the advantages of recommending a transfer to a general education setting.
- Educators should seek ways to have children and youth with disabilities participate with their general education class peers in social, extracurricular, and nonacademic school and community activities, even if they remain in segregated settings. Many parents may be reluctant to give up programs that they have struggled so hard to obtain and return their children to a setting that has been unrewarding. Nonetheless, systematic attempts should be made to increase the in-

clusion of students with exceptionalities into normalized situations as much as possible.

- Educators must be able to offer a continuum of educational placement alternatives for students with exceptionalities. With choices available, parents and educators will be able to select from those placements that seem most appropriate for a given student.

There is no question that decisions relating to inclusion (especially full inclusion) of children and youth with disabilities in general education settings require prudent consideration of a number of factors. It is also clear that this emotionally charged issue will be the source of a good deal of disagreement for some professionals and parents. Thus, as Simpson and Sasso (1992) pointed out, individuals considering issues related to the least restrictive environment and inclusion should acknowledge parents' and professionals' positive regard for students with disabilities, regardless of their full-inclusion viewpoint. The vast majority of professionals and parents involved in rearing, educating, and treating individuals with disabilities are decent, honest, and compassionate people, and thus the differences of opinion they hold regarding full inclusion should be viewed as arising from different attitudes, training, and experiences. It should also be apparent that these differences are not only natural but a potentially rich catalyst for cooperative problem solving. Simpson and Sasso (1992) also offered the following observations regarding the focus of full-inclusion discussions and debates:

> Too much energy has already been invested in the full-inclusion debate in terms of defining who is the "most right," who cares most about children, who has the most worthy values, and so on. We contend that the vast majority of individuals associated with children and youth [with disabilities] are committed to promoting the best interests of these individuals. By assuming this attitude, differences of opinion over full inclusion can be used to stimulate creative and mutually beneficial problem solving. Consequently, the debate can be redirected to focus on the utility of full inclusion, as opposed to whether one group's values are as good as those of another. (p. 11)

We should recognize how unrealistic it is to expect that children and youth without disabilities and general education teachers and staff will independently and exclusively make all necessary adjustments to accommodate students with disabilities in full-time general education settings. Furthermore, expecting that all the necessary accommodations related to inclusion will be made by general education students and educators implies that students with disabilities are unable to positively change their behavior and that special educators are incapable of providing effective instruction. Current strategies provide remarkable opportunities for behavioral, social, language, and cognitive change. Thus, when provided appropriate training and intervention, students with disabilities can make significant gains. Accordingly, the most appropriate program is that which most effectively serves the individualized needs of the student, regardless of its physical setting.

In spite of its positive aspects, full inclusion of all such students violates the concept of individualized education, as does any procedure that is advocated for all children. Full inclusion should be viewed as one of several placement options, not the default placement of all students. Thus, children and youth with disabilities should be integrated on an individual basis after consideration of a variety of placement alternatives, including (but not limited to) general education classrooms.

Moreover, full inclusion may be appropriate during one phase of a student's school program but not at other times. For example, some students with severe disabilities may require skills that are better developed and trained in a segregated setting (e.g., self-help, toileting). In such situations, skill development may progress more rapidly and effectively in a special education setting. In addition, community integration and functional-skill development constitute two core curricular areas for many children and youth with severe disabilities. Concern for contact with peers without disabilities should not completely overshadow the need for functional skills that are necessary for persons with disabilities to live an independent adult life.

Full-inclusion plans for students with disabilities should consider the needs of children and youth both with and without disabilities. Integration experiences rely on the involvement of typically developing and achieving peers. Though integration primarily benefits students with disabilities, children and youth without disabilities also gain from these interactions. Unfortunately, special education policies such as inclusion have been perceived by some general educators, administrators, parents, and members of the general population as a factor associated with the poor performance of some general education students. Accordingly, appropriate educational experiences for all children and youth must be ensured. With regard to inclusion decisions, teams must consider the needs of both students with disabilities and their regular education peers.

Clearly, for many parents the entrance of their child into elementary school brings the additional challenge of negotiating between multiple placement options and the ongoing debate regarding inclusion. Some parents may be unsure that their child's individual needs will be met and feel uncertain about how their child will fare in a general education class (Duhaney & Salend, 2000; J. Johnson & Duffett, 2002; Lindsay & Dockrell, 2004). Others may emphasize the advantages of and advocate for an inclusive placement (Buchan, 2000; Duhaney & Salend, 2000; D. S. Palmer, Fuller, Arora, & Nelson, 2001). Regardless of the nature or extent of inclusion for an individual student, effective efforts necessitate the involvement of parents in the program planning process.

Participation and Accommodation in Assessment

The Elementary and Secondary Education Act, now known as the No Child Left Behind Act (2001), has increased the emphasis on accountability for schools by requiring states to implement an assessment system for students, including those with disabilities, to demonstrate that all students have access to and are succeeding in the general curriculum (Simpson, LaCava, & Graner, 2004). Schools must demonstrate that *all* students are making adequate yearly progress (based on state proficiency standards). Therefore, in addition to the overall scores of students in individual grades and content areas, the scores must be disaggregated for subgroups of students who (a) are economically disadvantaged, (b) are from diverse racial and ethnic groups, (c) have diagnosed disabilities, and (d) have limited English proficiency (Yell, Katsiyannas, & Shriner, 2006).

Although standardized testing has a long history in our educational system, there are concerns regarding high-stakes accountability testing and the inappropriateness for students with disabilities (National Center on Educational Outcomes, 2003; National Center for Learning Disabilities, 2006; Shriner, 2000). Some issues relate to the one-size-fits-all approach, the overreliance on a single test score, the potential for narrowing the curriculum to the areas assessed, and the limited utility these tests have in designing daily classroom instruction because they assess broad areas and so do not provide the specific information teachers need to modify their lessons. In addition, there is a delay in reporting scores back to the school, sometimes after the school year is over and the student has advanced to the next grade. If the delay is significant, the results may no longer accurately reflect the current skill level of the student.

Even with these drawbacks and limitations, standardized scores can contribute important information for policy and decision makers in improving the academic achievement of all students (Thurlow, 2000; Ysseldyke et al., 2004). In addition, on the basis of analyses of anecdotal (media reports) and empirical studies, Ysseldyke and colleagues (2004) concluded,

> High-stakes assessments seem to encourage better communication with parents about students' skill levels, accommodations, and the various options available to the students. Parents can ask better questions about what specific skills their child needs additional work on, and the parents, student, and teacher can collaborate on all avenues of learning within and outside the classroom setting. (p. 91)

Most states have constructed their own tests to ensure that they focus on important educational outcomes in that state and reflect student attainment of specific achievement targets (Stiggins, 2001). These tests typically include statewide standardized assessments and alternate assessments (Yell, Dragsow, & Lowrey, 2005). Standardized assessments are typically paper-and-pencil tests that are administered under established conditions in a group format on specified schoolwide testing days. Alternate assessments are designed to demonstrate the progress of students with significant cognitive disabilities who are unable to participate in the state or district standardized assessment, even with accommodations.

IDEA requires that parents, as part of the IEP team, be involved in deciding how the child will participate in district and state assessments (20 U.S.C. § 1414(d)(1)(A)). The IEP team may determine that the child will participate in the regular assessment under the standardized conditions, participate in the regular assessment with accommodations (e.g., extended time, orally read questions, larger print), or participate in an alternate assessment (e.g., videotape of a child independently performing a self-care task). If testing accommodations are in order, the team must also determine the appropriate and individualized accommodations for the student (Edgemon, Jablonski, & Lloyd, 2006; Elbaum, 2007; Salend, 2008b) and identify who will implement and monitor those accommodations to ensure consistency between what is listed on the IEP and what is actually provided (Shriner & Destefano, 2003). Conferencers must ensure that parents understand the assessment program and possible accommodations so that they can contribute fully in making decisions regarding how their child will participate.

For students with severe disabilities participating in an alternate assessment, parental input may be even more valuable. Parents can help establish a realistic profile of their child's present level of functioning that will enable the school to document change over time (Campbell, Reilly, & Henley, 2008). They may also identify familiar activities and interests that can be incorporated into the assessment to ensure a more accurate evaluation of the child's skills (Vacca, 2007).

The assessment results are reported to parents in the form of school report cards that illustrate where their own child stands academically, as well as whether their school and district are succeeding in meeting state standards for all students, including those in the disaggregated groups (Yell et al., 2005). Although most parents have heard of the large-scale assessment programs in their school, they may not be aware of how the test results will be used to impact the general curriculum of the school and that of their own child (N. Frey, 2005) or of the possible sanctions such as supplemental service (e.g., tutoring) that may be available to them (Howell, 2006). Conferencers must be able to explain to parents how to interpret these scores and how the scores reflect one measure of their child's level of academic achievement as compared to that of their peers.

Some parents welcome the effect these assessment systems have on establishing higher expectations for achievement for their children with disabilities. Other parents, such as Mandy's mother in the opening vignette, have concerns about the appropriateness of having their child take a test that is beyond their ability and that includes material that the child has not yet been taught:

> State testing came up last spring. Mandy wasn't severe enough to be able to do the other stuff, portfolio work [alternate assessment], but they put in for her to be able to have modified testing with accommodations. It was way too stressful for her. The week that they did the testing, she was so drained. She felt like she had to do perfectly on it, and she couldn't do any of it. She stresses about tests, and her anxiety level is really high anyway. She cries about these tests. You can't push her too much, or she just falls apart, and what's the purpose of that?

Clearly, schools must work with parents to identify barriers to students' success on large-scale and high-stakes assessments and to alter those barriers that can be changed. They must also ensure that the child's special education program and assessments are aligned to state content standards (Browder et al., 2004; Roach, Elliott, & Webb, 2005) and that access is provided to a general curriculum demonstrated to be effective for most students (Malmgren, McLaughlin, & Nolet, 2005). Finally, schools must make sure that the accommodations that a child needs to participate are provided (Thurlow, House, Scott, & Ysseldyke, 2000) and that meaningful opportunities for remediation are available for students to achieve proficiency levels in core academic areas (National Center for Learning Disabilities, 2006; Quenemoen, Lehr, Thurlow, & Massanari, 2001).

Homework

Another topic that is often included in information exchange conferences is homework. Homework is regularly given to elementary-age students to promote independent work habits, to develop fluency on important skills by providing practice or review of material presented in class, and to acquire content knowledge (Bursuck et al., 1999; H. Cooper, Robinson, & Patall, 2006). It is not surprising that students with disabilities often struggle to complete homework assignments and spend more time completing these assignments than do their peers without disabilities (Harniss, Epstein, Bursuck, Nelson, & Jayanthi, 2001). Given the increasing importance of homework as an instructional practice in inclusive classrooms, there is a need for enhancing the effectiveness of homework for students with disabilities, including improving home–school communication (M. H. Epstein, 1999).

Homework may serve as a communication tool between teachers and parents to share information regarding topics taught in class, the child's progress in the curriculum, and ways that parents can support that progress (H. Cooper et al., 2006; J. L. Epstein & Van Voorhis, 2001; Polloway, Bursuck, & Epstein, 2001). There are a number of specific strategies schools can use to improve home–school communication. Schools can establish a homework hotline that parents can call during evening homework hours or a homework link on the school's Web site to provide parents with Internet access to homework policies, practices, and assignments (Olsen & Fuller, 2003; Salend, Duhaney, Anderson, & Gottschalk, 2004).

Schools can also implement a homework planner or notebook system where students are required to record daily assignments, the date they are due, and any specific directions for completing the assignment and then have their parents sign the notebook each evening. In fact, in a nationwide survey of 120 parents of children with disabilities and 140 parents of children without disabilities, parents in both groups ranked daily assignment books as the most effective action teachers could take to improve home–school communication and ranked checking with their child daily about homework as the most effective recommendation for parents (Harniss et al., 2001). Regardless of the particular strategy employed, decisions regarding homework communication strategies should be dynamic and collaborative processes whereby conferencers and parents can identify effective and feasible strategies (Bursuck et al., 1999; M. H. Epstein, 1999; J. S. Nelson, Jayanthi, Brittain, Epstein, & Bursuck, 2002).

In addition to getting information regarding the assignments, parents will need to know if homework assignments will be adapted for their child and in what ways. For example, time during the school day to complete assignments, opportunities for extra credit, student effort as a factor in grading, how teachers check for understanding of homework assignments in class, and how assignments are altered in terms of deadlines, content, or length (J. S. Nelson, Epstein, Bursuck, Jayanthi, & Sawyer, 1998) should be explained to parents. In addition, with the increased focus on inclusive educational placements, most students with disabilities are in general education classes. Hence, parents need to know which teacher they should contact if they have questions or concerns regarding their child's homework (Munk et al., 2001).

Margolis (2005) offered these suggestions to elicit parental support for homework: (a) initiate and maintain contact with parents and learn about parents' concerns, views, talents, interests, and availability; (b) help parents develop a support plan that includes a quiet, distraction-free place and materials; (c) suggest specific support activities, such as listening to their child read or reviewing concepts by discussing photos; (d) provide homework information; (e) ask parents to limit homework if their child is frustrated or has spent reasonable time on it, and then inform the teacher of the child's efforts and difficulties; and (f) invite parents to participate in a school–home reinforcement system where they agree to provide their child a predetermined reinforcer for successfully completed homework.

The focus of parent–professional discussions at the elementary-age level shifts from community to public school and from readiness and development to more traditional academic concerns. As noted, the need for information is among the most common parental needs; consequently, strategies designed to satisfy this need will create a basis for effective program progress.

Needs for Service and Advocacy

Parents of school-age children with exceptionalities are initially concerned about locating appropriate educational and treatment alternatives for their children. Given the impact of federal legislation and school policy changes that have produced an increased number of program options for children with exceptionalities—thus relieving many parental concerns for direct service—attention has shifted somewhat from location of services to the quality of those services. Specifically, attention is increasingly focused on the use of empirically based interventions and highly qualified teachers implementing those interventions.

The No Child Left Behind Act requires schools to use scientifically based instructional programming to improve student achievement. In essence, it calls on schools to rely on science when they make decisions about all aspects of education (Yell, 2006). This emphasis on sound scientific research that demonstrates the effectiveness of an intervention or program prevents programming based on fads and will result in more effective instruction (Kauffman, Mock, Tankersley, & Landrum, 2008; O'Neill, 2004).

It is difficult not only for parents but also for professionals to judge the scientific validity of the myriad interventions available to them. This is not surprising given, as Simpson (2003) suggested, that "there is fierce debate over which options hold the most promise, and decisions regarding methodology selections are often based on hype and other nonscientific factors" (p. 193). Teachers must be aware of the empirical evidence supporting the interventions and methods they include in a student's educational program, the anticipated outcomes, and the most effective means of evaluating a particular method or approach (Simpson, 2005). Simpson, de Boer-Ott, and colleagues (2005) presented an overview and analysis of the utility and efficacy of commonly used and purported interventions and treatments for individuals with autism-related disabilities. They suggested differentiating between interventions that have significant and convincing empirical efficacy and support from those that are promising practices or that have limited empirical support. Teachers must be able to critically evaluate and select instructional methods that have the highest probability of success and to communicate to parents the empirical bases for making those determinations. This is critical not only for compliance with current law but also as it reflects best practice methods for delivering services to children with disabilities.

Both the No Child Left Behind Act and IDEA require all teachers to be highly qualified to teach the subjects assigned to them. Under IDEA, states must ensure that personnel are appropriately and adequately prepared and trained and have the content knowledge and skills to serve children with disabilities. For special education teachers at the elementary level, this requires a bachelor's degree, certification as a special education teacher, and a license to teach in that state. If special education teachers are also responsible for teaching a core academic subject, they must meet the same requirements applied to any general elementary or middle school teacher under the No Child Left Behind Act or demonstrate competence in core academic subjects by completing the state-developed high objective uniform state standard of evaluation. Teachers of students with severe disabilities, those assessed against alternate achievement standards, can demonstrate subject matter competency by passing a test at their students' level of instruction (Yell, 2006).

Starr et al. (2006) surveyed parents of children with autism spectrum disorders, Down syndrome, and learning disabilities regarding their perceptions of the education their child was receiving. In responding to questions concerning the implementation of best practices, these parents showed dissatisfaction by reporting low agreement with statements that suggested that components generally considered desirable in delivering special education services (and that parents felt their child needed) were actually being provided to their child. In addition, 86% of the children discussed in this study spent at least a portion of their school day in a general education class. In a study by Munk and colleagues (2001), parents reported the perception that teachers do not have enough information about their child's needs to help with or appropriately adapt homework assignments. Clearly, if students with disabilities are going to have meaningful access to the general curriculum, they must have teachers highly trained in instructional techniques and strategies that support that access. Teachers must be knowledgeable and experienced in implementing scientifically based management, communication, social interaction, independent living, and cognitive and academic skill instructional interventions (Simpson, 2003, 2004). In addition, all teachers working with students with disabilities must be trained to implement curriculum adaptations and augmentation strategies that might promote student involvement and progress in the general curriculum (Browder & Cooper-Duffy, 2003; Lee et al., 2006).

Parents are frequently interested in augmenting professional services and meeting the school-related needs of their children, but they may be unaware of the range of services available. Bos and Vaughn (2006) suggested that teachers provide parents with a list of community resources that provide structured programs for children and youth with disabilities during unstructured times, particularly during the summer months. These programs might include public library literacy programs; programs at children's museums; acting, cinema, and stage design with local theater groups; public parks and recreation activities; summer camps; and special programs offered by universities or colleges (p. 504).

Because parents have a vested interest in the policies and administrative procedures that govern service delivery, they should be encouraged to serve in local, state, or national organizations as members or officers to impact the policies and procedures on a broader scale. In short, it is a good idea for them to expand their contact with professionals, other constituency groups, and other parents of children with disabilities.

Finally, in addition to advocacy and involvement training, parents and families must be directed to appropriate counseling, support groups, and social agencies whenever it would be helpful. As suggested, the infrequency of this need in no way discounts its importance.

Summary

The needs of parents with elementary-age children are as varied and individualized as those of parents with preschoolers, yet they tend to fall within the same basic areas: emotional support and understanding, information exchange opportunities, and mechanisms for identifying, implementing, and evaluating needed services. With the increased emphasis on serving students with disabilities in general education classrooms, conferencers must be able to work collaboratively with parents to determine the least restrictive environment for the child that will, by definition, provide the necessary supports and services to enable the child to receive meaningful educational benefit. A critical part of this collaborative process is the development of the IEP and the implementation of empirically based interventions by qualified personnel.

Exercises

1. Prepare a handbook on the Individuals with Disabilities Education Improvement Act for parents and family members of the children in your classroom. Include pertinent information for parents on their roles and responsibilities in the development of their child's IEP and in program planning. Ensure that the language you use is free from professional jargon and accessible to the full range of parents with whom you collaborate.

2. Prepare a list of ways that parents can support and advocate for their elementary-age child, such as monitoring homework completion, balancing school-related requirements and extracurricular activities, following their child's progress and

contacting teachers when they have questions or concerns, and providing input at IEP and other conferences.

3. Design an ongoing school–home communication system appropriate for elementary-age children.

4. Observe an IEP meeting of a student with an exceptionality. Following the meeting, use the IEP conference evaluation form in Figure 11.1 to evaluate the conferencer(s). For those skills not apparent, consider ways that the conferencer might have been more effective.

Chapter 12

Parents and Families of Youth and Young Adults With Exceptionalities

Vignette

Rachel is 16. She is a precious person. She has a head full of common sense. I think she's really perceptive about people. She has a strong values system, and family is very important to her. She has a real strong moral sense, too. . . . She's very kind hearted, very sensitive to others' needs. Academically she's doing great. She's a hard worker; sometimes I think she puts too much pressure on herself academically because she's so afraid of being embarrassed and that somebody else will think that she's dumb. That's still the stressor in her life. The beginning of every school year is a new stressor. Tears and anxiety, and actually she has gastritis—she has always had belly aches related to school. She's beautiful. She's athletic . . . no signs of competitiveness . . . doesn't like the confrontation . . . she's running cross-country track.

Because I mentioned values and morals, that's kind of a relief . . . because that was something I was worried about when she was younger. Her self-esteem has taken a major blow in all of this, and I was just afraid that she would be at high risk for all of the things we don't want our kids involved in, and as of right now we're doing great. Socially she's still very intimidated in a lot of social situations. The principal with whom I have very good communication and rapport . . . we know her on the side so she has been around Rachel a lot . . . she made a comment, she said Rachel is a silent leader. I think it's true. She would love to be part of the "the popular group," she always has wanted that, but she's not a follower. She won't just hang out and be on the fringes because she feels uncomfortable. She has slowly . . .

a little group of kids has evolved or developed around her, and she is the core.

One thing that Rachel asks for and that she really needs is a trust thing, totally. She needs to know that the teachers understand her and know what her weaknesses are and that they won't hang her out to dry. In elementary school the first day of every year I would meet with the teacher, and I would basically say I am most concerned about her self-esteem and I want her to learn to love school. So I wouldn't say it just like this, but please don't set her up in front of her peers. That's her biggest concern. This year all of the teachers have been wonderful—I made my point in elementary school, for them to realize that my child needed a little special care.

College is a given. We always talk like that, and we always have. Right now, I think she's thinking along those lines—that she'll go to college. I anticipate that I may have to make her move out of the house perhaps at some point, at least for a little while, because home and family are big security nets for her. This year she went to all of her teachers because she has to learn to advocate for herself, and she did. She rehearsed what she was going to say. I was really proud of her.

I wonder how much of a stigma may be attached to "resource," because that's where she receives her special education help. I have somewhat encouraged her to think about giving up the special education resource room support so that she could take an elective, and she's not interested. That is still her sanctuary, basically. She knows she has that support. It makes her nervous to be called on in class. She still lags behind in reading and English, but she's making progress, and her spelling, oh my gosh, she still has spelling issues. We send her to a math tutor once a week so she can earn her high school math credits.

Adolescence can be an exciting time full of change and opportunity. It can also be a time of anxiety and apprehension for children and their families. Children with and without disabilities must wrestle with issues of identity, independence, and autonomy; school transitions; emerging sexuality; social relationships; and the changing nature of parent–child relationships. Expectations in secondary schools typically include increased independence for academic and behavioral functioning, greater emphasis on academic requirements that lead to graduation, more homework, a larger student body, and more rigorous academic content provided within a whole-group instructional model. In addition, the gap between the performance of students with and without disabilities widens, particularly for students with moderate or severe disabilities. Clearly, the challenges are greater for adolescents and young adults with disabilities than for their peers without disabilities (T. E. C. Smith, Polloway, Patton, & Dowdy, 2004; Wagner, Newman, & Cameto, 2004).

For example, learning to drive and obtaining a license is considered a rite of passage for adolescents; however, students with disabilities may struggle to obtain this ubiquitous symbol of emerging independence, freedom, and responsibility. As one student with physical disabilities articulated, "Freedom! It's horrible, especially at my age, when everybody else is driving, um, when you've still got to have your big brother take you around like you're some 2-year-old or something. Or you can't even find your own way to school. It's like you're in elementary school, like all over again" (McGill & Vogtle, 2001, p. 458).

As a result of legislative mandates, litigation, and advocacy efforts, secondary-age students and young adults with special needs are beginning to receive a greater variety of services. Families have advocated for expanded opportunities to participate in school life, access to vocational and rehabilitation services, and integration in all school environments (Brolin & Loyd, 2004). Utilizing the supports and resources that parents and families can provide is particularly crucial for adolescents with disabilities given the current information on the long-term outcomes for these students.

Longitudinal studies on the community transition of students with disabilities have found higher dropout rates, lower employment rates, low wages, and higher arrest rates among those students than among their peers without disabilities (Cheney & Bullis, 2004; Hallahan & Kauffman, 2003; U.S. Department of Education, 2002). In a survey of 277 young adults with learning disabilities or emotional or behavioral disorders, Scanlon and Mellard (2002) concluded that 71% dropped out before completing 11th grade, and most reported having problems in school that are interest or attendance related as well as having disability-based difficulties. Given the prevalence of these students' dropping out and the resultant negative impact on economic, academic, and social independence after leaving school, it is imperative that schools work collaboratively with parents to identify and address risk factors for dropping out (National Center on Secondary Education and Transition, 2004; Scanlon & Mellard, 2002). The following strategies are suggested by the National Center on Secondary Education and Transition (2006) in a parent brief on the role of parents in dropout prevention: Parents can (a) maintain contact with their child's teachers throughout high school, (b) monitor school attendance, (c) encourage extracurricular activities or employment where students can develop positive relationships and experience success outside of school, (d) help their child explore career options that interest them, (e) let their child know that individuals with a high school diploma (or equivalency) are likely to earn twice as much as those who do not have one, (f) help their child identify graduation as a priority by keeping track of credits earned toward graduation, and (g) help their child identify postsecondary goals.

Self-Determination

Another important factor that can influence students' intention to complete high school is their development of self-determination. A relevant curricular outcome for secondary students would be to successfully describe their disability, understand its significance in day-to-day activities, and understand their rights and responsibilities as a person with disabilities (Scanlon & Mellard, 2002). In addition, students should demonstrate choice making, goal setting, problem solving, self-evaluation, and self-advocacy, all characteristics associated with self-determination (Eisenman, 2007; Wehmeyer, Agran, & Hughes, 2000).

Self-determination interventions can help students with disabilities develop the internal structures of motivation to achieve success in school and as young adults, thereby increasing the likelihood of engagement in academic learning and school activities and of graduation (Eisenman, 2007). Unfortunately, limited opportunities to exercise self-determination and self-advocacy during the school years may be masked by the procedural protections and safeguards provided by school personnel. In the postsecondary adult world, however, the absence of these skills can have significant negative impact (T. E. C. Smith, Gartin, Murdick, & Hilton, 2006). Although not mentioned explicitly in the requirements for transition services, self-determination skills are implied in the language of the Individuals with Disabilities Education Improvement Act (IDEA, 2004), where it is pointed out that discussion of needed transition services must occur within the context of the student's needs, preferences, and interests.

The implementation of strategies to teach and support self-determination behaviors have been shown to improve students' self-regulation, help them identify and attain goals (J. E. Martin et al., 2003; Mithaug & Mithaug, 2003; Wehmeyer, Palmer, Agran, Mithaug, & Martin, 2000), improve performance on academic skills (Fowler, Konrad, Walker, Test, & Wood, 2007), increase financial independence and independent living (Wehmeyer & Palmer, 2003), and enhance postsecondary educational opportunities (Field, Sarver, & Shaw, 2003; Kosine, 2007).

In an investigation of the self-determination skills and opportunities for adolescents with learning and/or emotional disorders, teachers' ratings of students' capacity for self-determination were significantly lower than the students' self-appraisals (Carter, Lane, Pierson, & Glaeser, 2006). In addition, both parents and special educators rated the capacity of adolescents with emotional disorders to engage in self-determination behavior significantly lower than the capacity of adolescents with learning disorders. Furthermore, although educators reported that few self-determination opportunities existed for students at home, parents felt that diminished opportunities exist at school, which suggests that little communication is occurring between school professionals and parents regarding efforts to promote self-determination in their respective settings (Carter et al., 2006).

In a survey of parents and teachers of students ages 16 to 21 with mild or moderate disabilities regarding beliefs about self-determination, parents and caregivers strongly supported teaching the skills and competencies underlying self-determination, such as setting goals and expressing interests and personal abilities. In addition, these parents and caregivers believed that their child not only should attend but also be taught the how to participate in their own Individualized Education Program (IEP) meetings (Grigal, Neubert, Moon, & Graham, 2003). Interestingly, parents and caregivers responded that they only slightly agree that these skills are taught to their child. This is not surprising given that the responses of the teachers who participated in this study indicated only slight familiarity with the concept of self-determination and how to teach it, which suggests that schools can do more to support the development of self-determination skills (Grigal et al., 2003).

Schools can support the development of self-determination skills through a variety of approaches, such as implementing person-centered planning methods that include the student's vision of his or her life, needs, interests, and abilities (e.g., Holburn & Vietz, 2002; Miner & Bates, 2002); implementing self-determination and self-instruction models (e.g., Benitez, Lattimore, & Wehmeyer, 2005; Wehmeyer, Agran, et al., 2000); using strategies to help students participate in meetings (e.g., Miner & Bates, 2002); and integrating instruction in self-determination skills across the day (e.g., Held, Thomas, & Thomas, 2004). Regardless of the specific approach utilized, current literature suggests that self-determination makes a significant difference in the life of students with disabilities and should be a component of programming at the secondary level (T. L. Smith, Polloway, Smith, & Patton, 2007).

Parents can also support the development of self-determination skills by allowing their child to take risks, test their abilities and limitations, develop problem-solving skills, make age-appropriate choices, and learn from the natural consequences of their choices (Lindstrom, Doren, Metheny, Johnson, & Zane, 2007; National Center on Secondary Education and Transition, 2006; Test, Aspel, & Everson, 2006).

Age of Majority

Another issue related to self-determination of adolescents and young adults is guardianship. Under IDEA (2004), parental rights transfer to the child when he or she reaches the age of majority in that state. Those rights transfer unless the child has been determined to be incompetent or unable to provide informed consent. Research by Millar and Renzaglia (2002) and Millar (2003) indicated that a primary reason guardians are appointed is the perception that the children involved are not capable of making decisions or are limited in their ability to make decisions—an important aspect of self-determination. In another study, Millar (2007) concluded that special educators and parents had a limited understanding of guardianship and its alternatives (such as case management, trust funds, and power of attorney) and did not recognize the disconnect between guardianship and self-determination. One teacher shared this experience:

> This last year, I had a student who was almost 20 years old and her mother was her appointed guardian. Her mother made all, and I do mean all, decisions for her. My co-workers and I were so disturbed by the relationship. I had known the student for years and felt that she had extremely regressed in all aspects. The young lady that I was working with had always expressed a desire to pursue her education. Sadly, I know that my ex-student is continuing to remain at home with no tangible future in sight. I truly believe that it is her mother that is unable to function independently of the student; not the other way around. (p. 126)

It is important that conferencers, parents, and families have accurate information related to guardianship and its relationship to the development of self-determination skills and behaviors, including ways to empower young adults with disabilities. Schools should encourage the student's development of independence and adult functioning while recognizing the important role parents and families may continue to play in the young adult's life. Although it may be necessary for a guardian to be appointed to serve the best interests of a young adult with disabilities, the guardianship process should be based on ongoing assessment of the student's strengths, needs, preferences, and interests and be intertwined with the transition process to ensure that students, families, and professionals are considering all adult roles and the supports needed. In this way, less intrusive options to guardianship might be possible (Payne-Christiansen & Sitlington, 2008).

Although it is important for adolescents and young adults to assert their independence and self-direct their life and plans for their future, parents and families continue to play a critical role in the developmental process of growing from childhood to adulthood. It is clear that many parents and families of youth and young adults with special needs are motivated to work with schools, agencies, and professionals on behalf of their children. These parents and families must be afforded the same opportunities for individualized involvement as their counterparts whose children are younger (Brolin & Loyd, 2004; T. E. C. Smith et al., 2006; R. L. Taylor, Smiley, & Richards, 2009). In fact, their needs generally fall within the same domain. Specifically, one can expect them to experience a need for emotional support, information exchange opportunities, and advocacy and service.

Need for Emotional Support

Although this need is not as widely recognized with adolescents and young adults with disabilities as with young children, parents and families nonetheless require emotional support and attention to help them cope with the exceptionality of their family member. This need exists regardless of the time lapsed since the initial diagnosis and interpretation and the services subsequently rendered.

Adolescence is a critical period of development, and the challenges inherent in moving from childhood to adulthood can be stressful for parents as well as their child. A natural part of adolescent development is to demand independence from parents and become dependent on the opinions of peers, yet the behavior of adolescents often indicates they still require security and supervision (Algozzine, O'Shea, & Algozzine, 2001). Conferencers must be supportive of parents as they wrestle with the fact that it is a natural impulse for their adolescent child to pull away from them and gravitate to peers, and parents must balance the necessity for supervision and direction with appropriate opportunities for the child to gain independence and develop his or her own autonomy.

In addition, parents might struggle with the seemingly contradictory emotions of wanting to protect their child from disappointments, isolation, and unknown dangers in the future while at the same time worrying about how to best prepare their child for that future. The mother of a young adult with autism reported that when her son was of elementary-school age, she periodically would break into tears upon seeing him attempt to interact with his siblings and their friends. She noted, however, that because he has now completed school and spends most of his time at home, her concerns are much different: "Will he qualify for a community workshop if space becomes available?" "Will his behavior allow him to be maintained at home?" "What will eventually happen to our son?"

Professionals should be aware of and sensitive to parents' and siblings' needs for support even after their family member has grown up. Such sensitivity and awareness may be manifested by recognizing individual feelings and attitudes relative to living with the person who has an exceptionality, being willing to listen to concerns and perceptions, and being attentive to the issues parents and siblings must deal with. For example, the mother of an 18-year-old with Down syndrome reported that her neighbors at one time considered her son cute, but many of them now considered him a threat even though he had never shown any aggressive or antisocial inclinations. The parents of an adolescent girl with retardation and physical impairments revealed that they were revisiting emotional issues and stages they thought had been resolved years before. For instance, these parents noted that with their daughter's passage into puberty came the realization that her condition was truly permanent. Specifically, they experienced renewed feelings of anger and frustration over recognizing that she likely could never live completely independently. Other parents and family members of youth and adults with disabilities have reported problems in dealing with such issues as sex, living arrangements, and marriage (Oliver, Anthony, & Leimkuhl, 2002; Raffaelli & Ontai, 2001).

When youth and young adults classified as exceptional on the basis of school-related criteria become able to function independently in normalized settings upon leaving school, their parents generally experience a sense of relief. Conversely, parents whose children have more severe disabilities will encounter even more frustration as they see their children growing up. Accordingly, the educational conferencer must stay mindful that family members' need for emotional support cannot be expected to vanish once a child leaves an elementary-level program (Dunst, 2002; Levinson, McKee, & DeMatteo, 2000).

Need for Information Exchange Systems

Even without the side issues of exceptionality, the nature of the psychological and developmental changes associated with adolescence and young adulthood can be highly unpredictable. The interaction between adolescence and a disability, though, can result in a period of even greater instability (Bos & Vaughn, 2006; T. E. C. Smith et al., 2004). Thus, although adolescence is typically a stage when peer groups replace parents as the primary social influence, an exceptionality may require the parents and families to continue to serve in a more prominent and supportive role for their adolescent or young adult. Accordingly, parents and siblings frequently desire information relating to the changes associated with their family member's puberty and young adulthood and to the many issues associated with this period. In addition, many families seek opportunities to share information about their family member who has special needs with his or her teacher and other professionals. Algozzine and colleagues (2001) listed some of the particular youth-related problems about which parents desire information: drug and alcohol abuse, school violence, depression and suicide, and teen sexuality. Parents also are interested in learning strategies instruction. Because of the significance of these and related issues, parents and families of youth and young adults with exceptionalities, contrary to popular opinion, are often motivated to interact with professionals for the purpose of exchanging information.

In addition, based on research findings, conferencers can expect parents and family members of adolescents and young adults with exceptionalities to show interest in discussing the results of various types of assessment measures descriptive of their family member's abilities. Thus, rather than being satiated or totally familiar with their adolescent son's or daughter's strengths and weaknesses, these parents sometimes have a strong interest in more of this type of information. Perhaps because at this time they are also considering nonacademic alternatives for their children (e.g., workshops, competitive employment, independent living) or because they are more realistic about a disability, many families consider diagnostic data a topic of interest during this period of a child's life.

Diploma

Awarding a diploma to a student with disabilities can be a monumental event for school professionals as well as for parents and the student (Livovich, 2004). Simply remaining in high school for 4 years or until graduation, however, does not guarantee students with disabilities will earn their diploma. Each state has the authority to set the standards and requirements for earning a high school diploma and, as such, can either modify or hold constant the requirements for students with disabilities (Lanford & Cary, 2000). States vary in their requirements, and some students with disabilities earn certificates of attendance or effort, modified diplomas, or IEP diplomas. Approximately 80% of the states provide an alternative to the standard diploma (e.g., certificate of attendance) that does not specify the student's skill level or the course of study (Test et al., 2006). Other options include a modified diploma for students who do not pass the required state tests or the requirement that students pass an alternative test for a diploma (Brigham, Morocco, Clay, & Zigmond, 2006). Roughly 10% of the states use completion of the student's IEP goals and objectives, or an alternative course of study, to qualify for a standard diploma (Test et al., 2006). Given the importance of a high school diploma for postsecondary educational opportunities as well as employment options, it is critical that conferencers communicate clearly to parents the relationship between participating in alternate assessment or alternative courses of study and graduating with a standard diploma (Byrnes, 2004; Guy, Shin, Lee, & Thurlow, 2000).

Educational Programming

Although students with disabilities have a variety of educational needs, reading is a problem area for many that persists into high school; students struggle to understand and remember what they read across the range of content areas typical in a high school curriculum. Although instruction in the basic skills associated with literacy becomes more difficult as the student grows older, quality instruction includes explicit instruction, promotion of cognitive and collaborative engagement, multiple opportunities for distributed practice, and teacher feedback (Denton & Vaughn, 2008; Faggella-Luby & Deshler, 2008). The essential features of adolescent literacy instruction include word study (e.g., decoding multisyllable words), fluency (e.g., increasing reading speed as well as accuracy), vocabulary development (e.g., using direct instruction of key words), comprehension (e.g., using visual representations such as graphic organizers), and motivation (e.g., providing interesting texts) (Roberts, Torgesen, Boardman, & Scammacca, 2008). For example, one common strategy is to use high-interest–low-level-vocabulary reading materials (for students who read at levels lower than expected for their age) to help improve the literacy skills of adolescents with disabilities (Lewis & Doorlag, 2006). Whatever the strategies used, it is vital that students with disabilities continue to receive instruction in literacy skills while at the same time accessing the content of academic classes through instructional supports and accommodations. In other words, even if students require intensive individual reading instruction, they must be able to participate in and have access to the academic content provided to their peers.

Many high schools are organized to provide academic instruction to homogeneous groups of students, which is sometimes called *tracking*. Tracking at all levels of education has been controversial, but it perhaps is more entrenched in the culture of secondary schools. High school teachers are often viewed as content specialists who are responsible to convey the content of their discipline. They are math teachers, for example, with greater training in mathematics than in pedagogy, and they often have limited training in teaching students with disabilities. Composing classes with students who have similar needs and abilities enables high school teachers to convey their subject matter more easily and with less need for differentiating instruction, because learner diversity is minimized within each track. Tracking may serve to legitimize separate classrooms and programs for students with disabilities (Stodden, Galloway, & Stodden, 2003) and to inappropriately remove students from more rigorous content courses. There are a variety of feasible strategies and supports, such as modifying assignments, providing outlines or study guides, creating rubrics to assess critical skills, and making content enhancements, such as those developed by the University of Kansas Center for Research on Learning, that can be implemented to maintain the integrity of content courses while at the same time meeting the diverse needs of students both with and without disabilities (Lynch & Bruhl, 2005). Conferencers must be vigilant in working within the high school culture to ensure that the educational program designed for each student not only meets individual goals but also represents equity and access to the general high school curriculum (Alston & Hampton, 2000; Jimenez, Browder, & Courtade, 2008; Valadez, 2002; Wehmeyer, Lance, & Bashinski, 2002).

Typical high schools are organized by academic departments (e.g., English, math, science) with teachers assigned to one or more department. Curricular policies are often decided at the department level and communicated to school administrators via the department chair or head. Although this organizational structure may promote the workings of the school as a whole, it may inhibit collaborative activities across departments on behalf of individual students. Conferencers must pay careful attention to the fidelity of implementation of all supports and services required by the students across content areas, not simply within the special education program. This will require ongoing communication with teachers in various content areas as well as with individual members of the adolescent's IEP team.

Some students function within the standard general education track with appropriate supports and services, whereas others participate in a parallel track (e.g., occupational or vocational). Those with more significant disabilities may be assigned to an alternate curriculum (Friend, 2005). Decisions regarding how the student's curriculum will address state learning standards and impact adult outcomes must be made within the context of the options currently available in the school or district as well as the full continuum of services that must be made available to meet students' needs.

Although individual programs will vary, some information is available regarding effective practices and indicators of quality programming for adolescents with disabilities. Brigham et al. (2006) conducted a 3-year study of high schools that have strong participation and positive results for their students with disabilities. From the three high schools studied, the researchers articulated five schoolwide strategies for educating students with disabilities: These schools (a) provided a broad array of academic course and program options, (b) provided schoolwide support structures that could be combined and customized to the needs and strengths of the individual students, (c) worked intentionally to connect students to the school and build their motivation to succeed (e.g., tap into students' interests and encourage participation in extracurricular activities), (d) created a connected and caring adult community to serve students' academic and social and personal needs (e.g., a community characterized by shared responsibility for all students), and (e) developed responsive leaders who managed the tensions inherent in the commitment to prepare students with disabilities to be successful in their life beyond school (e.g., balancing individual student success with accountability for groups of students).

There are a number of things conferencers can do to encourage parent support of the high school program. At the start of the year, and preferably during an on-site orientation session, parents should receive information regarding daily schedules, procedures for absences and tardiness, behavioral expectations and discipline policies, grading and makeup work policies, curricular and extracurricular options, parent organizations or activities, and whom to contact with questions. Conferencers should strive to present a balanced view of the child and not limit contacting parents only to the times when there is a problem. One high school mailed "positive note" postcards to parents to inform them of specific laudable behaviors or examples of achievement of their child. On the other side of the coin, teachers can also implement an early warning system (e.g., phone calls, e-mail messages, PDA messages) to inform parents if their child's performance has declined or if they are at risk of failing an academic class. Many schools have Web sites where parents can access their child's attendance and behavioral records, current grades, and any outstanding homework assignments. Parents should receive hands-on training on how to access the Web site and their child's record.

Transition

One of the most prominent information exchange needs involving parents and families and teachers and other professionals relates to the future of the person with exceptionalities. This discussion may focus on determining whether the person's needs can be best served in a competitive work environment, on the status and adequacy of the school district's transition services, on whether he or she is eligible or appropriate for particular types of services, and on the impact of an exceptionality on the youth's postschool adjustment. Current research on postsecondary outcomes for adolescents and young adults with disabilities indicates these to be priority topics for discussion (Katsiyannis, Zhang, Woodruff, & Dixon, 2005; T. E. C. Smith et al., 2006).

In addition to the requirements for an IEP, a transition plan must be in effect when the student is 16 and updated annually thereafter. The contents must include the following: (a) appropriate measurable postsecondary goals based on age-appropriate transition assessments related to training, education, employment, and, where appropriate, independent living skills; (b) the transition services (including courses of study) needed to assist the child in reaching those goals; and (c) a statement, beginning no later than 1 year before the child reaches the age of majority under state law, that the child has been informed of the child's rights that will transfer to the child when he or she reaches the age of majority (20 U.S.C. § 1414(d)(A)).

The transition of students with disabilities thus differs from that of their peers without disabilities in that a specific plan is created to ensure that the necessary supports and services are in place to facilitate their preparation for adult life. During the middle and high school years, schools can offer functional curricula, social skills training, school-based functional learning opportunities, employment skill development, and functional assessment to prepare students and to ensure positive adult outcomes (Carter & Lunsford, 2005; Storey, Bates, & Hunter, 2002; D. Zhang, Ivester, & Katsiyannis, 2005).

Transition services must include a coordinated set of activities for a child with a disability that are designed to be results oriented and are focused on improving the academic and functional achievement of the child. These activities should facilitate the child's movement from school to post-school activities, including postsecondary education, vocational education, integrated employment (including supported employment), continuing and adult education, adult services, independent living, or community participation. The identified services are based on the individual child's needs, taking into account the child's strengths, preferences, and interests (20 U.S.C. 1401 § 1401(34)).

To design the most effective transition plan for an adolescent with disabilities, all IEP and transition team members must have critical information regarding available services and postsecondary school options. Respondents in a study examining the perceptions of parents and siblings of high school students with significant cognitive disabilities reported a lack knowledge regarding postschool options such as employment, daily living, postsecondary education, social relationships, and leisure and recreation (Chambers, Hughes, & Carter, 2004). They were concerned about an employer's willingness to hire for pay and whether the family member would receive adequate support to enable success on the job. They also reported that although they perceived employment and independent or supported living to be important areas of postschool transition, they predicted that their family member would work in a segregated employment setting and live in their parents' home (Chambers et al., 2004).

Another consideration related to employment is the need for some students from low socioeconomic status levels to contribute to the family through early employment or caretaking roles for other family members (Lindstrom et al., 2007). Conferencers should be aware of and sensitive to this fact.

Although some parents may be unfamiliar with the particular services and postschool options that are available, they still have information that can be critical to the transition planning process. As Brolin and Loyd (2004) articulated,

> Families are a repository of information about the student with special learning and/or behavior needs, his/her strengths and abilities, likes and dislikes, interests, limitations, and idiosyncrasies. They can tell you how a student . . . spends his/her spare time, his/her hobbies and interests, and whether she/he has ever maintained a checkbook or has access to a computer. The student's siblings can tell you how many friends she/he has in the neighborhood. Parents and family members can tell you whether the student . . . can cook

a simple meal, has ever interviewed for a job, or reads the paper daily. There are not enough checklists available to encompass the amount of information to be gained by family members. (p. 101)

It is particularly imperative, then, that conferencers dialogue with parents during the transition planning process to harvest the important information they can provide to increase the likelihood of positive adult outcomes for the child. In fact, the quality of the relationship parents of adolescents with disabilities have with service providers has been identified by those parents as a key factor in their level of involvement in the transition planning process (deFur, Todd-Allen, & Getzel, 2001).

Another important consideration in the transition planning process is the need for conferencers to maintain "an awareness of and sensitivity to the impact culture has on the planning process, use of services, and desired outcomes of the people they serve" (J. R. Patton, 2006, p. 446). For example, professionals may believe that their view of the importance of self-determination and independence is shared by all families; however, some families may believe that it is the responsibility of the mother to care for the child with disabilities and that responsibility rightly transfers to a sibling or other family member upon the mother's death (Rueda, Monzo, Shapiro, Gomez, & Blacher, 2005). In addition, the views and input of the young adult in the transition process may not be seen by all parents as a necessary component or even a priority (Rueda et al., 2005). Likewise, some families from culturally or linguistically diverse groups believe the launching of an adolescent into adulthood stems from family and community rather than from school experiences (Geenen, Powers, & Lopez-Vasquez, 2001). If this is the case, conferencers may mistakenly view families as being uninvolved in the transition process, when in fact they are highly involved but in activities outside the scope of school.

In a study by Hogansen, Powers, Geenen, Gil-Kashiwabara, and Powers (2008), examples of the impact of gender and cultural expectations were noted. One teacher observed,

Well, there's the other cultural differences for boys and girls, how females and males talk to each other. And we . . . ran into that with a Chinese family where women are not supposed to contradict men, women are not supposed to talk back to men. So the whole concept of advocacy and going up to the boss and saying, "I can't do it this way. I need to do it that way" or . . . "I need this to be changed," no, you don't do that. A girl doesn't go up to a man and say that. But the [work training] boss happens to be male, so she can't do that. And she is not comfortable doing that because that's the culture she was raised in. (Hogansen et al., 2008, p. 225)

Clearly, open discussion with parents and families regarding their expectations, goals, and aspirations for their family member with disabilities is most effectively accomplished within a framework that recognizes the impact of culture.

PARTICIPANTS IN IEP AND TRANSITION MEETINGS

Transition planning requires the active participation of a variety of team members such as the child's current teachers, assessment specialists, transition specialists, and representatives from community colleges, universities, and technical and vocational schools and from agencies such as social services and mental health, public health, and vocational rehabilitation, in addition to the parents and the child. The particular members will be determined on an individual student basis; however, the adolescent is probably the most critical member of the team and the focus of all activities and discussions. Active student involvement in the transition planning process ensures that the student's interests, preferences, and values are represented, which in turn can be linked to personally meaningful employment goals and other adult outcomes (Carter & Lunsford, 2005). It may also provide families with new insight into their child's goals and dreams and may serve as a catalyst for the family members to reconsider their expectations for the student (Childre & Chambers, 2005). Unfortunately, many students with disabilities do not attend or actively participate in their IEP or transition planning meetings (J. Martin, Marshall, & Sale, 2004; J. E. Martin, Van Dycke, Greene, et al., 2006). In particular, a study by Katsiyannis et al. (2005) found that students with mental retardation were less involved and less likely to provide input in discussing transition plans or to take leadership during the transition planning process than were students with learning disorders or behavior disorders. In a survey of 523 educators regarding students' involvement in IEP meetings, most responded that although self-determination activities such as student involvement in IEP meetings were very important, actual student involvement was minimal (C. Mason, Field, & Sawilowsky, 2004).

Students with disabilities can be instructed in how to lead or self-direct their IEP meetings and to take more ownership of their education (C. Y. Mason, McGahee-Kovac, & Johnson, 2004; Myers & Eisenman, 2005). When students take an active leadership role in directing the meeting, they attend more meetings, increase their active participation, and express their interests, skills, and limits (J. E. Martin, Van Dycke, Christensen, et al., 2006). They also report feeling they have a greater understanding of the IEP process and a greater voice in planning for their future (Arndt, Konrad, & Test, 2006). Finally, students who receive instruction in how to self-direct their meetings had more comprehensive postschool transition statements than students who did not receive training (Martin, Van Dycke, Christensen, et al., 2006,).

As mentioned previously, parents and families have a wealth of important information regarding their family member, and their involvement is essential in the transition planning and IEP processes. One piece of information that is invaluable is the ability of family members to talk about the child's gifts and capacities while developing the personal profile of the child. This can help the team see beyond the deficits and weaknesses so prominent in school records and develop a person-centered transition plan that is based on appropriately high expectations for the child (Loyd, Wehmeyer, & Davis, 2004; Miner & Bates, 2002; Test et al., 2006). Miner and Bates (2002) provided an example of the impact of working from a more holistic perspective of the child:

> Steve was finishing his junior year in high school. He had always been a quiet, well-mannered student and the teachers at the high school liked him. When Steve's person-centered planning meeting began, he didn't say much, but just seemed to agree with most of the things that were said by his parents.
>
> When discussing where he would live in the future, his mom suggested that it would have to be near public transportation as Steve didn't drive. Later, when the action steps were being identified, Steve stated that he wanted to take driver's education during his senior year. His mom objected, saying that it would be dangerous for Steve to drive. What if he was too slow to react and has a wreck?
>
> Steve reminded his mom that one of his gifts was persistence. It was agreed that he could talk to Mr. McCoy, the special education teacher, about taking the classroom portion of the driver's education course. During his senior year, Steve completed driver's education, got a license, and later bought a red pickup truck. Dreaming of a future for Steve was much different when planning from a capacities perspective rather than focusing on his deficits. (p. 21)

There are a number of other ways that parents and families can contribute to the transition planning process, such as advocating for their child, becoming familiar with the demands of adulthood, and actively participating in the transition process (Levinson et al., 2000; J. R. Patton, 2006; T. E. C. Smith et al., 2006). In addition, because parents of students with disabilities often take over the role of service coordinator when their child leaves high school, they must be supported in planning for their role in the transition process after school services have been terminated (Flexer, Simmons, Luft, & Baer, 2005). See Table 12.1 for a listing of suggestions to increase parental involvement in the transition planning process.

Finally, it is the responsibility of school personnel to bring together the representatives from other agencies as needed (e.g., vocational rehabilitation, community college) to participate in the transition planning process. The number and diversity of participants in a transition planning meeting may pose a challenge to smooth communication and coordination of services. The skills discussed in Chapter 3 for effective communication will be critical during these meetings. In addition, if a participating agency does not provide the agreed-on transition services, it is the responsibility of the school to reconvene the IEP team and identify alternative ways to meet the transition objectives. Obviously, this requires interagency collaboration and cooperation. It is imperative that conferencers have knowledge of the agency services and linkages that might be appropriate for their students so that they can facilitate agency participation and effective transition planning.

TRANSITION TO POSTSECONDARY EDUCATIONAL SETTINGS

Although there has been an increase in the number of students with disabilities who attend postsecondary schools, many are unprepared for the academic and social demands of those settings (National Council on Disability, 2004). It is important to note that although the IEP requirements are in place for students until they turn age 21 or graduate from high school, the requirements for individualized services do not apply to colleges and universities (Getzel & Wehman, 2005; Madaus, 2005). This change may pose a particularly difficult challenge for students who are accustomed to intensive levels of individualized support. One way that conferencers and parents can work together to ensure adolescents possess the skills necessary for success is by providing instruction and support in four areas students with disabilities encounter on a regular, sometimes daily, basis: (a) problem-solving skills (e.g., asking questions to resolve concerns), (b) evaluation skills (e.g., recognizing own improvement or lack of progress), (c) monitoring skills (e.g., using rehearsal strategies to learn content), and (d) communication skills (e.g., developing effective speaking, negotiating, and conversational skills) (Hong, Ivy, Gonzalez, & Ehrensberger, 2007). In addition, students can be taught to take responsibility for their own learn-

---

TABLE 12.1.
Suggestions to Improve Parent Participation in Transition and Individualized Education Program (IEP) Meetings

- Schedule meetings at times and places that are convenient for parents.
- Invite parents to bring siblings or other family members who may make a positive contribution to the planning meeting.
- Have an agenda for the meeting that includes introduction of all participants, a statement of the student's current goals, a collaborative discussion of the challenges and supports needed, the roles and responsibilities of each team member, and a summary of the meeting and action steps to be taken.
- Help the child prepare for participating in the meeting and for self-directing it if appropriate.
- Ask parents to identify the transition goals they have for their child. Don't dismiss their dreams but help them differentiate between ideal and possible outcomes.
- Ask parents to complete a survey of their child's strengths, needs, and interests.
- Have parents list natural supports (such as a potential mentor) that may be available in their community or within the family's circle of friends.
- Actively encourage the parents to participate as contributing members during each meeting through effective questioning and listening techniques.
- Discuss ways that parents can encourage the development of self-determination and self-advocacy skills in their child.
- Give parents the opportunity to help with the implementation of one of the IEP or transition goals.
- Have parents identify potential employment or volunteer opportunities for their child during high school.
- Provide parents with a directory of resources and services in their community (e.g., day service programs, housing supports) that can support successful transition.
- Identify a staff member who will coordinate transition services and maintain contact with the parents.
- Encourage parents to visit local postsecondary schools, colleges, and universities.

---

ing needs and advocate for themselves (Hadley, 2006; Sahlen & Lehmann, 2006) and to develop their own written self-advocacy plan (e.g., including the accommodations they require) to use as an advanced organizer to improve communication with their professors. They also can learn how to contact the college or university office of support services for students with disabilities (Lock & Layton, 2001). In preparation, transition teams can assist students in identifying and gathering the information required by postsecondary educational institutions to document their disability, thereby enabling them to access the disability supports and services that are available (Madaus & Shaw, 2006). Finally, high school students and their families can attend 1-day conference-type events at community colleges or universities to develop awareness of college services and support programs for students with disabilities. These events may include a tour of the campus to learn about the campus facilities and departments; meet with students with disabilities; gain information regarding college recreation programs, disability services, tutoring, and advisement; and attend special sessions for parents on how to support their child and help him or her navigate the programs (Kato, Nulty, Olszewski, Doolittle, & Flannery, 2006).

Effective transition planning takes coordination and collaboration among all stakeholders, and as articulated by T. E. C. Smith and colleagues (2006), "Although there are no guarantees that implementing well-planned transition services will result in smooth transitions, without them the likelihood is substantially diminished" (p. 230).

WHEN SCHOOLS AND PARENTS DISAGREE

It is not surprising that given the importance of decisions made regarding the preparation for postsecondary life, conferencers and parents may sometimes disagree. Disagreements may arise concerning the type of employment or the work schedule, the place where the young adult will live, the differences in expectations, or the fear that the child is not prepared for a community-based experience (Test et al., 2006). Conferencers should be sensitive to parents' concerns while providing a positive image of the adolescent as a capable employee or community member to create a framework that allows parents to move beyond previously held stereotypes and expectations when they are inappropriate (Loyd et al., 2004). According to Levinson et al. (2000),

> When school professionals and parents differ regarding a child's post-high school plans, it is extremely important that school staff avoid negative judgments about parents and make every effort to view the situation from the parents' perspective. As frustrating as it might be, the only thing schools can do in some cases is to provide parents with the information and resources which they might use in the future when they are ready to deal with transition issues. (pp. 421–422)

Chapter 9 contains additional information regarding resolving conflicts.

Programs for Students Ages 18 to 21

A final topic of educational programming relates to students who continue to need special education services and supports after their classmates have graduated from high school. For these students, ages 18 to 21, services designed and provided by high school personnel are sometimes located in community colleges or other community sites to provide a more normalized setting (Grigal, Neubert, & Moon, 2002). In addition, students can access the facilities and services their peers without disabilities have access to, such as the cafeteria, fitness center, computer lab, and library (Test et al., 2006). For students ages 18 to 21 who continue to receive services and supports, Wehmeyer, Garner, Yeager, Lawrence, and Davis (2006) identified seven indicators of high-quality services for students with mental retardation and severe disabilities:

- Quality educational services are provided in age-appropriate environments that allow for social interactions and community inclusion.
- Quality services are ecologically valid and community based.
- Academic instruction in quality programs is functional and focused on outcomes.
- Quality services emphasize person-centered planning.
- Quality services involve active participation of adult service providers in planning and implementation.
- Quality services implement best practices in transition such a job shadowing, job sampling, and leisure training.
- Quality services foster active student involvement and promote self-determination.

Finally, many parents and families of children with special needs, particularly those with severe disabilities, will wish to discuss the options available to their family member upon their own death. Although some parents and family members may be reluctant to initiate discussions that focus on their child's future, such reticence cannot be interpreted as a lack of interest in the topic.

Service and Advocacy Needs

The first issue parents must deal with is the culture change from elementary school to high school. The large size, increased diversity of the student population, and scale and level of issues within a complex organization may be intimidating to many parents. The personal relationships established between parents and educators in elementary school may seem impossible in high school with the wide range of professionals with whom parents and families may now interact. Effective trust building and communication strategies will be critical to establish and support collaborative relationships with parents and adolescents.

Wrestling with issues of equality and equity, secondary school principals may focus their actions on the best interests of the student body in general and struggle to balance that approach with also meeting the needs of each individual student (Frick & Faircloth, 2007). Interestingly, in their research on what makes a good high school, Brigham and colleagues (2006) concluded, "When a school sets out deliberately to create an environment in which students with disabilities can succeed, they tend to create a school that serves all students well" (p. 189).

Some parent advocates contend that school personnel view themselves as the knowledgeable and professional experts in special education and that parent knowledge is often dismissed or devalued as overly experiential, subjective, anecdotal, or personal (Zaretsky, 2005). And yet the results of a survey of parents' beliefs and knowledge about special education (e.g., learning and the general curriculum, transition, the least restrictive environment as defined by IDEA, parental involvement) indicate that parents of students enrolled in special education consistently demonstrated a more accurate awareness of the IDEA mandates and reported being more informed than parents of students enrolled in general education (Nutting, Porfeli, Queen, & Algozzine, 2006).

Parents who have become accustomed to a wide range of educational services often discover after their offspring's completion of public school that suitable programs and services are either unavailable or severely scarce (D. R. Johnson, Stodden, Emanuel, Luecking, & Mack, 2002). Faced with this dilemma, one can expect many parents of youth and young adults with disabilities to focus on identifying, developing, and advocating for acceptable direct service options for their sons and daughters.

In addition to providing direct services, educators and other professionals must be able to identify and help families access psychological, social, vocational, welfare, medical, dental, housing, and other types of services.

Parents of adolescents and young adults with exceptionalities may require the assistance of the conferencer in structuring their home environment and in developing behavior management strategies for their son or daughter. Some of the parent-applied procedures and consequences appropriate for managing the behavior of adolescents and young adults differ from those applicable to younger children. For example, the mother of a 200-pound teenage boy with mental retardation remarked that a time-out procedure ceased to be effective the day her son told her that he would no longer go to the time-out area. In addition, conferencers can work closely with parents to identify and structure age-appropriate leisure and recreational activities in the natural environments of home and community (Algozzine et al., 2001).

Some parents feel that it is developmentally appropriate for them to be less engaged in their child's high school program as they make their way from childhood to young adulthood (Dunst, 2002). Other parents, from lower socioeconomic levels, report that barriers to participation such as work schedules, day care, and transportation prevent them from attending school functions during the week (A. Y. Ramirez, 2001). Still other parents may lose interest in being involved in their child's educational program after watching the child fail for an extended period of time and after determining that professionals lack a cure for the child's condition. As a result, some professionals have concluded that parents of older children lack an interest in being involved in their child's program, and consequently, these professionals fail to put forth the effort necessary to encourage such participation.

Professionals must recognize that parent and family noninvolvement has been associated with issues that can be abated, at least to some extent. Accordingly, professionals must consider their role to consist in part of finding ways to facilitate cooperation behavior between parents and educators rather than assuming an attitude of noninvolvement and lack of interest among parents of older individuals with exceptionalities. Thus, educators must identify a variety of formal and informal ways for parents to interact with school personnel, as well as identify and eliminate barriers to parent and family involvement.

An increase in parent–professional communication opportunities must also be accompanied by changes in the nature of parent–professional interactions. In particular, professionals must strive to foster parity-based collaborative relationships that allow parents to become more broadly involved in their children's school activities instead of their simply receiving information provided by professionals. Obviously, such changes will not occur easily, but the advantages of pursuing such relationships appear well worth the effort.

Summary

High school presents a new set of challenges for adolescents with disabilities and their families. Effective conferencers will support parents in their efforts to be actively involved in their child's educational program while at the same time recognizing the need to enable their child to develop a sense of autonomy and independence.

Training students in self-determination and empowerment skills may help them feel ownership of their transition plans. In addition, students taking an active role in their education may provide parents with a more accurate image of their child and serve to build their confidence in the child's postsecondary adult outcomes.

The transition from high school to postsecondary settings requires even greater collaboration between educators, service providers, and families. It will be critical for conferencers to facilitate this collaboration and to consider the important role families will continue to play in the successful transition of their family member. As always, conferencers must demonstrate cultural sensitivity as they consider the concerns, priorities, and goals of the family members with whom they collaborate to develop successful program and transition plans.

Exercises

1. Prepare a sample handbook on the rules, routines, and expectations for high school students. Include items such as procedures for absences, homework, discipline policies, and so on that would be helpful for parents and students.

2. Identify services available in your community for adolescents and young adults with disabilities such as rehabilitation, day service programs, and housing supports.

3. Design an ongoing school–home communication system appropriate for high school students. Consider the use of technology in your system.

4. Review sample transition plans for adolescents. Pay particular attention to the goals and how they reflect the students' needs, preferences, and interests.

References

Aaroe, L., & Nelson, J. R. (2000). A comparative analysis of teachers', Caucasian parents', and Hispanic parents' views of problematic school survival behaviors. *Education and Treatment of Children, 23*(3), 314–324.

Abreu, J. M., Consoli, A. J., & Cypers, S. J. (2004). Treatment issues with Hispanic clients. In D. R. Atkinson (Ed.), *Counseling American minorities* (6th ed., pp. 317–338). Boston: McGraw-Hill.

Adams, K. S., & Christenson, S. L. (2000). Trust and the family–school relationship: Examination of parent–teacher differences in elementary and secondary grades. *Journal of School Psychology, 38*(5), 477–497.

Adams, L. D. (1999–2000). Conferring with Amanda's mom [Electronic version]. *Childhood Education, 76*(2), 106–107.

Adelizzi, J. U., & Goss, D. B. (2001). *Parenting children with learning disabilities.* Westport, CT: Bergin & Garvey.

Afifi, T. D., Huber, F. N., & Ohs, J. (2006). Parent's and adolescents' communication with each other about divorce-related stressors and its impact in their ability to cope positively with the divorce. *Journal of Divorce and Remarriage, 45*(1/2), 1–30.

Alberto, P. A., Mechling, L., Taber, T. A., & Thompson, J. (1995). Using videotape to communicate with parents of students with severe disabilities. *Teaching Exceptional Children, 27*(3), 18–21.

Alberto, P. A., & Troutman, A. C. (2009). *Applied behavior analysis for teachers (8th ed.).* Upper Saddle River, NJ: Pearson Education.

Algozzine, K., O'Shea, D. J., & Algozzine, B. (2001). Working with families of adolescents. In D. J. O'Shea, L. J. O'Shea, R. Algozzine, & D. J. Hammitte (Eds.), *Families and teachers of individuals with disabilities* (pp. 179–204). Boston: Allyn & Bacon.

Al-Hassan, S., & Gardner, R., III. (2002). Involving immigrant parents of students with disabilities in the educational process. *TEACHING Exceptional Children, 34*(5), 52–58.

Alston, R. J., & Hampton, J. L. (2000). Science and engineering as viable career choices for students with disabilities: A survey of parents and teachers. *Rehabilitation Counseling Bulletin, 43*(3), 158–164.

Alter, P. J., Conroy, M. A., Mancil, G. R., & Haydon, T. (2008). A comparison of functional behavior assessment methodologies with young children: Descriptive methods and functional analysis. *Journal of Behavioral Education, 17*(2), 200–219.

Altshuler, S. J. (2003). From barriers to successful collaboration: Public schools and child welfare working together. *Social Work, 48*(1), 52–63.

Amato, P. R. (2000). The consequences of divorce for adults and children. *Journal of Marriage and Family, 62*(4), 1269–1287.

American Civil Liberties Union. (1999). *Fact sheet: Overview of lesbian and gay parenting, adoption and foster care.* Retrieved March 5, 2004, from www.aclu.org/LesbianGayRights/LesbianGayRights.cfm?ID=9212&c=104

Anderson, C. M., & McMillan, K. (2001). Parental use of escape extinction and differential reinforcement to treat food selectivity. *Journal of Applied Behavior Analysis, 34*(4), 511–515.

Anderson-Butcher, D., & Ashton, D. (2004). Innovative models of collaboration to serve children, youths, families, and communities. *Children and Schools, 26*(1), 39–53.

Arndt, S. A., Konrad, M., & Test, D. W. (2006). Effects of the self-directed IEP on student participation in planning meetings. *Remedial and Special Education, 27*(4), 194–207.

Arreaga-Mayer, C., Utley, C. A., Perdomo-Rivera, C., & Greenwood, C. R. (2003). Ecobehavioral assessment of instructional contexts in bilingual special education programs for English language learners at risk for developmental disabilities. *Focus on Autism and Other Developmental Disabilities, 18*(1), 28–40.

Artiles, A. J., & Bal, A. (2008). The next generation of disproportionality research: Toward a comparative model in the study of equity in ability differences. *Journal of Special Education, 42*(1), 4–14.

Artiles, A. J., Harry, B., Reschly, D. J., & Chinn, P. C. (2002). Over-identification of students of color in special education: A critical overview. *Multicultural Perspectives, 41*(1), 3–10.

Artiles, A. J., Rueda, R., Salazar, J. J., & Higareda, I. (2005). Within-group diversity in minority disproportionate representation: English language learners in urban school districts. *Exceptional Children, 71*(3), 283–300.

Atkinson, D. R. (2004). *Counseling American minorities* (6th ed.). Boston: McGraw-Hill.

Babcock, S., & Backlund, J. (2001). Proactive parent communication [Electronic version]. *Instructor, 110*(6), 34–35.

Bailey, D. B., Jr. (2001). Evaluating parent involvement and family support in early intervention and preschool programs. *Journal of Early Intervention, 24*(1), 1–14.

Bailey, D. B., Jr., Hebbeler, K., Scarborough, A., Spiker, D., & Mallik, S. (2004). First experiences with early intervention: A national perspective. *Pediatrics, 113*(4), 887–896.

Bailey, D. B., Jr., Hebbeler, K., Spiker, D., Scarborough, A., Mallik, S., & Nelson, L. (2005). Thirty-six-month outcomes for families of children who have disabilities and participated in early intervention. *Pediatrics, 116*(6), 1346–1352.

Bailey, D. B., Jr., McWilliam, R. A., Darkes, L. A., Hebbeler, K., Simeonsson, R. J., Spiker, D., & Wagner, M. (1998). Family outcomes in early intervention: A framework for program evaluation and efficacy research. *Exceptional Children, 64*(3), 313–328.

Bailey, D. B., Jr., & Simeonsson, R. J. (1998). Assessing needs of families with handicapped infants. *Journal of Special Education, 22*(1), 117–127.

Bailey, D. B., Skinner, D., Rodriguez, P., Gut, D., & Correa, V. (1999). Awareness, use, and satisfaction with services for Latino parents of young children with disabilities. *Exceptional Children, 65*(3), 367–381.

Baker, L. (2003). The role of parents in motivating struggling readers. *Reading and Writing Quarterly, 19*, 87–106.

Bandura, A. (1969). *Principles of behavior modification*. New York: Holt, Rinehart & Winston.

Bannon, W. M., & McKay, M. M. (2005). Are barriers to service and parental preference match for service related to urban child mental health service use? *Families in Society, 86*(1), 30–34.

Barclay, K. H. (2005). *Together we can: Uniting families, schools, and communities to help all children learn*. Dubuque, IA: Kendall/Hunt.

Barrera, I., Corso, R., & Macpherson, D. (2003). *Skilled dialogue: Strategies for responding to cultural diversity in early childhood.* Baltimore: Brookes.

Barry, L. M., & Singer, G. H. S. (2001). Reducing maternal psychological distress after the NICU experience through journal writing. *Journal of Early Intervention, 24*(4), 287–297.

Bateman, B. D., & Herr, C. M. (2006). *Writing measurable IEP goals and objectives.* Verona, WI: Attainment Company.

Bateman, B. D., & Linden, M. A. (2006). *Better IEPs: How to develop legally correct and educationally useful programs* (4th ed.). Verona, WI: Attainment Company.

Baxter, C., Cummins, R. A., & Yiolitis, L. (2000). Parental stress attributed to family members with and without disability: A longitudinal study. *Journal of Intellectual and Developmental Disability, 25*(2), 105–118.

Bayles, E. E., & Hood, B. L. (1966). *Growth of American educational thought and practice.* New York: Harper & Row.

Becker, W. C., & Gersten, R. (2001). Follow-up of follow through: The later effects of the direct instruction model on children in fifth and sixth graders. *Journal of Direct Instruction, 1*(2), 45–52.

Behring, S. T., Cabello, B., Kushida, D., & Murguia, A. (2000). Cultural modifications to current school-based consultation approaches reported by culturally diverse beginning consultants. *School Psychology Review, 29*(3), 354–367.

Benitez, D. T., Lattimore, J., & Wehmeyer, M. L. (2005). Promoting the involvement of students with emotional and behavioral disorders in career and vocational planning and decision-making: The self-determined career development model. *Behavioral Disorders, 30*(4), 431–447.

Benjamin, A. (1969). *The helping interview.* Boston: Houghton Mifflin.

Bentley, J. P., Tinney, M. V., & Chia, B. H. (2005). Intercultural Internet-based learning: Know your audience and what it values. *Educational Technology Research and Development, 53*(2), 117–127.

Berliner, B. (2002). *Educating homeless students.* Retrieved March 18, 2004, from http://www.wested.org/pub/doc/431

Bersoff, D. N., & Grieger, R. M. (1971). An interview model for psycho-situational assessment of children's behavior. *American Journal of Orthopsychiatry, 41*(3), 483–493.

Billingsley, B. S. (2002). *Special education teacher retention and attrition: A critical analysis of the literature.* Gainesville: University of Florida, Center on Personnel Studies in Special Education.

Bireda, M. R. (2002). *Eliminating racial profiling in school discipline: Cultures in conflict.* Lanham, MD: Scarecrow Press.

Birenbaum, A. (2002). Poverty, welfare reform, and disproportionate rates of disability among children. *Mental Retardation, 40*(3), 212–218.

Black, S. (2005). Rethinking parent conferences. *American School Board Journal, 192*(10), 46–48.

Blackburn, C., & Read, J. (2005). Using the Internet? The experiences of parents of disabled children. *Child: Care, Health and Development, 31*(5), 507–515.

Blair, C., & Scott, K. G. (2002). Proportion of LD placements associated with low socioeconomic status: Evidence for a gradient? *Journal of Special Education, 36*(1), 14–22.

Blanchett, W. J., Mumford, V., & Beachum, F. (2005). Urban school failure and disproportionality in a post-Brown era. *Remedial and Special Education, 26*(2), 70–81.

Blue-Banning, M., Summers, J. A., Frankland, H. C., Nelson, L. L., & Beegle, G. (2004). Dimensions of family and professional partnerships: Constructive guidelines for collaboration. *Exceptional Children, 70*(2), 167–184.

Bock, S. J., Stoner, J. B., Beck, A. R., Hanley, L., & Prochnow, J. (2005). Increasing functional communication in non-speaking preschool children: Comparison of PECS and VOCA. *Education and Training in Development Disabilities, 40*(3), 264–278.

Bos, C. S., & Vaughn, S. (2006). *Strategies for teaching students with learning and behavior problems* (6th ed.). Boston: Person Education.

Boschen, K., Gargaro, J., Gan, C., Gerber, G., & Brandys, C. (2007). Family interventions after acquired brain injury and other chronic conditions: A critical appraisal of the quality of the evidence. *NeuroRehabilitation, 22*, 19–41.

Boushey, H., Brocht, C., Gundersen, B., & Bernstein, J. (2001). *Hardships in America: The real story of working families.* Washington, DC: Economic Policy Institute.

Bowen, G. L., & Richman, J. M. (Eds.). (2002). Schools in the context of communities [Special issue]. *Children and Schools, 24*(2).

Boyer, L., & Mainzer, R. W. (2003). Who's teaching students with disabilities? *Teaching Exceptional Children, 35*(6), 8–11.

Bradley, B., Brown, I., & Mack, J. (2000). Modes of conflict. In N. W. Ragin (Ed.), *Strategies for resolving conflict* (pp. 37–44). *Orangeburg, SC: South Carolina State University, Department of Educational Leadership and Counselor Education.* (ERIC Document No. ED453458).

Brady, S. J., Peters, D. L., Gamel-McCormick, M., & Venuto, N. (2004). Types and patterns of professional–family talk in home-based early intervention. *Journal of Early Intervention, 26*(2), 146–159.

Brigham, N., Morocco, C. C., Clay, K., & Zigmond, N. (2006). What makes a high school a good high school for students with disabilities. *Learning Disabilities Research and Practice, 21*(3), 184–190.

Brody, G. H., Dorsey, S., Forehand, R., & Armistead, L. (2002). Unique and protective contributions of parenting and classroom processes to the adjustment of African American children living in single parent families. *Child Development, 73*(1), 274–286.

Brolin, D. E., & Loyd, R. J. (2004). *Career development and transition services: A functional life skills approach* (4th ed.). Upper Saddle River, NJ: Pearson Education.

Bronfenbrenner, U. (1974). *A report on longitudinal evaluations of preschool programs: Is early intervention effective?* (Vol. 2). Washington, DC: Department of Health, Education and Welfare, Office of Human Development.

Browder, D. M., & Cooper-Duffy, K. (2003). Evidence-based practices for students with severe disabilities and the requirement of accountability in "No Child Left Behind." *Journal of Special Education, 37*(2), 157–163.

Browder, D., Flowers, C., Ahlgrim-Delzell, L., Karvonen, M., Spooner, F., & Algozzine, R. (2004). The alignment of alternate assessment content with academic and functional curricula. *Journal of Special Education, 37*(4), 211–223.

Brown, D., Pryzwansky, W., & Schulte, A. (2001). *Psychological consultation: Introduction to theory and practice* (5th ed.). Boston: Allyn & Bacon.

Brown, L., Nietupski, J., & Hamre-Nietupski, S. (1976). The criterion of ultimate functioning and public school service for severely handicapped students. In L. Brown, N. Certo, K. Belmore, & T. Crowner (Eds.), *Madison alternative for zero exclusion: Papers and programs related to public school services for secondary age severely handicapped students* (pp. 113–139). Madison, WI: Madison Public Schools.

Brown, W. H., Odom, S. L., & Conroy, M. (2001). An intervention hierarchy for promoting preschool children's peer interactions in naturalistic environments. *Topics in Early Childhood Special Education, 21,* 162–175.

Bruce, E., & Schultz, C. (2002). Non-finite loss and challenges to communication between parents and professionals. *British Journal of Special Education, 29*(1), 9–13.

Bruder, M. B. (2005). Service coordination and integration in a developmental systems approach to early intervention. In M. J. Guralnick (Ed.), *A developmental systems approach to early intervention: National and international perspectives* (pp. 23–42). Baltimore: Brookes.

Bryk, A. S., & Schneider, B. (2002). *Trust in schools: A core resource for improvement.* New York: Russell Sage Foundation.

Buchan, J. (2000). When different is the same. *Exceptional Parent, 30*(9), 71–73.

Buck, P. S. (1950). *The child who never grew.* New York: Day.

Burns, B. J., Phillips, S. D., Wagner, H. R., Barth, R. P., Kolko, D. J., Campbell, Y., & Landsverk, J. (2004). Mental health needs and access to mental health services by youths involved with child welfare: A national survey. *Child and Adolescent Psychiatry, 43*(8), 960–970.

Burns, B. J., Schoenwald, S. K., Burchard, J. D., Faw, L., & Santos, A. B. (2000). Comprehensive community-based interventions for youth with severe emotional disorders: Multisystemic therapy and the wraparound process. *Journal of Child and Family Studies, 9,* 283–314.

Bursuck, W. D., Harniss, M. K., Epstein, M. H., Polloway, E. A., Jayanthi, M., & Wissinger, L. M. (1999). Solving communication problems about homework: Recommendations of special education teachers. *Learning Disabilities Research and Practice, 14*(3), 149–158.

Burt, M., & Aron, L. (2000). *America's homeless II: Populations and services.* Washington, DC: Urban Institute.

Buschbacher, P., Fox, L., & Clarke, S. (2004). Recapturing desired family routines: A parent–professional behavioral collaboration. *Research and Practice for Persons With Severe Disabilities, 29*(1), 25–39.

Byrnes, M. (2004). Alternate assessment FAQs (and answers). *Teaching Exceptional Children, 36*(6), 58–63.

Calabrese, N. M. (2006). Video technology: A vehicle for educators to enhance relationships with families. *Education, 127,* 155–160.

Campbell, D. J., Reilly, A., & Henley, J. (2008). Comparison of assessment results of children with low incidence disabilities. *Education and Training in Developmental Disabilities, 43*(2), 217–225.

Cannella, H. I., O'Reilly, M. F., & Lancioni, G. (2005). Choice and preference assessment research with people with severe to profound developmental disabilities: A review of the literature. *Research in Developmental Disabilities, 26*(1), 1–15.

Carkhuff, R. R. (1985). *Productive parenting skills.* Amherst, MA: Human Resource Development.

Carlisle, E., Stanley, L., & Kemple, K. M. (2005). Opening doors: Understanding school and family influences on family involvement. *Early Childhood Education Journal, 33*(3), 155–162.

Carnegie, D. (1936). *How to win friends and influence people.* New York: Simon & Schuster.

Carter, E. W., Lane, K. L., Pierson, M. R., & Glaeser, B. (2006). Self determination skills and opportunities of transition-age youth with emotional disturbance and learning disabilities. *Exceptional Children, 72*(3), 333–346.

Carter, E. W., & Lunsford, L. B. (2005). Meaningful work: Improving employment out-comes for transition-age youth with emotional and behavioral disorders. *Preventing School Failure, 49,* 63–69.

Cartledge, G., & Kourea, L. (2008). Culturally responsive classrooms for culturally di-verse students with and at risk for disabilities. *Exceptional Children, 74,* 351–371.

Cartledge, G., Tillman, L. C., & Johnson, C. T. (2001). Professional ethics within the context of student discipline and diversity. *Teacher Education and Special Educa-tion, 24*(1), 25–37.

Chambers, C. R., Hughes, C., & Carter, E. W. (2004). Parent and sibling perspectives on the transition to adulthood. *Education and Training in Developmental Disabilities, 39*(2), 79–94.

Chandler, L. K., & Dahlquist, C. M. (2006). *Functional assessment: Strategies to prevent and remediate challenging behavior in school settings.* Upper Saddle River, NJ: Mer-rill Prentice Hall.

Charlop-Christy, M. H., & Carpenter, M. H. (2000). Modified incidental teaching ses-sions: A procedure for parents to increase spontaneous speech in their children with autism. *Journal of Positive Behavior Interventions, 2*(2), 98–112.

Cheldelin, S. I., & Lucas, A. F. (2004). *The Jossey-Bass academic administrator's guide to conflict resolution.* San Francisco: John Wiley.

Cheney, D., & Bullis, M. (2004). The school-to-work transition of adolescents with emo-tional and behavioral disorders. In R. B. Rutherford, M. M. Quinn, & S. R. Mathur (Eds.), *Handbook of research in emotional and behavioral disorders* (pp. 369–384). New York: Guilford.

Childre, A., & Chambers, C. R. (2005). Family perceptions of student centered plan-ning and IEP meetings. *Education and Training in Developmental Disabilities, 40*(3), 217–233.

Cho, S. J., Singer, G. H. S., & Brenner, M. (2000). Adaptation and accommodation to young children with disabilities: A comparison of Korean and Korean American parents. *Topics of Early Childhood Special Education, 20*(4), 236–249.

Cho, S., Singer, H. S., & Brenner, B. (2003). A comparison of adaptation to childhood disability in Korean immigrant and Korean mothers. *Focus on Autism and Other Developmental Disabilities, 18*(1), 9–19.

Chrispeels, J. H., & Rivero, E. (2001). Engaging Latino families for student success: How parent education can reshape parents' sense of place in the education of their chil-dren. *Peabody Journal of Education, 76*(2), 119–170.

Christenson, S. L. (2004). The family–school partnership: An opportunity to promote the learning competence of all students. *School Psychology Review, 33*(1), 83–104.

Christenson, S. L., & Cleary, M. (1990). Consultation and the parent–education partner-ship: A perspective. *Journal of Education and Psychological Consultation, 1,* 219–241.

Christenson, S. L., & Sheridan, S. M. (2001). *School and families: Creating essential con-nections for learning.* New York: Guilford.

Christian, L. G. (2006). Understanding families: Applying family systems theory to early childhood practice. *Young Children, 61*(1), 12–20.

Cihak, D., Alberto, P. A., & Fredrick, L. D. (2007). Use of brief functional analysis and intervention evaluation in public settings. *Journal of Positive Behavior Interventions, 9*(2), 80–93.

Clark, D., & Fiedler, C. R. (2003). Building family–school relationships during the assess-ment and intervention process. In M. J. Breen & C. R. Fiedler (Eds.), *Behavioral approach to assessment of youth with emotional/behavioral disorders: A handbook for school-based practitioners* (pp. 561–585). Austin, TX: PRO-ED.

Clarke-Stewart, K. A., Vandell, D. L., McCartney, K., Owen, M. T., & Booth, C. (2000). Effects of parental separation and divorce on very young children. *Journal of Family Psychology, 14,* 304–326.

Cohen, P. N., & Petrescu-Prahova, M. (2006). Gendered living arrangements among children with disabilities. *Journal of Marriage and Family, 68,* 630–638.

Cooley, E. L., & Triemer, D. M. (2002). Classroom behavior and the ability to decode nonverbal cues in boys with severe emotional disturbance. *Journal of Social Psychology, 142*(6), 741–751.

Cooper, H., Robinson, J. C., & Patall, E. A. (2006). Does homework improve academic achievement? A synthesis of research, 1987–2003. *Review of Educational Research, 76*(1), 1–62.

Cooper, J. O., Heron, T. E., & Heward, W. L. (2007). *Applied behavior analysis.* Upper Saddle River, NJ: Pearson Education.

Cormier, S., & Nurius, P. S. (2003). *Interviewing and change strategies for helpers: Fundamental skills and cognitive behavioral interventions* (5th ed.). Pacific Groves, CA: Brooks/Cole.

Correa, V. I., & Jones, H. (2000). Multicultural issues related to families of children with disabilities. In M. J. Fine & R. L. Simpson (Eds.), *Collaboration with parents and families of children and youth with exceptionalities* (pp. 133–154). Austin, TX: PRO-ED.

Correa, V. I., Jones, H. A., Thomas, C. C., & Morsink, C. V. (2005). *Interactive teaming: Enhancing programs for students with special needs* (4th ed.). Upper Saddle River, NJ: Pearson Education.

Couchenour, D., & Chrisman, K. (2000). *Families, schools, and communities: Together for young children.* New York: W. W. Norton.

Courtade-Little, G. C., & Browder, D. M. (2005). *Aligning IEPs to academic standards for students with moderate and severe disabilities.* Verona, WI: Attainment Company.

Coutinho, M. J., & Oswald, D. P. (2000). Disproportionate representation in special education: A synthesis and recommendations. *Journal of Child and Family Studies, 9,* 135–156.

Coutinho, M. J., Oswald, D. P., & Best, A. M. (2002). The influence of sociodemographics and gender on the disproportionate identification of minority students as having learning disabilities. *Remedial and Special Education, 23*(1), 49–59.

Covey, S. R. (1989). *The 7 habits of highly effective people.* New York: Simon & Schuster.

Crnic, K., & Leconte, J. (1986). Understanding siblings need and influences. In R. Fewell & P. Vadasy (Eds.), *Families of handicapped children: Needs and supports across the lifespan* (pp. 75–98). Austin, TX: PRO-ED.

Cronin, M., Slade, D. L., Bechtel, C., & Anderson, P. (1992). Home–school partnerships: A cooperative approach to intervention. *Intervention in School and Clinic, 27,* 286–292.

Cushner, K., McClelland, A., & Safford, P. (2003). *Human diversity in education: An integrative approach* (4th ed.). New York: McGraw-Hill.

Cuskelly, M., & Gunn, P. (2006). Adjustment of children who have a sibling with Down syndrome: Perspectives of mothers, fathers, and children. *Journal of Intellectual Disability Research, 50,* 917–925.

Dabkowski, D. M. (2004). Encouraging active parent participation in IEP team meetings. *Teaching Exceptional Children, 36*(3), 34–39.

Damiani, V. B. (1999). Responsibility and adjustment in siblings of children with disabilities: Update and review. *Families in Society, 80*(1), 34–40.

Darch, C., Miao, Y., & Shippen, P. (2004). A model for involving parents of children with learning and behavior problems in schools. *Preventing School Failure, 48*(3), 24–34.

Darling-Hammond, L. (2004). Inequality and the right to learn: Access to qualified teachers in California's public schools. *Teachers College Record, 106*(10), 1936–1960.

Dattilio, F. M. (2005). The restructuring of family schemas: A cognitive-behavior perspective. *Journal of Marital and Family Therapy, 31*(1), 15–30.

Davern, L. (2004). School-to-home notebooks: What parents have to say. *Teaching Exceptional Children, 36*(5), 22–27.

Day-Vines, N. L., & Day-Hairston, B. O. (2005). Culturally congruent strategies for addressing the behavioral needs of urban, African American male adolescents. *Professional School Counseling, 8*(3), 236–243.

DeFur, S. H., Todd-Allen, M., & Getzel, E. E. (2001). Parent participation in the transition planning process. *Career Development for Exceptional Individuals, 24*, 19–36.

Demarle, D. J., & le Roux, P. (2001). The life cycle and disability: Experiences of discontinuity in child and family development. *Journal of Loss and Trauma, 6*, 29–43.

Demmert, W. G. (2005). The influences of culture on learning and assessment among Native American students. *Learning Disabilities Research and Practice, 20*(1), 16–23.

Dempsey, I., & Dunst, C. J. (2004). Helpgiving styles and parent empowerment in families with a young child with a disability. *Journal of Intellectual and Developmental Disability, 29*(1), 40–51.

DeNavas-Walt, C., Proctor, B. D., & Lee, C. H. (2006). *Income, poverty, and health insurance coverage in the United States: 2005* (Current Population Reports, P60-231). Washington, DC: U.S. Government Printing Office.

DeNavas-Walt, C., Proctor, B. D., & Mills, R. J. (2004). *Income, poverty, and health insurance coverage in the United States: 2003* (Current Population Reports, P60-226). Washington, DC: U.S. Government Printing Office.

Deno, S. L. (2003). Developments in curriculum-based measurement. *Journal of Special Education, 37*(3), 184–192.

Deno, S. L. (2005). Problem-solving assessment. In R. Brown-Chidsey (Ed.), *Assessment for intervention: A problem-solving approach* (pp. 10–40). New York: Guilford.

Deno, S. L., Fuchs, L. S., Marston, D., & Shin, J. (2001). Using curriculum-based measurement to establish growth standards for students with learning disabilities. *School Psychology Review, 30*(4), 507–524.

Denton, C. A., & Vaughn, S. (2008). Reading and writing interventions for older students with disabilities: Possibilities and challenges. *Learning Disabilities Research and Practice, 23*(2), 61–62.

Dettmer, P., Dyck, N., & Thurston, L. P. (2005). *Consultation, collaboration, and teamwork for students with special needs* (5th ed.). Boston: Allyn & Bacon.

Dettmer, P., Thurston, L., Knackendoffel, A., & Dyck, N. J. (2009). *Consultation, collaboration, and teamwork for students with special needs* (6th ed.). Upper Saddle River, NJ: Pearson.

DeVito, J. A. (2001). *The interpersonal communication book* (9th ed.). New York: Longman.

Devlin, S. D., & Harber, M. M. (2004). Collaboration among parents and professionals with discrete trial training in the treatment for autism. *Education and Training in Developmental Disabilities, 39*(4), 291–300.

Dew, A., Balandin, S., & Llewellyn, G. (2008). The psychosocial impact of siblings of people with lifelong physical disabilities. *Journal of Developmental and Physical Disabilities, 20*(5), 485–507.

Dewey, J. (1938). *Experience and education.* New York: Collier.

Diamond, K. E., & Kontos, S. (2004). Families' resources and accommodations: Toddlers with Down syndrome, cerebral palsy, and developmental delay. *Journal of Early Intervention, 26*(4), 253–265.

Dillenburger, K., Keenan, M., Gallagher, S., & McElhinney, M. (2004). Parent education and home-based behavior analytic intervention: An examination of parents' perceptions of outcome. *Journal of Intellectual and Developmental Disability, 29*(2), 119–130.

Dodge, N., Keenan, S., & Lattanzi, T. (2002). Strengthening the capacity of schools and communities to serve students with serious emotional disturbance. *Journal of Child and Family Studies, 11*(1), 23–34.

Doe v. Withers, 20 IDELR 442 (W.Va. Cir. Ct. 1993).

Dominguez, C. (2003). Involving parents, motivating students. *Principal Leadership (Middle School Ed.), 4*(4), 43–46.

Donley, C. R., & Williams, G. (1997). Parents exhibit children's progress at a poster session. *Teaching Exceptional Children, 29*(4), 46–51.

Donovan, S., & Cross, C. (Eds.). (2002). *Minority students in special and gifted education.* Washington, DC: National Academy Press.

Drasgow, E., & Yell, M. L. (2001). Functional behavioral assessment: Legal requirements and challenges. *School Psychology Review, 30,* 239–251.

Drasgow, E., Yell, M. L., & Robinson, T. R. (2001). Developing legally correct and educationally appropriate IEPs. *Remedial and Special Education, 22*(6), 359–378.

Duhaney, L. M. G., & Salend, S. J. (2000). Parental perceptions of inclusive educational placements. *Remedial and Special Education, 21*(2), 121–128.

Duncan, L. W., & Fitzgerald, P. W. (1969). Increasing the parent–child communication through counselor–parent conferences. *Personnel and Guidance Journal, 48,* 514–517.

Dunlap, G., & Fox, L. (2007). Parent–professional partnerships: A valuable context for addressing challenging behaviors. *International Journal of Disability, Development and Education, 54*(3), 273–285.

Dunlap, G., Newton, J. S., Fox, L., Benito, N., & Vaughn, B. (2001). Family involvement in functional assessment and positive behavior support. *Focus on Autism and Other Developmental Disabilities, 16*(4), 215–221.

Dunn, L. M. (1968). Special education for the mildly retarded—Is much of it justifiable? *Exceptional Children, 23,* 5–22.

Dunst, C. J. (2000). Revisiting "rethinking early intervention." *Topics in Early Childhood Special Education, 20,* 95–104.

Dunst, C. J. (2002). Family-centered practices: Birth through high school. *Journal of Special Education, 36*(2), 139–147.

Dunst, C. J., & Bruder, M. B. (2002). Valued outcomes of service coordination, early intervention, and natural environments. *Exceptional Children, 68,* 361–375.

Dunst, C. J., Hambry, D., Trivette, C. M., Raab, M., & Bruder, M. B. (2000). Everyday family and community life and children's naturally occurring learning opportunities. *Journal of Early Intervention, 23,* 151–164.

Dunst, C. J., & Trivette, C. M. (1996). Empowerment, effective helpgiving practices, and family-centered care. *Pediatric Nursing, 22,* 334–337, 343.

Dunst, C. J., Trivette, C. M., & Snyder, D. M. (2000). Family–professional partnerships: A behavioral science perspective. In M. J. Fine & R. L. Simpson (Eds.), *Collaboration with parents and families of children and youth with exceptionalities* (2nd ed., pp. 27–48). Austin, TX: PRO-ED.

Duquette, S. M., Ragin, N. W., & Stewart, P. D. (2000). Managing intergroup conflict. In N. W. Ragin (Ed.), *Strategies for resolving conflict* (pp. 1–9). Orangeburg, SC: South Carolina State University, Department of Educational Leadership and Counselor Education. (ERIC Document No. ED453458)

Duvall, S. F., Delquadri, J. C., & Ward, D. L. (2004). A preliminary investigation of the effectiveness of home school instructional environments for students with attention-deficit/hyperactivity disorder. *School Psychology Review, 33*(1), 140–158.

Duvall, S. F., Ward, D. L., Delquadri, J. C., & Greenwood, C. R. (1997). An exploratory study of home school instructional environments and their effects on the basic skills of students with learning disabilities. *Education and Treatment of Children, 20,* 150–172.

Dyson, L. L. (1996). The experiences of families of children with learning disabilities: Parental stress, family functioning, and sibling self-concept. *Journal of Learning Disabilities, 29*(3), 280–286.

Dyson, L. L. (2003). Children with learning disabilities within the family context: A comparison with siblings in global self-concept, academic self-perception, and social competence. *Learning Disabilities Research, 18*(1), 1–9.

Edgemon, E. A., Jablonski, B. R., & Lloyd, J. W. (2006). Large-scale assessments: A teacher's guide to making decisions about accommodations. *Teaching Exceptional Children, 38*(3), 6–11.

Eisenman, L. (2007). Self-determination interventions: Building a foundation for school completion. *Remedial and Special Education, 28*(1), 2–8.

Elbaum, B. (2007). Effects of an oral testing accommodation on the mathematics performance of secondary students with and without learning disabilities. *Journal of Special Education, 40*(4), 218–229.

Elhoweris, H., Mutua, K., Alsheikh, N., & Holloway, P. (2005). Effect of children's ethnicity on teachers' referral and recommendation decisions in gifted and talented programs. *Remedial and Special Education, 26*(1), 25–31.

Elwy, A. R. (2005). Programs and services for children with disabilities: Parents lack information. *The Exceptional Parent, 35*(3), 72, 74.

Emerson, E. (2007). Poverty and people with intellectual disabilities. *Mental Retardation and Developmental Disabilities Research Review, 13,* 107–113.

Emerson, J., & Lovitt, T. (2003). The educational plight of foster children in the schools and what can be done about it. *Remedial and Special Education, 24*(4), 199–203.

Engels, T. C., & Andries, C. (2007). Feasibility of family-focused intervention for the prevention of problem behavior in early adolescents. *Child and Family Therapy, 29*(1), 71–79.

Epstein, J. L. (1992). School and family partnerships: Leadership roles for school psychologists. In S. Christenson & J. Conoley (Eds.), *Home–school collaboration: Enhancing children's academic and social competence* (pp. 499–515). Silver Springs, MD: National Association of School Psychologists.

Epstein, J. L., & Sanders, M. G. (2000). Connecting home, school, and community: New directions for social research. In M. T. Hallinan (Ed.), *Handbook of the sociology of education* (pp. 285–306). New York: Kluwer Academic/Plenum.

Epstein, J. L., & Van Voorhis, F. L. (2001). More than minutes: Teachers' roles in designing homework. *Educational Psychologist, 36*(3), 181–193.

Epstein, M. H. (1999). Strategies for improving home–school communication about homework for students with disabilities. *Journal of Special Education, 33*(3), 166–177.

Erion, J. (2006). Parent tutoring: A meta-analysis. *Education and Treatment of Children, 29*(1), 79–106.

Essex, N. L. (2004). Confidentiality and student records: Ten ways to invite legal challenges. *The Clearing House, 77*(3), 111–113.

Evans, A. (2003). Empowering families, supporting students. *Educational Leadership, 61*(2), 35–37.

Faggella-Luby, M. N., & Deshler, D. D. (2008). Reading comprehension in adolescents with LD: What we know; what we need to learn. *Learning Disabilities Research and Practice, 23*(2), 70–78.

Family Educational Rights and Privacy Act, 20 U.S.C. § 1232 *et seq.*

Ferguson, P. M. (2002). A place in the family: An historical interpretation of research on parental reactions to having a child with a disability. *Journal of Special Education, 36*(3), 124–130.

Ferri, B. A., & Connor, D. J. (2005). In the shadow of Brown: Special education and overrepresentation of students of color. *Remedial and Special Education, 26*(2), 93–100.

Feuerstein, A. (2000). School characteristics and parent involvement: Influences on participation in children's schools. *Journal of Educational Research, 94*(1), 29–40.

Fidler, D. J., Lawson, J. E., & Hodapp, R. M. (2003). What do parents want? An analysis of education-related comments made by parents of children with different genetic syndromes. *Journal of Intellectual and Developmental Disability, 28*(2), 196–204.

Fiedler, C. R., Simpson, R. L., & Clark, D. M. (2007). *Parents and families of children with disabilities: Effective school-based support services.* Upper Saddle River, NJ: Prentice Hall.

Fiedler, C. R., & Swanger, W. H. (2000). Empowering parents to participate: Advocacy and education. In M. Fine & R. Simpson (Eds.), *Collaboration with parents and families of children and youth with disabilities* (2nd ed., pp. 437–464). Austin, TX: PRO-ED.

Field, S., Sarver, M. D., & Shaw, S. F. (2003). Self-determination: A key to success in post-secondary education for students with learning disabilities. *Remedial and Special Education, 24*, 339–349.

Fields, J. (2003). *America's families and living arrangements: 2003* (Current Population Reports, P20-552). Washington, DC: U.S. Census Bureau.

Fields, J., & Casper, L. M. (2001). *America's families and living arrangements: Population characteristics* (Current Population Reports, P20-537). Washington, DC: U.S. Census Bureau.

Fields-Smith, C. (2005). African American parents before and after Brown. *Journal of Curriculum and Supervision, 20*(2), 129–135.

File, N. (2001). Family–professional partnerships: Practice that matches philosophy. *Young Children, 56*(4), 70–74.

Fine, M. J., & Nissenbaum, M. S. (2000). The child with disabilities and the family: Implications for professionals. In M. J. Fine & R. L. Simpson (Eds.), *Collaboration with parents and families of children and youth with exceptionalities* (2nd ed., pp. 3–26). Austin, TX: PRO-ED.

Fine, M. J., & Simpson, R. L. (2000). *Collaboration with parents and families of children and youth with exceptionalities* (2nd ed.). Austin, TX: PRO-ED.

Fisher, R. J. (1994). Generic principles for resolving intergroup conflict. *Journal of Social Issues, 50*(1), 47–66.

Fitzpatrick, M., & Reeve, P. (2003). Grandparents' raising grandchildren—A new class of disadvantaged Australians. *Family Matters, 66,* 54–57.

Flaugher, P. (2006). Two dimensions of parent participation in an inner school district. *Education and Urban Society, 38*(2), 248–261.

Fleischmann, A. (2004). Narratives published on the Internet by parents of children with autism: What do they reveal and why is it important? *Focus on Autism and Other Developmental Disabilities, 19,* 35–45.

Fleming, A. (2004). My brother is autistic. *Scholastic Choices, 20*(2), 16–19.

Flexer, R. W., Simmons, T. J., Luft, P., & Baer, R. M. (2005). *Transition planning for secondary students with disabilities* (2nd ed.). Upper Saddle River, NJ: Pearson Education.

Florian, L., Hollenweger, J., Simeonsson, R. J., Wedell, K., Riddell, S., Terzi, L., & Holland, A. (2006). Cross-cultural perspectives on the classification of children with disabilities: Part I; Issues in the classification of children with disabilities. *Journal of Special Education, 40*(1), 36–46.

Force, L. T., Botsford, A., Pisano, P. A., & Holbert, A. (2000). Grandparents raising children with and without a developmental disability: Preliminary comparisons. *Journal of Gerontological Social Work, 33*(4), 5–21.

Ford, B. A. (2004). Preparing special educators for culturally responsive school–community partnerships. *Teacher Education and Special Education, 27*(3), 224–230.

Ford, D. Y., Grantham, T. C., & Whiting, G. W. (2008). Culturally and linguistically diverse students in gifted education: Recruitment and retention issues. *Exceptional Children, 74,* 289–306.

Fowler, C. H., Konrad, M., Walker, A. R., Test, D. W., & Wood, W. M. (2007). Self-determination interventions' effects on the academic performance of students with developmental disabilities. *Education and Training in Developmental Disabilities, 42*(3), 270–285.

Fox, L., Dunlap, G., & Cushing, L. (2002). Early intervention, positive behavior support, and transition to school. *Journal of Emotional and Behavioral Disorders, 10*(3), 149–157.

Fox, L., Vaughn, B. J., Wyatte, M. L., & Dunlap, G. (2002). "We can't expect other people to understand": Family perspectives on problem behavior. *Exceptional Children, 68,* 437–450.

Freeman, B., Dieterich, C., & Rak, C. (2002). The struggle for language: Perspectives and practices of urban parents of children who are deaf or hard of hearing. *American Annals of the Deaf, 147*(5), 37–44.

Freeman, S. H., & Alkin, M. C. (2000). Academic and social attainment of children with mental retardation in general education and special education settings. *Remedial and Special Education, 21*(1), 3–18.

Freund, P. J., Boone, H. A., Barlow, J. H., & Lim, C. I. (2005). Healthcare and early intervention collaborative supports for families and young children. *Infants and Young Children, 18*(1), 25–36.

Frey, A. (2002). Predictors of placement recommendations for children with behavioral or emotional disorders. *Behavioral Disorders, 27*(2), 126–136.

Frey, N. (2005). Retention, social promotion, and academic redshirting: What do we know and need to know? *Remedial and Special Education, 26*(6), 332–346.

Frick, W. C., & Faircloth, S. C. (2007). Acting in the collective and individual "best interest of students." *Journal of Special Education Leadership, 20*(1), 21–32.

Friend, M. (2008). *Special education: Contemporary perspectives for school professionals* (2nd ed.). Boston: Merrill.

Friend, M., & Cook, L. (2003). *Interactions: Collaboration skills for school professionals* (4th ed.). Boston: Allyn & Bacon.

Friend, M., & Cook, L. (2007). *Interactions: Collaboration skills for school professionals* (5th ed.). Boston: Merrill.

Frowe, I. (2005). Professional trust. *British Journal of Educational Studies, 53*(1), 34–53.

Fujiura, G. T., & Yamaki, K. (2000). Trends in demography of childhood poverty and disability. *Exceptional Children, 66*(2), 187–199.

Fuller, M. L. (2008). Poverty: The enemy of children and families. In G. Olsen & M. L. Fuller (Eds.), *Home-school relations: Working successfully with parents and families* (pp. 271–285). Boston: Allyn & Bacon.

Gallagher, D. J. (2001). Neutrality as a moral standpoint, conceptual confusion, and the full inclusion debate. *Disability and Society, 16*, 637–654.

Gallagher, P. A., Fialka, J., Rhodes, C., & Arceneaux, C. (2004). Working with families: Rethinking denial. In E. Horn, M. M. Ostrosky, & H. Jones (Eds.), *Family-based practices: Monograph of the Division for Early Childhood of the Council for Exceptional Children* (Series No. 5, pp. 3–12). Longmont, CO: Sopris West.

Gallagher, P. A., & Rhodes, C. A. (2004, December). *Brothers and sisters in early intervention*. Paper presented at the 20th annual DEC International Conference, Chicago, IL.

Gallagher, P. A., Rhodes, C. A., & Darling, S. M. (2004). Parents as professionals in early intervention: A parent educator model. *Topics in Early Childhood Special Education, 24*(1), 5–13.

Ganong, L., & Coleman, M. (2004). *Stepfamily relationships: Development, dynamics, and interventions*. New York: Kluwer Academin/Plenum.

Garland, A. F., Landsverk, J. A., & Lau, A. S. (2003). Racial/ethnic disparities in mental health service use among children in foster care. *Child Youth Services Review, 25*, 491–507.

Garrett, M. T. (2004). Profiles of Native Americans. In D. R. Atkinson (Ed.), *Counseling American minorities* (6th ed., pp. 147–170). Boston: McGraw-Hill.

Garriott, P. P., Wandry, D., & Snyder, L. (2000). Teachers as parents, parents as children: What's wrong with this picture? [Electronic version]. *Preventing School Failure, 45*(1), 37–43.

Gay, G. (2000). *Culturally responsive teaching: Theory, research, and practice*. New York: Teachers College Press.

Geenen, S., Powers, L., & Lopez-Vasquez, A. (2001). Multicultural aspects of parents' involvement in transition planning. *Exceptional Children, 67*(2), 265–282.

Gentry, J., & Luiselli, J. (2008). Treating a child's selective eating through parent implemented feeding intervention in the home setting. *Journal of Developmental and Physical Disabilities, 20*(1), 63–70.

Getzel, E. E., & Wehman, P. (2005). *Going to college: Expanding opportunities for people with disabilities*. Baltimore: Brookes.

Gill, A. G., Wagner, E. F., & Vega, W. A. (2000). Acculturation, familism, and alcohol use among adolescent males: Longitudinal relations. *Journal of Community Psychology, 28*(4), 443–458.

Gill, H., Boies, K., Finegan, J., & McNally, J. (2005). Antecedents of trust: Establishing a boundary condition for the relation between propensity to trust and intention to trust. *Journal of Business and Psychology, 19*(3), 287–301.

Gilliam, W. S., & Mayes, L. C. (2005). Developmental assessment of infants and toddlers. In C. H. Zeanah (Ed.), *Handbook of infant mental health* (2nd ed., pp. 236–248). New York: Guilford.

Ginther, D. K., & Pollak, R. A. (2004). Family structure and children's educational outcomes. *Demography, 41*(4), 671–696.

Glass, J. C., Jr., & Huneycutt, T. L. (2002). Grandparents parenting grandchildren: Extent of situation, issues involved, and educational implication. *Educational Gerontology, 28*(2), 139–161.

Goddard, R. D., Tschannen-Moran, M., & Hoy, W. K. (2001). A multilevel examination of the distribution and effects of teacher trust in students and parents in urban elementary schools. *Elementary School Journal, 102*(1), 3–17.

Goode, W. J. (1971). World revolution and family patterns. *Journal of Marriage and Family, 33*, 624–635.

Gortmaker, V. J., Daly, E. J., McCurdy, M., Persampieri, M., & Hergenrader, M. (2007). Improving reading outcomes for children with learning disabilities: Using brief experimental analysis to develop parent tutoring interventions. *Journal of Applied Behavior Analysis, 40*(2), 203–221.

Gravois, T. A., & Rosenfield, S. A. (2006). Impact of instructional consultation teams on the disproportionate referral and placement of minority students in special education. *Remedial and Special Education, 27*(1), 42–52.

Gresham, F. M. (2003). Establishing the technical adequacy of functional behavioral assessment: Conceptual and measurement challenges. *Behavioral Disorders, 28*, 282–298.

Grigal, M., Neubert, D. A., & Moon, M. S. (2002). Postsecondary options for students with significant disabilities. *Teaching Exceptional Children, 35*(2), 68–73.

Grigal, M., Neubert, D. A., Moon, M. S., & Graham, S. (2003). Self-determination for students with disabilities: Views of parents and teachers. *Exceptional Children, 70*(1), 97–112.

Grossman, H. (1995). *Special education in a diverse society.* Boston: Allyn & Bacon.

Guilar, J. D. (2001). *The interpersonal communication skills workshop.* New York: Amacom.

Gunn, I. (2003). IWPR: *Single mothers and their children suffered the most in the last year with persistently high poverty; Gender wage gap stagnant.* Institute for Women's Policy Research. Retrieved May 7, 2008, from http://www.scienceblog.com/community/older/archives/K/2/pub2934.html

Guralnick, M. J. (Ed.). (2005). *A developmental systems approach to early intervention: National and international perspectives.* Baltimore: Brookes.

Guy, B., Shin, H., Lee, S., & Thurlow, M. (2000). State graduation requirements for students with and without disabilities. In D. R. Johnson & E. J. Emanuel (Eds.), *Issues influencing the future of transition programs and services in the United States* (pp. 85–110). Minneapolis: University of Minnesota, National Transition Network.

Hadden, D. S. (2004). Entering preschool: Supporting family involvement in the age three transition. In E. Horn, M. M. Ostrosky, & H. Jones (Eds.), *Family-based practices: Monograph of the Division for Early Childhood of the Council for Exceptional Children* (Series No. 5, pp. 77–87). Longmont, CO: Sopris West.

Hadley, W. M. (2006). LD students' access to higher education: Self-advocacy and support. *Journal of Developmental Education*, 30, 10–16.

Hall, T. (2000). Never say never—Keep on keeping on. *Focus on Autism and Other Developmental Disabilities*, 15(1), 208–210.

Hall, T. E., Wolfe, P. S., & Bollig, A. A. (2003). The home–school notebook: An effective communication strategy for students with severe disabilities. *Teaching Exceptional Children*, 36(2), 68–73.

Hallahan, D. P., & Kauffman, J. M. (2003). *Exceptional learners (9th ed.)*. Boston: Allyn & Bacon.

Hallahan, D. P., Kauffman, J. M., & Pullen, P. C. (2009). *Exceptional learners: An introduction to special education* (11th ed.). Boston: Pearson Education.

Halpern-Meekin, S., & Tach, L. (2008). Heterogeneity in two-parent families and adolescent well-being. *Journal of Marriage and Family*, 70, 435–451.

Hamilton, C. (with Parker, C.). (2001). *Communicating for results: A guide for business and professionals* (6th ed.). Belmont, CA: Wadsworth.

Hammitte, D. J., & Nelson, B. M. (2001). Families of children in early childhood special education. In D. J. O'Shea, L. J. O'Shea, R. Algozzine, & D. J. Hammitte (Eds.), *Families and teachers of individuals with disabilities: Collaborative orientations and responsive practices* (pp. 129–154). Boston: Allyn & Bacon.

Hanhan, S. F. (2003). Parent–teacher communication: Who's talking? In G. Olsen & M. L. Fuller (Eds.), *Home–school relations: Working successfully with parents and families* (2nd ed., pp. 111–133). Boston: Allyn & Bacon.

Hanson, M. J., & Lynch, E. W. (2004). *Understanding families: Approaches to diversity, disability, and risk*. Baltimore: Brookes.

Harbin, G., Rous, B., & McLean, M. (2005). Issues in designing state accountability systems. *Journal of Early Intervention*, 27(3), 137–164.

Hardman, M. J., Drew, C. J., & Egan, M. W. (2002). *Human exceptionality: Society, school and family* (7th ed.). Boston: Allyn & Bacon.

Harniss, M. K., Epstein, M. H., Bursuck, W. D., Nelson, J., & Jayanthi, M. (2001). Resolving homework-related communication problems: Recommendations of parents of children with and without disabilities. *Reading and Writing Quarterly*, 17, 205–225.

Harrison, M. E., McKay, M. M., & Bannon, W. M. (2004). Inner-city child mental health service use: The real question is why youth and families do not use services. *Community Mental Health Journal*, 40(2), 119–131.

Harry, B. (2002). Trends and issues in serving culturally diverse families of children with disabilities. *Journal of Special Education*, 36(3), 132–140.

Harry, B. (2008). Collaboration with culturally and linguistically diverse families: Ideal versus reality. *Exceptional Children*, 74, 327–388.

Harry, B., Allen, N., & McLaughlin, M. (1995). Communication versus compliance: African-American parents' involvement in special education. *Exceptional Children*, 61(4), 364–377.

Harry, B., & Klinger, J. K. (2006). *Why are so many minority students in special education? Understanding race and disability in schools*. New York: Teachers College Press.

Heflin, J., & Simpson, R. (2002). Understanding intervention controversies. In B. Scheuermann & J. Webber (Eds.), *Autism: Teaching does make a difference* (pp. 248–277). Belmont, CA: Wadsworth/Thomson Learning.

Held, M. F., Thomas, C. A., & Thomas, K. (2004). "The John Jones Show": How one teacher facilitated self-determined transition planning for a young man with autism. *Focus on Autism and Other Developmental Disabilities*, 19(3), 177–188.

Heller, K. W., Forney, P. E., Alberto, P. A., Schwartzman, M. N., & Goeckel, T. M. (2000). *Meeting physical and health needs of children with disabilities: Teaching physician and health management skills.* Belmont, CA: Thompson.

Henderson, A. T., & Mapp, K. L. (2002). *A new wave of evidence: The impact of school, family, and community connections on student achievement. Annual synthesis, 2002.* Austin, TX: National Center for Family and Community Connections With Schools.

Henderson, A. T., Mapp, K. L., Johnson, V. R., & Davies, D. (2007). *Beyond the bake sale: The essential guide to family–school partnerships.* New York: New Press.

Hepworth-Berger, E. (2000). *Parents as partners in education* (5th ed.). Columbus, OH: Merrill.

Herring, R. D. (2004). Physical and mental health needs of Native American Indian and Alaska Native populations. In D. R. Atkinson (Ed.), *Counseling American minorities* (6th ed., pp. 171–192). Boston: McGraw-Hill.

Hetherington, E. M. (2002). Should we stay together for the sake of the children? In E. M. Hetherington (Ed.), *Coping with divorce, single-parenting, and remarriage: A risk resiliency perspective* (pp. 93–116). Mahwah, NJ: Lawrence Erlbaum.

Heward, W. L. (2006). *Exceptional children* (8th ed.). Columbus, OH: Pearson Prentice Hall.

Heward, W. L. (2009). *Exceptional children: An introduction to special education* (9th ed.). Upper Saddle River, NJ: Pearson Education.

Hoagwood, K. E. (2005). Family-based services in children's mental health: A research review and synthesis. *Journal of Child Psychology and Psychiatry, 46*(7), 690–713.

Hobbs, F. (2005). *Examining American household composition: 1990 and 2000.* Washington, DC: U.S. Census Bureau.

Hodapp, R. M. (2007). Families of persons with Down syndrome: New perspectives, findings, and research and service needs. *Mental Retardation and Developmental Disabilities Research Reviews, 13,* 279–287.

Hodapp, R. M., & Urbano, R. C. (2007). Adult siblings of individuals with Down syndrome versus with autism: Findings from a large-scale U.S. survey. *Journal of Intellectual Disability Research, 51*(12), 1018–1029.

Hodgkinson, H. (1992). *A demographic look at tomorrow.* Washington, DC: Institute for Educational Leadership.

Hoffman, C. D., Sweeney, D. P., Lopez-Wagner, M. C., Hodge, D., Nam, C. Y., & Botts, B. H. (2008). Children with autism: Sleep problems and mothers' stress. *Focus on Autism and Other Developmental Disabilities, 23*(3), 155–165.

Hoffman, M. L. (2001). Toward a comprehensive empathy-based theory of prosocial moral development. In A. C. Bohart & D. J. Stip (Eds.), *Constructive and destructive behavior: Implications for family, school, and society* (pp. 61–86). Washington, DC: American Psychological Association.

Hogansen, J. M., Powers, K., Geenen, S., Gil-Kashiwabara, E., & Powers, L. (2008). Transition goals and experiences of females with disabilities: Youth, parents, and professionals. *Exceptional Children, 74*(2), 215–234.

Holburn, C. S., & Vietz, C. (2002). *Person-centered planning: Research, practice, and future directions.* Baltimore: Brookes.

Holloway, J. (2001). Inclusion and students with learning disabilities. *Educational Leadership, 58*(6), 86–88.

Holzman, M. (2004). *Public education and Black male students: A state report card.* Cambridge, MA: Scott Foundation for Public Education.

Hong, B. S. S., Ivy, W. F., Gonzalez, H. R., & Ehrensberger, W. (2007). Preparing students for postsecondary education. *Teaching Exceptional Children, 40*(1), 32–38.

Hooste, A. V., & Maes, B. (2003). Family factors in the development of children with Down syndrome. *Journal of Early Intervention, 25*(4), 296–309.

Horn, E., Ostrosky, M. M., & Jones, H. (Eds.). (2003). *The Young Exceptional Child Monograph Series No. 5: Family-based practices.* Longmont, CO: Sopris West.

Hornby, G. (1994). *Counseling in child disability.* London: Chapman & Hall.

Hosp, J. L., & Reschly, D. J. (2002). Predictors of restrictiveness of placement for African American and Caucasian students with learning disabilities. *Exceptional Children, 68,* 225–238.

Hosp, J. L., & Reschly, D. J. (2003). Referral rates for intervention or assessment: A meta-analysis of racial differences. *Journal of Special Education, 37*(2), 67–80.

Howell, W. (2006). Switching schools? A closer look at parents' initial interest in and knowledge about the choice provisions of No Child Left Behind. *Peabody Journal of Education, 81*(1), 140–170.

Hoy, W. K. (2002). Faculty trust: A key to student achievement. *Journal of School Public Relations, 23*(2), 88–103.

Hughes, M. T., Valle-Riestra, D. M., & Arguelles, M. E. (2002). Experiences of Latino families with their child's special education program. *Multicultural Perspective, 4*(1), 11–18.

Hundt, T. A. (2002). Videotaping young children in the classroom: Parents as partners. *Teaching Exceptional Children, 34*(3), 38–43.

Hunt, P., Soto, G., Maier, J., & Doering, K. (2003). Collaborative teaming to support students at risk and students with severe disabilities in general education classrooms. *Exceptional Children, 69*(3), 315–332.

Hussey, D. L., & Guo, S. (2005). Characteristics and trajectories of treatment foster care youth. *Child Welfare, 84*(4), 485–506.

Hutton, A. M., & Caron, S. L. (2005). Experience of families with children with autism in rural New England. *Focus on Autism and Other Developmental Disabilities, 20,* 180–189.

Idol, L., Nevin, A., & Paolucce-Whitcomb, P. (2000). *Collaborative consultation* (3rd ed.). Austin, TX: PRO-ED.

Indian Health Service. (2002). *Trends in Indian health.* Washington, DC: Author.

Individuals With Disabilities Education Improvement Act of 2004. 20 U.S.C. § 1400 *et seq.* (2004).

Institute for Community Inclusion. (2005). *Answers to parents' questions on mental retardation.* Retrieved June 14, 2007, from http://www.communityinclusion.org

Isenhart, M. W., & Spangle, M. (2000). *Collaborative approaches to resolving conflict.* Thousand Oaks, CA: Sage.

Ivey, A. E., & Ivey, M. B. (2003). *Intentional interviewing and counseling: Facilitating client development in a multicultural society* (5th ed.). Pacific Grove, CA: Brooks/Cole.

Ivey, A., Ivey, M., & Simek-Downing, L. (1987). *Counseling and psychotherapy: Integrating skills, theory, and practice.* Englewood Cliffs, NJ: Prentice Hall.

Jackson, C. W., & Turnbull, A. (2004). Impact of deafness on family life: A review of the literature. *Topics in Early Childhood Special Education, 24*(1), 15–29.

Jacobson, L. (2005). E-mail opens lines of communication for teachers. *Education Week, 24*(30), 8.

Jason, L. A., & Fries, M. (2004). Helping parents reduce children's television viewing. *Research on Social Work Practice, 14,* 121–131.

Jehn, K. A., & Chatman, J. A. (2000). The influence of proportional and perceptual conflict composition on team performance. *The International Journal of Conflict Management, 11*(1), 56–73.

Jeynes, W. H. (1999). The effects of remarriage following divorce on the academic achievement of children. *Journal of Youth and Adolescents, 28,* 385–393.

Jeynes, W. H. (2001). The effects of recent parental divorce on their children's consumption of alcohol. *Journal of Youth and Adolescence, 30*(3), 305–319.

Jimenez, B. A., Browder, D. M., & Courtade, G. R. (2008). Teaching algebraic equations to high school students with moderate developmental disabilities. *Education and Training in Developmental Disabilities, 43*(2), 266–274.

Johnson, D. R., Stodden, R. A., Emanuel, E. J., Luecking, R., & Mack, M. (2002). Current challenges facing secondary education and transition services: What research tells us. *Exceptional Children, 68,* 519–531.

Johnson, H. P., & O'Brien-Strain, M. (2000). Underlying population tends. In *Getting to know the future customers of the Office of Child Support: Projections report for 2004 and 2009.* Retrieved April 11, 2005, from www.acf.dhhs.gov/programs/cse/pubs/reports/projections

Johnson, J., & Duffett, A. (2002). *When it's your own child: A report on special education and the families who use it.* New York: Public Agenda.

Johnson, L. J., Pugach, M. C., & Hawkins, A. (2004). School–family collaboration: A partnership. *Focus on Exceptional Children, 36*(5), 1–12.

Judge, S. (2002). Family-centered assistive technology assessment and intervention practices for early intervention. *Infants and Young Children, 15*(1), 60–68.

Jung, L. A., Gomez, C., & Baird, S. (2004). Family-centered intervention: Bridging the gap between IFSPs and implementation. In E. Horn, M. M. Ostrosky, & H. Jones (Eds.), *Family-based practices: Monograph of the Division for Early Childhood of the Council for Exceptional Children* (Series No. 5, pp. 61–76). Longmont, CO: Sopris West.

Kahne, J., & Westheimer, J. (1993). Building school communities: An experience based model. *Phi Delta Kappan, 74*(4), 324–329.

Kaiser, A. P., & Hancock, T. B. (2003). Teaching parents new skills to support their young child's development. *Infants and Young Children, 16*(1), 9–21.

Kalyanpur, M., & Harry, B. (1999). *Culture in special education.* Baltimore: Brookes.

Kampwirth, T. J. (2003). *Collaborative consultation in the schools: Effective practices for students with learning and behavior problems* (2nd ed.). Upper Saddle River, NJ: Merrill.

Kampwirth, T. J. (2006). *Collaborative consultation in the schools: Effective practices for students with learning and behavior problems* (3rd ed.). Upper Saddle River, NJ: Merrill.

Kapinus, C. A., & Johnson, M. P. (2003). The utility of family life cycle as a theoretical and empirical tool: Commitment and family life-cycle stage. *Journal of Family Issues, 24*(2), 155–184.

Karnes, M. B., & Beauchamp, K. D. F. (1993). PEECH: A nationally validated early childhood special education model. *Topics in Early Childhood Special Education, 13*(1), 120–136.

Kato, M. M., Nulty, B., Olszewski, B. T., Doolittle, J., & Flannery, K. B. (2006). Postsecondary academies: Helping students with disabilities transition to college. *Teaching Exceptional Children, 39*(1), 18–23.

Katsiyannis, A., Zhang, D., Woodruff, N., & Dixon, A. (2005). Transition supports to students with mental retardation: An examination of data from the National Longitudinal Transition Study 2. *Education and Training in Developmental Disabilities, 40*(2), 109–116.

Kauffman, J. M. (2005). *Characteristics of emotional and behavioral disorders of children and youth* (8th ed.). Upper Saddle River, NJ: Pearson Education.

Kauffman, J. M., & Hallahan, D. P. (2005). *The illusion of full inclusion* (2nd ed.). Austin, TX: PRO-ED.

Kauffman, J. M., & Landrum, T. (2009). *Characteristics of emotional and behavioral disorders of children and youth* (9th ed.). Upper Saddle River, NJ: Prentice Hall.

Kauffman, J. M., Mock, D. R., Tankersley, M., & Landrum, T. (2008). Effective service delivery models. In R. J. Morris & N. Mather (Eds.), *Evidence-based interventions for students with learning and behavioral challenges* (pp. 359–378). Mahwah, NJ: Lawrence Erlbaum.

Kaufman, H. O. (2001). Skills for working with all families. *Young Children, 56*(4), 81–83.

Kavale, K. A., & Forness, S. R. (2000). History, rhetoric, and reality: Analysis of the inclusion debate. *Remedial and Special Education, 21*(5), 279–296.

Keller, B. (2004). Parent communication. *Education Week, 23*(34), 16–24.

Kelly, J., & Emery, R. (2003). Children's adjustment following divorce: Risk and resilience perspectives. *Family Relations, 52*(4), 352–362.

Keogh, B. K., Garnier, H. E., Bernheimer, L. P., & Gallimore, R. (2000). Models of child–family interactions for children with developmental delays: Child-driven or transactional? *American Journal on Mental Retardation, 105*, 32–46.

Kershaw, S. (2000). Living in a lesbian household: The effect on the children. *Child and Family Social Work, 5*, 365–371.

Keyes, C. R. (2002). A way of thinking about parent/teacher partnerships for teachers. *International Journal of Early Years Education, 10*(3), 177–191.

Kieff, J., & Wellhousen, K. (2000). Planning family involvement in early childhood programs. *Young Children, 55*(3), 18–25.

Kim, A. U. (2004). Asian Americans: A practical history and overview. In D. R. Atkinson (Ed.), *Counseling American minorities* (6th ed., pp. 217–238). Boston: McGraw-Hill.

Kirschenbaum, H. (2000). From values clarification to character education: A personal journey. *Journal of Humanistic Counseling, Education, and Development, 39*(1), 4–21.

Kluth, P., Villa, R., & Thousand, J. (2002). "Our school doesn't offer inclusion" and other legal blunders. *Educational Leadership, 83*(4), 24–27.

Kochhar-Bryant, C. A. (2008). *Collaboration and system coordination for students with special needs: From early childhood to the postsecondary years.* Upper Saddle River, NJ: Prentice Hall.

Koegel, R. L., Symon, J. B., & Koegel, L. K. (2002). Parent education for families of children with autism living in geographically distant areas. *Journal of Positive Behavior Interventions, 4*(2), 88–103.

Kosine, N. R. (2007). Preparing students with learning disabilities for postsecondary education: What research literature tells us about transition programs. *Journal of Educational Leadership, 20*(2), 93–104.

Kroth, R. L., & Edge, D. (2007). *Communicating with parents and families of exceptional children* (4th ed.). Denver, CO: Love.

Kroth, R. L., & Simpson, R. L. (1977). *Parent conferences as teaching strategies.* Denver, CO: Love.

Kübler-Ross, E. (1969). *On death and dying.* New York: Macmillan.

Kuhn, S. A. C., Lerman, D. C., & Vorndran, C. M. (2003). Pyramidal training for families of children with problem behavior. *Journal of Applied Behavior Analysis, 36*(1), 77–88.

Kyriakides, L. (2005). Evaluating school policy on parents working with their children in class. *Journal of Educational Research, 98*(5), 281–298.

Lafasakis, M., & Sturmey, P. (2007). Training parent implementation of discrete-trial teaching: Effects on generalization of parent teaching and child correct responding. *Journal of Applied Behavior Analysis, 40*(4), 685–689.

Lai, Y., & Ishiyama, F. I. (2004). Involvement of immigrant Chinese Canadian mothers of children with disabilities. *Exceptional Children, 71*(1), 97–108.

Lake, J. L., & Billingsley, B. S. (2000). An analysis of factors that contribute to parent–school conflict in special education. *Remedial and Special Education, 21*(4), 240–251.

Lambie, R. (2000a). *Family systems within educational contexts* (2nd ed.). Denver, CO: Love.

Lambie, R. (2000b). Working with families of at-risk and special needs students: A systems change model. *Focus on Exceptional Children, 32*(6), 1–23.

Lambie, R., & Daniels-Mohring, D. (1993). *Family systems within educational contexts.* Denver, CO: Love.

Lamme, L. L., & Lamme, L. A. (2001/2002). Welcoming children from gay families into our schools. *Educational Leadership, 59*(4), 65–69.

Lamme, L. L., & Lamme, L. A. (2003). *Welcoming children from sexual-minority families into our school.* Bloomington, IN: Phi Delta Kappa Educational Foundations.

Lamorey, S. (2002). The effects of culture on special education services: Evil eyes, prayer meetings, and IEPs. *Teaching Exceptional Children, 34*(5), 67–71.

Lanford, A. D., & Cary, L. G. (2000). Graduation requirements for students with disabilities: Legal and practical considerations. *Remedial and Special Education, 21*(3), 152–160.

LaParo, K. M., Pianta, R. C., & Cox, M. J. (2000). Teachers' reported transition practices for children transitioning into kindergarten and first grade. *Exceptional Children, 67*, 7–20.

LaRocco, D. J., & Bruns, D. A. (2005). Advocacy is only a phone call away. *Young Exceptional Children, 8*(4), 11–18.

Laumann-Billings, L., & Emery, R. E. (2000). Distress among young adults in divorced families. *Journal of Family Psychology, 14*, 671–687.

Lawrence-Lightfoot, S. (2004a). Building bridges from school to home. *Instructor, 114*(1), 24–27.

Lawrence-Lightfoot, S. (2004b). *The essential conversation: What parents and teachers can learn from each other.* New York: Random House.

Lawson, H. A., & Sailor, W. (2000). Integrating services, collaborating, and developing connections with schools. *Focus on Exceptional Children, 33*(2), 1–22.

Lechtenberger, D., & Mullins, F. E. (2004). Promoting better family–school–community partnerships for all of America's children. *Beyond Behavior, 14*(1), 17–22.

Lee, S., Amos, B. A., Gragoudas, S., Lee, Y., Shogren, K. A., Theoharis, R., & Wehmeyer, M. L. (2006). Curriculum augmentation and adaptation strategies to promote access to the general curriculum for students with intellectual and developmental disabilities. *Education and Training in Developmental Disabilities, 41*(3), 199–212.

Leiter, V., & Krauss, M. W. (2004). Claims, barriers, and satisfaction: Parents requests for additional special education services. *Journal of Disability Policy Studies, 15*(3), 135–146.

Leon, K. (2003). Risk and protective factors in young children's adjustment to parental divorce: A review of the research. *Family Relations, 52*(3), 258–270.

Lessenberry, B. M., & Rehfeldt, R. A. (2004). Evaluating stress levels of parents with disabilities. *Exceptional Children, 70*, 231–244.

Levinson, E. M., McKee, L., & DeMatteo, F. J. (2000). The exceptional child grows up: Transition from school to adult life. In M. J. Fine & R. L. Simpson (Eds.), *Collaboration with parents and families of children and youth with exceptionalities* (pp. 409–435). Austin, TX: PRO-ED.

Lewis, R. B., & Doorlag, D. H. (2006). *Teaching special students in general education classrooms* (7th ed.). Upper Saddle River, NJ: Pearson Prentice Hall.

Lin, S. L. (2000). Coping and adaptation in families of children with cerebral palsy. *Exceptional Children, 66*(2), 201–218.

Lindsay, G., & Dockrell, J. E. (2004). Whose job is it? Parents' concerns about the needs of their children with language problems. *Journal of Special Education, 37*(4), 225–235.

Lindstrom, L., Doren, B., Metheny, J., Johnson, P., & Zane, C. (2007). Transition to employment: Role of the family in career development. *Exceptional Children, 73*(3), 348–366.

Livovich, M. (2004). The high school diploma: A standards-based passport or reward for effort? *Journal of Special Education Leadership, 17*(2), 126–127.

Lock, R. H., & Layton, C. A. (2001). Succeeding in postsecondary ed through self-advocacy. *TEACHING Exceptional Children, 34*(2), 66–71.

Logan, K. R., & Gast, D. L. (2001). Conducting preference assessment and reinforcer testing for individuals with profound multiple disabilities: Issues and procedures. *Exceptionality, 9*(3), 123–134.

Lopez, E. C. (2000). Conducting instructional consultation through interpreters. *School Psychology Review, 29*(3), 378–388.

Losen, D. J., & Orfield, G. (Eds.). (2002). *Racial inequality in special education.* Cambridge, MA: Harvard Education Press.

Lovett, D. L., & Haring, K. A. (2003). Family perceptions of transitions in early intervention. *Education and Training in Developmental Disabilities, 38*(4), 370–377.

Loyd, R. J., Wehmeyer, M., & Davis, S. (2004). Family support. In D. E. Brolin & R. J. Loyd (Eds.), *Career development and transition services: A functional life skills approach* (4th ed., pp. 94–116). Upper Saddle River, NJ: Merrill Prentice Hall.

Lucyshyn, J., Dunlap, G., & Albin, R. W. (Eds.). (2002). *Families, family life, and positive behavior support: Addressing the challenge of problem behaviors in family contexts.* Baltimore: Brookes.

Lucyshyn, J. M., Horner, R. H., Dunlap, G., Albin, R. W., & Ben, K. R. (2002). Positive behavior support with families. In J. M. Lucyshyn, G. Dunlap, & R. W. Albin (Eds.), *Families and positive behavior support: Addressing problem behavior in family contexts* (pp. 3–43). Baltimore: Brookes.

Lundahl, B., Risser, H. J., & Lovejoy, M. C. (2006). A meta-analysis of parent training: Moderators and follow-up effects. *Clinical Psychology Review, 26*(1), 86–104.

Lustig, D. C. (2002). Family coping in families with a child with a disability. *Education and Training in Mental Retardation and Developmental Disabilities, 37*, 14–22.

Lynch, P., & Bruhl, S. (2005). Inclusive practices in secondary settings. In P. Zionts (Ed.), *Inclusion strategies for students with learning and behavior problems: Perspectives, experiences, and best practices* (pp. 93–109). Austin, TX: PRO-ED.

Lytle, R. K., & Bordin, J. (2001). Enhancing the IEP team: Strategies for parents and professionals. *Teaching Exceptional Children, 33*(5), 40–44.

MacMillan, D. L., & Reschly, D. J. (1998). Overrepresentation of minority students: The case for greater specificity or reconsiderations of the variables examined. *Journal of Special Education, 32*(1), 15–24.

Madaus, J. W. (2005). Navigating the college transition maze: A guide for students with learning disabilities. *Teaching Exceptional Children, 37*(3), 32–37.

Madaus, J. W., & Shaw, S. F. (2006). The impact of the IDEA 2004 on the transition to college for students with learning disabilities. *Learning Disabilities Practice, 21*(4), 273–281.

Malmgren, K. W., McLaughlin, M. J., & Nolet, V. (2005). Accounting for the performance of students with disabilities on statewide assessments. *Journal of Special Education, 39*(2), 86–96.

Mandell, C. J., & Murray, M. M. (2005). Innovative family-centered practices in personnel preparation. *Teacher Education and Special Education, 28*(1), 74–77.

Mandlawitz, M. (2007). *What every teacher should know about IDEA 2004 laws and regulations.* Boston: Pearson Education.

Mapp, K. L. (2002, April). *Having their say: Parents describe how and why they are involved in their children's education.* Paper presented at the annual meeting of the American Educational Research Association, New Orleans, LA.

Margolis, H. (1999). Mediation for special education conflicts: An opportunity to improve family–school relationships. *Journal of Educational and Psychological Consultation, 10*(1), 91–101.

Margolis, H. (2005). Resolving struggling learners' homework difficulties: Working with elementary school learners and parents. *Preventing School Failure, 50*(1), 5–12.

Marino, M. T., Marino, E. C., & Shaw, S. F. (2006). Making informed assistive technology decisions for students with high incidence disabilities. *Teaching Exceptional Children, 38*(6), 18–25.

Marsh, T. Y., & Cornell, D. G. (2001). The contribution of student school experiences to understanding ethnic differences in high-risk behaviors at school. *Behavioral Disorders, 26*(2), 152–163.

Marshak, L. E., & Prezant, F. (2007). *Married with special needs children: A couples guide to keeping connected.* Bethesda, MD: Woodbine House.

Martin, E. J., & Hagan-Burke, S. (2002). Establishing a home–school connection: Strengthening the partnership between families and school. *Preventing School Failure, 46*(2), 62–65.

Martin, J., Marshall, L. H., & Sale, P. (2004). A 3-year study of middle, junior high, and high school IEP meetings. *Exceptional Children, 70*(3), 285–297.

Martin, J. E., Mithaug, E., Cox, P., Peterson, L. Y., Van Dycke, J. L., & Cash, M. E. (2003). Increasing self-determination: Teaching students to plan, work, evaluate, and adjust. *Exceptional Children, 69*(4), 431–447.

Martin, J. E., Van Dycke, J. L., Christensen, W. R., Greene, B. A., Gardener, J. E., & Lovett, D. L. (2006). Increasing student participation in IEP meetings: Establishing the self-directed IEP as an evidence-based practice. *Exceptional Children, 72*(3), 299–316.

Martin, J. E., Van Dycke, J. L., Greene, B. A., Gardener, J. E., Christensen, W. R., Woods, L. L., & Lovett, D. L. (2006). Direct observation of teacher-directed IEP meetings: Establishing the need for student IEP meeting instruction. *Exceptional Children, 72*(2), 187–200.

Mason, C., Field, S., & Sawilowsky, S. (2004). Implementation of self-determination activities and student participation in IEPs. *Exceptional Children, 70*(4), 441–451.

Mason, C. A., Chapman, D. A., & Scott, K. G. (1999). The identification of early risk factors for severe emotional disturbances and emotional handicaps: An epidemiological approach. *American Journal of Community Psychology, 27*(3), 357–382.

Mason, C. Y., McGahee-Kovac, M., & Johnson, L. (2004). How to help students lead their IEP meetings. *Teaching Exceptional Children, 36*(3), 18–25.

Masten, A. (2001). Ordinary magic: Resilience processes in development. *American Psychologist, 56*(3), 227–238.

Mathur, S., & Smith, R. M. (2003). Collaborate with families of children with ADD. *Intervention in School and Clinic, 38,* 311–315.

Matuszny, R. M., Banda, D. R., & Coleman, T. J. (2007). A progressive plan for building collaborative relationships with parents from diverse backgrounds. *TEACHING Exceptional Children, 39*(4), 24–31.

Maurice, C., & Taylor, B. A. (2005). Early intensive behavioral intervention for autism challenges and opportunities. In W. L. Heward, T. E. Heron, N. A. Neef, S. M. Peterson, D. M. Sainato, G. Cartledge, R. Gardner, L. D. Peterson, S. B. Hersh, & J. C. Dardig (Eds.), *Focus on behavior analysis in education* (pp. 31–52). Upper Saddle River, NJ: Pearson Education.

McAfee, J. K., & Vergason, G. A. (1979). Parent involvement in the process of special education: Establishing the new partnership. *Focus on Exceptional Children, 11*(2), 1–15.

McDonough, C. S., Covington, T., Endo, S., Meinberg, D., Spencer, T. D., & Bicard, D. F. (2005). The Hawthorne Country Day School: A behavioral approach to schooling. In W. L. Heward, T. E. Heron, N. A. Neef, S. M. Peterson, D. M. Sainato, G. Cartledge, R. Gardner, L. D. Peterson, S. B. Hersh, & J. C. Dardig (Eds.), *Focus on behavior analysis in education* (pp. 188–210). Upper Saddle River, NJ: Pearson Education.

McEwan, E. K. (2005). *How to deal with parents who are angry, troubled, afraid, or just plain crazy.* Thousand Oaks, CA: Corwin Press.

McGill, T., & Vogtle, L. K. (2001). Driver's education for students with physical disabilities. *Exceptional Children, 67*(4), 455–466.

McKay, M. M., Lynn, C. J., & Bannon, W. M. (2005). Understanding inner city child mental health need and trauma exposure: Implications for preparing urban service providers. *American Journal of Orthopsychiatry, 75*(2), 201–210.

McKay, M. M., Pennington, J., Lynn, C. J., & McCadam, K. (2001). Understanding urban child mental health services use: Two studies of child, family, and environmental correlates. *Journal of Behavioral Health Services and Research, 28*(4), 475–483.

McKenzie, H. S., Clark, M., Wolf, M. M., Kothera, R., & Benson, C. (1968). Behavior modification of children with learning disabilities using grades as tokens and allowances as back up reinforcers. *Exceptional Children, 34*(10), 745–752.

McKinney-Vento Homeless Assistance Act of 2001. 42 U.S.C. § 11431 *et seq.* (2001).

McLaughlin, M. J., Dyson, A., Nagle, K., Thurlow, M., Rouse, M., Hardman, M., Norwich, B., Burke, P. J., & Perlin, M. (2006). Cross-cultural perspectives on the classification of children with disabilities: Part II; Implementing classification systems in schools. *Journal of Special Education, 40*(1), 46–58.

McLean, M., & Shaeffer, M. (2003). Family involvement in special education. In G. Olson & M. L. Fuller (Eds.), *Home–school relations* (2nd ed., pp. 183–196). Boston: Allyn & Bacon.

McLoyd, V. C., Cauce, A. M., Takeuchi, D., & Wilson, L. (2000). Marital process and parental socialization in families of color: A decade review of research. *Journal of Marriage and Family, 62,* 1070–1093.

McMillen, J. C., Scott, L. D., Auslander, W. F., Munson, M. R., Ollie, M. T., & Spitznagel, E. L. (2005). Prevalence of psychiatric disorders among older youths in the foster care system. *Journal of the American Academy of Child and Adolescent Psychiatry,* *44*(1), 88–95.

McNair, R., Dempsey, D., Wise, S., & Perlesz, A. (2002). Lesbian parenting: Issues, strengths and challenges. *Family Matters, 63,* 40–49.

McWilliam, R. A., Wolery, M., & Odom, S. L. (2001). Instructional perspectives in inclusive preschool classrooms. In M. J. Guralnick (Ed.), *Early childhood inclusion: Focus on change* (pp. 503–527). Baltimore: Brookes.

Mendez, L. M. R., Knoff, H. M., & Ferron, J. M. (2002). School demographic variables and out of school suspension rates: A quantitative and qualitative analysis of a large, ethnically diverse school district. *Psychology in the Schools, 39*(3), 259–277.

Millar, D. S. (2003). Age of majority, transfer of rights and guardianship: Considerations for families and educators. *Education and Training in Developmental Disabilities,* *38*(4), 378–397.

Millar, D. S. (2007). "I never put it together": The disconnect between self-determination and guardianship; Implications for practice. *Education and Training in Developmental Disabilities, 42*(2), 119–129.

Millar, D. S., & Renzaglia, A. (2002). Factors affecting guardianship practices for young adults with disabilities. *Exceptional Children, 68,* 465–484.

Millbank, J. (2002). *Meet the parents: A review of the research on lesbian and gay families, Gay and Lesbian Rights Lobby (NSW).* Retrieved March 20, 2004, from http://www. glrl.org.au

Mills, G. E., & Duff-Mallams, K. (2000). Special education mediation. *Teaching Exceptional Children, 32*(4), 72–78.

Miltenberger, R. (2004). *Behavior modification principles and procedures* (3rd ed.). Belmont, CA: Wadsworth.

Miner, C., & Bates, P. (2002). Person-centered transition planning: Creating lifestyles of community inclusion and autonomy. In K. Storey, P. Bates, & D. Hunter (Eds.), *The road ahead: Transition to adult life for persons with disabilities* (pp. 7–24). St. Augustine, FL: Training Resource Network.

Minino, A. M., & Smith, B. L. (2001). Deaths: Preliminary data for 2000. *National Vital Statistics Report, 49*(12), 1040.

Minke, K. M., & Anderson, K. J. (2003). Restructuring routine parent–teacher conferences: The family–school conference model. *The Elementary School Journal, 104*(1), 49–69.

Mira, M. (1970). Results of behavior modification training programs for parents and teachers. *Behavior Research and Therapy, 8,* 309–311.

Miretzky, D. (2004). The communication requirements of democratic schools: Parent–teacher perspectives on their relationships. *Teachers College Record, 106*(4), 814–851.

Mithaug, D. K., & Mithaug, D. E. (2003). The effects of choice opportunities and self-regulation training on the self-engagement and learning of young children with disabilities. In D. E. Mithaug, D. K. Mithaug, M. Agran, J. E. Martin, & M. Wehmeyer (Eds.), *Self-determined learning theory: Predictions, prescriptions, and practice* (pp. 141–157). Mahwah, NJ: Lawrence Erlbaum.

Mobayed, K. L., Collins, B. C., Strangis, D. E., Schuster, J. W., & Hemmeter, M. L. (2000). Teaching parents to employ mand-model procedures to teach their children requesting. *Journal of Early Intervention, 23*(3), 165–179.

Moes, D. R., & Frea, W. D. (2000). Using family context to inform intervention planning for the treatment of a child with autism. *Journal of Positive Behavior Interventions,* *2*(1), 40–47.

Moes, D. R., & Frea, W. D. (2002). Contextualized behavioral support in early intervention for children with autism and their families. *Journal of Autism and Developmental Disorders, 32*(6), 519–533.

Montgomery, D. J. (2005). Communicating without harm: Strategies to enhance parent–teacher communication. *Teaching Exceptional Children, 37*(5), 50–55.

Moore, K. (2003). Making the home–school connection. *Early Childhood Today, 18*(1), 14.

Morrison, G. S. (2004). *Early childhood education today* (9th ed.). Upper Saddle River, NJ: Merrill Prentice Hall.

Mullis, F., & Edwards, D. E. (2001). Consulting with parents: Applying family systems concepts and techniques. *Professional School Counseling, 5*(2), 116–123.

Mundschenk, N. A., & Foley, R. M. (1997). Collaboration: Strategies for building effective teams. In P. Zionts (Ed.), *Inclusion strategies for students with learning and behavior problems* (pp. 57–81). Austin, TX: PRO-ED.

Mundschenk, N. A., & Foley, R. M. (2000). Building blocks to effective partnerships: Meeting the needs of students with emotional or behavioral disorders and their families. In M. J. Fine & R. L. Simpson (Eds.), *Collaboration with parents and families of children and youth with exceptionalities* (pp. 369–387). Austin, TX: PRO-ED.

Mundschenk, N. A., Foley, R. M., & Swedburg, K. A. (2005). Collaboration: Building teams to facilitate inclusive practices. In P. Ziontz (Ed.), *Inclusion strategies for students with learning and behavior problems* (2nd ed., pp. 57–91). Austin, TX: PRO-ED.

Munk, D. D., Bursuck, W. D., Epstein, M. H., Jayanthi, M., Nelson, J., & Polloway, E. A. (2001). Homework communication problems: Perspectives of special and general education parents. *Reading and Writing Quarterly, 17,* 189–203.

Murdick, N., Shore, P., Chittooran, M. M., & Gartin, B. (2004). Cross-cultural comparison of the concept of "otherness" and its impact on persons with disabilities. *Education and Training in Developmental Disabilities, 39*(4), 310–316.

Mutua, N. K. (2001). Policied identities: Children with disabilities. *Educational Studies, 32*(3), 289–300.

Myers, A., & Eisenman, L. (2005). Student-led IEPs: Take the first step. *Exceptional Children, 37*(4), 52–58.

Najdowski, A. C., Wallace, M. D., Doney, J. K., & Ghezzi, P. M. (2003). Parental assessment and treatment of food selectivity in natural settings. *Journal of Applied Behavior Analysis, 36*(3), 383–386.

National Association for Retarded Citizens. (1973). *The right to choose.* Arlington, TX: Author.

National Association for the Education of Young Children. (2005). *Early childhood program standards and accreditation criteria.* Washington, DC: Author.

National Center for Educational Statistics. (2003). *Institute for Education Sciences.* Washington, DC: Author.

National Center for Learning Disabilities. (2006). *Understanding high-stakes testing and its impact on students with learning disabilities.* Retrieved May 7, 2008, from http://www.LD.org

National Center on Educational Outcomes. (2003). *Accountability for assessment results in the No Child Left Behind Act: What it means for children with disabilities.* Minneapolis: University of Minnesota, National Center on Educational Outcomes. Retrieved May 7, 2008, from http://cehd.umn.edu/nceo/OnlinePubs/NCLBdisabilities.pdf

National Center on Secondary Education and Transition. (2004). *Dropout and graduation: Frequently asked questions.* Retrieved June 5, 2008, from http://www.ncset.org/topics/dropout/faq.asp?topic=36

National Center on Secondary Education and Transition. (2006). *The role of parents in dropout prevention: Strategies that promote graduation and school achievement.* Retrieved July 10, 2008, from http://www.ncset.org/publications/printresource.asp?id=3135

National Clearinghouse on Child Abuse and Neglect Information. (2004). *Child maltreatment 2002: Summary of key findings.* Washington, DC: Author.

National Collaboration on Diversity in the Teaching Force. (2004). *Assessment of diversity in America's teaching force: A call to action.* Retrieved June 12, 2005, from http://www.nea.org/teacherquality/images/diversityreport.pdf

National Council on Disability. (2004). *Higher education fact sheet.* Washington, DC: Author. Retrieved July 10, 2008, from http://www.ncd.gov/newsroom/publications/2004/pdf/hea_factsheet.pdf

National Population Projections. (2002). *Projections of the resident population by race, Hispanic origin, and nativity: Middle series.* U.S. Census Bureau, Population Division, Populations Branch. Retrieved April 19, 2005, from http://www.census.gov/population/projections/natsum=T5.html

Ndura, E., Robinson, M., & Ochs, G. (2003). Minority students in high school advanced placement courses: Opportunity and equity denied. *American Secondary Education, 32*(1), 21–38.

Nelson, J. S., Epstein, M. H., Bursuck, W. D., Jayanthi, M., & Sawyer, V. (1998). The preference of middle-school students for homework adaptations made by general education teachers. *Learning Disabilities Research and Practice, 13,* 119–127.

Nelson, J. S., Jayanthi, M., Brittain, C. R., Epstein, M. H., & Bursuck, W. D. (2002). Using the nominal group technique for homework communication decisions. *Remedial and Special Education, 23*(6), 397–386.

Nelson, L. G., Summers, J. A., & Turnbull, A. (2004). Boundaries in family–professional relationships: Implications for special education. *Remedial and Special Education, 25*(3), 153–165.

Neville, H. A., & Walters, J. M. (2004). Contextualizing Black Americans' health. In D. R. Atkinson (Ed.), *Counseling American minorities* (6th ed., pp. 83–103). Boston: McGraw-Hill.

Nissenbaum, M. S., Tollefson, N., & Reese, R. M. (2002). The interpretive conference: Sharing a diagnosis of autism with families. *Focus on Autism and Other Developmental Disabilities, 17*(1), 30–43.

No Child Left Behind Act of 2001, 20 U.S.C. 70 § 6301 *et seq.* (2002).

Nutting, B., Porfeli, E., Queen, J. A., & Algozzine, B. (2006). Parent beliefs and knowledge about special education and the Individuals With Disabilities Education Act. *Journal of Special Education Leadership, 19*(2), 48–61.

Obiakor, F. E., Algozzine, B., & Ford, B. (1993). Urban education, the general education initiative, and service delivery to African-American students. *Urban Education, 28*(3), 313–327.

Obiakor, F. E., & Ford, B. A. (2002). *Creating successful learning environments for African American learners with exceptionalities.* Thousand Oaks, CA: Corwin Press.

Odom, S. L., Horn, E., Marquart, J. M., Hanson, M. J., Wolfberg, P., Beckman, P., Lieber, J., Li, S., Schwartz, I., Janko, S., & Sandall, S. (2000). On the forms of inclusion:

Organization context and individualized service models. *Journal of Early Intervention, 22*, 185–199.

Odom, S. L., & Strain, P. S. (2002). Evidence-based practices in early intervention/early childhood special education: Single-subject design research. *Journal of Early Intervention, 25*(2), 151–162.

Odom, S. L., & Wolery, M. (2003). A unified theory of practice in early intervention/early childhood special education: Evidence-based practices. *Journal of Special Education, 37*(3), 164–173.

Ogletree, B. T., Bull, J., Drew, R., & Lunnen, K. Y. (2001). Team-based service delivery for students with disabilities: Practice options and guidelines for success. *Interventions in School and Clinic, 36*, 138–145.

Okum, B. F. (2002). *Effective helping: Interviewing and counseling techniques* (6th ed.). Pacific Grove, CA: Brooks/Cole.

Oliver, M. N. I., Anthony, A., & Leimkuhl, T. T. (2002). Attitudes toward acceptable socio-sexual behaviors for persons with mental retardation: Implications for normalization and community integration. *Education and Training in Mental Retardation and Developmental Disabilities, 37*(2), 193–201.

Olsen, G., & Fuller, M. L. (2003). *Home–school relations: Working successfully with parents and families* (2nd ed.). Boston: Allyn & Bacon.

Olson, L. (2000). Finding and keeping competent teachers: Quality counts—Who should teach? *Education Week, 19*(18), 12–17.

O'Neill, P. T. (2004). *No Child Left Behind compliance manual*. New York: Brownstone.

Orfield, G., & Lee, C. (2005). *Why segregation matters: Poverty and educational inequality*. Cambridge, MA: Civil Rights Project at Harvard University.

Orfield, G., Losen, D., Wald, J., & Swanson, C. (2004). *Losing our future: How minority youth are being left behind by the graduation rate crisis*. Cambridge, MA: Civil Rights Project at Harvard University.

Orsmond, G. I., & Seltzer, M. M. (2000). Brothers and sisters of adults with mental retardation: Gendered nature of the sibling relationship. *American Journal on Mental Retardation, 105*(6), 486–508.

Orsmond, G. I., & Seltzer, M. M. (2007). Siblings of individuals with autism spectrum disorders across the life course. *Mental Retardation and Developmental Disabilities Research Reviews, 13*, 313–320.

Orsmond, G. I., Seltzer, M. M., Greenberg, J. S., & Krauss, M. W. (2006). Mother–child relationship quality among adolescents and adults with autism. *American Journal on Mental Retardation, 111*, 121–137.

Osborne, A. G., & Russo, C. J. (2006). *Special education and the law: A guide for practitioners*. Thousand Oaks, CA: Corwin Press.

O'Shea, D. J., O'Shea, L. J., Algozzine, R., & Hammitte, D. J. (2001). *Families and teachers of individuals with disabilities: Collaborative orientations and responsive practices*. Boston: Allyn & Bacon.

O'Sullivan, K. R., & Russell, H. (2006). Parents and professionals: Breaking cycles of blame. *Reclaiming Children and Youth, 15*(1), 37–39.

Oswald, D. P., & Coutinho, M. J. (2001). Trends in disproportionate representation in special education: Implications for multicultural education. In C. A. Utley & F. E. Obiakor (Eds.), *Special education, multicultural education, and school reform* (pp. 53–73). Springfield, IL: Thomas.

Owen-DeSchryver, J. S., Carr, E. G., Cale, S. I., & Blakeley-Smith, A. B. (2008). Promoting social interactions between students with autism spectrum disorders and their peers in inclusive school settings. *Focus on Autism and Other Developmental Disabilities, 23*(1), 15–28.

Palmer, A. (2004). Parent perspective. *The Exceptional Parent, 34*(9), 34–35.

Palmer, D. S., Fuller, K., Arora, T., & Nelson, M. (2001). Taking sides: Parent views on inclusion for their children with severe disabilities. *Exceptional Children, 67*(4), 467–484.

Parette, H. P., & Brotherson, M. J. (2004). Family-centered and culturally responsive assistive technology decision making. *Infants and Young Children, 17*(4), 355–367.

Parette, H. P., Brotherson, M. J., & Huer, M. B. (2000). Giving families a voice in augmentative and alternative communication decision-making. *Education and Training in Mental Retardation and Developmental Disabilities, 35*(2), 177–190.

Parette, H. P., Huer, M. B., & Wyatt, T. A. (2002). Young African American children with disabilities and augmentative and alternative communication issues. *Early Childhood Education Journal, 29*(3), 201–207.

Parette, H. P., & Petch-Hogan, B. (2000). Approaching families: Facilitating culturally/linguistically diverse family involvement. *Teaching Exceptional Children, 33*(2), 4–10.

Parish, S. L., Rose, R. A., Grinstein-Weiss, M., Richman, E. L., & Andrews, M. E. (2008). Material hardship in U.S. families raising children with disabilities. *Exceptional Children, 75*(1), 71–92.

Park, J., Hoffman, L., Marquis, J., Turnbull, A. P., Poston, D., Mannan, H., Wang, M., & Nelson, L. L. (2003). Toward assessing family outcomes of service delivery: Validation of a family quality of life survey. *Journal of Intellectual Disability Research, 47*(4/5), 367–384.

Park, J., Turnbull, A. P., & Turnbull, H. R. (2002). Impacts of poverty on quality of life in families of children with disabilities. *Exceptional Children, 68*(2), 151–170.

Parrish, L. (2002). Racial disparities in the identification, funding, and provision of special education. In D. J. Losen & G. Orfield (Eds.), *Racial inequity in special education* (pp. 15–37). Cambridge, MA: Harvard Education Press.

Patterson, C. (2000). Family relationships of lesbians and gay men. *Journal of Marriage and Family, 62*(2), 1052–1069.

Patterson, G. R. (1982). *Coercive family processes.* Eugene, OR: Castalia Press.

Patton, J. M. (1998). The disproportionate representation of African Americans in special education: Looking behind the curtain for understanding and solutions. *Journal of Special Education, 32,* 25–31.

Patton, J. R. (2006). Transition planning and transition education. In C. S. Bos & S. Vaughn (Eds.), *Strategies for teaching students with learning and behavior problems* (pp. 428–450). Boston: Allyn & Bacon.

Pauken, P. D., & Daniel, P. T. K. (1999, December). Race and disability discrimination in school discipline: A legal and statistical analysis. *Education Law Reporter, 139,* 766–768.

Paul, J. L., & Simeonsson, R. J. (1993). *Children with special needs.* Ft. Worth, TX: Harcourt Brace Jovanovich.

Payne, R. (2005). *A framework for understanding poverty.* Highlands, TX: aha! Process, Inc.

Payne-Christiansen, E. M., & Sitlington, P. L. (2008). Guardianship: Its role in the transition process for students with developmental disabilities. *Education and Training in Developmental Disabilities, 43*(1), 3–19.

Pemberton, J. B. (2003). Communicating academic progress as an integral part of assessment. *Teaching Exceptional Children, 35*(4), 16–20.

Pemberton, J. R., & Borrego, J. (2007). Increasing acceptance of behavioral child management techniques: What do parents say? *Child and Family Behavior Therapy, 29*(2), 27–45.

Peña, D. C. (2000). Parent involvement: Influencing factors and implications. *Journal of Educational Research, 94*(1), 42–54.

Pennsylvania Association for Retarded Children (PARC) v. Commonwealth of Pennsylvania, 343 F. Supp. 279 (E.D. Pa. 1972).

Perry, D. F., Greer, M., Goldhammer, K., & Mackey-Andrews, S. D. (2001). Fulfilling the promise of early intervention: Rates of delivered IFSP services. *Journal of Early Interventions, 24*(2), 90–102.

Persampieri, M., Gortmaker, V., Daly, E. J., Sheridan, S. M., & McCurdy, M. (2006). Promoting parent use of empirically supported reading interventions: Two experimental investigations of child outcomes. *Behavioral Interventions, 21,* 31–57.

Peterson, P., Carta, J. J., & Greenwood, C. (2005). Teaching enhanced milieu language teaching skills to parents in multiple risk families. *Journal of Early Intervention, 27*(2), 94–109.

Pierangelo, R., & Giuliani, G. (2006). *Learning disabilities: A practical approach to foundations, assessment, diagnosis, and teaching.* Boston: Pearson Education.

Pluviose, D. (2006). New GED chief faces sagging testing rates despite high minority dropout numbers. *Diverse Issues in Higher Education, 23*(12), 15–17.

Pogoloff, S. M. (2004). Twenty ways to facilitate positive relationships between parents and professionals. *Intervention in School and Clinic, 40*(2), 116–119.

Polloway, E. A., Bursuck, W. D., & Epstein, M. H. (2001). Homework for students with learning disabilities: The challenge of home–school communication. *Reading and Writing Quarterly, 17,* 181–187.

Powell-Smith, K. A., Stoner, G., Shinn, M. R., & Good, R. H. (2000). Parent tutoring in reading using literature and curriculum materials: Impact on student reading achievement. *School Psychology Review, 29*(1), 5–27.

Poyadue, F. S. (1993). Cognitive coping at Parents Helping Parents. In A. P. Turnbull, J. M. Paterson, S. K. Behr, D. L. Murphy, J. G. Marquis, & M. J. Blue-Banning (Eds.), *Cognitive coping, families, and disability* (pp. 95–110). Baltimore: Brookes.

Praisner, C. L. (2003). Attitudes of elementary school principals toward the inclusion of students with disabilities. *Exceptional Children, 69*(2), 135–145.

Prevent Blindness America. (2005). *Signs of possible eye problems in children.* Retrieved December 15, 2006, from http://www.preventblindness.org/children/trouble_signs.html

Pugach, M. C., & Johnson, L. J. (2002). *Collaborative practitioners, collaborative schools* (2nd ed.). Denver, CO: Love.

Quenemoen, R. F., Lehr, C. A., Thurlow, M. L., & Massanari, C. B. (2001). *Students with disabilities in standards-based assessment and accountability systems: Emerging issues, strategies, and recommendations* (Synthesis Report 37). Minneapolis: University of Minnesota, National Center on Educational Outcomes. Retrieved May 7, 2008, from http://education.umn.edu/NCEO/OnlinePubs/Synthesis37.html

Raffaelli, M., & Ontai, L. L. (2001). "She's 16 years old and there's boys calling over to the house": An exploratory study of sexual socialization in Latino families. *Culture, Health and Sexuality, 3*(3), 295–310.

Rafferty, Y., & Griffin, K. W. (2005). Benefits and risks of reverse inclusion for preschoolers with and without disabilities: Perspectives of parents and providers. *Journal of Early Intervention, 27*(3), 173–192.

Ramirez, A. Y. (2001). "Parent involvement is like apple pie": A look at parental involvement in two states. *The High School Journal, 85,* 1–9.

Ramirez, F. (2001). Technology and parental involvement. *Clearing House, 75*(1), 30–31.

Ramos, K. (1995). Advocacy: Friend or foe? *Preventing School Failure, 39*(1), 37–40.

Raver, S. A. (2004). Monitoring child progress in early childhood special education settings. *Teaching Exceptional Children, 36*(6), 52–57.

Rea, P. J., McLaughlin, V. L., & Walther-Thomas, C. (2002). Outcomes for students with learning disabilities in inclusive and pullout programs. *Exceptional Children, 68*(2), 203–222.

Reese, R. M., Richman, D. M., Zarcone, J., & Zarcone, T. (2003). Individualizing functional assessments for children with autism: The contribution of perseverative behavior and sensory disturbances to disruptive behavior. *Focus on Autism and Other Developmental Disabilities, 18*(2), 87–92.

Reid, M. J., Webster-Stratton, C., & Baydar, N. (2004). Halting the development of conduct problems in Head Start children: The effects of parent training. *Journal of Clinical Child and Adolescent Psychology, 33*(2), 279–292.

Reschly, D. J. (2000). Assessment and eligibility determination in the Individuals With Disabilities Education Act of 1997. In C. Telzrow & M. Tankersley (Eds.), *IDEA Amendments of 1997: Practice guidelines for school-based teams* (pp. 65–104). Bethesda, MD: National Association of School Psychologists.

Reyno, S. M., & McGrath, P. J. (2006). Predictors of parent training efficacy for child externalizing behavior problems: A meta-analytic review. *Journal of Child Psychology and Psychiatry, 47*(1), 99–111.

Reynolds, G. P., Wright, J. V., & Beale, B. (2003). The roles of grandparents in educating today's children. *Journal of Instructional Psychology, 30*(4), 316–325.

Risley, T. R., & Wolf, M. M. (1966). Experimental manipulation of autistic behaviors and generalization into the home. In R. Ulrich, T. Stachnik, & J. Mabry (Eds.), *Control of human behavior* (pp. 193–220). Austin, TX: PRO-ED.

Roach, A. T., Elliott, S. N., & Webb, N. L. (2005). Alignment of an alternate assessment with state academic standards. *Journal of Special Education, 38*(4), 218–231.

Roberts, G., Torgesen, J. K., Boardman, A., & Scammacca, N. (2008). Evidence-based strategies for reading instruction of older students with learning disabilities. *Learning Disabilities Research and Practice, 23*(2), 63–69.

Robinson, E., & Fine, M. J. (1995). Developing collaborative home–school relationships. *Preventing School Failure, 39*(1), 9–15.

Rock, M. L. (2000). Parents as equal partners: Balancing the scales in IEP development. *Teaching Exceptional Children, 32*(6), 30–37.

Rogers, C. R. (1962). The interpersonal relationship: The core of guidance. *Harvard Educational Review, 32*(4), 416–429.

Rooker, L. S. (1997, October 2). *FERPA memorandum: Access to test protocols and test answer sheet.* Retrieved October 10, 2005, from http://www.fetaweb.com/04/ferpa.rooker.ltr.protocols.htm

Rosenkoetter, S. E., & Squires, S. (2004). Writing outcomes that make a difference for children and families. In E. Horn, M. M. Ostrosky, & H. Jones (Eds.), *Family-based practices: Monograph of the Division for Early Childhood of the Council for Exceptional Children* (Series No. 5, pp. 51–60). Longmont, CO: Sopris West.

Rosenzweig, C. (2001, April). *A meta-analysis of parenting and school success: The role of parents in promoting students' academic performance.* Paper presented at the annual meeting of the American Educational Research Association, Seattle, WA.

Rossiter, L., & Sharpe, D. (2001). The siblings of individuals with mental retardation: A quantitative integration of the literature. *Journal of Child and Family Studies, 10,* 65–85.

Rudawsky, D. J., Lundgren, D. C., & Grasha, A. F. (1999). Competitive and collaborative responses to negative feedback. *The International Journal of Conflict Management, 10*(2), 172–190.

Rueda, R., Monzo, L., Shapiro, J., Gomez, J., & Blacher, J. (2005). Cultural models of transition: Latina mothers of young adults with developmental disabilities. *Exceptional Children, 71*(4), 401–414.

Ruiz-Primo, M. A. (2006). *A multi-method and multi-source approach for studying fidelity of implementation.* Center for the Study of Evaluation Report 677. Retrieved May 10, 2005, from http://www.vanderbilt.edu/lsi/expert/documents/fidelityofimplementation .pdf

Rupiper, M., & Marvin, C. (2004). Preparing teachers for family centered services: A survey of preservice curriculum content. *Teacher Education and Special Education, 27*(4), 384–395.

Rush, D. D., Shelden, M. L., & Hanft, B. E. (2003). Coaching families and colleagues: A process for collaboration in natural settings. *Infants and Young Children, 16*(1), 33–47.

Rutherford, R. B., & Edgar, E. (1979). *Teachers and parents: A guide to interaction and cooperation.* Boston: Allyn & Bacon.

Sahlen, C. A. H., & Lehmann, J. P. (2006). Requesting accommodations in higher education. *Teaching Exceptional Children, 38,* 28–34.

Sailor, W. (1991). Special education in the restructured school. *Remedial and Special Education, 12*(6), 8–22.

Sailor, W. (2002). *Whole school success and inclusive education: Building partnerships for learning, achievement, and accountability.* New York: Teachers College Press.

Sainato, D. S., & Morrison, R. S. (2001). Transition to inclusive environments for young children with disabilities: Toward a seamless system of service delivery. In M. J. Guralnick (Ed.), *Early childhood inclusion: Focus on change* (pp. 293–306). Baltimore: Brookes.

Salas, L. (2004). Individualized educational plan (IEP) meetings and Mexican American parents: Let's talk about it. *Journal of Latinos and Education, 3*(3), 181–192.

Salend, S. J. (2005). Report card models that support communication and differentiation of instruction. *Teaching Exceptional Children, 37*(4), 28–34.

Salend, S. J. (2008a). *Creating inclusive classrooms: Effective and reflective practices.* Upper Saddle River, NJ: Pearson Education.

Salend, S. J. (2008b). Determining appropriate testing accommodations: Complying with NCLB and IDEA. *Teaching Exceptional Children, 40*(4), 14–22.

Salend, S. J., Duhaney, D., Anderson, D. J., & Gottschalk, C. (2004). Using the Internet to improve homework communication and completion. *Teaching Exceptional Children, 36*(3), 64–73.

Salend, S. J., & Taylor, L. (1993). Working with families: A cross-cultural perspective. *Remedial and Special Education, 14,* 25–32.

Salvia, J., Ysseldyke, J., & Bolt, S. (2007). *Assessment in special and inclusive education* (10th ed.). Boston: Houghton Mifflin.

Sandall, S., Hemmeter, M. L., Smith, B. J., & McLean, M. E. (2005). *DEC recommended practices: A comprehensive guide for practical application in early intervention/early childhood special education.* Longmont, CO: Sopris West.

Sanders, M. R., Mazzucchelli, T. G., & Studman, L. J. (2004). Stepping Stones Triple P: The theoretical basis and development of an evidence-based positive parenting program for families with a child who has a disability. *Journal of Intellectual and Developmental Disability, 29*(3), 265–284.

Sands, D. J., Kozleski, E. B., & French, N. K. (2000). *Inclusive education for the twenty-first century.* Belmont, CA: Wadsworth/Thomson Learning.

Sands, R. G., & Goldberg-Glen, R. S. (2000). Factors associated with stress among grandparents raising their grandchildren. *Family Relations, 49*(1), 97–111.

Sarafino, E. P. (2001). *Behavior modification: Principles of behavior change.* Mountain View, CA: Mayfield.

Sasso, G. M., Conroy, M., Stichter, J., & Fox, J. (2001). Slowing down the bandwagon: The misapplication of functional assessment for students with emotional and behavioral disorders. *Behavioral Disorders, 26,* 282–296.

Scanlon, D., & Mellard, D. F. (2002). Academic and participation profiles of school-age dropouts with and without disabilities. *Exceptional Children, 68*(2), 239–258.

Scarborough, A. A., Hebbeler, K. M., & Spiker, D. (2006). Eligibility characteristics of infants and toddlers entering early intervention services in the United States. *Journal of Policy and Practice in Intellectual Disabilities, 3*(1), 57–64.

Scarborough, A. A., Spiker, D., Mallik, S., Hebbeler, K. M., Bailey, D. B., Jr., & Simeonsson, R. J. (2004). A national look at children and families entering early intervention. *Exceptional Children, 70*(4), 469–483.

Schwartz, I. S., & Rodriguez, P. B. (2001). A few issues to consider: The who, what, and where of family support. *Journal of Early Intervention, 24*(1), 19–21.

Scorgie, K., & Sobsey, D. (2000). Transformational outcomes associated with parenting children who have disabilities. *Mental Retardation, 38,* 195–206.

Seery, M. E., Davis, P. M., & Johnson, L. J. (2000). Seeing eye-to-eye: Are parents and professionals in agreement about the benefits of preschool inclusion? *Remedial and Special Education, 21*(5), 268–278.

Seligman, M. (2000). *Conducting effective conferences with parents of children with disabilities.* New York: Guilford.

Seligman, M., & Darling, R. B. (2007). *Ordinary families, special children.* New York: Guilford.

Serna, L., Forness, S. R., & Nielson, M. E. (1998). Intervention versus affirmation: Proposed solutions to the problem of overrepresentation in special education. *Journal of Special Education, 32,* 48–51.

Shackelford, J. (2004). *State and jurisdictional eligibility definitions for infants and toddlers with disabilities under IDEA* (NECTAC Notes No. 14). Chapel Hill: University of North Carolina, Child Development Institute, National Early Childhood Technical Assistance Center.

Shannon, P., Grinde, L. R., & Cox, A. W. (2003). Families' perceptions of the ability to pay for early intervention services. *Journal of Early Intervention, 25*(3), 164–172.

Shapiro, E. S., & Clemens, N. H. (2005). Conducting systematic direct classroom observations to define school-related problems. In R. Brown-Chidsey (Ed.), *Assessment for intervention: A problem-solving approach* (pp. 175–199). New York: Guilford.

Shealey, M. W., Lue, M. S., Brooks, M., & McCray, E. (2005). Examining the legacy of Brown: The impact on special education teacher practice. *Remedial and Special Education, 26*(2), 113–121.

Sheldon, S. B. (2002). Parents' social networks and beliefs as predictors of parent involvement. *The Elementary School Journal, 102*(4), 301–316.

Sheridan, S. M. (2000). Considerations of multiculturalism and diversity in behavioral consultation with parents and teachers. *School Psychology Review, 29*(3), 344–353.

Sheridan, S. M., & McCurdy, M. (2005). Ecological variables in school-based assessment and intervention planning. In R. Brown-Chidsey (Ed.), *Assessment for intervention: A problem-solving approach* (pp. 43–64). New York: Guilford.

Shriner, J. G. (2000). Legal perspectives on school outcomes assessment for students with disabilities. *Journal of Special Education, 33,* 232–239.

Shriner, J. G., & Destefano, L. (2003). Participation and accommodation in state assessment: The role of individualized education programs. *Exceptional Children, 69*(2), 147–161.

Shumow, L., & Lomax, R. (2001, April). *Parental efficacy: Predictor of parenting behavior and adolescent outcomes.* Paper presented at the annual meeting of the American Educational Research Association, Seattle, WA. Sicley, D. (1993). Effective methods of communication: Practical interventions for classroom teachers. *Intervention in School and Clinic, 29*(2), 105–108.

Simmons, B. J. (2003). Facilitative conferences: Parents and teachers working together. *Journal of Educational Strategies, Issues and Ideas, 76*(2), 88–93.

Simon, J. B. (2006). Perceptions of the IEP process. *Teacher Education and Special Education, 29*(4), 225–235.

Simonsen, F., & Gunter, L. (2001). Best practices in spelling instruction: A research summary. *Journal of Direct Instruction, 1*(2), 97–105.

Simpson, R. (1988). Needs of parents and families whose children have learning and behavior problems. *Behavior Disorders, 14*(1), 40–47.

Simpson, R. L. (2003). Policy-related research issues and perspectives. *Focus on Autism and Other Developmental Disabilities, 18*(3), 192–196.

Simpson, R. L. (2004). Finding effective intervention and personnel preparation practices for students with autism spectrum disorders. *Exceptional Children, 70*(2), 135–144.

Simpson, R. L. (2005). Evidence-based practices and students with autism spectrum disorders. *Focus on Autism and Other Developmental Disabilities, 20,* 140–149.

Simpson, R. L., & Carter, W. (1993). Comprehensive, inexpensive, and convenient services for parents and families of students with behavioral disorders. *Preventing School Failure, 37,* 21–25.

Simpson, R. L., de Boer-Ott, S. R., Griswold, D. E., Myles, B. S., Byrd, S. E., Ganz, J. B., et al. (2005). *Autism spectrum disorders: Interventions and treatments for children and youth.* Thousand Oaks, CA: Corwin Press.

Simpson, R. L., de Boer-Ott, S. R., & Smith-Myles, B. (2003). Inclusion of learners with autism spectrum disorders in general education settings. *Topics in Language Disorders, 23*(2), 116–133.

Simpson, R. L., & Fiedler, C. R. (1989). Parent participation in individualized educational program (IEP) conferences: A case for individualization. In M. Fine (Ed.), *The second handbook on parent education: Contemporary perspectives* (pp. 145–171). New York: Academic Press.

Simpson, R. L., LaCava, P., & Graner, P. (2004). The No Child Left Behind Act (NCLB): Challenges and implications for educators. *Intervention in School and Clinic, 40*(20), 67–75.

Simpson, R. L., McKee, M., Teeter, D., & Beytien, A. (2007). Evidence-based methods for children and youth with autism spectrum disorders: Stakeholder issues and perspectives. *Exceptionality, 15*(4), 203–217.

Simpson, R. L., Myles, B. S., Simpson, J., & Ganz, J. (2005). Inclusion of students with disabilities in general education settings: Structuring for successful management. In P. Zionts (Ed.), *Inclusion strategies for students with learning and behavior problems* (pp. 193–216). Austin, TX: PRO-ED.

Simpson, R. L., & Poplin, M. S. (1981). Parents as agents of change: A behavioral approach. *School Psychology Review, 10*(1), 15–25.

Simpson, R. L., & Sasso, G. M. (1992). Full inclusion of students with autism in general education settings: Values versus science. *Focus on Autistic Behavior, 7*(3), 1–13.

Simpson, R. L., & Simpson, J. D. (1994). Needs of parents and families of at-risk and disabled students. *Preventing School Failure, 39*(1), 21–25.

Simpson, R. L., & Zionts, P. (2000). *Autism: Information and resources for parents, families, and professionals* (2nd ed.). Austin, TX: PRO-ED.

Simpson, R. L., & Zurkowski, J. K. (2000). Parent and professional collaborative relationships in an era of change. In M. J. Fine & R. L. Simpson (Eds.), *Collaboration with parents and families of children and youth with exceptionalities* (2nd ed., pp. 89–102). Austin, TX: PRO-ED.

Singer, G. H. S. (2002). Suggestions for a pragmatic program of research on families and disability. *Journal of Special Education, 36*, 148–154.

Skiba, R. J., Simmons, A. B., Ritter, S., Gibb, A. C., Rausch, M. K., Cuadrado, J., & Chung, C. (2008). Achieving equity in special education: History, status, and current challenges. *Exceptional Children, 74*(3), 264–288.

Skinner, B. F. (1948). *Walden two.* New York: Macmillan.

Smith, B. J., Strain, P. S., Snyder, P., Sandall, S. R., McLean, M. E., Broudy-Ramsey, A., & Sumi, W. C. (2002). DEC recommended practices: A review of 9 years of EI/ECSE research literature. *Journal of Early Intervention, 25*(2), 108–119.

Smith, C. (1993). Cultural sensitivity in working with children and families. In J. L. Paul & R. J. Simeonsson (Eds.), *Children with special needs: Family, culture and society* (pp. 113–121). Ft. Worth, TX: Harcourt Brace Jovanovich.

Smith, D. D. (2007). *Introduction to special education: Making a difference (6th ed.).* Boston: Allyn & Bacon.

Smith, T. E. C., Gartin, B. C., Murdick, N. L., & Hilton, A. (2006). *Families and children with special needs: Professional and family partnerships.* Upper Saddle River, NJ: Pearson Prentice Hall.

Smith, T. E. C., Polloway, E. A., Patton, J. R., & Dowdy, C. A. (2004). *Teaching students with special needs in inclusive settings* (4th ed.). Boston: Allyn & Bacon.

Smith, T. L., Polloway, E. A., Smith, J. D., & Patton, J. R. (2007). Self-determination for persons with developmental disabilities: Ethical considerations for teachers. *Education and Training in Developmental Disabilities, 42*(2), 144–151.

Soodak, L. C., & Erwin, E. J. (2000). Valued member or tolerated participant: Parents' experiences in inclusive early childhood settings. *Journal of the Association for Persons With Severe Handicaps, 25*(1), 29–41.

Spann, S. J., Kohler, F. W., & Soenksen, D. (2003). Examining parents' involvement in and perceptions of special education services: An interview with families in a parent support group. *Focus on Autism and Other Developmental Disabilities, 18*(4), 228–237.

Stainback, S., & Stainback, W. (1992). Schools as inclusive communities. In W. Stainback & S. Stainback (Eds.), *Controversial issues confronting special education* (pp. 29–43). Boston: Allyn & Bacon.

Stainton, T., & Besser, H. (1998). The positive impact of children with an intellectual disability on the family. *Journal of Intellectual and Developmental Disability, 23*(1), 57–70.

Starr, E., Foy, J. B., Cramer, K. M., & Singh, H. (2006). How are schools doing? Parental perceptions of children with autism spectrum disorders, Down syndrome and learning disabilities: A comparative analysis. *Education and Training in Developmental Disabilities, 41*(4), 315–332.

Sterling-Turner, H. E., Watson, T. S., Wildmon, M., Watkins, C., & Little, E. (2001). Investigating the relationship between training type and treatment integrity. *School Psychology Quarterly, 16*, 56–67.

Stevens, B. A., & Tollafield, A. (2003). Creating comfortable and productive parent/teacher conferences [Electronic version]. *Phi Delta Kappan, 84*(7), 521–524.

Stiggins, R. J. (2001). *Student-involved classroom assessments* (3rd ed.). Upper Saddle River, NJ: Prentice Hall.

Stodden, R., Galloway, L. M., & Stodden, J. M. (2003). Secondary school curricula issues: Impact on postsecondary students with disabilities. *Exceptional Children, 70*(1), 9–25.

Stoneman, Z., & Berman, P. W. (Eds.). (1993). *The effects of mental retardation, disability, and illness on sibling relationships: Research issues and challenges.* Baltimore: Brookes.

Stoner, J. B., Bock, S. J., Thompson, J. R., Angell, M. E., Heyl, B. S., & Crowley, E. P. (2005). Welcome to our world: Parents' perceptions of interactions between parents of young children with ASD and education professionals. *Focus on Autism and Other Developmental Disabilities, 20*(1), 39–51.

Storey, K., Bates, P., & Hunter, D. (Eds.). (2002). *The road ahead: Transition to adult life for persons with disabilities.* St. Augustine, FL: Training Resource Network.

Strain, P. S., & Joseph, G. E. (2004). Engaged supervision to support recommended practices for young children with challenging behavior. *Topics in Early Childhood Special Education, 24*(1), 39–50.

Strom, P. S., & Strom, R. D. (2002). Teacher–parent communication reforms. *High School Journal, 86*(2), 14–21.

Substance Abuse and Mental Health Services Administration. (2003). *National survey on drug use and health.* Washington, DC: U.S. Department of Health and Human Services.

Sun, C. M. (2007). The impact of inclusion-based education on the likelihood of independence for today's students with special needs. *Journal of Special Education Leadership, 20*(2), 84–92.

Swick, K. J. (2003). Communication concepts for strengthening family–school–community partnerships. *Early Childhood Education Journal, 30*(4), 275–280.

Swick, K. J., & Bailey, L. B. (2004). Communicating effectively with parents and families who are homeless. *Early Childhood Education Journal, 32*(3), 211–215.

Symon, J. B. (2001). Parent education for autism: Issue in providing services at a distance. *Journal of Positive Behavior Interventions, 3*(3), 160–174.

Symon, J. B. (2005). Expanding interventions for children with autism: Parents as trainers. *Journal of Positive Behavior Interventions, 7*(3), 159–173.

Talbott, E., & Fleming, J. (2003). The role of social contexts and special education in the mental health problems of urban adolescents. *Journal of Special Education, 37*(2), 111–123.

Tasker, F. (1999). Children in lesbian-lead families: A review. *Clinical Child Psychology and Psychiatry, 4*(2), 153–166.

Tate, C., & Audette, D. (2001). Theory and research on "race" as a natural kind of variable in psychology. *Theory and Psychology, 11*, 495–520.

Taunt, H. M., & Hastings, R. P. (2002). Positive impact of children with disabilities on their families: A preliminary study. *Education and Training in Mental Retardation and Developmental Disabilities, 37*, 410–420.

Taylor, G. (2000). *Parental involvement: A practical guide for collaboration and teamwork for students with disabilities.* Springfield, IL: Charles C. Thomas.

Taylor, R. L., Smiley, L. R., & Richards, S. B. (2009). *Exceptional students: Preparing teachers for the 21st century.* New York: McGraw-Hill.

Tein, J., Sandler, I. N., & Zautra, A. J. (2000). Stressful life events, psychological distress, coping, and parenting of divorced mothers: A longitudinal study. *Journal of Family Psychology, 14*(1), 27–41.

Test, D. W., Aspel, N. P., & Everson, J. M. (2006). *Transition methods for youth with disabilities.* Upper Saddle River, NJ: Pearson Education.

Thurlow, M. L. (2000). Standards-based reform and student with disabilities: Reflections on a decade of change. *Focus on Exceptional Children, 33*(3), 1–16.

Thurlow, M. L., House, A. L., Scott, D. L., & Ysseldyke, J. (2000). Students with disabilities in large-scale assessments: State participation and accommodation policies. *Journal of Special Education, 34*(3), 154–163.

Tillett, G., & French, B. (2006). *Resolving conflict: A practical approach.* Oxford: Oxford University Press.

Tingley, S. C. (2006). *How to handle difficult parents: A teacher's survival guide.* Fort Collins, CO: Cottonwood Press.

Tomlin, A. M. (2002). Partnering with parents with personality disorders: Effective strategies for early intervention providers. *Infants and Young Children, 14*(4), 68–75.

Trenholm, S. (2005). *Thinking through communication: An introduction to the study of human communication* (4th ed.). Boston: Allyn & Bacon.

Trivette, C. M., & Dunst, C. J. (2005). DEC recommended practices: Family-based practices. In S. Sandall, M. L. Hemmeter, B. J. Smith, & M. E. McLean (Eds.), *DEC recommended practice: A comprehensive guide for practical application in early intervention/early childhood special education* (pp. 107–126). Longmont, CA: Sopris West.

Trumbull, E., Rothstein-Fisch, C., Greenfield, P. M., & Quiroz, B. (2001). *Bridging cultures between home and school: A guide for teachers.* Mahwah, NJ: Lawrence Erlbaum.

Trussell, R. P., Hammond, H., & Ingalls, L. (2008). Ethical practices and parental participation in rural special education. *Rural Special Education Quarterly, 27*(1/2), 19–23.

Tsai, L. Y. (2000). I learn about autism from my son and people like him. *Focus on Autism and Other Developmental Disabilities, 15*(1), 202–205.

Tschannen-Moran, M., & Hoy, W. K. (2000). A multidisciplinary analysis of the nature, meaning, and measurement of trust. *Review of Educational Research, 70*(4), 547–593.

Tucci, V., Hursh, D. E., & Laitinen, R. E. (2004). The competent learner model: A merging of applied behavior analysis, direct instruction, and precision teaching. In D. J. Moran & R. W. Malott (Eds.), *Evidence-based education methods* (pp. 109–123). London: Elsevier Academic Press.

Turbiville, V. P., Umbarger, G. T., & Guthrie, A. C. (2000). Fathers' involvement in programs for young children. *Young Children, 55*(4), 74–79.

Turnbull, A., & Turnbull, R. (2001). *Families, professionals, and exceptionality: Collaborating for empowerment.* Upper Saddle River, NJ: Prentice Hall.

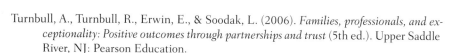

Turnbull, A., Turnbull, R., Erwin, E., & Soodak, L. (2006). *Families, professionals, and exceptionality: Positive outcomes through partnerships and trust* (5th ed.). Upper Saddle River, NJ: Pearson Education.

Turnbull, A. P., Summers, J. A., & Brotherson, M. J. (1983). *Working with families with disabled members: A family systems perspective.* Lawrence: University of Kansas, Research and Training Center on Independent Living.

Turnbull, R., Huerta, N., & Stowe, M. (2006). *The Individuals With Disabilities Education Act as amended in 2004.* Upper Saddle River, NJ: Merrill Prentice Hall.

Turnbull, R., Turnbull, A., Shank, M., & Smith, S. J. (2004). *Exceptional lives: Special education in today's schools* (4th ed.). Upper Saddle River, NJ: Merrill Prentice Hall.

Turner, P. H. (2000). The developmental nature of parent–child relationships: The impact of disabilities. In M. J. Fine & R. L. Simpson (Eds.), *Collaboration with parents and families of children and youth with exceptionalities* (2nd ed., pp. 103–130). Austin, TX: PRO-ED.

Tyler, N. C., Yzquierdo, Z., Lopez-Reyna, N., & Flippin, S. S. (2004). Cultural and linguistic diversity and the special education workforce: A critical overview. *Journal of Special Education, 38*(1), 22–38.

Ulrich, M. E., & Bauer, A. M. (2003). Levels of awareness: A closer look at communication between parents and professionals. *Teaching Exceptional Children, 35*(6), 20–24.

Unger, D. G., Jones, C. W., Park, E., & Tressell, P. A. (2001). Promoting involvement between low-income single caregivers and urban early intervention programs. *Topics of Early Childhood Special Education, 21*(4), 197–212.

U.S. Census Bureau. (2003). Annual estimates of the population by race alone and Hispanic or Latino origin for the United States and states. Washington, DC: U.S. Government Printing Office.

U.S. Census Bureau. (2002). *Statistical abstract of the United States: 2002.* Retrieved December 15, 2004, from http://www.census.gov/prod/2003pubs/02statab/statistical-abstract-02.html

U.S. Census Bureau. (2008). *Income, poverty, and health insurance coverage in the United States: 2007* (Current Population Reports, P60-235). Washington, DC: U.S. Government Printing Office.

U.S. Department of Education. (2002). *Twenty-fourth annual report to Congress on implementation of the Individual With Disabilities Education Act.* Washington, DC: Author.

U.S. Department of Education. (2007). *Twenty-ninth annual report to Congress on the implementation of the Individuals with Disabilities Education Act.* Washington, DC: Author.

U.S. Department of Education. (2004, August 13). *Letter to parent re: amendment of special education records.* Retrieved October 10, 2005, from http://www.ed.gov/policy/gen/guid/fpco/ferpa/library/parent.html

U.S. Department of Education. (2008). *Public school graduates and dropouts from the common core of data: School year 2005–06* (NCES No. 2008-353). Retrieved August 28, 2008, from http://nces.ed.gov/pubsearch/pubsinfo.asp?pubid=2008353

U.S. Department of Health and Human Services, Administration for Children and Families. (2001). *Adoption and foster care analysis and reporting system.* Washington, DC: Author.

U.S. General Accounting Office. (2000). *At-risk youth: School–community collaboration focus on improving student outcomes* (GAO-01–66). Washington, DC: Author.

Vacca, J. J. (2001). Promoting positive infant–caregiver attachment: The role of the early interventionist and recommendations for parent training. *Infants and Young Children*, *13*(4), 1–10.

Vacca, J. J. (2007). Incorporating interests and structure to improve participation of a child with autism in a standardized assessment: A case study. *Focus on Autism and Other Developmental Disabilities*, *22*(1), 51–59.

Vacca, J., & Feinberg, E. (2000). Why can't families be more like us? Henry Higgins confronts Eliza Dolittle in the world of early intervention. *Infants and Young Children*, *13*(1), 40–48.

Valadez, J. R. (2002). The influence of social capital on mathematics course selection by Latino high school students. *Hispanic Journal of Behavioral Sciences*, *24*(3), 319–339.

Valleley, R. J., Evans, J. H., & Allen, K. D. (2002). Parent implementation of an oral reading intervention: A case study. *Child and Family Behavior Therapy*, *24*(4), 39–50.

Volkmar, F. R., & Wiesner, L. A. (2004). *Healthcare for children on the autism spectrum: A guide to medical, nutritional, and behavioral issues*. Bethesda, MD: Woodbine House.

Wacharasin, C., Barnard, K. E., & Spieker, S. J. (2003). Factors affecting toddler cognitive development on low-income families: Implications for practitioners. *Infants and Young Children*, *16*(2), 175–181.

Wade, C. M., Ortiz, C., & Gorman, B. S. (2007). Two-session group parent training for bedtime noncompliance in Head Start preschoolers. *Child and Family Therapy*, *29*(3), 23–55.

Wagner, M., & Cameto, R. (2004). *NLTS2 data brief: The characteristics, experiences, and outcomes of youth with emotional disturbances*. Report from the National Longitudinal Transition Study-2. Retrieved July 7, 2007, from www.ncset.org/publications/default.asp#nlts2

Wagner, M., Cameto, R., & Newman, L. (2003). *Youth with disabilities: A changing population*. Menlo Park, CA: SRI International.

Wagner, M., Newman, L., & Cameto, R. (2004). *Changes over time in the secondary school programs of students with disabilities: A report of findings from the National Longitudinal Transition Study and the National Longitudinal Transition Study-2 (NLTS2)*. Menlo Park, CA: SRI International.

Waldman, B. W., & Perlman, S. P. (2008). Homeless children with disabilities. *Exceptional Parent Magazine*, *38*(6), 56–57.

Waldrop, D. P., & Weber, J. A. (2001). From grandparents to caregiver: The stress and satisfaction of raising grand children. *Families in Society*, *82*(5), 461–472.

Walker, J. E., & Shea, T. M. (1999). *Behavior management: A practical approach for educators* (7th ed.). Upper Saddle River, NJ: Merrill.

Walker, J. S., & Schutte, K. M. (2004). Practice and process in wraparound teamwork. *Journal of Emotional and Behavioral Disorders*, *12*(3), 182–192.

Walker-Dalhouse, D., & Dalhouse, A. D. (2001). Parent–school relation: Communicating more effectively with African American parents. *Young Children*, *56*(4), 75–80.

Wallace, T., Espin, C. A., McMaster, K., Deno, S. L., & Foegen, A. (2007). CBM progress monitoring within a standards-based system: Introduction to the special series. *Journal of Special Education*, *41*(2), 66–67.

Walther-Thomas, C. S., Korinek, L., McLaughlin, V. L., & Williams, B. T. (2000). *Collaboration for inclusive education: Developing successful programs*. Boston: Allyn & Bacon.

Webber, J., Simpson, R. L., & Bentley, J. K. (2000). Parents and families of children with autism. In M. J. Fine & R. L. Simpson (Eds.), *Collaboration with parents and families of children and youth with exceptionalities* (2nd ed., pp. 303–324). Austin, TX: PRO-ED.

Webster-Stratton, C. (2005). The Incredible Years: A training series for the prevention and treatment of conduct problems in young children. In E. D. Hibbs & P. S. Jensen (Eds.), *Psychosocial treatments for child an adolescent disorders: Empirically based strategies for clinical practice* (2nd ed., pp. 507–555). Washington, DC: American Psychological Association.

Webster-Stratton, C., Reid, M. J., & Hammond, M. (2001). Preventing conduct problems, promoting social competence: A parent and teacher training partnership in Head Start. *Journal of Clinical Child Psychology, 30*(3), 283–303.

Webster-Stratton, C., Reid, M. J., & Hammond, M. (2004). Treating children with early-onset conduct problems: Intervention outcomes for parent, child, and teacher training. *Journal of Clinical and Adolescent Psychology, 33*(1), 105–125.

Wedell, K. (2003). What's in a label? *British Journal of Special Education, 30*(2), 107.

Weist, M. D., Myers, C. P., Danforth, J., McNeil, D. W., Ollendick, T. H., & Hawkins, R. (2000). Expanded school mental health services: Assessing needs related to school level and geography. *Community Mental Health Journal, 36*, 259–273.

Welch, M., & Tulbert, B. (2000). Practitioners' perspectives of collaboration: A social validation and factor analysis. *Journal of Educational and Psychological Consultation, 11*(3/4), 357–378.

Westling, D. L., & Fox, L. (2009). *Teaching students with severe disabilities* (4th ed.). Upper Saddle River, NJ: Prentice Hall.

Whaley, A. L. (2001a). Cultural mistrust and mental health services for African Americans: A review and meta-analysis. *The Counseling Psychologist, 29*(4), 513–531.

Whaley, A. L. (2001b). Cultural mistrust of White mental health clinicians among African Americans with severe mental illness. *Journal of Orthopsychiatry, 71*(2), 252–256.

Wehmeyer, M. L., Agran, M., & Hughes, C. (2000). A national study of teachers' promotion of self-determination and student directed learning. *Journal of Special Education, 34*, 58–68.

Wehmeyer, M. L., Garner, N., Yeager, D., Lawrence, M., & Davis, A. K. (2006). Infusing services into 18–21 services for students with intellectual or developmental disabilities: A multi-stage, multiple component model. *Education and Training in Developmental Disabilities, 41*(1), 3–13.

Wehmeyer, M. L., Lance, G. D., & Bashinski, S. (2002). Promoting access to the general curriculum for students with mental retardation: A multi-level model. *Education and Training in Mental Retardation and Developmental Disabilities, 37*, 223–234.

Wehmeyer, M. L., Palmer, S., Agran, M., Mithaug, D., & Martin, J. (2000). Promoting casual agency: The Self-Determined Learning Model of Instruction. *Exceptional Children, 66*, 439–453.

White, L. (2001). Sibling relationships over the life course: A panel analysis. *Journal of Marriage and Family, 63*, 555–568.

White, T. B. (2005). Consumer trust and advice acceptance: The moderating roles of benevolence, expertise, and negative emotions. *Journal of Consumer Psychology, 15*(2), 141–154.

Wicker, L. R., & Brodie, R. E., II. (2004). The physical and mental health needs of African Americans. In D. R. Atkinson (Ed.), *Counseling American minorities* (6th ed., pp. 105–124). Boston: McGraw-Hill.

Wilds, M. (2001). It's about time! Computers as assistive technology for infants and toddlers with disabilities. *Zero to Three, 22*(2), 32–41.

Wilford, S. (2004). Resolving teacher–parent differences. *Scholastic Early Childhood Today, 18*(6), 9–10.

Williams, C. D. (1959). The elimination of tantrum behavior by extinction procedures. *Journal of Abnormal and Social Psychology, 59,* 269.

Wolery, M., & Bailey, D. B., Jr. (2002). Early childhood special education research. *Journal of Early Intervention, 25*(2), 88–99.

Woods, J., & Goldstein, H. (2003). When the toddler takes over: Changing challenging routines into conduits for communication. *Focus on Autism and Other Developmental Disabilities, 18*(3), 176–181.

Worcester, J. A., Nesman, T. M., Raffaele Mendez, L. M., & Keller, H. R. (2008). Giving voice to parents of young children with challenging behavior. *Exceptional Children, 74*(4), 509–525.

Yeh, M., McCabe, K., Hough, R. L., Dupuis, D., & Hazen, A. (2003). Racial/ethnic differences in parental endorsement of barriers to mental health services for youth. *Mental Health Services Research, 5*(2), 65–77.

Yell, M. L. (2006). *The law and special education* (2nd ed.). Upper Saddle River, NJ: Pearson/Prentice Hall.

Yell, M. L., Drasgow, E., & Lowrey, K. A. (2005). No Child Left Behind and students with autism spectrum disorders. *Focus on Autism and Other Developmental Disabilities, 20*(3), 130–139.

Yell, M. L., Katsiyannas, A., & Shriner, J. G. (2006). The No Child Left Behind Act, adequate yearly progress, and students with disabilities. *Teaching Exceptional Children, 38*(4), 32–39.

Ysseldyke, J., Nelson, J. R., Christenson, S., Johnson, D. R., Dennison, A., Triezenberg, H., et al. (2004). What we know and need to know about the consequences of high-stakes testing for students with disabilities. *Exceptional Children, 71*(1), 75–94.

Zaidman-Zait, A., & Jamieson, J. R. (2007). Providing Web-based support for families of infants and young children with established disabilities. *Infants and Young Children, 20*(1), 11–25.

Zanglis, I., Furlong, M. J., & Casas, J. M. (2000). Case study of a community mental health collaborative: Impact of identification of youths with emotional or behavioral disorders. *Behavioral Disorders, 25,* 359–371.

Zaretsky, L. (2005). Parent advocates' and principals' perceptions of professional knowledge and identity in special education. *Journal of Special Education Leadership, 18*(2), 30–40.

Zetlin, A. G., & Weinberg, L. A. (2004). Understanding the plight of foster youth and improving their educational opportunities. *Child Abuse and Neglect, 28,* 917–923.

Zetlin, A., Weinberg, L., & Luderer, J. W. (2004). Problems and solutions to improving education services for children in foster care. *Preventing School Failure, 48*(2), 31–36.

Zhang, C., & Bennett, T. (2003). Facilitating the meaningful participation of culturally and linguistically diverse families in the IFSP and IEP process. *Focus on Autism and Other Developmental Disabilities, 18*(1), 51–59.

Zhang, D., Ivester, J., & Katsiyannis, A. (2005). Teachers' view of transition services: Results from a statewide survey in South Carolina. *Education and Training in Developmental Disabilities, 40*(4), 360–367.

Zhang, D., & Katsiyannis, A. (2002). Minority representation in special education. *Remedial and Special Education, 23*(3), 180–187.

Zigmond, N. (2003). Where should students with disabilities receive special education services? Is one place better than another? *Journal of Special Education, 37*(3), 193–199.

Zima, B. T., Bussing, R., Freeman, S., Xiaowei, Y., Belin, T. R., & Forness, S. R. (2000). Behavior problems, academic skills delays and school failure among school-aged children in foster care: Their relationship to placement characteristics. *Journal of Child and Family Studies, 9*(1), 87–103.

Zionts, L. T., Zionts, P., Harrison, S., & Bellinger, O. (2003). Urban African American families' perceptions of cultural sensitivity within the special education system. *Focus on Autism and Other Developmental Disabilities, 18*(1), 41–50.

Zionts, P., & Simpson, R. (1988). *Understanding children and youth with emotional and behavioral problems.* Austin, TX: PRO-ED.

Zionts, P., Zionts, L., & Simpson, R. L. (2002). *Emotional and behavioral problems: A handbook for understanding and handling students.* Thousand Oakes, CA: Corwin Press.

Zirpoli, T. J. (2008). *Behavior management applications for teachers.* Upper Saddle River, NJ: Pearson Education.

Zolko, M. E. (1991). Counseling parents of children with disabilities: A review of the literature and implications for practice. *Journal of Rehabilitation, 57*(2), 29–34.

Initial Interview

Role-Playing Materials

These materials are to be used in conjunction with the exercises at the end of Chapter 5. See those exercises for specific directions.

Teddy, Age 13

Diagnosis: Gifted, Emotional and Behavioral Disorder

BACKGROUND INFORMATION

Medical History. Teddy is a 13-year-old male. According to his mother he is healthy and had few medical problems as a young child. His mother carried him to full term during her pregnancy and had little trouble during delivery. As a child Teddy reached all of his developmental milestones in a timely manner.

Teddy's parents were divorced when he was in first grade. By the end of first grade, his behaviors had become a serious problem. The family doctor referred Teddy to a specialist, and he was diagnosed with attention-deficit/hyperactivity disorder (ADHD) at the end of his first-grade year. His mother was reluctant to medicate Teddy and tried a variety of alternative homeopathic methods before she finally agreed to permit him to receive the medical treatment for ADHD recommended by his physician while he was in the third grade. He continues to receive medication for his ADHD.

When Teddy was in seventh grade, his mother suspected that he might have depression. Teddy was subsequently diagnosed with depression at the age of 13 and prescribed antidepression medication. Teddy continues to be prescribed antidepression treatment, although he frequently resists or forgets to take his medications.

Social History. Teddy's mother reported that her son has never been particularly social, and even as a young child he had little interest in others. When he initiates social contact, it is usually with adults. He most enjoys talking about things that interest him, including astronomy, numbers, mathematical equations, computers, and computer software. He bluntly states that he is not particularly interested in his peers, and until recently he rarely attempted to engage them in typical age-related conversations.

Within the past year Teddy has shown an interest in girls his own age. He appears to be interested in interacting and forming relationships with them, but he does not appear to have the social skills required for age-appropriate conversations and interactions. Teddy's female classmates generally fail to respond to his clumsy attempts to engage them in conversations. When they rebuff him Teddy becomes verbally aggressive.

Academic History. Teddy attended a Montessori preschool during his first year of education. After preschool Teddy was enrolled in public schools, and throughout elementary school he attended general education classes. Beginning in the third grade, he began receiving gifted education services. In spite of his abilities, however, Teddy did not consistently excel in academics. He did well in math and science classes but had little interest in English and social studies and received relatively poor marks in those subjects. Beginning in the early elementary grades, Teddy's teachers labeled him as a "problem child." He was especially a concern to his teachers because he attempted to bully his peers.

In middle school Teddy is enrolled in a gifted program class for 1 hour each day. He is also enrolled in an advanced math and science class as well as a special education resource program for 2 hours daily. His special education program focuses on reading comprehension and social skills.

General Educator Reports. According to his general education teachers, Teddy is a bright student, and his teachers judge him to be capable of doing grade-level academic work. He has demonstrated the ability to independently complete classroom assignments; however, he routinely either fails to complete assigned work or turns in partially completed or late assignments. When confronted by teachers about turning in incomplete work, Teddy comments, "The stuff you give me to do is stupid and boring," and he becomes confrontational. His teachers also observed that Teddy chronically daydreams and is easily distracted by peers. Teddy's teachers described him as having poor social skills and being immature for his age. Teddy does not work well in groups and is frequently a problem during group work because he is verbally aggressive toward his peers.

Special Education Teacher Report. Teddy was referred for special education placement because of his disruptive behaviors in general education classes. Teddy is an intelligent student who likes to be the center of attention. He responds well to direct and small-group instruction. He will work hard for the teacher if he feels he will be recognized for his accomplishments. His teachers reported that Teddy has consistently been aggressive and confrontational with his peers during his time in special education. Accordingly, Teddy's IEP goals and objectives have accentuated instruction and other programs to encourage appropriate interactions with peers and alternatives to verbal and other forms of aggressive behavior.

Gifted Teacher Report. Teddy receives services from a gifted education teacher for 1 hour each day. His academic goals within this program have primarily focused on vocabulary development, computer skills, and accelerated reading. He currently is reading at the seventh-grade reading level, with reading comprehension at the sixth-grade level.

As in other settings Teddy has difficulty working in groups in the gifted program. He requires assistance with anger management and reportedly has meltdowns (i.e., severe tantrums) when other students fail to share his opinions or he does not like the assignment his group is given. The teacher and his peers reported that he has been known to provoke altercations to get out of unwanted group activities. Other students make fun of Teddy's behavior, and he has no friends in the gifted classroom. Teddy prefers to work independently, primarily on puzzles and computer research projects.

School Psychologist Report. Results of individualized psychoeducational assessments revealed that Teddy functions within the gifted ability range. He scored 2 deviations above the mean on verbal expression tasks, spatial tasks, and overall performance. He scored significantly below grade level in the area of receptive language skills. Teddy scored above grade level on reading recognition, math, and science. He scored below his grade level on reading comprehension and social studies skills.

The school psychologist also reported that Teddy has a hard time following multiple-step directions and staying in his seat. He was described as showing hyperactive and aggressive behaviors when he is out of his seat. Once these behaviors start, teachers and others have a difficult time calming him down. The school psychologist also reported that Teddy does not interact appropriately with his peers. He tries to be the center of attention, but if he does not get this attention, he becomes aggressive. Teddy was also observed to display signs of depression.

PARENT PERCEPTIONS

Family Structure and Parent Information. Teddy's parents are divorced. Teddy lives with his mother, a 35-year-old legal assistant. The father is a high school graduate with 2 years of technical training in auto mechanics and welding. The mother reported that for approximately the past year, she has been dating a 37-year-old construction worker. She reported that her boyfriend frequently visits the home and occasionally sleeps over on the weekends. The mother reported that her 9-year-old daughter is a typically developing child who is doing well in school in both academic and social areas. The mother also reported that the maternal grandparents, who live near the family, are actively involved in their children's lives. The biological father reportedly has little contact with the children.

The mother reported that Teddy can be very disruptive around the house when he does not get his way. She noted that Teddy can be vindictive and has been known to set booby traps around the house so that he can watch people become upset. She also reported that Teddy is particularly defiant when visitors come to the house. These problems take the form of Teddy's talking back to his mother, displaying physical and verbal aggression, using profanity, punching walls, and slamming doors.

The mother stated that over the years she has received numerous calls from Teddy's teachers reporting his behavior problem at school. Several principals have communicated that Teddy is disruptive in class, talks back to teachers, and bullies and threatens peers. When Teddy's mother confronts him about these incidents, he denies any wrongdoing. When confronted by the mother's boyfriend about his behavior, Teddy replies, "Shut up, you are not my dad." These incidents often lead to arguments between the mother and her boyfriend; Teddy appears to enjoy these interactions.

The mother reported that Teddy agitates his sister. At the same time, however, he is also described as being very protective of her. Teddy appears to have low self-esteem. He has poor relationships with his peers, and he has no neighborhood friends. In fact many parents in the neighborhood will not permit their children to play with Teddy. Teddy was recently required by his mother to attend a Boys and Girls Club after-school program 3 days a week. He was expelled from the program because of disruptive behavior.

Teddy's mother indicated she is authoritarian. She indicated she would like to see her boyfriend be more assertive when Teddy becomes defiant. The mother reported she frequently spanks Teddy when he becomes defiant, and she threatens to take away his PlayStation as an attempt to get him to become more compliant. She stated, however, that as Teddy has become larger and stronger, she is fearful of trying to spank him.

Teddy's mother is pleased with his gifted abilities but is concerned about his behavior and poor record of completing his schoolwork. Teddy tells his mother he is bored in his general education classes and the other students are mean to him. She is increasingly concerned about his destructive behavior at home. He also has been accused of vandalizing neighbors' homes and torturing neighborhood animals. She is also very concerned that he has a long pattern of poor peer social interactions. He does not enjoy playing outside with the other children on the block; he would rather play violent video games. Teddy has a tendency to pick on his little sister, especially when he is mad at other people. Teddy's behavior is something that the mother feels needs to be under control before he enters high school.

Development. According to his mother, from the ages of birth to 6 years, Teddy developed typically. He was completely toilet trained by 3 and a half years old and never had a problem with bed-wetting. He began talking at age 17 months and was talking in short sentences by age 2 and a half years.

Teddy attended a Montessori preschool and was able to read upon entering kindergarten. During first grade his parents divorced. Subsequent to the separation the mother reported that she began receiving calls from Teddy's teacher informing her that Teddy was displaying aggressive behaviors. At the end of first grade, Teddy was diagnosed with ADHD. The doctor who diagnosed Teddy's ADHD recommended medication treatment. His mother was reluctant to medicate Teddy, however, and tried a variety of alternative homeopathic methods before she finally agreed to the recommended medical treatment when Teddy was in the third grade. Teddy continues to receive medication for his ADHD. Teddy was also diagnosed with depression at the age of 13 and subsequently prescribed medication treatment. He reportedly resists taking his medication, however, and will often go for several days without following the prescribed treatment.

Parent's Expectations for the Future. Teddy's mother is concerned with her son's poor social skills, aggressive behavior, and lack of peer relationships. She believes that this is the reason that Teddy has become withdrawn and lacks the motivation to learn new things. She is also concerned that Teddy's emotional stability is deteriorating and his academic progress is not keeping pace. She bluntly stated that she does not know what will become of Teddy in the future.

Teddy's Expectations and Plans for the Future. Teddy would like to be able to work independently at school because "everyone hates me." He would like to focus his annual goals on problem-solving activities and computer programming. He hopes to be released from all group-activity requirements and not be forced to participate in district testing. Teddy reported that working in a group is stupid because "they don't understand what I mean." He plans to attend college at MIT to get away from his mother and to pursue his interest in computer programming.

Terri, Age 7

Diagnosis: Autism, Mental Retardation

BACKGROUND INFORMATION

Medical History. Terri was the product of a full-term pregnancy and uncomplicated delivery. She was a typically developing infant the first 30 months of her life. Subsequent to this point in her development, she began losing the ability to talk, and there was deterioration in her social interaction interests and skills. These developments led her parents to seek medical attention. Subsequent to several referrals to various specialists, Terri was diagnosed with autism at age 3. Terri has no physical limitations; she has, however, significant cognitive, language, and social delays. She also displays a variety of aberrant behaviors. For the past several years, Terri has followed a strict diet that is designed to mitigate the impact of her autism. Terri also takes medication for behavior control, specifically impulsiveness.

Social History. Terri developed at a typical social pace for the first 30 months of her life. At approximately 30 months of age, she stopped talking. She also began avoiding eye contact and shunned social situations. Terri rarely responds to peers. She does, however, seek out adults for attention. She is responsive to her parents and seems to enjoy interacting with them, albeit for short periods of time.

Her parents reported that Terri became interested in another girl in her preschool class. Terri and the other girl have maintained periodic contact for the past several years, and this typically developing child is virtually Terri's only source of peer social interaction.

Terri has almost no age-appropriate expressive language skills. She screams and makes facial grimaces to communicate her needs. She is being instructed to use an augmentative communication system, the Picture Exchange Communication System, at school and home.

Academic History. Terri began early intervention services at 3 years of age. These services were provided at a public school early education site and included 3 hours per week of occupational therapy and physical therapy, 5 hours per week of speech and language training, and 10 hours per week of applied behavior analysis training.

Terri began attending a public elementary school in kindergarten. Her kindergarten class was an inclusion program, with approximately half the students in the class having diagnosed disabilities. After her kindergarten year Terri was placed in a self-contained classroom for learners with moderate to severe disabilities. She was included for classes in music, art, and physical education with her first-grade peers without disabilities. Currently, she spends approximately half of each day in a self-contained classroom and half of her day in a general education classroom. In her self-contained special education classroom, Terri works on communication and language skill development, social interaction activities, self-help and independent living skills, and functional academic skills. While Terri is in the general education setting, she has a paraprofessional with her at all times.

Special Education Teacher Report. Terri was recommended for special education placement because of significant academic, communication, functional behavior, and social deficiencies. Terri requires constant supervision; hence, she has her own paraeducator. She is easily distracted by peers, although she rarely initiates contact with them or responds to their initiations. Terri will flap her hands excessively and twist her fingers when she becomes upset. Throughout the day Terri receives stickers as reinforcement for appropriate behavior and for completing assigned work. She is able to trade these stickers for preferred activities and other reinforcers.

Terri's curriculum emphasizes development of skills in the areas of communication, functional academics, social interaction, and self-help and independent living. Terri is generally compliant and appears to enjoy school. She is by and large positive in her responses to her teacher and paraeducator.

General Education Teacher Report. With the assistance of a paraeducator, Terri spends about half of each day in a general education classroom. She has her own work space, where her visual schedule and "penny board" (token reinforcement program) are kept, as well as a desk in the main classroom with the other students.

Terri's paraeducator adapts and supports her participation in the classroom. For example, the paraeducator assists and prompts Terri so that she can participate in PE, music, and art. While the other members of the class are working on independent reading and other grade-level activities, the paraeducator reads to Terri or engages her in other activities that are parallel adaptations of what her peers are doing.

Many of the students are eager to assist Terri, but she tends to ignore them. Approximately once every 7 to 10 days, Terri has a meltdown (i.e., severe tantrum), during which time the paraeducator removes her from the classroom.

School Psychologist Summarized Report. Terri's intellectual and overall cognitive levels were determined to fall within the moderate range of mental retardation. She also has moderate to severe autism, as evidenced by severe communication and language delays, minimal interest in others, poor social skills, and a variety of self-stimulatory and other aberrant behaviors.

Occupational Therapist Summarized Report. Terri receives 45 minutes of occupational therapy each week. A portion of this time is devoted to sensory integration therapy. This is provided through a variety of activities that are designed to assist her to respond better to sensory stimuli, particularly noises and unfamiliar sounds. The occupational therapist also works with Terri on motor skills (e.g., holding a pencil to write, balancing her lunch tray, using eating utensils) and independent living skills (e.g., buttoning, zipping, and pulling on clothing). Terri is reported to enjoy these activities and is making good progress.

Speech and Language Therapist Summarized Report. Terri receives 60 minutes per week of speech and language therapy. Her speech and language therapist also consults with her special and general education teachers on programs that can be used to support and train improved communication skills within the classroom. Terri's individual therapy sessions primarily focus on training her to use her augmentative communication program, the Picture Exchange Communication System.

Autism Specialist Summarized Report. According to the school district's autism specialist, Terri responds well to a structured learning environment. Accordingly, this consulting teacher has assisted Terri's general and special education teachers in using structured teaching methods, physical organization strategies, and strategic scheduling of activities. She has also been encouraging staff to design and implement programs to encourage Terri to interact more with her peers.

PARENT PERCEPTIONS

Family Structure and Parent Information. Terri's parents are married. Terri is an only child. They live in a high socioeconomic suburb in a medium-size Midwestern community. Her father is a psychologist who works for a community mental health program, and her mother has a professional degree and license in graphic design. Subsequent to Terri's disability diagnosis, however, her mother became a stay-at-home mother. They have the means to send Terri to a private program but decided that public school would be the most beneficial to Terri for social development. Terri's mother is very involved in her daughter's life and education. She has taken classes on how to set up a home program for Terri. The parents have high expectations for their daughter's education. If their expectations are not met, they have implied that they are willing to consider due process. They are very active in the autism community and organizations.

Terri's mother has created a structured environment for her daughter at home. The program emphasizes routines, clear expectations, contingencies for appropriate behavior and correct performance, and consistency. She frequently urges school personnel to visit the home so that school staff can replicate these structuring efforts. Terri has her own sensory room in the basement where Christmas lights, a tactile wall, and music are used to train her to be more tolerant of sensory stimuli. Terri receives private music therapy every Saturday. The parents also have participated in various experimental intervention and treatment studies wherein Terri is subjected to various programs that purport to advance the needs of students with autism. The parents, particularly the mother, have consistently and rigidly followed a special gluten-free and casein-free diet that is designed to calm Terri.

Terri's parents consistently and rigidly follow a behavior modification token economy system with their daughter at home. She earns rewards for showing appropriate behavior, following daily living skill development routines, and using her communication system. In spite of this program, Terri continues to show self-stimulatory behavior, especially when she is tired or stressed. She also has meltdowns several times a week.

Terri's parents are concerned that their daughter is not progressing as fast as they would like, and they hold school personnel responsible for her modest progress. They have concerns about her tantrums and meltdowns and think more should be done to improve her behavior. They are also very concerned that she has not developed verbal speech and think school personnel should be more aggressive in looking for alternative treatments and interventions to improve her language and communication skills. At home they regularly discuss transferring Terri to another school if she fails to make significant improvements in the future. They also discuss the advantages and disadvantages of legal action to force school personnel to be more accountable for effectively teaching their daughter.

Development. According to Terri's parents, Terri developed typically as an infant. She crawled at age 11 months, walked at 15 months, and started babbling at 18 months. At 30 months, however, she began to regress. This pattern of regression led to diagnoses of autism and mental retardation at age 3. As previously noted Terri is nonverbal, generally disinterested in interacting with most peers, and prone to displaying aberrant and self-stimulatory behavior when stressed, upset, or tired.

Parents' Expectations for the Future. Terri's parents are optimistic about their daughter's future and are hopeful that she will develop verbal language and improved behavior. They think that if these outcomes occur, she will demonstrate better learning potential and will be able to fit more into the general curriculum that is followed by learners without disabilities. They are concerned about her poor social skills and lack of social interaction interests albeit less so than for her language and behavioral improvement needs. They would like to believe that Terri's school personnel have the skills and motivation to help her significantly improve. Candidly, however, they are increasingly inclined to believe that school personnel simply lack the commitment and skills to be effective with their daughter.

Initial Conference Evaluation Form

Date: _____

Student (Teddy or Terri): _____

Person Playing Parent Role: _____

Person Playing Conferencer Role: _____

Circle the response that most closely describes the performance of the individual being evaluated. Verbal feedback and evaluative information are recommended subsequent to completing the role-play exercise and this evaluation form.

General Conference Evaluation

1. Clearly informed parents of the purpose of the conference

1	2	3	4	5
Poor	Needs Improvement	Acceptable Performance	Strong Performance	Excellent Performance

2. Conducted the conference in a systematic, fluid, and organized manner

1	2	3	4	5
Poor	Needs Improvement	Acceptable Performance	Strong Performance	Excellent Performance

3. Kept the conference flowing and on course

1	2	3	4	5
Poor	Needs Improvement	Acceptable Performance	Strong Performance	Excellent Performance

4. Solicited and responded to parents' questions and concerns

1	2	3	4	5
Poor	Needs Improvement	Acceptable Performance	Strong Performance	Excellent Performance

5. Clearly and effectively summarized the conference

1	2	3	4	5
Poor	Needs Improvement	Acceptable Performance	Strong Performance	Excellent Performance

Evaluation of Information Requested From Parents

6. Clearly and effectively sought parents' information, including perceptions of relevant issues and problems

1	2	3	4	5
Poor	Needs Improvement	Acceptable Performance	Strong Performance	Excellent Performance

7. Appropriately noted and resolved differences between professionals' and parents' perceptions of issues and problems

1	2	3	4	5
Poor	Needs Improvement	Acceptable Performance	Strong Performance	Excellent Performance

8. Clearly and effectively sought parents' developmental history information

1	2	3	4	5
Poor	Needs Improvement	Acceptable Performance	Strong Performance	Excellent Performance

9. Clearly and effectively sought parents' relevant school history information

1	2	3	4	5
Poor	Needs Improvement	Acceptable Performance	Strong Performance	Excellent Performance

10. Clearly and effectively sought information about parents' expectations for their child and the school

1	2	3	4	5
Poor	Needs Improvement	Acceptable Performance	Strong Performance	Excellent Performance

(continues)

11. Clearly and effectively sought appropriate information about the family and relevant social information

1	2	3	4	5
Poor	Needs Improvement	Acceptable Performance	Strong Performance	Excellent Performance

Evaluation of Information Given to Parents

12. Clearly and effectively disseminated appropriate assessment and diagnostic information to parents

1	2	3	4	5
Poor	Needs Improvement	Acceptable Performance	Strong Performance	Excellent Performance

13. Clearly and effectively disseminated appropriate information to parents about the educational program to be used with their child

1	2	3	4	5
Poor	Needs Improvement	Acceptable Performance	Strong Performance	Excellent Performance

14. Clearly and effectively disseminated information to parents on procedures for evaluating the progress of pupils and the manner this information will be communicated to parents

1	2	3	4	5
Poor	Needs Improvement	Acceptable Performance	Strong Performance	Excellent Performance

15. Clearly and effectively sought parents' school history information

1	2	3	4	5
Poor	Needs Improvement	Acceptable Performance	Strong Performance	Excellent Performance

16. Clearly and effectively disseminated information to parents regarding appropriate community supports, school problem-solving supports and resources, and related family and child supports and programs

1	2	3	4	5
Poor	Needs Improvement	Acceptable Performance	Strong Performance	Excellent Performance

Additional Summary and Evaluative Information and Narrative Comments

_____

_____

_____

_____

_____

_____

_____

_____

_____

_____

_____

_____

_____

_____

_____

_____

_____

_____

_____

_____

Training Parents and Family Members to Be Treatment and Intervention Agents

Role-Playing Materials

These materials are to be used in conjunction with the exercises at the end of Chapter 6. See those exercises for specific directions. There are no materials designated for the person playing the role of the conferencer; however, background information on the two students and their families is provided in Appendix A.

Teddy, Age 13

Teddy, a 13-year-old male who is gifted and has been diagnosed as having an emotional and behavioral disorder, has increasingly become a concern to his family because of his "pouting" behavior. When displeased, Teddy will show his displeasure by making facial grimaces, stomping around the house, and sulking. This is a long-standing behavior; however, it has recently become more pronounced.

This behavior is pervasive, and Teddy displays it whenever he is at home, regardless of who is there. Because his mother and sister are most frequently at home with him, they experience it most. It appears that the behavior is primarily designed to secure attention.

The mother has tried scolding him, isolating him, ignoring him, and reasoning with him when attempting to deal with the problem, albeit with little success. The mother's boyfriend contends that Teddy is seeking punishment when he pouts and that he is not going to disappoint the youth by ignoring him.

Terri, Age 7

Terri is a 7-year-old girl who has autism and mental retardation. Terri has virtually no age-appropriate expressive language skills. She is being instructed to use an augmentative communication system, the Picture Exchange Communication System, at school and home. Terri, however, frequently resists using her communication system. Instead she prefers to stomp, scream, and make facial grimaces when she wants something. For example, if she wants a soda or glass of water, she will seek out one of her parents and begin whining and stomping. She will continue to escalate these behaviors to the point of a full tantrum until someone delivers whatever it is she wants.

Terri has chronically resisted using her augmentative communication system; this problem, however, has become more evident. Both parents have experienced the problem, and it is most evident when Terri is stressed or tired. The mother experiences it the most, likely because she is the most available. A formal functional analysis of the behavior has not yet been conducted. It is generally assumed, however, that the behavior is designed to acquire attention and to resist the nonpreferred augmentative communication alternative. Terri's teacher and her colleagues appear to be far more successful in training Terri to use the augmentative communication system. The parents are pleased that Terri has demonstrated that she can learn and functionally use the alternative communication program, yet they are distressed that they have been unable to make similar progress at home.

Terri's parents seem to be very savvy in terms of understanding how to implement the alternative communication program. Then again, they acknowledged that they do not like to see their daughter upset and that it is sometimes just easier and far more expedient to forego using the augmentative system in favor of presenting Terri with various items (e.g., glass of water, preferred toy) until they find one that satisfies her needs. The parents concede that this inconsistency is a barrier to their daughter's improving her communication skills.

Behavior Management Conference Evaluation Form

Part 1

Date: _____

Student (Teddy or Terri): _____

Person Playing Parent Role: _____

Person Playing Conferencer Role: _____

Circle the response that most closely describes the performance of the individual being evaluated. Verbal feedback and evaluative information are recommended subsequent to completing the role-play exercise and this evaluation form.

General Conference Evaluation

1. Clearly informed parents of the purpose of the conference

1	2	3	4	5
Poor	Needs Improvement	Acceptable Performance	Strong Performance	Excellent Performance

2. Conducted the conference in a systematic, fluid, and organized manner

1	2	3	4	5
Poor	Needs Improvement	Acceptable Performance	Strong Performance	Excellent Performance

3. Kept the conference flowing and on course

1	2	3	4	5
Poor	Needs Improvement	Acceptable Performance	Strong Performance	Excellent Performance

4. Solicited and responded to parents' questions and concerns

1	2	3	4	5
Poor	Needs Improvement	Acceptable Performance	Strong Performance	Excellent Performance

5. Clearly and effectively summarized the conference, including subsequent steps and procedures

1	2	3	4	5
Poor	Needs Improvement	Acceptable Performance	Strong Performance	Excellent Performance

Evaluation of First Session Procedural Steps

6. Clearly and effectively assisted the parents in identifying an appropriate target behavior and operational definition of the target response

1	2	3	4	5
Poor	Needs Improvement	Acceptable Performance	Strong Performance	Excellent Performance

7. Clearly and effectively assisted the parents in appropriate methods for measuring the agreed-on target behavior

1	2	3	4	5
Poor	Needs Improvement	Acceptable Performance	Strong Performance	Excellent Performance

8. Clearly and effectively assisted the parents in identifying and understanding appropriate antecedent variables connected to the agreed-on target behavior, including settings, personnel, time, activities, and so forth

1	2	3	4	5
Poor	Needs Improvement	Acceptable Performance	Strong Performance	Excellent Performance

9. Clearly and effectively assisted the parents in identifying and understanding appropriate motivational variables connected to the agreed-on target behavior

1	2	3	4	5
Poor	Needs Improvement	Acceptable Performance	Strong Performance	Excellent Performance

10. Clearly and effectively ended the conference, including ensuring the parents understand their assignment for measuring and understanding the agreed-on target behavior and subsequent steps and procedures for dealing with the problem behavior

1	2	3	4	5
Poor	Needs Improvement	Acceptable Performance	Strong Performance	Excellent Performance

Additional Summary and Evaluative Information and Narrative Comments

Behavior Management Conference Evaluation Form

Part 2

Date: _____

Student (Teddy or Terri): _____

Person Playing Parent Role: _____

Person Playing Conferencer Role: _____

Circle the response that most closely describes the performance of the individual being evaluated. Verbal feedback and evaluative information are recommended subsequent to completing the role-play exercise and this evaluation form.

General Conference Evaluation

1. Clearly informed parents of the purpose of the conference

1	2	3	4	5
Poor	Needs Improvement	Acceptable Performance	Strong Performance	Excellent Performance

2. Conducted the conference in a systematic, fluid, and organized manner

1	2	3	4	5
Poor	Needs Improvement	Acceptable Performance	Strong Performance	Excellent Performance

3. Kept the conference flowing and on course

1	2	3	4	5
Poor	Needs Improvement	Acceptable Performance	Strong Performance	Excellent Performance

4. Solicited and responded to parents' questions and concerns

1	2	3	4	5
Poor	Needs Improvement	Acceptable Performance	Strong Performance	Excellent Performance

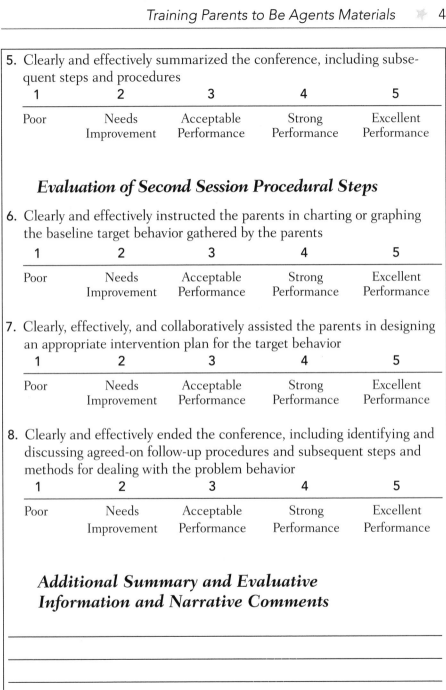

5. Clearly and effectively summarized the conference, including subsequent steps and procedures

1	2	3	4	5
Poor	Needs Improvement	Acceptable Performance	Strong Performance	Excellent Performance

Evaluation of Second Session Procedural Steps

6. Clearly and effectively instructed the parents in charting or graphing the baseline target behavior gathered by the parents

1	2	3	4	5
Poor	Needs Improvement	Acceptable Performance	Strong Performance	Excellent Performance

7. Clearly, effectively, and collaboratively assisted the parents in designing an appropriate intervention plan for the target behavior

1	2	3	4	5
Poor	Needs Improvement	Acceptable Performance	Strong Performance	Excellent Performance

8. Clearly and effectively ended the conference, including identifying and discussing agreed-on follow-up procedures and subsequent steps and methods for dealing with the problem behavior

1	2	3	4	5
Poor	Needs Improvement	Acceptable Performance	Strong Performance	Excellent Performance

Additional Summary and Evaluative Information and Narrative Comments

_____

_____

_____

_____

_____

_____

_____

Conflict Resolution

Role-Playing Materials

These materials are to be used in conjunction with the exercises at the end of Chapter 9. See those exercises for specific directions.

Teddy, Age 13

Diagnosis: Gifted, Emotional and Behavioral Disorder

EDUCATOR AND PROFESSIONAL INFORMATION

As a means of motivating Teddy to complete his assignments, his special education teacher has implemented a program whereby he is allowed to earn free time and break time when he completes a prescribed amount of work. The program has been relatively successful at school as judged by the fact that Teddy has increased his work output. Teddy has vocalized his dislike for the program (e.g., "This is illegal and patently un-American torture"); the teacher is not particularly concerned with these protests. After being denied a break, Teddy will sulk, attempt to create disturbances with other students, and occasionally swear at the teacher. The teacher is concerned about these behaviors but is not sure if there is anything that she can do to improve the situation. When all is considered the teacher believes the program should be continued because it seems to be helping Teddy complete his work and it is teaching him discipline.

The teacher has received word from Teddy's mother that she believes the school program is negatively impacting Teddy's behavior at home. The teacher is concerned with this development and wants to be supportive of the family's situation and concerns. In spite of that, she strongly believes the program's success is justification for its continuation and that with time Teddy's behavior at home will improve.

Data supportive of the program's impact on Teddy's completion of assignments are shown in the following table.

Percentage of Assignments Completed: Baseline and Work-Contingency Program Intervention			
	Baseline		After Intervention Program Implementation
Day 1	47%	Day 1	67%
Day 2	18%	Day 2	79%
Day 3	33%	Day 3	84%
Day 4	0%	Day 4	61%
Day 5	21%	Day 5	82%
		Day 6	74%
		Day 7	88%
		Day 8	71%
		Day 9	86%
		Day 10	78%

PARENT INFORMATION

Teddy's mother was consulted regarding her son's special education teacher's wanting to create a program requiring that he earn free time at school by completing his assignments. She agreed with the objectives of the program and endorsed the use of the program with her son.

Shortly after the program was initiated, the mother and Teddy's sister noticed a significant increase in Teddy's pouting, aggressiveness, and antisocial behavior. When confronted by his mother and her boyfriend, Teddy indicated that he was angry because he was being denied free time at school. He elaborated that he was being "abused" and that "this un-American act" was making him a target for peer ridicule and teasing.

Teddy's mother freely acknowledged that she agreed to the intervention program at school. She also admitted that she is conflicted by the situation. On one hand, she is pleased that Teddy is completing more school assignments. At the same time, she is concerned that denying Teddy a break at school will further exacerbate his problems of interacting with his peers. She concluded that if he is denied a break, he will never learn to play and work with other students. She is also frustrated and angry that the school program is creating additional behavior problems for her family at home. As a result she determined that this particular intervention strategy should be abandoned immediately.

Terri, Age 7

Diagnosis: Autism, Mental Retardation

EDUCATOR AND PROFESSIONAL INFORMATION

Terri splits her time at school between a self-contained special education classroom and a general education classroom. Her school team is in agreement that Terri has significant disabilities and that she requires a highly structured program and intensive intervention. Yet the team members also believe that she has benefitted from her time in general education. They are particularly encouraged that she recently appears to be more aware of her peers and believe that she may soon be more receptive to peer social interaction program efforts. They also hold the opinion that she is more apt to use her augmentative communication system in a general education classroom than she would if she were exclusively in a special education classroom. Finally they are of the opinion that the general education teacher has created a highly supportive environment for Terri and that there are ample opportunities for intensive individualized work in both her special education classroom and her general education classroom.

School personnel recently heard from Terri's parents that they would like to have their daughter withdrawn from general education and placed exclusively in a special education classroom. It is their understanding that the parents are recommending that the time their daughter is spending in general education be replaced with one-to-one intensive behavioral training based on applied behavior analysis methodology. School personnel have informally discussed this recommendation among themselves and determined that Terri will have difficulty tolerating additional one-to-one intensive behavioral treatment, especially in the afternoon. They pointed out that Terri's parents were the ones who initially argued for Terri's placement in general education and that she is receiving significant benefit from the present program configuration.

PARENT INFORMATION

Terri's mother and father initially argued for an inclusion program for their daughter. They favored placement of Terri in a program with children without disabilities because it would provide her "normal models" and a connection with a "normal curriculum and world." They were pleased with the decision to have their daughter split her time between a special education classroom and a general education classroom.

More recently the parents have changed their opinion about the benefits of placing Terri in a general education classroom. They now believe that their daughter's needs demand additional intensive one-to-one training. They believe that only through such training will Terri develop the skills necessary for her to have a more normal life. They also have come to believe that Terri's time in general education is frequently wasted because she does not have the skills to do what the other students are doing and as a result she often sits with a paraeducator and does nothing. They also have decided that whatever benefits Terri might derive from being around children without disabilities are outweighed by the skills she would acquire through intensive one-to-one behaviorally based instruction.

The parents have determined that an immediate program change is needed. They have decided that they are willing to use whatever means necessary to ensure that an appropriate program is created for their daughter.

Conflict Resolution Conference Evaluation Form

Date: _____

Student (Teddy or Terri): _____

Person Playing Parent Role: _____

Person Playing Conferencer Role: _____

Circle the response that most closely describes the performance of the individual being evaluated. Verbal feedback and evaluative information are recommended subsequent to completing the role-play exercise and this evaluation form.

General Conference Evaluation

1. Informed or assisted parents in understanding the purpose of the conference

1	2	3	4	5
Poor	Needs Improvement	Acceptable Performance	Strong Performance	Excellent Performance

2. Conducted the conference in a systematic, fluid, and organized manner

1	2	3	4	5
Poor	Needs Improvement	Acceptable Performance	Strong Performance	Excellent Performance

3. Kept the conference flowing and on course

1	2	3	4	5
Poor	Needs Improvement	Acceptable Performance	Strong Performance	Excellent Performance

4. Solicited and responded to parents' questions and concerns

1	2	3	4	5
Poor	Needs Improvement	Acceptable Performance	Strong Performance	Excellent Performance

5. Clearly and effectively summarized the conference

1	2	3	4	5
Poor	Needs Improvement	Acceptable Performance	Strong Performance	Excellent Performance

Evaluation of Communication Skills

6. Effectively established and maintained rapport

1	2	3	4	5
Poor	Needs Improvement	Acceptable Performance	Strong Performance	Excellent Performance

7. Effectively used active listening skills

1	2	3	4	5
Poor	Needs Improvement	Acceptable Performance	Strong Performance	Excellent Performance

8. Clearly and effectively identified areas of mutual agreement and disagreement

1	2	3	4	5
Poor	Needs Improvement	Acceptable Performance	Strong Performance	Excellent Performance

9. Demonstrated the ability to be constructively open during the conference

1	2	3	4	5
Poor	Needs Improvement	Acceptable Performance	Strong Performance	Excellent Performance

Evaluation of Conflict Resolution Process

10. Objectively and constructively listened and responded to parents' concerns

1	2	3	4	5
Poor	Needs Improvement	Acceptable Performance	Strong Performance	Excellent Performance

11. Demonstrated the ability to be empathic and sensitive to parents' concerns while also demonstrating appropriate assertiveness

1	2	3	4	5
Poor	Needs Improvement	Acceptable Performance	Strong Performance	Excellent Performance

12. Clearly identified the problem and the individuals associated with the conflict

1	2	3	4	5
Poor	Needs Improvement	Acceptable Performance	Strong Performance	Excellent Performance

13. Clearly and effectively facilitated a discussion and evaluation of possible solutions to the identified conflict and problem

1	2	3	4	5
Poor	Needs Improvement	Acceptable Performance	Strong Performance	Excellent Performance

14. Clearly and effectively identified a mutually agreed-on problem-solving strategy and procedures for evaluating the strategy

1	2	3	4	5
Poor	Needs Improvement	Acceptable Performance	Strong Performance	Excellent Performance

15. Clearly and effectively ended the conference, including identifying and discussing agreed-on follow-up procedures and subsequent steps

1	2	3	4	5
Poor	Needs Improvement	Acceptable Performance	Strong Performance	Excellent Performance

Additional Summary and Evaluative Information and Narrative Comments

_____

_____

_____

_____

_____

Index

About the Authors

Richard L. Simpson, EdD, is a professor of special education at the University of Kansas. He has also been a special education teacher, school psychologist, and coordinator of a community mental health outreach program. His other professional experiences include directing several University of Kansas and University of Kansas Medical Center demonstration programs for students with autism spectrum disorders and coordinating numerous federal grant programs related to students with autism spectrum disorders and other disabilities. He has authored numerous books, articles, and tests on the topic of students with disabilities. His research interests include students with emotional–behavioral disorders, parent–family participation, effective practices for students with disabilities, and autism spectrum disorders.

Nancy A. Mundschenk, PhD, is an associate professor in the Department of Educational Psychology and Special Education at Southern Illinois University. Dr. Mundschenk provides ongoing staff development and consultation to parents, schools, teachers, and administrators in problem solving in a three-tier model of school supports and increasing meaningful parent participation in the educational decision-making process. She co-directed a 3-year federally funded interdisciplinary collaboration training project, and she currently serves as a regional coordinator for a state-funded project to support early intervening services and response to intervention within a collaborative problem-solving model. Her research interests include students with emotional–behavioral disorders, collaborative service delivery, parent–family participation, data-based decision making, and autism spectrum disorders.